Grosse Pointe Yacht Club

100 Years: 1914 – 2014

PRINCESS TINA

Flagship for GPYC 2003 Fleet Review
owned by member George Milidrag

Grosse Pointe Yacht Club
100 Years: 1914 – 2014

Larry W. Stephenson, M.D.
Editor

Past Com. James L. Ramsey
Associate Editor

Carol E. Stephenson
Associate Editor

GPYC Centennial Book Project Committee

Past Com. Sloane R. Barbour Jr.   Director Joseph P. Schaden
Com. Kevin B. Granger   Larry W. Stephenson, Chair
Past Com. James N. Martin   Ross B. Stone
Past Com. James L. Ramsey   Past Com. William C. Vogel Jr.

Dorian Naughton Publishing
Grosse Pointe Farms, Michigan

NOTICE TO READERS

Each author is responsible for the accuracy of his or her content as well as obtaining permission to use photographs, other images, and materials that were not their own. Statements made by them, including opinions, are not necessarily shared by the editors, other members of the Grosse Pointe Yacht Club, or the publisher.

First Edition
ISBN: 978-0-578-15908-9

Publisher: Dorian Naughton Publishing (a division of dstudio74 LLP)

Cover design: Cynthia Naughton

For information on book distributors or translations, please contact the Grosse Pointe Yacht Club, 313-884-2500.

Library of Congress Cataloging in Publication Data: 2015903729

Stephenson, Larry W. (Larry Warren), 1944 –

Includes index.
ISBN: 978-0-578-15908-9

Grosse Pointe Yacht Club, 100 Years: 1914 – 2014/ Publisher Dorian Naughton Publishing — 1st Edition includes bibliographical references and index.

Table of Contents

Table of Contents

Foreword

Publishing a book of one hundred years of history requires a significant commitment and an enormous amount of work. This centennial book for the Grosse Pointe Yacht Club was no exception.

For more than two years, several GPYC members volunteered their time to review countless documents, photographs, newspaper clippings, books, etc., in order to draft the story and write the history of the venerable Grosse Pointe Yacht Club.

That commitment and effort has resulted in this wonderful book, and special recognition and thanks need to be given to those individuals for their *pro bono* work.

First and foremost, to Dr. Larry Stephenson. Dr. Larry was the chair of the committee, the principal editor and researcher, and the driving force in getting the job done. A very close second is Past Commodore Jim Ramsey. Jim's writing ability, communications background, and even temperament aided in all areas. Dr. Stephenson's wife, Carol, spent countless hours writing and rewriting, typing and retyping, and editing.

Others to be recognized include: Ross Stone, who shared his historical knowledge; John Martin, Tom Kliber, and Shelley Schoenherr, who donated their photographic skills; Director Joe Schaden, who provided historic material and artistic advice; and so many other members of the Club who contributed in a variety of ways. We would also like to acknowledge publishers Jim Dorian and Cynthia Naughton for their outstanding design skills and photography expertise, including the book's cover design, and Club Manager Tom Trainor for his thoughtful insight.

This book chronicles one hundred years of history of one of the country's premier yacht clubs, and is a welcome addition to the Club's centennial celebration. Thank you all for your unwavering commitment.

Commodore Kevin B. Granger, 2015
Past Commodore James N. Martin, 2014

Preface

It was not a date that will live in immortality, but on Monday evening, January 7, 2013, a small group of members and spouses gathered in the Commodores' Room to discuss the possibility of producing a book to celebrate the centennial year of the Grosse Pointe Yacht Club. Board members present were Commodore William and Sue Vogel, Vice Commodore James and Louann (Van Der Wiele) Martin, Rear Commodore Kevin and Julie Granger, and Director Joe Schaden. Also in attendance were Past Commodore James Ramsey, Archives Committee member Ross Stone, member Dr. Larry Stephenson, and Club Manager Tom Trainor. Past Commodore Sloane Barbour Jr. was unable to attend.

Initial discussion centered on the enormous amount of research that would be required to produce a quality product. Could a group of members do it? Could they do it in a timely fashion, in order to publish the book in Spring 2015? Or would it be prudent to hire outside professionals to do the job? Some of those present were either strongly for or against entrusting the project to members (read: amateurs). Those against were especially concerned that the production deadline would be so short that the book could not possibly be finished in 2015 as expected. Little good would be served by publishing a centennial history years after the event was over.

The meeting ended with Larry Stephenson agreeing to be the temporary chair of a committee that would give more in-depth study to the subject. Members of the committee would be Messrs. Vogel, Martin, Granger, Schaden, Ramsey, Stone, and Barbour.

At the second meeting, held on February 6, it was decided to entrust the project to the membership. Larry Stephenson was asked to become the permanent chair of the existing committee. Larry and others brought several club centennial books to the meeting as examples, and their various design formats were discussed by the committee. It was agreed that a letter would be sent to the membership to announce the book project and solicit members' help.

Following that meeting, letters were sent to all members enclosed with their February statements. Members were asked to share any historical information they might have, especially regarding the formative years of the Club. Volunteers were requested for help with research and writing. The letter was also published in *The Mast* and several times in *The Buzz*.

Meanwhile, work had begun on a proposed format. On April 11, a meeting was held with those members who responded to the call for help. Research and writing assignments were given. The final format was chosen, incorporating certain elements that had been noted in other club centennial books; but the finished product would be unique to our Club. When the board met on April 25, it was officially agreed that the project would receive financing, and work could begin in earnest.

The next several months were a dervish of activity. In many cases, it was nothing short of amazing to discover how much we did not know about our Club, especially during the early years of its existence; also how much we thought we knew but really did not. Writing, rewriting, correcting, and proof-reading were constant activities as the early chapters began to unfold. More letters were published in *The Mast*, reminding members to be on the lookout for historical memorabilia.

In February 2014, requests for cost proposals were sent to eleven publishers, seven in southeast Michigan and four from out-of-state. All when previously contacted had expressed interest in the project. They were asked to submit bids for publishing, along with samples of their work, and include printing cost estimates if possible. The committee then met in March, with all committee members present, to discuss the proposals. After carefully reviewing the bids and inspecting samples of previous projects, a publisher was selected.

Per the format that was developed back in 2013, Part I of the book would contain eleven chapters relating the history of the Club, roughly by decade, with the final chapter highlighting the actual centennial year at the Club. Part II would contain nine monographs about people and events that were deemed too important, and in some cases too lengthy, to be included as part of the year-to-year chronology of the Club. Part III would be devoted to the Club's various committees and activities, and to the fleet officers. For inclusion purposes, the head of each committee and activity, along with the 2014 fleet officers, were contacted and given the opportunity to include a write-up for the book, and a great many did so. The Appendices section would contain basic facts about the Club. There readers would find lists of Club officers and managers down through the years and a compiled roster of early members from 1914 to 1935.

So many wonderful photographs and illustrations were uncovered during development of the book; we wish we could have included them all, but length and budget constraints forced us to choose what we felt were the very best, or occasionally the most appropriate. It has been quite a journey. We believe we speak for everyone who contributed in some way to this book when we say that, although the labor was lengthy, and often intense, it has been a true labor of love. We hope you enjoy what you see and read.

Larry W. Stephenson, M.D.
Committee Chairman,
GPYC Centennial Book Project
Past Commodore James L. Ramsey

Acknowledgements

A number of people have already been recognized for their contributions to this project by Commodore Kevin Granger and Past Commodore James Martin in the book's foreword. Those members who supplied photos and other images for the book are appropriately acknowledged in the section of the book where the photos or images appear.

Grosse Pointe Yacht Club staff who were particularly helpful to this project include Maureen Nance, Michele Penoyer, Tom Trainor, Aaron Wagner, and Gene Gellert. Former Club Manager Jack Sullivan was contacted a number of times regarding Club issues and private clubs in general. Members Bob Hackathorn, William "Joe" Cook, Ross Stone, Doug Dossin, Mary Huebner, and Past Commodore Sloane Barbour provided valuable archival information. Member Tom Hathaway and Liz Rader, along with husband Past Commodore Bob Rader, answered the call for writers and wrote three of the chapters in Part I. Kelley Vreeken also answered that call and wrote the history of the junior sailing program. Past Commodore Ronald A. Schaupeter strongly encouraged us to feature the Club's artwork in the book. Legal committee member Bob Joslyn gave counsel, advice, and related services as the project progressed.

Several people from other private clubs in the area were very helpful to this project. From Bayview Yacht Club: Past Commodore and Club Historian Brian Geraghty and Fred Woolsey. From Detroit Yacht Club: Past Commodore, Club Historian, and DRYA Historian Ed Theisen and Membership Coordinator Margaret Gmeiner, who spent a considerable amount of her time locating important historical documents. From Detroit Athletic Club: Ken Voyles. From Grosse Pointe Club: Club Manager Justin Jones.

Other valuable information deserving special recognition was provided by the following people: Tom Krolczyk, Grosse Pointe Shores Village office; Elizabeth Clemens, Walter P. Reuther Archives, Wayne State University; Romie Minor and Dawn Eurich, Burton Historical Collection, Detroit Public Library; Isabelle "Izzy" Donnelly and Jean Dodenhoff, Grosse Pointe Historical Society; Cynthia Bieniek, St. Clair Shores Public Library; Todd Walsh, State of Michigan Historical Commission; Carol Mowery and Louisa Wadrous, Mystic Seaport Museum Archives; Kevin Martin, Hagley Museum Archives; Barbara Watson, Club Historian, St. Petersburg Yacht Club; Jim Orr, Benson Ford Archives; Captain John Sarns, International Shipmasters Association; Joel Stone, senior curator, Detroit Historical Society; John Polacsek, former curator, Dossin Great Lakes Museum; and Matt Wolfe and William Chapin, Automotive Hall of Fame.

The front cover illustration was provided by the Grosse Pointe Yacht Club. The image of the motor yacht *Nakhoda* is from the Pusey and Jones Corporation. The photo of the sailing yacht *Royono III* is courtesy of the Mystic Seaport Museum archives.

A very special thank you goes to Robert and Dorothy Roney for graciously hosting a gathering at their residence, the former home of Commodore R. George Marsh, which was the site of the first organizational meeting of the Club one hundred years ago. It was indeed a memorable occasion.

Having discovered that a small painting of *Sea Witch* had been commissioned as a model for the much larger *Sea Witch* painting hanging in the GPYC Ballroom, we are grateful to Conrad "Duke" Williams III, great-grandson of our fourth commodore, John H. French, for bringing that painting to the Club for display during the centennial year.

To honor the significance of iceboating in the Club's early history, John Woodhouse Jr. and William Waugaman donated a trophy, circa 1900 to 1905, from the former Grosse Pointe Ice Yacht Club. The family of GPYC founding member and avid iceboater George Hendrie was especially helpful in researching the GPYC connection to iceboating.

Special thanks also to the following for services rendered: Donna Hammond for typing; Jennifer Backer for proofreading and copy editing of style consistency in Part I; Robert Hackathorn, Joe Schulte, and Robert Joslyn who helped with the final proofreading; Brad Stephenson for obtaining artwork; member Beline Obeid for due-diligence in locating a scrapbook with valuable historical information.

PART I

Introduction

By Past Com. James L. Ramsey

Like the journey of a thousand miles that begins with a first step, this 100-year chronicle flows from a single word: Ice.

Ice was the start of it all.

It was ice, in the form of moving glaciers, that carved the basin of the Great Lakes 10,000 years ago. The force of the ice left huge footprints in the earth, sometimes hundreds of miles across and hundreds of feet deep. The melting ice left behind massive amounts of water which filled the cavities, forming Lakes Ontario, Erie, Huron, Michigan and Superior.

Located among them was a relative pond, just 25 miles across, shallow and mostly placid, connected by two strong, deep rivers. The early natives called it Waawiyaataan, then Otsiketa, and later, under the French, Lac Sainte-Claire.

In the winter, Lake St. Clair became an attractive body of frozen water, forming hard and thick from shore to shore for four months of the year. And when the winter winds blew across its smooth, uninterrupted surface, it became a natural playground for iceboats, which, before the advent of steam and gasoline power, were among the fastest manmade craft on earth. In the 1800s, a 60-mph ride on an iceboat across a frozen lake, with two blades slicing into the ice and the third hiked high in the air, must have been the ultimate speed thrill, and arguably still is.

Ice was centermost in the minds of a group of winter sportsmen who gathered at the turn of the 19th century to form an organization dedicated to the sport of iceboat racing on Lake St. Clair.

Legend has it that these iceboaters, who founded an organization known as the Grosse Pointe Ice Boat Club, were also the founders of the Grosse Pointe Yacht Club. Other folklore claims that the Grosse Pointe Ice Boat Club was absorbed by a group of sailboaters who in 1914 reformed it into the Grosse Pointe Yacht Club. Yet another tale tells that the devotees were "just a bunch of teenagers," but that, too, turns out to be only partly correct. At least those are the popular versions of the story that have been passed along.

But the real truth is so clouded in ambiguity and conflicting documentation it may never be known exactly what happened at the inception. The latest and best evidence, however, strongly suggests that the Grosse Pointe Yacht Club was founded separately from any iceboat club.

Although the founders were primarily sailors, many were iceboaters, which is perhaps the cause of the confusion. Sailing was a popular passion in the early 1900s, and some devotees pursued the sport in both winter and summer. In any event, it appears certain that the Grosse Pointe Yacht Club was from the beginning exactly that — a yacht club.

One of the new club's first priorities was to gain access to Lake St. Clair. It so happened that the Village of Grosse Pointe Shores owned lakefront property near the intersection of Lake Shore and Vernier Roads. And by happy coincidence, the Shores was about to begin construction of a 1,300-foot municipal pier with a protected harbor at the end. When it was complete, the Club proceeded to lease space there. It gave members a place to tie up their boats, year-round.

That old municipal pier must have been one solid structure. It is recalled that many years later, when the Club's present-day outer harbor was being installed, the pilings of the old pier were so firmly planted in the ground that construction crews built around them rather than try to remove them. The remnants of the original pier are still in place beneath the present-day construction — a silent, century-old reminder of the beginnings of one of the country's foremost yacht clubs.

■ ⬌ ■

Figure 1. Circa 1914–29. Preparing for the Grosse Pointe Yacht Club trophy iceboat races.

By Larry W. Stephenson, M.D.

1914 to November 1925

The founding meetings of the Yacht Club

Early articles about the history of the Grosse Pointe Yacht Club all agree that twenty-five sailors interested in organizing a new club held their first meeting at the home of George Marsh[1-4] in Grosse Pointe Shores on December 3, 1913. Minutes were taken at that meeting with a heading that reads, "Grosse Pointe Yacht Club." Officers elected were R. George Marsh, commodore; John R. Long, vice commodore; William C. Roney, secretary; William E. Roney, treasurer; Dr. George L. Renaud, fleet surgeon; William Granger, official measurer. William Granger and Joseph Dwyer were assigned to write the constitution and bylaws. Committees were formed and their members were mentioned by name. (fig. 4)

The next three meetings were also held at the Marsh home at 840 Lake Shore Road. At the second meeting it was moved and adopted that R. George Marsh, John R. Long, William E. Roney, and O.D. Henry be made directors for the year 1914. A proposed constitution and bylaws were read, discussed and approved. A resolution was passed stating that, "no one except members be allowed to sail on any boat in any race."

Nine new members were voted in at the third meeting and are listed in the minutes. Included on that list are George M. Slocum and his father, Grant. George would later become one of the Club's most significant commodores when he led the GPYC into and out of receivership from 1935 to 1938. Harold Chapoton was chosen as the club's baseball manager. In the minutes there is a reference to "Judge Dwyer," who is probably the Joseph Dwyer assigned to work on the

Figure 2. First membership card
Note sailboat at the top.

1

Grosse Pointe Yacht Club.

First Meeting held at the residence of R. George Marsh, Grosse Pointe Shores, Michigan December, 3. 1913.

Meeting called to order at 7⁴⁵ P. M. at residence of R. George Marsh.

On motion, Mr. R. George Marsh was elected temporary chairman, and Wm. C. Roney as temporary secretary.

Mr. Marsh explained the object of the meeting. The following permanent officers were elected.

Commodore R. George Marsh.
vice-Commodore J. R. Long
Secretary Wm. C. Roney
Treasurer Wm. E. Roney
Fleet Surgeon Dr. George. L. Renaud
Official Measurer Wm Granger

On motion duly made & seconded the permanent officers assumed office.
The following committees were appointed.
Regatta. Carlyle Long
Bradford Larned
Orginazation. Cortland Larned
Cornelius Long
Edward Roney
Constitution & By Laws. Wm. Granger
Joseph Dwyer.

Meeting adjourned to meet Dec. 10. 1913 at 7³⁰ P. M.

Above, figure 3.
1914–GPYC iceboat
racers receiving trophies:

Back row standing: Bill Long,
George Hendrie, Carlyle Long,
Ignatius Backman, William C. Roney,
Bill Hendrie, Wilfred Backman,
Wally Hock, John Aukland.

Seated front: Harold "Chappie" Chapoton
Commodore George Marsh,
Vice Commodore John R. Long,
Frank Center.

Left, figure 4. Minutes from the first
meeting of the Grosse Pointe Yacht
Club dated December 3, 1913.

constitution and bylaws. At that same meeting, "cups" were awarded, which presumably were trophies for iceboat racing.

The minutes of the fourth meeting are not dated, but begin with "Fourth Regular Meeting…" in the same way that the first three sets of minutes begin. This meeting most likely was held in the waning months of 1914 because directors were once again elected, presumably for 1915. They were R. George Marsh, John R. Long, Robert C. Hupp and William E. Roney.

The earliest membership list as we know it

None of the minutes from the first four meetings gives the names of all the attendees at each meeting, but a total of twenty-eight different names appears in those minutes. No membership roster for 1914 is currently known to exist. There is a photograph, given to the Club in 1989, of thirteen men, their names written in, titled "The Founders of the Grosse Pointe Yacht Club." This photo appeared in a 1989 issue of *The Grosse Pointer* and in the book published to celebrate the 75th anniversary of the GPYC clubhouse in 2004.[5–6] Eleven of these men are mentioned in the minutes of the first four meetings; the two who are not are Wilfred Backman and Frank Center.

"The Founders" and "The Founding Fathers" captions of the photographs in the two publications are a bit misleading for these reasons. A number of men whose names appear in the minutes of the first two meetings, including some elected officers, are not pictured. According to those minutes, three of the men in the photo were voted in as members at the third meeting. The photograph could have been taken at that third meeting, as it includes Commodore Marsh, Vice Commodore Long, and eleven younger members, who appear to have received trophies for iceboat racing. (fig.3) Another copy of that same photograph provided by the Backman family is simply labeled "Ice Sail Trophies." Whatever the case, the photo is only a partial representation of our founding members.

Table 1 lists the thirty-three known Club members in 1914. The minutes from the first four meetings show that only at the third meeting was there any mention of new members (nine) being elected. So those nine plus the twenty-five who were present at the first meeting seem to indicate that the list of names contained in table 1 is fairly accurate.

The book that was written for the 75th anniversary of the clubhouse states, "The Club was originally organized by a bunch of teen-agers and one adult."[7] But as table 1 shows, of the thirty-three known members of the Club in 1914, there are twenty-two whose ages have been determined. Of those twenty-two, eleven members ranged in age from thirty-six to fifty-five and five were in their twenties. There certainly were some teenagers, however, including Ignatius Backman(19), William Hendrie(19), George Hendrie(17), William C. Roney(16), Edward Roney(15), and Courtland Larned(13). William Roney and his brother Edward were sons of founding member William E. Roney. Courtland Larned and his brother Bradford were sons of Abner E. Larned, who is known to be an early member.

Table 1
GPYC Founding Members

Name	Date of Birth	Age 1914	
1. Auckland, John**	10/11/1893	21	3*, 4, P (also sp. 'Aukland')
2. Backman, Ignatius**	2/26/1895	19	3*, P
3. Backman, Wilfred**	8/16/1892	22	P
4. Center, Frank			P (also sp. 'Centers')
5. Chapoton, Harold**	1893	21	3, 4, P
6. Dwyer, Joseph L	1878	36	1, 3, 4
7. Granger, William			1
8. Hager, Julius**			3
9. Harrigan, Edward C.**	1894	20	2
10. Hendrie, George**	1897	17	3, P
11. Hendrie, William**	1895	19	3*, P
12. Henry, O.D.			2
13. Hickey, Edward J.**	11/18/1863	51	2
14. Hock, Walter**			2, 4, P
15. Hupp, Robert C	1876	38	3*, 4
16. Hurley, Ignatius B**.		37	2
17. Larned, Bradford**			1, 3
18. Larned, Courtland**		13	1 (also sp. 'Cortland')
19. Long, Carlyle			1, 3, 4, P
20. Long, Cornelius			1, 3
21. Long, John R**			1, 2, 3, 4, P
22. Long, William P.			P
23. Marsh, R. George**	12/27/1869	45	1, 2, 3, 4, P
24. Osius, George**◊	11/14/1859	55	
25. Renaud, Dr. George L.**	1870	44	1
26. Roney, Edward**	10/21/1899	15	1
27. Roney, William C.**	3/2/1898	16	1, P
28. Roney, William E.**	8/30/1868	46	1, 2, 4
29. Sanders, George**			3* (also sp. 'Saunders')
30. Scherer, Dr. Otto**	1862	52	3*
31. Shelden, George**	1862	52	3* (also sp. 'Sheldon')
32. Slocum, George M.**	1/24/1889	25	3*
33. Slocum, Grant**	1864	50	3*

Explanations:
1, 2, 3, 4 – name appears in minutes of 1st, 2nd, 3rd, and 4th meetings
3* – became member at 3rd meeting
P – Present in 1914 GPYC group photograph
** – also listed as a member on the GPYC 1923-24 membership roster
◊ Osius listed as a 1914 member in the following three sources:
References, 1, 2, 18

Figure 22. *French Boy* with George Russell French at the tiller on Lake St. Clair, winner of Class "A" Championship, 1920. In background is the French family home, 936 Lake Shore Rd. *French Boy* was co-owned by GPYC members George and John H. French Jr., sons of GPYC Commodore John French Sr., and is likely the same *French Boy* iceboat that is now on display in the Fo'c'sle Room.

The birthplace and headquarters of the GPYC until the mid-1920s

In December 1913, a group of men convened at the home of R. George Marsh at 840 Lake Shore Road in Grosse Pointe Shores with the intention of forming a yacht club. In the early months of 1914, after three more meetings were held in the same location, the end result was the establishment of the Grosse Pointe Yacht Club, with George Marsh at the helm as the Club's first commodore.

Of course this new club without a clubhouse had to meet somewhere, and quite often during the next several years, George Marsh's home was used for that purpose. We know that meetings were occasionally held at the Shores Municipal Building, at the Lochmoor Club, and often hosted by other members in their homes, but 840 Lake Shore Road came to be considered the headquarters for the fledgling GPYC.[1,3]

It is believed that the home was originally built for George Marsh and his wife Margaret and completed in 1907 or early 1908. The Marshes, who had no children, used their lakefront home as a summer residence, spending the winter months in downtown Detroit at the prestigious Hotel Tuller on Grand Circus Park, known as the "Grand Dame on Grand Circus." Their home in the Shores, unoccupied during the winter months but well-heated with a furnace and several fireplaces, would have become a natural meeting place for the new club.

In the early 1900s there were few homes along the Lake St. Clair shoreline in the Vernier Road vicinity. When the Marsh home was built, the original address was "Jefferson Avenue, two north of Vernier Road." After George Marsh died in 1937, his widow continued to live in the home until her death in 1958. In 1961, the home was purchased from the Marsh estate by architect Robert Roney. Mr. Roney made some much-needed improvements and changes to the home, and continues to reside there to this day. One of his favorite stories about the house came from a member of the Schwartz family who owned a plumbing business for many years in Grosse Pointe Farms. Mr. Schwartz recalled his father telling him that when he was in his late teens, he had helped to salvage lumber from the old St. Paul rectory for use in building the Marsh home. This first St. Paul rectory had been located just north of the site of the new Marsh home and had been torn down at some point due to the church's relocation to the Farms.

When Mr. Roney purchased the home, he fondly remembers the numerous boat photos hanging on walls all over the house. There were large boats and small boats, sailboats, powerboats and iceboats. His particular favorites were the photos of the Marsh backyard which was two lakefront lots wide, virtually covered with boats of different sizes and types pulled up on the lawn. He recalls thinking that poor Margaret Marsh probably was constantly complaining to her husband about all those boats cluttering her yard. Maneuvering through them just to reach the shoreline must have been a real challenge!

Figure 23. Marsh home facing the lake. Photograph taken in 1961 when present owner purchased the house, which was in poor condition.

Figure 24. Marsh home facing Lake Shore Road.

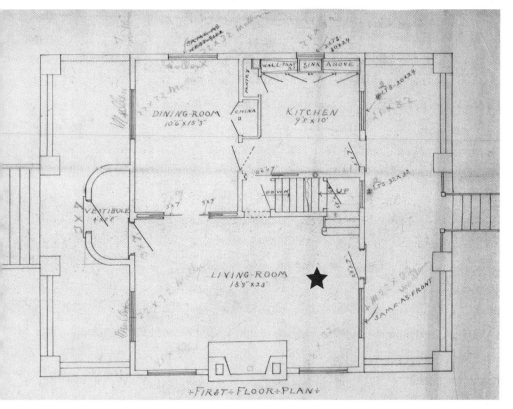

Figure 25. Blueprint of Marsh home, the living room indicated with a red star. Below the living room is a similar room with a fireplace and billiard table. It is believed these two rooms were alternately used for the first organizational meetings of the GPYC and served for several years as the Club's unofficial clubhouse.

IMAGE ACKNOWLEDGEMENTS

Frontispiece
Photography by Jim Dorian

Introduction
Photography on page 2 ©MarkGraf. Composition by Cynthia Naughton.

Chapter One
1. George Hendrie family
2.–3. Backman family
4. GPYC
5. Hendrie family
6. Grosse Pointe Historical Society
7. GPYC
8. Percell Siniff/ Dorothy Jewett family
9. *The Rudder* magazine, January 1906/ Joe Schaden
10. Detroit Yacht Club, *Main Sheet*, January 1918
11. Burton Historical Collection, Detroit Public Library
12. Grosse Pointe Historical Society
13. Jim Johnson
14. *Lloyd's Register of American Yachts*, 1919 edition.
15. GPYC
16.–17. Detroit Athletic Club
18. Detroit Yacht Club, *Main Sheet*, March 1917
19.–21. George Hendrie family
22. Grosse Pointe Historical Society
23.–25. Robert Roney

Figure 1. The way it will be: Before construction of the clubhouse began in 1928, several breezy artists' conceptions of the way it would look were circulated among the membership. Club leaders were undoubtedly not only looking for member buy-in to what would be an expensive undertaking, but also hoping to entice new members with the projected beauty of the place. The watercolor renderings were packaged in an elegant parchment portfolio, befitting the aspirations of the planners.

By Past Com. James L. Ramsey and
Larry W. Stephenson, M.D.

CHAPTER TWO

December 1925 through June 1938

The 1920s: Boom — and bust

The 1920s were a flamboyant time in America. After the sobering shock of World War I, the nation was collectively ready to get on with the pleasure of living and put the morbid past behind. As returning veterans reentered the workforce and the marketplace, the American economy began to boom, setting off a period of sustained prosperity that made the United States one of the richest countries in the world. For the first time in history, more Americans lived in cities than on farms, while in many regions of the country telephone lines, indoor plumbing, and sewage systems were installed for the first time. The decade also gave rise to the first large-scale use of automobiles, motion pictures, and electricity. Jazz, Art Deco, and flappers added a distinct flair to the era, while heroes such as Babe Ruth, Gar Wood, and Charles Lindbergh gave the public something to cheer about.[1] As an example of the country's postwar preeminence, when Germany was unable to pay its war reparations to England, France, and other Allies, the

Daily News
Evening Edition
40 PAGES   30th Year NO. 29
Tuesday, October 29, 1929

MARKET CRASHES, WALL STREET IN PANIC

Figure 2. October 29, 1929, the day that became known as "Black Tuesday." The bottom fell out of the U.S. stock market, leaving millions of investors with worthless holdings frequently purchased with borrowed money. It was the beginning of the Great Depression, which would last for the next ten years. It spelled serious financial trouble for many members of the new Grosse Pointe Yacht Club.

United States stepped in and paid what was owed. This in turn enabled England, France, and the Allies to repay their war debts to this country, so the money the United States gave out flowed right back into its own coffers.[2] It is one of many reasons why the total wealth of the United States doubled between 1920 and 1929, and why the "Roaring Twenties" in the early part of the decade evolved into the "Golden Twenties" in the latter half.

The Grosse Pointe area, too, was transformed by the prosperity of the times. What was once an agricultural community with long, narrow "ribbon" farms (many of which predated the American Revolution) that were interrupted only by a few summer homes owned by the wealthy, began to evolve into a year-round suburb of Detroit. Prosperous patriarchs, many of them captains of a rapidly growing automobile industry, moved their families permanently into the area to escape the confines of the big city. It was only natural for many of them to look for private clubs where they could relax, take in the lake, and, despite the restrictions of Prohibition, enjoy the company of other successful Grosse Pointers.

Figure 3. Old Lake Shore Road in the vicinity of Vernier Road: No median and trees on both sides of the road.

From unbounded optimism a dream takes shape

It was in the midst of this national hubris that early leaders of the GPYC began to envision a clubhouse and harbor for their club that would surpass anything else in the region. For the first years of its existence, the Club's only meeting places were in members' homes, the Grosse Pointe Shores municipal building, or occasionally the Lochmoor Club. Although the idea of a head-quarters for the Yacht Club had existed from almost the beginning, the size and grandeur of the concept grew more and more ambitious with the times. By the mid-1920s, Club leadership was thinking far beyond a warming-hut clubhouse with a couple of meeting rooms.

Their thoughts took an even more positive turn at a board meeting in December 1925 when Commodore George Marsh recognized member and Grosse Pointe Shores Village President George Osius. Mr. Osius not only blessed the idea of a prestigious home for the Club in his municipality, he pledged to devote his energies — and surely his considerable political clout — to the successful realization of the project.

The momentum continued into the following summer. On July 28, 1926, the first of two meetings was held to completely reorganize the Grosse Pointe Yacht Club. Prior to the meeting, a committee was formed and assigned the task of writing an entirely new set of bylaws for the Club. Those bylaws were presented, discussed and unanimously approved. New directors were then elected.

The second meeting on August 11 was long and intense, but when the board finally adjourned, the "new" Club had officially become a reality. On that day, on the watch of newly elected Commodore Edsel B. Ford, the board resolved at its meeting "to build and erect a Club House and appurtenances and fully furnish and equip the same." At the same meeting, the board resolved "to work with the Village of Grosse Pointe Shores to build a mutual harbor."

The board also entertained a report, signed by the leaders of the newly formed building committee, consisting of Clarence Ayres, George

Figure 4. July 1927: Harbor construction looking westward toward the shoreline.

Hilsendegen, and Past Commodore George Marsh. Among other things, the committee recommended the purchase of a certain piece of property from Mr. Ayres and signing a lease with the Village of Grosse Pointe Shores for an adjoining parcel that would give the Club 160 feet of lakefront access. The report also outlined the committee's intent to fill in the land in question to accommodate the building of a clubhouse.

The name Clarence Ayres is noteworthy here. Mr. Ayres was a successful lawyer and insurance executive who owned an office building in downtown Detroit and lived in a fine home along Lake Shore Road to the north of the Club. An enthusiastic member of the Club, Ayres was a strong proponent of making the GPYC a standout among yacht clubs. On his own initiative, Ayres purchased a parcel of property with lakefront access and its riparian rights at the corner of Lake Shore and Vernier Roads for $28,000. The property would be the ideal location for an impressive new clubhouse and

yacht harbor. He then offered the parcel to the Club at no profit, on whatever terms and repayment schedule the Club saw fit. Ayres also loaned the Club $6,000 to help pay for the fill necessary to raise the property above the ever-changing levels of the lake.

At that same August meeting, the board moved to purchase the property in question from Mr. Ayres. But $28,000 was a lot of money in 1926. And with annual dues of only $5, the Club lacked a sufficient revenue stream to pay for the property. The board looked at the Club's growing roster of members and concluded the Grosse Pointe area had many more potential members where those originals came from. The needed funds would come from the creation of several new classes of membership: Life, Active, Junior, Non-Resident, and Associate (a structure very similar to the one in effect at GPYC today). Dues from the new memberships were expected to contribute $225,000 to the building effort, while another $100,000 would come from the sale of private bonds. The projected numbers were deemed adequate because the total estimated cost of the land, the new clubhouse, and the new harbor was optimistically set at $200,000. Typical of the giddy thinking of the 1920s, the estimates were sorely out of touch with the reality that was in store. As further evidence of their optimism, the board took a thirty-year lease on an adjoining parcel of land 90 x 325 feet owned by the Shores, and purchased an additional lot adjoining Ayres's property to the south for $65,000 from member John Hurley, who, like Ayres, generously offered it to the Club at no profit. The necessary funds were borrowed from the American Insurance Company.

Now that they had the land on which to build their headquarters, Club leaders immediately bid out the building of a new harbor and seawall with several hundred feet of landfill extending eastward from the existing shoreline to accommodate the new clubhouse. The bid for the seawall went to the A.J. Dupuis Company. The landfill bid, at ninety cents per square foot, was awarded to Liberty Construction Company, although Liberty soon defaulted on the deal and the job had to be reassigned to the Dunbar-Sullivan Company for completion. With the harbor and landfill projects underway, construction of the new clubhouse would follow shortly.

All that was needed was a design — and, of course, a designer.

Enter Boston architect Guy Lowell

It appears that the building committee favored noted East Coast architect and Harvard/MIT graduate Guy Lowell for the task from the outset, despite the presence of several highly respected architectural resources in Detroit. There was Albert Kahn Associates, who had designed numerous area landmarks including the Packard Plant, the Edsel and Eleanor Ford House, and the Grosse Pointe Shores municipal building across the street, as well as the famed firm of Smith, Hinchman and Grylls, who created the J.L. Hudson Building, the Buhl Building, and Meadow Brook Hall.

But in all fairness to the selection committee, the aristocratic Lowell also had more than a few architectural accomplishments to his credit,

Figure 5. A portrait of architect Guy Lowell created by renowned artist John Singer Sargent.

including the Boston Museum of Fine Art and the New York Supreme Court building. Lowell's initial rough sketches no doubt impressed Marsh, Ayres, and the others, but it may have been his credentials as an accomplished ocean sailor that made the real difference. He had been a member of the U.S. Sailing Team and belonged to one of the oldest yacht clubs in America, the Eastern Yacht Club in Massachusetts. Lowell's nautical background may well have been perceived as a plus that would give him a more intuitive "feel" for what a prestigious yacht clubhouse should be.

Whatever the case, in January 1927, Lowell was awarded the assignment of designing the home of the Grosse Pointe Yacht Club. The agreed-upon fee for his services would be 7.5 percent of the cost of the building's construction, plus a fee of $50 per month for Lowell's onsite representative. If the total cost of the building as originally estimated came in at $200,000, Lowell would receive $15,000 for his efforts, which seems like a bargain, even at 1920s prices.

Figure 6. Different interpretations of a given theme. These rough sketches, based on Guy Lowell's original idea, show that the clubhouse could have looked very different from the way it turned out.

Unfortunately, none of Lowell's initial rough sketches has survived. It is therefore difficult to determine how closely the completed building follows his conceptual thinking. The sad irony here is that Lowell died just eighteen days after he won the assignment. Fittingly enough, he died aboard a boat at sea, amid the Madeira Islands off the coast of Portugal. But tragically, he would never see the completion of his work, not even the start of construction.

Now meet Henry and Richmond

With Lowell's untimely demise, the job of designing and executing the architectural plans for the GPYC clubhouse fell to two of his colleagues, Ralph Henry and Henry Richmond, who formed the firm of Henry and Richmond to carry on the project. It is to this duo that much of the credit for the beauty of the clubhouse must be given. The two architects traveled to the site where construction would commence and were immediately struck by the flatness of the terrain and the lake. For them, it was both a challenge and an inspiration, and they both agreed that there should be a strong vertical element in the architecture — something that would contrast sharply with the topography. [3] As Henry wrote in retrospect:

> To the architectural imagination, the natural setting and the immediate program of the yacht club problem were equally captivating. The outstanding characteristics of this region of the lake country are its apparently limitless extent of water surface, almost equally level and limitless terrain and a rich vegetation. It was at once apparent that the program demanded the informal and the picturesque in plan, and that the composition required, for piquancy and flavor, some element of contrasting verticality in a region where all else is horizontal. The convincing first thought of an element to fulfill this function was of the campanile; why not one of slender proportions and marked height, with a large bell in its lantern to strike the hours and half-hours of the dial-less ship's clock; why not one whose height would be doubled by its reflection in the mirror of the calm water surface; why not one with a modern aviation beacon at its apex?[4]

Whether the original idea for the campanile came from Lowell or from Henry and/or Richmond isn't important; what is important is that the concept for the clubhouse remained intact. The fact is, a slender 187-foot bell tower and steeple became the dominant feature of the clubhouse's Venetian design, a style of architecture that frequently featured towers, or campaniles, as navigational aids. And it is certainly through the diligence of Henry and Richmond as executors of the idea that detailed building plans were developed, revised repeatedly, and completed in time for the start of construction in 1928. They are the unsung heroes of the clubhouse project.

As the design progressed on the drawing boards in Boston, it became clear to everyone that the original cost estimates for the building were way below what they should have been. Two months after the contract was signed, the first revised estimate came in at more than twice what was originally envisioned — or about $500,000. In somewhat of a panic, the board immediately ordered the architects to scale back the design to $350,000. Compromises ensued: features were revised or dropped and an extensive cost-shaving effort by the designers helped trim expense from the ambitious undertaking.

A popular legend has it that one of the victims of the cost cutting was the indoor swimming pool that can be found today underneath the Club bowling alley. But that is not the case. In fact, the pool was completed, and despite its attractiveness it was never used — not because of construction costs, but because of potential legal problems. It seems one of the other Detroit-area clubs had an indoor pool in which a drowning occurred and a huge lawsuit ensued. Apparently the directors of the GPYC, already antsy over mounting costs, decided that the liability issue was too great and never opened the pool to members. The present-day display cases in the Club's trophy hall were originally windows to allow parents to watch their children and friends while they played in the water.

In any case, once the real cost trimming was complete, bids were let out to several Detroit-area construction firms. The winning constructor was Corrick Brothers, with a bid of $380,000 plus a $20,000 contingency fee to cover unforeseen expenses.

As construction begins, reality sets in

If there was an official ribbon-cutting or ground-breaking ceremony at the start of construction in February 1928, it is not recorded in Club chronicles, although it is almost certain there was one. All that is known from existing financial records is that cost overruns at both the clubhouse and harbor construction sites began almost immediately, and board members must have watched with growing anxiety as the project of their dreams that they had set in motion so optimistically began to soar out of their control.

Even so, construction proceeded. The new harbor, shared by the municipality and the Club, was completed that same year; it featured an inner harbor closest to the shore for swimming and small boats and a larger, outer harbor of 450 x 550 feet with deeper water for bigger boats. Meanwhile, the clubhouse began to rise slowly but surely above the newly placed fill atop more than a thousand wood pilings that had been driven deep into the ground to support the weight of the structure.

The board's fiscal strategy was straight-forward, though fatally flawed: They would pay for the project with revenue from dues and initiations — period. During the 1926 reorganization, a provision in the newly adopted bylaws stated, "Active members ...shall be limited to two-hundred," which realistically meant that the total membership, all categories included, would likely be around 250 members. That made for a very exclusive club. Now, however, the board had a change of heart. More members, plus more dues, plus more initiation fees equal more revenue. That was the logic, anyway. And so they began a series of increases in the price of dues and initiation fees, along with steady increases in the number of members allowed into the Club. At a meeting of the board in May 1927, the restriction limiting membership to residents of the then-four Grosse Pointes was rescinded to allow more prospects into the mix. By January 1929, the cap on Active membership was raised from two hundred to five hundred. What had begun as an organization with approximately two dozen members at $1 per year, had grown to 100, then 150, then 200, and finally 250 members. In less than three years, from October 1926 to January 1929, initiation fees had climbed from $5 to $500, then to $750, then to $1,250, then to $2,000, then to $2,750, then to $3,000, and finally to $3,300,

Figure 7. Harbor construction at full-steam — literally. From east looking west, steam-powered dredging equipment scoops up lake bottom, which was transported by barge to help fill the land around the clubhouse. Note the wooded shoreline in the background.

Figure 8.

Figure 9.

Top left, figure 8. Steam -powered pile driver pounding sharpened wood pilings into the frozen ground to support the foundation for the GPYC clubhouse.

Bottom left, figure 9. Winter 1928: Early construction of the clubhouse foundation. The portion shown here is thought to be the footing for the indoor swimming pool that was never opened.

Top right, figure 10. The club-house, despite its massive size and intricate Mediterranean architecture, was completed in just sixteen months.

Bottom right, figure 11. Without landscaping, the approach to the new clubhouse was a bit barren.

Figure 10.

Figure 11.

Figure 12. The clubhouse in the final phase of construction, circa spring 1929.

which in today's dollars was the equivalent of more than $40,000. Despite that, there was no shortage of prospective members who were willing and able to pay the price of belonging. By early 1929, with a strong and growing membership roster, Club receipts had soared to nearly $400,000 annually.

It wasn't enough.

Price increases could in no way keep pace with the costs that were mounting at the construction site. As early as August 1927, the directors had begun to have misgivings about their strategy of using initiation fees and dues as the sole means of covering costs, and talk of a mortgage ensued. By now, the board's only choice was to borrow the needed money. A loan of $250,000 from the National Bank of Commerce was followed by one for $240,000 from People Wayne Company, and another for $250,000 from Union Guardian Trust

Company. These loans, together with several private ones, put the Club's indebtedness at nearly a million dollars, despite the fact the doors to the clubhouse hadn't yet opened.

Today, with twenty-twenty hindsight, it is easy to look back more than eight decades and render judgment on the board of directors for lavish spending, fiduciary irresponsibility, woeful stewardship, and other misdeeds. But in truth, their actions were anything but frivolous. At the time, they were absolutely confident they could pay back the loans in question. After all, the American economy was booming, the directors themselves were engaged in highly successful businesses, the Grosse Pointes were filling with affluent people, and there was no shortage of solid new dues-paying members to fill the ranks of the Club. An Active membership totaling five hundred was envisioned, and the dues and initiation fees that would flow from such a large base would surely be more than enough to erase the temporary indebtedness. Moreover, the directors made themselves personally responsible for repayment of some of the loans in the unlikely event the Club could not meet its obligations. Of course the directors had no way of knowing what was ahead. For them, like so many others, the nation was on an upward-bound escalator that seemingly had no end. The sky was the limit, if there was a limit.

A bell for the belfry

As construction progressed and the clubhouse bell tower rose above the landscape, the time had come to obtain a bell to reside there. Because of spiraling costs, consideration was given to not installing a bell at all, at least for the time being. But a bell tower without a bell is like a singer without a song, and the cost of a retrofit would have been totally impractical. So the decision was made to purchase a bell from one of America's most acclaimed bell makers, the Meneely Company of Watervliet, New York. (Meneely bells currently hang above Independence Hall, at West Point, and aboard the *U.S.S. Constitution*, aka "Old Ironsides.") The finished bell was massive, measuring over five feet high, five inches thick, and weighing more than two tons. Its $4,000 price tag was equally imposing, and it was only through a series of urgent phone calls to prosperous members that the needed funds were raised.[5,6]

The bell was soon hoisted into position, but because of continuing financial concerns it was installed without a remote-controlled clapper, which meant that when it needed to be rung, some poor person theoretically had to climb Quasimodo-like to the belfry of the 187-foot tower and strike it by hand. Forty years would pass before a remote clapper mechanism was installed; but even then, its complicated design proved unreliable. An essay in retrospect by Past Commodore George Kriese put it this way: "The device coupled a clock to many gears, cams and electro-mechanical relays that, if all functioned properly, would send a signal to the bell tower

A tale of two burgees: original and current

Not long after the Club founding, leaders saw the need for an "emblem" that would help identify the new organization. It would be used as a letterhead on Club stationery, but more importantly as a burgee to fly from members' boats. The design they adopted around 1917 was a "swallowtail" shape with red lettering and a blue "X" on a white field. That rather straightforward look would serve as the Club trademark for over a decade.

But as plans for the new clubhouse and harbor took shape, and the vision for the Club grew increasingly ambitious, it appears that some of the leadership felt the need for a logo that would better express the Club's elite status. A new design with white letters and a red "X" on a blue field was proposed and approved. It bore an uncanny resemblance to

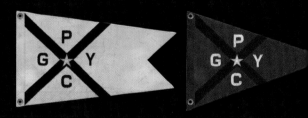

that of the New York Yacht Club and first flew over the new harbor in 1928, a year before the clubhouse was complete.

But nothing changes at the GPYC without some controversy. There seems to have been a faction that favored retention of the original white burgee, which in fact adorned Club stationery into the 1930s. It was also a prominent design feature in the china that was ordered for the clubhouse grand opening. So, for a period of time, the GPYC had two burgees. One can imagine members on either side of the issue proudly flying their burgee of choice to register their opinion.

Over time, proponents of the new burgee won out. After the Club reopened in 1938, the original burgee was no longer used. The red-and-white-on-blue design remains today as the GPYC burgee.

where a solenoid would pull a lanyard running over a pulley to cause the clapper to strike the bell."[5] That is, if all functioned properly. In 2002, thanks to the efforts of Commodore Kriese, the defunct device was replaced with an electronically controlled striking system. The giant bell now tolls perfect ship's time across the harbor, measuring the day in four-hour "watches" as is done aboard ship.

Complete at last – now the Grand Opening

After just sixteen months of construction, the Club's new home was ready. The board happily convened its first meeting there on May 28, 1929, followed by the Club's Grand Opening on July 4, 1929. It was a day marked by great fanfare, with competitive swimming, diving, and sailing events, much frivolity, and most of the Club's two hundred-plus members in attendance.

Detroit newspapers treated the Grand Opening of the Yacht Club as one of the great social events of the year and gave it generous coverage for days before and after the celebration. The Detroit News called it "The most pretentious ever attempted on the lakefront." For a time, the concerns of the past year and a half were forgotten in the hoopla.

The Detroit News society editor was in attendance and obviously charmed by the experience. On July 5, 1929, she wrote:

> The newly completed Grosse Pointe Yacht Club yesterday presented one of the most picturesque spots about the countryside for celebration of the holiday. The day marked the club's formal opening and smart society gathered there for hours of delightful leisure and entertainment in a setting brilliant with mid-summer beauty. All about the clubhouse and grounds myriad flags fluttered in the steady breeze and on one side of the lawn a Hawaiian orchestra played in the afternoon. The other side was gay with children of club members busy at games and various sports arranged for their amusement. The broad balcony across the front of the clubhouse was filled with smartly-clad spectators and the

Figure 13. This artist's rendering of the Club Room (today's Ballroom) shows the way it was intended to look upon completion. Note the large chart of Lake St. Clair over the fireplace. Perhaps that was a proposed decoration before Commodore John French commissioned the more dramatic *Sea Witch*, which has hung there for eighty-five years.

Right, figure 14. This is the way the Club Room (now Ballroom) actually looked at the time of the Grand Opening. It was decorated to feel like a luxurious hotel lobby, with cushiony chairs and oriental rugs that invited members to sit and chat.

Figure 15. The East Lawn the way it looked on Grand Opening day, July 4, 1929. Note two large yachts tied up along what is today the Guest Dock. A piece of harbor construction equipment remains in the background. In an era without the luxury of air conditioning, awnings were hung over the windows of the Main Dining Room to dampen the effects of the sun. Most of the Club's east and west windows were similarly shaded.

many yachts anchored at the club presented striking color effects with pennants flying and constantly moving groups of guests, the women particularly charming in their many colored sports ensembles.

Within the clubhouse the walls were brilliant with flowers, large vases and deep jars of phlox and delphinium placed about the halls and in the great, shaded lounge. The long buffet table in the dining room bore masses of garden flowers and each table was centered with blooms. There were numerous luncheon and dinner parties at the club, and several hosts entertained their guests at bridge and dinner aboard their yachts.

(See Table 1 for a list of yachts in the harbor that day.)

Figure 16. Before there was a swimming pool, bathers could descend for a dip in the harbor using these steps in the east wall. The position of the Guest Dock to the north appears to be much the same as today.

Figure 17. The "new" and very large Club burgee, ready to be flown from the old mast on the east lawn.

Another writer, Vera Brown from the Detroit Times, described an earlier visit to the Club this way:

> The club exterior, gorgeous in close view, is even more impressive from Lake Shore Road. The flat, gray stone structure, relieved only by the red roof and bits of green shrubbery, is completed by the campanile which raises its 187 feet of Venetian beauty in the cloudy atmosphere of a northern winter. At sight of it, one almost feels the soft enchantment of the Adriatic.

Later, recalling the Grand Opening, she wrote:

> A brief recollection of a day last summer gives a typical picture of the club, a day when the lake was dotted with graceful yachts, when the balconies were crowded and commodores from all over the country assembled to honor a sister organization.[7]

Table One

Member Yachts Anchored in Harbor July 4, 1929

Owner	Yacht Name	Length
Murray W. Sales	*Sea Sails III*	78 ft.
Com. John H. French	*Siele*	124 ft.
Charles F. Kettering	*Olive K*	97 ft.
B. F. Stephenson (shown in opening day video)	*Anona*	117 ft.
Robert Oakman	*Mamie O*	101 ft.
George Russell French	*Corsair*	unknown
Judge William Connolly	*Noremac*	45 ft.**
Thomas E. Currie	*Banty II*	47 ft.
Carl Bonbright	*Bonnie II*	58 ft.
V. Com. C. Hayward Murphy	*Althea**	106 ft.

Source: Brown, Vera, "A Bit of Spain", reproduced from 1929 Detroit newspaper article, The Grosse Pointer Yearbook 1943, 96. Boat lengths added by Chapter 2 authors.

*Also mentioned in article but not yet completed

**Estimated

Below, figure 18. No detail was spared to make sure the new Club trumpeted elegance. Even the china was custom-handcrafted in Bavaria. Several examples still remain.

The party's over

Ironically, the opening of the Club occurred less than four months before "Black Tuesday," October 29, 1929, when the U.S. stock market crashed, setting off the Great Depression that plunged the nation into hard times for the entire decade to follow. In the first week of the crash alone, stock values fell $30 billion, and in short order one out of four Americans would be unemployed.

The fledgling yacht club's doors had barely opened when resigning members began exiting through them. That was not at all what the board had in mind. Even weeks before the crash, there were signs that the U.S. economy was on shaky ground. Board minutes recorded sixteen resignations and expulsions due to nonpayment of dues and membership fees, and fifty other accounts were declared "delinquent." Not only was the board's dream of gaining throngs of new members not being realized, the size of the membership was actually in decline. The strategy of steadily increasing initiation fees and monthly dues had backfired. Now panicky, disillusioned members were abandoning ship.

As a means of stemming the negative flow, in late 1929 the board approved the creation of a new class of nonvoting membership, Class B, with a reduced initiation fee. Additional reductions in the price of dues and initiation fees followed in the coming months, but had little effect. The resignations and expulsions continued, while new memberships fell off. Board minutes record little of what was being said and discussed at the time, although the terseness of the entries suggests there was considerable tension in the room.

The 1930s: gloom, doom, and finally, recovery

Worse still, in November 1930, one of the big loans for $240,000 that had been underwritten by the board came due. In response, the board approved the sale of $750,000 worth of bonds—at 6 percent interest with a ten-year maturity — in the hope that members would come to the Club's rescue. And to demonstrate their faith in the validity of the bonds, the directors themselves signed personal notes in the amount of $10,000 and $20,000 apiece to account for $520,000 of the total.

Figure 19. The 1930 board of directors meeting. At the far side of the table, from left to right, are seated C. Hayward Murphy, Charles E. Sorensen, John H. French, Mark R. Hanna, George W. Carter, William G. Fitzpatrick, Charles F. Becker, Herbert J. Woodall, Dr. George L. Renaud, and Arthur J. Scully. From left to right on this side of the table, are: Charles T. Bush, George R. Osius, Conrad H. Smith, William C. Roney, William M. Mertz and Joseph L. Hickey.

It was an act, not only of hope, but of raw courage on their part. But by now there was widespread apprehension among the membership.

The attempted bond drive was not successful.

What is obvious from the board minutes of the era was that no one knew how deep the Great Depression really was or how long it would last. President Herbert Hoover himself made the mistake of declaring that the economy would recover within one year. It appears that many of the directors were of a similarly positive mind. They were convinced that the collapse was only a short-term setback. If only they could hang on a little longer by stalling creditors and cutting the cost of membership, everything would start to rebound and equilibrium would be restored.

But that was not to be. The Depression only grew worse, and the GPYC was not the only club in trouble. The Detroit Yacht Club, for example, saw its roster shrink from three thousand members in 1924 to just six hundred in 1932.[8]

As businesses and banks failed and unemployed workers multiplied into the millions, the future was indeed bleak for much of the U.S. population.

On January 13, 1930, the board minutes made note of "A great indebtedness" along with the warning that each board member and Club member should be "vitally interested in working out the financial programs of the Club." Perhaps as a means of fortifying their teetering status in the financial community, the board elected two powerful captains of the automobile industry to their midst: Charles F. Kettering, vice president of research at General Motors, and K.T. Keller, president of Chrysler.

Amid continued hope, a call for change

A year later, on January 12, 1931, the board discussed taking out another mortgage, this one for $650,000, an amount that was projected to carry the Club through the next two years "until the economy improves." In the meantime, the directors approved a relaxed delinquency policy that gave members who were in arrears more time to pay their dues. The board further confirmed its faith in the future by resolving to purchase six sailboats to form the Club's first competitive sailing

Iceboaters exit; an era ends

By 1926, looming clubhouse construction had revealed the need to generate more Club revenue. To that end, at the August 11, 1926, reorganizational meeting, a proposal was made and passed to significantly increase initiation fees and dues. New classes of membership were also created, each with its own set of initiation fees and dues. The new classifications were Life, Active, Junior, Non-Resident and Associate. Existing Club members were allowed to choose the classification they preferred; but everyone was then required to pay the initiation fee for their chosen class.

The Associate class of membership appears to have been created to accommodate young adult members, many of whom had joined in 1914 as iceboat racers. This class was limited to fifty members and had certain restrictions, most notably the ability to vote in Club elections. The initiation fee for Associate membership was $15 with annual dues of $5, compared to the Active membership initiation fee of $500 with $100 annual dues.

When the new membership classifications went into effect in 1927, most of the early iceboat racers chose to become Associate members, but the records show that from mid-1929 to late 1930, almost all of these members left the Club.[9]

The question arises, Why did that happen? During the Great Depression, many members were forced to drop their membership but rejoined after the Club reopened in 1938. For reasons that are unknown, nearly all of those early iceboating members chose never to return.

It is easy to assume that most members who left the Club after October 1929 did so as a result of the market crash and ensuing Depression. One can only speculate as to why the young iceboaters began leaving the Club in the months preceding the crash. As founding members and supporters of the Club in its early years, did they feel disenfranchised by their new membership status? Was there a disintegration of the bonds that once existed between the founding members? Did they decide that the growth of the Club as a yachting organization had devalued the importance of their winter sport? We will probably never know.

Figure 20. GPYC iceboaters line up on Lake St. Clair for the start of a race sometime between 1914 and 1921.

We do know, however, that when new membership classifications were established in 1927, the Active class was soon split into Active A and Active B, which corresponds to today's Active and Social classes. When the Club reopened in July 1938, all the previous classes of membership were retained, but no candidates were considered for Associate membership.[10] In addition, Club records from 1938 through 1949 do not contain the single name of any Associate member. This tends to reinforce the idea that Associate memberships were originally established with young — and less affluent — iceboating members in mind. But the board of the new GPYC apparently had other thoughts about the matter. Even so, they decided to keep the Associate membership category in the bylaws for possible use at some later date. If the category had been activated when the Club was restarted, perhaps with an accompanying reduction in initiation fees and dues, some of the iceboat racers might have returned to the Club. But that was not to be.

The departure of the iceboat racers brought to a close an important passage in the history of the Club. Although iceboating remained a popular winter sport for several decades after their exit, iceboat racers themselves were no longer a central part of the Club culture. By the 1970s, the popularity of the sport in the region had declined, largely as a result of warmer lake temperatures that reduced the quality and longevity of the ice on the lake. Nevertheless, the iceboat racers played a key role in the formative years of the Club, and their disappearance as a group represented a sad but perhaps inevitable change in the make-up of the membership.

Figure 21. July 1932: All dressed up and no place to go. The clubhouse looking lush and serene in the midst of the Great Depression.

fleet. (Despite their bullishness, the purchase would not take place until nine years later, in 1940, when four Lawley 110 sailboats were ordered, all of them funded by private member donations.)

In May 1931, the board received a letter from member George W. Carter that, while it may not have seemed like it at the time, was something of a prophetic look into the future of the Club and its new *raison d'etre*. Mr. Carter's letter was written out of concern for the Club's financial situation, and in it he proposed the need for a shift in the Club's solitary emphasis on "yachting features" to "taking care of the needs of the average family." What kind of consideration was given to George Carter's proposal at the time isn't recorded, but the ensuing years proved his vision to be spot-on. Over time, the GPYC's priorities did change, with strong emphasis given to family activities. And whether they listened to Mr. Carter or not, by 1939 the directors would

authorize the building of a new swimming pool, followed by a four-lane bowling alley, and later, tennis and badminton courts to add variety to the Club's palette of non-boating attractions.

That same month in 1931, in an attempt to gain new members, the board acted on another proposal by Mr. Carter: to harness the resources of the entire membership by forming the two hundred fifty-member roster into a giant membership committee, divided into eight subcommittees of thirty members each. The names of two hundred prospective new members in the Detroit area were identified and given to the eight subcommittees for action. It would be the responsibility of these eight groups to contact the individual prospects, hopefully meet with them and sell them on the idea of joining the Club. At the annual meeting on February 2, 1932, the board added a new class of Junior membership for people between the ages of twenty-one and twenty-seven. Additional discussion at the meeting was given to Mr. Carter's earlier suggestion of broadening the Club's focus to include swimming, tennis, competitive events, banquets, and business meetings. Several days later, at another meeting, the number of board members, which had swelled to thirty-six as a result of the crisis, was streamlined to nine. Initiation fees, which had soared to $3,300, now plummeted to $500.

Nothing seemed to work. At the May 18, 1932, meeting of the directors, 45 resignations were received, and in the minutes the first reference is made to the dreaded "f"-word — foreclosure — on the loan from Union Guardian Trust. Six months later, a plan to refinance the Club was presented by Treasurer B. F. Stephenson. Six months after that, in May 1933, General Manager V.C. Goetz was instructed to contact the Club's creditors and attempt to "adjust accounts payable on the most favorable basis." Yet another class of membership, Seasonal, with dues of $10.00 per month, was offered to attract part-time residents.

In December 1933, with the repeal of Prohibition, the directors saw an opportunity to add alcoholic beverages to the Club's menu of attractions. Regrettably, there was no money in the coffers to purchase a liquor license, so the board members took up a collection among themselves to pay the $750 fee. Thanks to their efforts, the Club was no longer a dry ship.

Despite board heroics, foreclosure

On November 14, 1934, the inevitable occurred: Liquidation. The board moved to close the clubhouse for the entire winter, beginning December 1. All employees were to be dismissed, "except those absolutely necessary to the protection of the Club's property in winter." At the same time, the directors implemented a liquidation plan proposed by the "Creditors' Committee" to address more than one million dollars in outstanding debt. A sign that the Depression was impacting the lives of almost everyone, the board at that meeting accepted the resignations of some of the Club's proudest names: William E. Roney, Joseph L. Hickey, Past Commodore John French, Oscar Webber and William Fisher. More resigna-

tions and expulsions followed in a steady stream over the ensuing three months. A long and tragic struggle was about to come to an end.

On February 28, 1935, a letter was sent to all the Club's creditors informing them that, "the Club is unable to meet its financial obligations and is considering reorganization under the Federal Bankruptcy Act." At this point, the Club was over a million dollars in debt with no means of repayment. As mute testimony to the severity of the situation, the board minutes from the mid-1930s are typed on the back of Club stationery, because that was apparently the only paper affordable at the time.

A caretaker, Mr. William Lancaster, under the title of assistant manager, was hired, along with his wife as housekeeper, and some other staff, for pay plus living quarters in the clubhouse.

Less than six years after the pomp and splendor of its Grand Opening, the Grosse Pointe Yacht Club officially closed its doors.

And so it ended — not with a bang, but with a dull thud.

During the twenty-seven months the Club was in receivership under the control of the Collateral Liquidation Corporation, the property was maintained and the clubhouse offered for rental to business organizations and private parties. In 1937, Paul Moreland, who was president of the Detroit chapter of the American Institute of Banking and who would later become commodore, negotiated the use of the Club for the institute's annual dinner dance. Around that time, future Commodore George Kriese, then a young man of nineteen, was dating a young lady from Liggett School, which was located in Indian Village in Detroit in those days. He recalls being invited by her to a Sunday afternoon tea dance at the Club. It was held in the Main Dining Room, with a string quartet providing the music. This was the first time Kriese, whose memory at age ninety-seven is enviably sharp, set foot in the clubhouse. But he remembers riding past it as a child, watching it being built, and marveling at what an impressive building it was. And recalling that long-ago tea dance, he remembers being in total awe of the Club's elegant interior.

Former and future members help Slocum regain the Club

The end of 1934 may have seen the end of GPYC members' access to their clubhouse, but the board of directors continued to hold meetings there. B.F. Stephenson was still commodore and treasurer, and a number of directors were known to have attended meetings under his leadership, including First Vice Commodore Walter F. Tant, Second Vice Commodore Thomas G. Wade, Rear Commodore John MacNeil Burns, Charles Bush, William Mertz, Edward Grace, and George Slocum.

The last known board minutes for 1935 are dated September 9, with another meeting that was supposed to occur on September 24. In the waning months of 1935, the entire assets of the Club were turned over to the Collateral Liquidation Corporation. During this same time period, George Slocum, founder of Automotive News, became commodore of the Club. Walter Tant continued as first vice commodore along with Second Vice Commodore Wade and Rear Commodore Burns. William Mertz was the secretary and Stephenson, although no longer commodore, remained as treasurer through 1936, when John Burns took over those duties. Writing in the July 1939 Grosse Pointer about his undoubtedly difficult years of leadership through 1936 and 1937, Slocum reflected:

> Every plan and method for bringing the Club out from its financial difficulties was tried. There was simply no hope, and during my second year as commodore we finally received approval of all parties to put Club properties under the friendly terms of 77B [Bankruptcy Reorganization, Section 77B] to establish the equities of those who had claims against the property and to bail out the water which everyone knew was foundering a good ship.[6]

A remarkable set of circumstances in 1938 ultimately turned matters around and led to the reemergence of the Club. In the September 1983 Grosse Pointer, Past Commodore Lynn Pierson described what happened:

> I was in Judge Lederle's office in the Federal Building one day, testifying in some

The U.S. Coast Guard comes to Lake St. Clair, thanks to GPYC

Between 1928 and 1932, the Village of Grosse Pointe Shores owned and operated a powerboat equipped with a ship-to-shore radio that was used for water rescue and other emergencies. But after discussion regarding the expense and upkeep of the boat, it was retired. After that, Norbert P. Neff, Grosse Pointe City clerk, used his own powerboat to respond to emergencies until the spring of 1936. Meanwhile, GPYC member Alger Shelden, who had achieved local prominence by winning the Port Huron-to-Mackinac race in 1930 and 1931, launched a campaign to have a U.S. Coast Guard boat stationed on Lake St. Clair.[25]

Back then, the nearest USCG base was located downriver at Trenton, Michigan. The Livingstone Channel at the mouth of the Detroit River was scheduled to open in August 1936, at which time the Trenton base would close, meaning the nearest Coast Guard stations would be at Port Huron, Michigan, and Marble Head, Ohio, each some sixty miles from the junction of Lake St. Clair and the Detroit River.[26]

Mr. Shelden obtained the help of several influential people, including Grosse Pointers Henry Webber, commodore of the Detroit River Yachting Association (DRYA); George Slocum, commodore of GPYC; Norbert Neff, Grosse Pointe City clerk; as well as Grosse Pointe City mayor H.B. Trix. The group devoted their personal time, energy, and money attempting to convince the federal government of the need to establish a USCG station on Lake St. Clair. Shelden on two occasions flew to Washington, D.C., and to the USCG base at Buffalo, New York, to plead his case. He also received help from local U.S. congressmen and three U.S. senators, including James J. Couzens.[27]

Much evidence of boating mishaps and sixty drownings on Lake St. Clair and the Detroit River was presented. The congressmen were reminded that Detroit, then with a population of 1.75 million, was the nation's fourth largest city and second only to Chicago in size on the Great Lakes. Chicago had three Coast Guard stations while Detroit had none.[28]

Figure 22. With the urging of Club leaders, Congress authorized the U.S. Coast Guard to establish its first year-round presence on Lake St. Clair with this seventy-five-foot cutter. *CG-192* motored to its new home at the GPYC on June 20, 1936.

Mr. Shelden persuaded U.S. Congressman Clarence J. McLeod to introduce a bill that would establish the Lake St. Clair Coast Guard station. The Grosse Pointe Yacht Club, despite being in receivership, was offered as a headquarters for the base, along with the harbor, jointly owned by the Yacht Club and the Village of Grosse Pointe Shores. The Club's bell tower would be available as a lookout station when needed by the USCG. [29]

Shelden and Congressman McLeod then convinced Coast Guard commandant H.G. Hamlet that a recent series of drownings on the lake created an emergency that must be addressed at once. The commandant endorsed the establishment of a Coast Guard station on Lake St. Clair. The bill that would establish the base was passed by Congress and signed by President Roosevelt on June 29, 1936. The Grosse Pointes had thus won an exception to the blanket presidential order that forbade the building of new Coast Guard stations during the Depression. [30]

U.S. Coast Guard Cutter #192 arrived at the GPYC harbor on June 20, 1936. The boat was seventy-five feet in length and cruised at sixteen knots. Armament for the crew of seven consisted of two one-pound cannon and one machine gun,

plus a complement of thirty-caliber rifles and forty-five-caliber pistols.[31] The boat also had a ship-to-shore radio that was monitored by the local police departments who were said to have a good working relationship with the Coast Guardsmen. In addition, the GPYC provided a dockside telephone: NIAGRA-6027. [32]

The duties of the Coast Guard were to protect life and property on the Detroit River and Lake St. Clair and to maintain active patrol within its district, which extended from Fighting Island, twelve miles south of the City of Detroit, to Marine City on the St. Clair River, a distance of approximately fifty miles. Their mission also included cruising Lake St. Clair, an area of four hundred square miles. The cutter would make numerous trips to help stranded lake freighters and render any assistance necessary. A second shallow-draft USCG vessel was stationed at the mouth of the Clinton River. [33]

Eventually the Coast Guard would build a station of its own in St. Clair Shores. But their reassuring presence on the lake today began with the persistence of one Grosse Pointe Yacht Club member and the willingness of the Club to give the USCG a home.

■ ◪ ■

case or another. I remember the judge suddenly calling me into his chambers, saying he had something to talk about. He then asked me if I lived in Grosse Pointe; I said yes. Then he asked if I was a member of the Club. I told him no. He asked if I knew that the Club was for sale for $125,000. I surely did not. Then the judge told me about the mortgage and all the debts against the Club, and he said that all those things would be wiped out for the price of $125,000. Abner Larned [a former GPYC director] was the receiver. Well, I hustled to get a group together at the Detroit Boat Club the next day around noon. I can't recall everyone, but there were Ward Peck, Jim Marks, John P. Fraser and others. We had a plan in no time. To raise money, we'd had to sell fifty lifetime memberships at $1,000 apiece. Initial dues for others who wanted to join as new members were $100 a year.

Following this meeting, Pierson contacted Commodore Slocum, informing him that he had just learned the Club was for sale and had organized a group with a plan to buy it. Working together, they brought more investors into the group and were ultimately successful in raising the $25,000 required in the court documents to proceed with the purchase of the Club's assets from the Collateral Liquidation Corporation. In Lynn Pierson's *Grosse Pointer* article, he tells of his own personal fund-raising efforts:

> I remember walking into K.T. Keller's office — he was the head of Chrysler, you know — and by the time I left he had sold six other guys the idea to join as lifetime members. He was a real wonder. Whenever we needed a boost, we just called in K.T.

Within this group of more than twenty investors, only seven had previously been members of the Club: Keller and Slocum, James Marks, Herbert Woodall, Thomas Wade, Alger Shelden, and E.R. Grace. In addition to Slocum, previous members James Marks and Herbert Woodall would ultimately serve as commodores. New members Lynn Pierson, Ward Peck and Frank Couzens would also serve in that capacity.

The first reorganizational meeting of the Club was held symbolically in the clubhouse on May 24, 1938, but it was at the second meeting, held the very next day at the Detroit Club and chaired by Lynn Pierson, where officers were elected. They were:

George M. Slocum . . Commodore
K.T. Keller . . . . First Vice Commodore
Frank Couzens . . . . . . Second Vice Commodore
Herbert J. Woodall . . Third Vice Commodore
H. Lynn Pierson . . . . Rear Commodore and
Treasurer
Ward H. Peck . . . . Secretary

And with that, the Grosse Pointe Yacht Club was back in business.

Figure 23. The GPYC as it looked in August 1937. Although the Club was in receivership from the Depression, boats were still kept in the harbor and private functions were held in the clubhouse. Note the Coast Guard cutter docked along the East Wall.

Figure 24. The seventy-five-foot USCG cutter is shown here patrolling the Deroit River.

The story of the *Sea Witch*

The highlight of the clubhouse Grand Opening in 1929 was a dinner dance, at which was unveiled the massive painting, ten by twenty feet, of the *Sea Witch*, by acclaimed East Coast marine artist Frank Vining Smith. The painting was created expressly for the Club, at a cost of $20,000, and depicts an actual New York-to-San Francisco ocean race in 1851 between the clipper ships *Sea Witch, Raven,* and *Typhoon.* The painting was donated to the Club by Commodore John French.

Time, however, took its toll. In the decades that followed, the work's dramatic images diminished due to the cigarette and cigar smoke that once permeated the Ballroom. The residue reached a point where the two ships in the background, *Raven* and *Typhoon*, disappeared completely from the scene, and were subsequently forgotten. It was not until the painting was given a professional cleaning in 1971 at the behest of Commodore French's family that the missing ships were rediscovered. Another cleaning in 2011 also revealed sailors the size of ants working high up in the rigging of *Sea Witch*. Regular maintenance now ensures that the original beauty and detail of the work still capture the attention of Ballroom visitors, just as they did when the painting was unveiled in 1929.

There is a final, recently uncovered story about the *Sea Witch* that deserves telling here. It turns out there is a second *Sea Witch* painting in existence. Before Commodore French commissioned the massive Ballroom painting from Mr. Smith, he had the artist create a much smaller version of it — approximately two by four feet — so he could see exactly what he was buying. Apparently French liked what he saw and gave the go-ahead. The smaller painting today graces the home of French's great-grandson, Conrad "Duke" Williams, in New Orleans.

◼▨◼

Above, figure 25. The *Sea Witch* by Frank Vining Smith is the Club's most prominent *objet d'art*. It measures ten by twenty feet, weighs eight hundred pounds, and has hung in the same commanding location in the Ballroom for eighty-five years. Photograph by John F. Martin.

Right, figure 26. The *Sea Witch* as it looked shortly after the Grand Opening.

Far right, figure 27. Marine artist Smith at work on his giant masterpiece. He was present at the Club when the painting was unveiled July 4, 1929.

Key players in the formative years of the Club

Edsel B. Ford I:
Our briefest-serving commodore

The membership of Edsel Bryant Ford I, son of Ford Motor Company founder Henry Ford I, is something of a Club mystery because detailed records of his time at the Club are non-existent. What is known is that Edsel Ford was proposed for membership at the Club by then Rear Commodore Clarence Ayres at the meeting of the board on July 28, 1926. Mr. Ford's membership was unanimously approved and later in the same meeting he was elected to the board of directors. At the reorganizational meeting on August 11, new flag officers were elected, at which time Mr. Ford was nominated and then elected commodore of the Club. His term, and that of the other flag officers, was to last until the next annual meeting in January 1927.

What tends to confuse the matter is that Mr. Ford resigned as commodore just forty days after assuming the office. It appears he was "unable to serve" in that capacity. His resignation has led some historians to conclude that Mr. Ford left the Club at the same time, but he did not. He remained an Active GPYC member until 1933.

Speculation also suggests that there was some sort of falling-out between Mr. Ford and the Club soon after he joined. But the minutes show that his letter of resignation was accepted with regret by the board, that "his wishes so kindly expressed in his letter to the [Club] secretary, should be respected."

So why did Edsel Ford resign as commodore? It is a guess — but a reasoned one — that his job as president of Ford Motor Company simply demanded too much of his time.[11] With the company undergoing mass retooling to replace the antiquated Model T with the new Model A, the pressures on him were enormous, some of which were probably coming from his father, insisting that he give his undivided attention to the family business.

If that was the case, Mr. Ford's decision to step down as commodore was conscientious and in the best interest of the Club, an act that was consistent with the character of the gentleman himself.

Edsel B. Ford I
1926

GPYC

Figure 28.

In 1933, in the thick of the Depression, the board voted to make him a Life member, "non-assessable and without dues," in view of the "distinctive services" he had provided to the Club. Clearly, Edsel Ford was a valued GPYC member.

John H. French:
The visionary "Clubhouse Commodore"

John H. French, known as "J.H." to his close friends, was one of our four-longest serving commodores, and arguably among the best. He steered the Club through some of its most formative and challenging years, from September 21, 1926, to 1931. He presided over the planning and building of the GPYC clubhouse and harbor, officiated at its Grand Opening, delighted in its initial success, and then stood tall when the Depression threatened its very existence. With the economy collapsing, he brought in automotive magnates Charles Kettering and K. T. Keller to stabilize the board and calm a panicky membership. Eighty-five years later, the painting, *Sea Witch*, which Mr. French commissioned for the Club and donated to it, still hangs proudly in the Ballroom.

John H. French
1926–1931

Figure 29.

C. Hayward Murphy
1931–1934

Figure 30.

In his own right, Commodore French was a successful industrialist and banker. He cofounded the Michigan Stamping Company, which merged with Briggs Manufacturing Company before Briggs itself became part of Chrysler Corporation. He retired from industry in 1924, only to return as vice president and general manager of the Briggs organization. Mr. French then went on to create the City Bank and also founded Jennings Memorial Hospital.[12,13] Mr. French resigned from the Club in 1934, but rejoined in 1940 after the Club reopened. He died of a heart attack in 1952. The French family's beloved iceboat, *French Boy*, was donated to the Club in 1999 and is on display in the Fo'c'sle Room today.

C. Hayward Murphy:
Taking the heat

It is difficult to say which of our Depression-era commodores drew the worst watch. There was B.F. Stephenson, who governed from 1934 to 1935 through the worst of the downturn. Or there was George Slocum, from 1935 to 1940, who formally ushered the Club into receivership. A third and likely candidate for this dubious

honor would surely be C. Hayward Murphy, who, as commodore from 1931 to 1934 in the early throes of the collapse, tried futilely to bail a sinking ship.

C. Hayward Murphy. The regal ring of his name alone might have been enough to install him as commodore, but in fact he was a person of considerable means and influence in the growing city of Detroit. He was a member of the Detroit Fire Commission by appointment of Detroit mayor John C. Lodge and served on the board of directors of several large Detroit institutions, including the Detroit National Bank and Detroit Guardian Trust Company. As a Yale graduate, Mr. Murphy had a lifestyle that was typically "good school" and he was a familiar figure at many area clubs where he was a member: the Country Club of Detroit, the Detroit Athletic Club, the Grosse Pointe Hunt Club, the Lochmoor Club, the Old Club, the Detroit Club, and the University Club, to name a few.

But it was Mr. Murphy's banking connections that were undoubtedly most responsible for putting him in the commodore's chair at the Grosse Pointe Yacht Club. When it became

H. Lynn Pierson
1942

Figure 31.

George M. Slocum
1935–1940

Figure 32.

apparent that the Club was strapped for money to pay for the new clubhouse and harbor, Murphy was instrumental in arranging for several large loans that would temporarily get the Club out of trouble. One of those loans, for $250,000, came directly from the Guardian Trust Company, of which he was a director. And when the Club was unable to make payment on the loan, Murphy himself interceded with Guardian Trust creditors to give the Club more time. Unfortunately for all parties, time was not enough.[14]

H. Lynn Pierson: Unsung

Commodore Lynn Pierson is one of the unsung heroes in the Club's recovery from bankruptcy. It was Pierson who took immediate action upon hearing about the Club being for sale for a fraction of the indebtedness that sent it into receivership. And it was he who quickly organized a meeting of investors to come up with the funding to buy back the Club from its creditors.

Mr. Pierson not only became a member of the re-formed Club, he went on to become commodore in 1942. Without his decisiveness and leadership, the GPYC as we know it might not exist.

George M. Slocum: A light at the end of the darkness

George Mertz Slocum served as commodore from late 1935 to January 1940, although the clubhouse was shuttered to the general membership for three of those years. Born into a publishing family in tiny Caro, Michigan, Slocum went to work as a typesetter at age twelve and always stayed close to his professional roots, eventually founding two successful publications, the *Michigan Business Farmer* and *Automotive Daily News*, which became *Automotive News*. While employed as an advertising copywriter, he joined the Adcraft Club of Detroit early enough in its existence to become one of its pioneer members. Mr. Slocum went on to become president of that organization in 1933, and from there, president of the Advertising Federation of America. Described as a dapper but conservative dresser who disliked golf and avoided horses, Slocum was an avid boater, the nephew of Joshua Slocum, the first person to sail solo around the world. Mr. Slocum owned a number of powerboats and sailboats, several of which were named *Spray* after his uncle's famous circumnavigating sailboat. One of his

Burnette F. Stephenson
1934–1935

Figure 33.

favorites was *Spray II*, a handsome forty-plus-foot Chris Craft that is shown elsewhere in this book.[15,16,17]

Mr. Slocum became commodore of the Club just in time to guide it into formal bankruptcy in late 1935. But the unflappable skipper never abandoned hope of restarting the organization. His hopes were realized less than three years later, on June 10, 1938, when the "new" Club was reorganized and he was reelected commodore. Three months afterward, Mr. Slocum presided over the new Club's first official board meeting and negotiated the terms of repayment that would lift the Club out of receivership. He also ushered in the very first issue of *The Grosse Pointer* as a color magazine, the same Club publication that members enjoy today. In his column in that inaugural issue, Slocum proudly announced that not only was the Club debt-free, but in a strong, cash-positive condition. Under Slocum's guidance, Club members began rejoining, and the GPYC never looked back. A new expanded harbor was opened, doubling the dock capacity of the old one. Simultaneously, plans for a new and improved swimming pool were unveiled.

On July 4, 1938, exactly nine years after the clubhouse Grand Opening, Commodore Slocum held a public ceremony in which the infamous mortgage was joyously burned. For a short time, at least until the outbreak of World War II, better times were here again.

In January 1940, at the annual meeting of the membership, George Slocum was officially recognized for his significant contributions to the Club.

Burnette F. Stephenson: Grace and perseverance in hard times

If you have kept an appointment in the Stephenson Building or taken a drive along Stephenson Highway, you have crossed paths, figuratively at least, with Commodore Burnette F. Stephenson, said to be an affable, easygoing person who amassed a considerable fortune from real estate. In the early 1900s, he began developing the area around Six Mile Road and Woodward near the Ford assembly plant in Highland Park, transforming it from an industrial complex into a thriving residential community. The key to Mr. Stephenson's success was that he didn't just sell lots; he completely developed them before the buyer took ownership, with electricity, water, sewage, telephone service, sidewalks, bus service, and so on. Moreover, he sold the lots for a price of $1 down and $1 a week. The idea was a tremendous hit. All told, Mr. Stephenson built an estimated five thousand homes in the Detroit area.[18]

In 1916, B.F. Stephenson, together with several colleagues, purchased a continuous stretch of acreage that ran from Six-and-a-Half-Mile Road to Nineteen Mile Road and was at the time mostly farmland. The key feature of the development was the Stephenson Super-Highway, a roadway and rail line that linked Highland Park with suburbs such as Royal Oak and helped create the city of Hazel Park, named after Stephenson's wife. Mr. Stephenson became, in the truest sense of the term, a real estate magnate, with his headquarters in the prosperous ten-story office building that bore his name in the New Center area of Detroit.[18]

Mr. Stephenson's fortunes took a downward turn soon after he became commodore of the GPYC in 1934. As reported, the Club was already in serious financial trouble by then, and Stephenson's year consisted mainly of holding off creditors, witnessing a relentless stream of member resignations, and finally acknowledging that the Club was bankrupt. Commodore Stephenson had the unenviable job of presiding over the Club as foreclosure loomed.

The Depression also hit Stephenson himself. His upscale Alta Marina development in St. Petersburg, Florida, fell on hard times and his personal fortune dwindled. According to his son James, the only thing that kept him from jumping off his own ten-story building was his farm in St. Clair, Michigan.[19]

Stephenson survived the Depression, but after that, the jovial gentleman was said to rarely smile again. He later ran for U.S. Senator and Governor, but without success. He died of pneumonia in 1954.[20]

Clarence L. Ayres:
Motivator and benefactor

As previously noted, it was Clarence Ayres who provided at no profit to himself the property on which the Club stands. But it was also his encouragement and enthusiasm that helped make the property into the exceptional clubhouse grounds and harbor that it eventually became. It was his urging, together with his own impressive stature in the community, that in no small part gave the board the confidence — or perhaps shove — it needed to move forward with a vision of building "the finest yacht club in the world."[6]

Mr. Ayres himself rose to the rank of rear commodore of the Club, although it is uncertain why he never went on to become its CEO. A reminder of his generosity resides today above the fountain in the Rotunda of the clubhouse. It is the sculpture of three female figures, titled *Rhythm of the Waves*, by the noted artist Wheeler Williams, which was donated to the Club by Mr. Ayres in honor of the 1929 Grand Opening. According to Club folklore, the model for the central figure was controversial dancer Isadora

Clarence L. Ayres

GPYC

Figure 34

Duncan. And while legends often pose as fact, records show that Ms. Duncan died in a motoring accident in 1927, a date that precedes the creation of the sculpture. However, it is still possible that Ms. Duncan's world-famous figure might have at least served as the inspiration for the piece. In 1934, Mr. Ayres was made an honorary member of the GPYC "in appreciation of his splendid services as a pioneer organizer and supporter of this Club, and to tender him a vote of thanks on behalf of the entire membership."

An undocumented story about Mr. Ayres relates that he went on to lose his considerable personal fortune in the Depression. According to the tale, Ayres salvaged enough cash to enable him, his wife, and his daughter to continue living in the Grosse Pointe area, but not in their luxurious Lake Shore home, which today is owned by Past Commodore John Boll and his wife Marlene. What exactly happened to Ayres is unknown, except that he remained president of his firm, the American Insurance Company, until at least 1938.[6, 21-24] A story of him disappearing from Grosse Pointe without a trace is unconfirmed,

Rhythm of the Waves: The grand gift that didn't arrive in time

Figure 35. *Ryhthm of the Waves* in the Rotunda

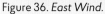

Figure 36. *East Wind.*

Figure 37. *West Wind.*

Clarence Ayres was looking for an imposing work that would grace the clubhouse rotunda and inspire onlookers with its presence. Could Williams come up with something that would capture the spirit of this proud new yacht club?

Williams' proposal was a garden sculpture—one of his favorite themes— depicting three well-endowed water nymphs by a fountain. The "Muses," as they were known in Greek mythology, were the goddesses of inspiration, science, and the arts — disciplines that would hopefully forever be part of the Club's culture. The flowing water of the fountain was meant to represent the timeless motion of the lake, giving rise to the work's title, *Rhythm of the Waves.* Two smaller sculptures also inspired by Greek mythology, *East Wind* and *West Wind*, would be placed on opposite sides of the Rotunda, to symbolize the prevailing lake winds.

Mr. Ayres was sold. He commissioned the young sculptor to execute the works in bronze and later paid the considerable sum of nearly thirty thousand dollars for them. Unfortunately, Williams failed to complete the assignment in time for the July Fourth Grand Opening, so it never received the acclaim it might have. Nevertheless, even when the works arrived some months later in the midst of a crumbling national economy, they were hailed as masterpieces.

Rhythm of the Waves, East Wind, and *West Wind* stand in the Rotunda today, reminders of Williams' genius and Ayres' generosity.

About the time Commodore John French was commissioning artist Frank Vining Smith to paint the massive *Sea Witch* as a gift to the Club, another wealthy member, Clarence Ayres, was in contact with East Coast sculptor Wheeler Williams about the creation of a piece of sculpture that would also be given to the Club to mark the Grand Opening of the clubhouse. Despite his youth, Williams was a promising up-and-comer whose sculpted works would eventually be displayed across Europe and the U.S. He had studied art at Yale, where he graduated *Magna cum Laude,* and at Harvard, where he earned his Masters of Architecture degree. In 1928, Williams was freshly back in the U.S. from advanced study at *Ecole des Beaux-Arts* in Paris.

although a search of the records reveals nothing of his life after 1938. All we know for certain is that Mr. Ayres died in the tiny border town of Edinburg, Texas, in 1941. He was sixty-seven years old.

Even so, when word was received of Ayres's death, the flag at the Club was flown at half-mast in his honor. It was testimony to the esteem in which he was held, many years after he was actively involved with the Club.

IMAGE ACKNOWLEDGEMENTS
Chapter Two

1. GPYC
2. Cynthia Naughton
3. Percell Siniff/Dorothy Jewett family
4. Village of Grosse Pointe Shores
5. Guy Lowell, *Wikimedia Commons*
6. *Pencil Points* magazine
7. Percell Siniff/Dorothy Jewett family
8. Ibid
9. Village of Grosse Pointe Shores
10. GPYC
11. Percell Siniff/Dorothy Jewett family
12. From the collections of the Henry Ford
13. GPYC
14. Ibid, Photograph by John Martin
15. WSU/ *Detroit News*
16. Joe Schaden
17. Ibid
18. GPYC
19. Ibid
20. Backman family
21. Dossin Family Collection
22. USCG
23. WSU / *Detroit News*
24. USCG
25. GPYC
26. Ibid
27. Hard Press Editions, Stockbridge
28. From the Collection of The Henry Ford
29. – 34. GPYC
35. – 37. Jim Dorian
38. Joe Schaden

Figure 38. Grosse Pointe Yacht Club truck with snowplow, circa 1929–1935. Note GPYC burgee painted on side.

Figure 1. The Club's first swimming pool officially opened July 4, 1939, shown here with harbor in background. Spectators are enjoying a swimming exhibition put on by members of the Detroit Athletic Club. For the first year of the Club's reopening in 1938, swimmers were relegated to a roped-off area in the lake known as the "swim court."

By Larry W. Stephenson, M.D.,

July 1938 through 1940

The "new" Grosse Pointe Yacht Club

The new Grosse Pointe Yacht Club was incorporated in May 1938 by Commodore George Slocum, Rear Commodore and Treasurer H. Lynn Pierson, and Secretary Ward H. Peck and received its charter on July 1, 1938.[1] The clubhouse reopened its doors to the membership in late June or early July,[2] at which point members began using the Club for such things as meetings and preparations for the formal reopening celebration, to be held on July fourth.[3]

The Grosse Pointer at that time was basically just a four-page newsletter. The headline of the July 1938 issue, probably mailed out to the membership sometime in June, reads, "Fourth of July Marks Ninth Anniversary and Eighth Annual Regatta of G.P.Y.C.", with a subtitle, "Full Program of Sailing, Swimming and Dancing Offered Members to Celebrate Formal Opening of New Club."[4]

That issue included the proposed schedule of events for the Fourth of July, beginning with the regatta at 10:45 am and ending with dancing on the terrace until midnight. At 10:00 pm there was to be a "Declaration of GPYC Independence and Bonfire of Old Bonds, Notes, Mortgages, 'worn-out bunting and slithered canvas' and burial-at-sea of the ashes thereof!"

An article guaranteed to warm the hearts of any board member, anytime, was titled, "All Boat Wells Filled" and declared that "The dock committee is already planning additional wells to accommodate new members." There was a list of boat owners with the names of their boats that were docked in the GPYC harbor on opening day.

Figure 2. *The Grosse Pointer* (July 1938) when it was still the Club's four-page newsletter.

—*Courtesy YACHTING.*

NOVEMBER 1938

Figure 3. Cover, first issue of *The Grosse Pointer* as a magazine, November 1938.

★ ★

Another article was titled, "Think of It—A Swim-Court." It states,

> You never heard of a swim court? Adjoining the pier south of the Club will run a board cat-walk for a distance of fifty feet. Floating markers will square off the rectangular area of seventy-five ft. long by forty ft. wide within the enclosure of which will be a raft, a water chute, springboard, etc. A lifeguard will be in attendance and depths in the swim-court will be marked so that everyone can swim with safety. The bottom of the lake at this point is smooth and free from stones and the entire area will be kept manicured and groomed so that the most fastidious may enjoy the sparkling, refreshing waters with peace of mind. There has been a lot of discussion about the open swimming pool at the Club, but any attempt to construct one this year would cause such a disturbance and upsetting of the grounds that it would spoil the season.[4]

Within two months of that grand July reopening, the Club had accepted 171 new members in the following categories: 41 Life; 77 Class A; and 53 Class B.[1] By the end of 1938 an additional 28 Class A and 27 Class B members had joined, for a grand total of 226 new members in just six months.

In November 1938 *The Grosse Pointer* was expanded from a newsletter into a full-fledged magazine. It was published with the aid of Cliff Warner, publisher of a number of other private club magazines in the Detroit area. In the first issue with the new format, Commodore Slocum stated, "The finances of the Club were never in better shape. Our treasurer, Rear-Commodore Lynn Pierson, reports that there are no outstanding current bills and he has maintained a healthy bank balance of many thousand dollars."[5]

He went on to state, "The improvement of the harbor under direction of Vice-Commodore K. T. Keller is progressing rapidly, the sheet-piling is already driven on the north side of the harbor and before the ice sets in it will be completed. This will give the Club a capacity of nearly double the number of boat wells and offer our boat-owning

GPYC

Figure 4. K. T. Keller, president of Chrysler Corporation, served as first vice commodore in 1938 and 1939. He played a significant role in bringing the Club out of bankruptcy in 1938.

members, for the first time since the Club was opened in 1929, a calm, safe harbor in a location second to no yacht club harbor on the Great Lakes."[3, 5]

1939: A return to "normalcy"

The summer of 1939 saw the clubhouse celebrating its tenth anniversary with a schedule of activities over the Fourth of July weekend that was said to rival a three-ring circus.[6] As part of the festivities, the Club's first outdoor swimming pool was formally opened, built to replace the "swim court" from 1938 that apparently was not as popular as was hoped.

The first Showboat Party took place on July 29 and was so popular that it became a major annual summer event for many years. This was also the first year that the GPYC sponsored the Bluenose Regatta, now an annual event that to this day continues to attract DRYA (Detroit River Yachting Association) sailors to the GPYC.

In the harbor, the number of boat wells increased from twenty-three to fifty-six. The construction of these new wells was financed by charging boat well renters three years of rental fees in advance.

Figure 5A. Figs. 5A, B, & C show different views of the hand-painted murals that graced the walls of the Grille Room, now the Spinnaker.

Inside the clubhouse, the Grille Room (now the Spinnaker) was transformed from "drab and uninviting" into a very attractive room for cocktails and lighter fare. Two well-known local artists, Russell Lange and Gerard VanderHeyden, painted the walls with colorful murals that depicted the full range of activities the Club offered to its members throughout the year.[7] For whatever reason, the following year the "e" was dropped from the name and it became the Grill Room. Construction was also begun on four new bowling alleys. The Club was fairly humming with activity.

Commodore Slocum's 1939 annual message began with these words: "No one could be more cognizant than your present commodore, of the necessity of brevity on the occasion of the annual meeting of any club." He went on to speak of the history of the Club, the untimely effects of the Depression on the new clubhouse, and then of the efforts to keep the Club afloat.

Now, having been only one of a group who went through the vicissitudes of the next nine years with the Club, I would just as soon let some impartial historian record that tragic era. Suffice it to say that a loyal group of officers, a

Figure 5B.

Figure 5C.

★ ★ ★

GPYC

Figure 6. Commodore George Slocum; photo taken circa 1938.

The stars seemed finally to be in alignment regarding the fortunes of the GPYC. But the most momentous event of 1939 was to occur just fourteen months after the Club had so triumphantly reopened.

On September 1 Germany invaded Poland, and Europe—once again—plunged into war. Members of the "old" GPYC had been forced to struggle with the challenges of the Great Depression almost from the day the clubhouse doors had opened. Now members of the "new" GPYC, having successfully returned the Club to financial stability and feeling so optimistic about the future, found themselves facing the uncertainties of a world at war and the awful possibility that the United States would one day be forced into the fray.

1940: War clouds gather; the Club welcomes the military

The Grosse Pointe Yacht Club began the new year with a new commodore. On January 11, Frank Couzens was elected to replace George Slocum, who had served in that position since the late fall of 1935. The Club was in good financial health, operating in the black, with monthly dues of $15.[2]

board of directors and many energetic and substantial citizens worked tirelessly, burned the midnight oil away from the bosom of their families many a night and broke into many a busy day with luncheon conferences, trying to find a way out for the old Grosse Pointe Yacht Club. From any impartial observer's viewpoint it was however obviously "just one of those 1929 things." So water-logged with bonds and mortgages that it was not only a white elephant but as out of line with Depression year values as a dinosaur returned to earth today! [8]

GPYC

Figure 7. Commodore Frank Couzens, 1940.

Contractor, Detroit Mayor, Bank Chairman, Commodore

Frank Couzens was thirty-seven when he took the reins of commodore in January 1940. He was the son of James J. Couzens and Margaret (Manning) Couzens. James Couzens had become secretary of the Ford Motor Company at its founding in 1903 and soon became vice president and general manager. He resigned from the company in 1915 and sold his Ford stock in 1919 for thirty million dollars. He went on to become mayor of Detroit and a U.S. senator, serving in the Senate for fourteen years until his death in 1936 at age sixty-four.

In 1922, Frank Couzens established a building construction company. That same year he married Margaret Lang; they had four sons and three daughters. In 1931 he served as president of the Detroit City Council and went on to be elected mayor, serving two terms from January 1934 to January 1938. After retiring from politics, Couzens founded the Wabeek Bank of Detroit and remained its chairman for the next twelve years. [12]

During World War II he joined the Army and served from 1942 to 1945, attaining the rank of colonel. He died in 1950 at the age of forty-eight after a long struggle with cancer.

In February, the four bowling lanes under construction were completed and opened for play. Four generous members stepped up to donate funds to purchase lockers for the bowlers. Three sailboats were donated to the sailing program and a fourth was purchased by the Club through member contributions.

Meanwhile in Europe, the war was escalating. On April 9, Germany invaded Norway and Denmark; on May 10, Luxembourg, The Netherlands, and Belgium fell, and only days later the German army entered France.

At the May 16 meeting of the board of directors, a special provision was put into the bylaws for prospective GPYC members serving as officers on active military duty. It read in part, "After discussion, a motion was made and passed recommending to the membership of the Club for consideration . . . memberships for commissioned officers of the regular Army and Navy of the United States, and membership of the clergy." In effect, the provision encouraged military officers on active duty in the area to become members. Their monthly dues would be reduced and the initiation fee waived. The same conditions would apply to members of the clergy. Residence requirements were set at no more than thirty miles from the city limits of Detroit.

GPYC members welcomed the summer of 1940 with sailing events, motorboat cruising, swim meets, parties, and relaxation in the sun. The flag mast at the entrance to the Club was donated and installed by member Clare Jacobs, just in time for racing signals to fly for the eleventh Annual Sailing Regatta on July 4. According to the September *Grosse Pointer*, several GPYC yachts had been cruising Georgian Bay throughout the summer.

And the war? On June 10, Italy sided with Germany and declared war on Britain. France fell on June 22, leaving Britain with no allies in western Europe. German military might had crushed six countries in three months. In the Far East, Japan had invaded and controlled most of eastern China and was becoming more belligerent toward its other neighbors. In August the massive air attack on England known as the

Figure 8. The Club's four original bowling lanes, 1940.

Battle of Britain began in earnest. In the United States, isolationist groups were urging neutrality, and Congress passed the Ludlow Amendment, requiring a national referendum to declare war, with the sole exception of invasion. But it was becoming increasingly clear to many people, both in the United States and abroad, that world dominance was the ultimate goal of the German and Japanese military forces, and the longer the United States remained uncommitted, the greater the struggle would be to overcome their powerful armies.[9]

At the direction of the U.S. government, U.S. factories began ramping up to supply Britain with war materials, and for Detroit that meant airplanes, tanks, and military vehicles. Among the leaders and key personnel at these Detroit companies were several members of the GPYC who would eventually play important roles in the

Figure 9. Member William S. Knudsen, president of General Motors, was appointed chairman of the Office of Production Management by President Roosevelt as war became more likely.

coming U.S. involvement in the war. One such gentleman was William S. Knudsen, president of General Motors, who was appointed by President Roosevelt that summer to be chairman of the Office of Production Management and a member of the National Defense Advisory Commission. He in turn asked fellow GPYC member K. T. Keller, president of Chrysler, to assist him in his duties. [10]

The Grosse Pointer 1940 yearbook contains the annual message from Commodore Couzens, which reads as follows:

> After almost two and one-half years since the re-organization of this Club, it gives me great pleasure to announce that our membership is almost at a close. An achievement which in the dark days of 1933 seemed almost impossible. This accomplishment was only obtained by the splendid cooperation of the entire membership, and from all indications we are on the upward trend.
>
> Operating in the black for the first time in the history of the Club, I take special pride in congratulating my associates on the board, the committees and the cooperation of the entire membership, in their faithful work in establishing one of the finest yacht clubs in America, together with a cuisine known in Detroit as the best. This was attained despite a high increase in taxes and food cost.
>
> Our present success does not cast any reflections on past operations, as you all know the membership was not complete last year, and the increase in dues was not in effect until February of this year.
>
> At this time I take the opportunity of thanking the whole membership; and with the activity and enthusiasm shown in the past there is no reason why this Club should not continue to be one of the most successful in the district.[11]

Grosse Pointe Yacht Club spars with *Grosse Pointe News* over name

by Elizabeth Vogel

Issue 1, volume 1 of the *Grosse Pointe News* was published on November 7, 1940. It was supposed to be published under another name, the *Grosse Pointer*. At least it was, that is, until Commodore Frank Couzens got wind of the news.

The feature story of the first issue, an article titled "Paper Is Requested to Change Name," begins, "The office of the *Grosse Pointe News*, a welter of hustle and bustle trying to get out its first issue late yesterday afternoon, was thrown into a state resembling panic when the following letter was hand delivered."

Figure 10. The Club's first yearbook, 1939, and the first *Grosse Pointer* issue to contain a roster of Club members.

The entirety of the firm letter from Commodore Couzens was printed and reads as follows:

Information has reached our Grosse Pointe Yacht Club that you are about to commence a publication of a periodical bearing the name, *Grosse Pointer*. This particular name is the name of our club publication, which we have used continuously since the 14th of May, 1936, for circulation not only as a club bulletin, but also as a magazine intended to cover the social activities of the entire Grosse Pointe residential area.

Furthermore, our name, *The Grosse Pointer*, has been registered with the Library of Congress, copyright office of the United States of America, in Washington, under Class B, 391-387, and the present reorganization of the club has duly succeeded to the rights of the original registrant and has duly continued the publication up to the present time.

Your proposed adoption of such a similar name cannot result otherwise than to confuse subscribers, the reading public, as well as prospective advertisers, and with so many other names open and available for your new publication, we must request that you desist the use of the name *Grosse Pointer*, or any name sufficiently similar to raise the possibility of confusion.

I am writing this letter before your first issue comes out so that you will be saved the expense of making a change of name. But in the event that my information is erroneous as to your plans and intentions, I hope you will regard this letter only as an effort on my part to protect us all from needless embarrassment. In other words, having received the above information, I wanted to write you as soon as possible without waiting to make verification of the actual issuance of your first number.

With very best wishes
I am very truly yours,
Frank Couzens
Commodore, Grosse Pointe Yacht Club

The editor responded.
Dear Mr. Couzens:

The name of our new weekly newspaper in the Grosse Pointes was selected by those interested some three weeks ago, at which time none of us had any knowledge that another publication with the same name was in existence. Since then we have brought out a dummy issue of 1,000 copies which have been distributed freely in the Grosse Pointes and the city of Detroit. There has been considerable talk about the new publication throughout all the Pointes. An office has been rented, phone and light service installed, all under the name of *The Grosse Pointer*.

Some ten days ago the fact that the Grosse Pointe Yacht Club issued a small house organ to its members under the same name, was brought to our attention. As we were about to register this name, we consulted with our lawyers. We were told that in the first place they could see no possibility of any conflict between the two publications with which we agreed, and that if the club had not registered the name in the courthouse here, we were legally entitled to use it.

There was no such registration and we thereupon had the name registered ourselves and went ahead with all plans for publication with no intention, we assure you, of ever encroaching upon any rights or privileges of your club.

We wish most earnestly the Club's objection, which we still don't understand, might have been lodged before we had a hand drawn mast-head executed, before we had set in type an entire paper of ads, news, and editorial matter filled with the original name. We wish that we hadn't been forced to waste so much time and spend so much money just a few hours before going to press, frantically making the changes to avoid bringing harm to your club. We wish most of all that our lawyers had properly covered all angles of the point in dispute.

We bow to the wishes of your club to keep the name of the publication undiluted.

We have made the necessary changes. We hope and trust there will be no trampling of toes.

Yours very truly,
Robert E. Edgar, Editor
Grosse Pointe News

Although the Grosse Pointe Yacht Club prevailed in keeping the name *The Grosse Pointer*, the editor made sure that their side of the story was heard. Couzens's letter, well intentioned as it was, did little to save cost to the new publication. The resentment in Edgar's response is thinly veiled, but his discontent was not without warrant.

Without fanfare or unnecessary drama, the paper acquiesced to Couzens's request and took the name the *Grosse Pointe News* before the first issue went to press. There was no follow-up article, and with so few even remembering that this conflict ever took place, it is possible that this exchange of letters marked both the beginning and the end of the issue.

IMAGE ACKNOWLEDGEMENTS
Chapter Three

1. Wayne State University / *Detroit News*

2. Past Com. Ralph Kliber family

3. Past Com. Ralph Kliber family

4. – 11. GPYC

Figure 11. The 49-ft. cutter *Sonata*, owned by R.R. Williams and skippered by his two sons Donald and Dave, sailed to victory in the racing-cruising class of the GPYC's Eleventh Annual Sailing Regatta in 1940. *Sonata* finished forty-two seconds behind Tommy Fisher's newly purchased *Apache*, but won on corrected time. This was the first race on Lake St. Clair for *Apache* since arriving here from the East Coast, but due to a dental operation, Tommy had to delegate the helm to brother Bill Fisher for the race.

Figure 1. Member Robert Oakman's 101-foot yacht *Mamie-O* was requisitioned by the U.S. Navy during the war and used to patrol shipping lanes along the East Coast. Note Navy personnel on deck and gun mounted on the bow. Over a dozen large yachts owned by GPYC members were summoned to wartime duty by the Navy.

By Larry W. Stephenson, M.D. and Carol Stephenson

1941 through 1950

1941: Life was beautiful until it wasn't

Commodore Herbert J. Woodall took the helm of the Grosse Pointe Yacht Club in 1941. According to the Club's yearbook, the membership had now grown to 409, almost doubling from the 226 members in the grand reopening year of 1938. This edition of the yearbook was the first to provide individual photos of the members.

There was no shortage of activities in 1941, especially during the summer months. The twelfth Annual Sailing Regatta held on July fourth was reported to be a gloriously successful event. There were other sailing regattas as well as power-boat cruises, swim meets, and several parties, including a Mexican Fiesta and a Power Squadron party.

The yearbook contains a picture of the Vere Wirwille Orchestra, which was reported to have been such a success the previous year that they were retained again for the summer season. The caption for the picture reads, in part, "Vere is an accomplished accordianist and pianist, and is well known to the smart set of Detroit. The Wirwille style of music lends distinctive interpretation to the Latin tempos of the Rhumba and Tango, and his band promises again to make the GPYC the popular summer spot for the Detroit younger set."[1]

Then in its second year of operation, the bowling facility was clearly a huge hit. The bowling committee reported that almost twenty-nine thousand games

Figure 2. Yearbook cover of *The Grosse Pointer*, 1943.

Figure 3. Pearl Harbor; the Japanese attack on the U.S. Navy Pacific Fleet, December 7, 1941.

were bowled on the four lanes, and enough revenue was generated to defray all operating expenses, with a surplus of nearly one thousand dollars. Plans were already in the works for pin-setting machines and the addition of two more lanes.

In his annual address to the membership, Commodore Woodall was full of enthusiasm for the outlook of the Club. He thanked everyone for their support and cooperation and wrote that "life is very beautiful and very much worthwhile."[2]

But in other parts of the world, life was no longer so beautiful. In June, Germany invaded Russia, and on July 25 forty thousand Japanese troops began occupying French Indo-China. President Roosevelt reacted by freezing Japanese assets in the United States and barring Japanese ships from using the Panama Canal, thus halting all trade with Japan.

It was becoming clear to many that U.S. involvement in the conflict was imminent. At the June 12 meeting of the GPYC board of directors,

Figure 4. Commodore Herbert J. Woodall, 1941.

the following motion was made and passed: "That payment of all dues of members drafted or enlisting in the Army, Navy or Marine Corps of the United States be waived during such service."

On Sunday, December 7, 1941, Japan attacked the U.S. Pacific Fleet at Pearl Harbor with approximately 360 aircraft from six aircraft carriers. Six battleships were sunk, three others were heavily damaged, and numerous smaller navy vessels were either sunk or damaged. More than two hundred military aircraft were destroyed or damaged. Over two thousand American lives were lost, and 1,178 were wounded. That same day other Japanese forces attacked the Philippines and U.S. garrisons on the islands of Guam, Wake, and Midway. The British were also attacked in Singapore, Hong Kong, and the Malay Peninsula. Four days later, Germany and Italy declared war on the United States.

For the United States, World War II, which would define the decade, had officially begun.

1942: Club members go to war

In January 1942, just one month after the United States officially entered the war, Club member William S. Knudsen, who had been president of General Motors, was appointed Director of Production, Office of the Under Secretary of War, and commissioned as a lieutenant general (three stars) in the U.S. Army. He was the only civilian to join the army with an initial rank that high. When the GPYC board of directors received his resignation from the Club owing to his departure for military service, they responded in a letter dated February 19, informing him that his "membership would be continued for the duration of the war without dues in consideration of his military activities." Shortly thereafter, Club member Alvan Macauley, president of Packard Motor Car Company, was asked to serve as chairman of the Automotive Council for War Production.

On that same day, the board passed a resolution that the clubhouse would be made available to Grosse Pointe Shores Civil Defense authorities as hospital space if needed. Board member George Lilygren, who had served in the U.S. Marine Corps in World War I, was designated as the Club's air raid warden. Lilygren gave a presentation at the May 8 board meeting on the procedures to follow in the event of an air raid. Club manager Emile Campenhout was instructed

Figure 5. Lieutenant General William S. Knudsen, Director of Production, Office of the Under Secretary of War.

Figure 6. Alvan Macauley, president of Packard Motor Car Company and chairman of the Automotive Council for War Production during World War II.

War rationing on the home front

Two of the first commodities to be rationed in the United States in January 1942 were automobile and truck tires. After the attack on Pearl Harbor, early targets of Japanese forces included the Malay Peninsula and many other areas in the Pacific where a significant number of rubber plantations were located. As 1942 progressed, gasoline, sugar, coffee, and finally diesel fuel and kerosene were added to the list of rationed items.

In 1943, the government began rationing processed foods such as canned meats, canned fish, canned milk, and canned fruit. Cheese and lard eventually made the list. These were foods that would travel well and could be easily furnished to feed U.S. troops.

In order to purchase these goods, consumers had to use ration books, which were issued with limited numbers of coupons for each item. Ordering rationed food items in a restaurant required the proper coupons for purchase. Cars and trucks were issued stickers for gasoline according to a government-established classification system.

Since gasoline and diesel fuel were not available for recreational boats, GPYC members were clearly restricted in their use of powerboats. Food rationing obviously limited the menu offerings. Members living any significant distance from the Club would have been forced to restrict their use of the Club according to the amount of gasoline they were able to obtain for their automobiles. Most people were limited to three to four gallons per week.

An effort was made to conserve tires and fuel by setting a top speed limit of thirty-five miles per hour on U.S. roads, but by all accounts it was largely ignored by the populace.

GPYC

Figure 7. Commodore H. Lynn Pierson, 1942.

to prepare the Fo'c'sle as a potential bomb shelter. At the July 25 meeting, the board recommended that bomb insurance be purchased at a cost of $585 for one year.

Looking back to the war news in the early months of 1942, it is understandable why people were apprehensive about a possible enemy attack. While the U.S. Pacific Fleet was desperately working to repair the damage from its devastating losses at Pearl Harbor, German and Japanese forces seemed to be gaining ground on all fronts.

During this difficult year, the Club's facilities remained open, albeit at a much subdued level. The plan to add two lanes to the bowling facility was implemented. The decision was made to include a special section of photographs of all members serving in the armed forces in the Club's yearbook. Commodore H. Lynn Pierson,[3] the attorney who had played such an important role in bringing the Club out of bankruptcy, summarized the war's impact on the Club in the following excerpts from his annual message to the membership:

At the start of the present year, we were all apprehensive as to the effect the war might have on our Club program and its activities. Sufficient time has now elapsed for us to get a

Figure 8. *White Cloud* shown here on the Detroit River was member Charles E. Sorensen's trim 60-foot cutter that carried the crew to victory in the 1942 Chicago-Mackinac Race, winning in a field of 39 starters and finishing more than 11 hours ahead of the second boat.

fairly clear picture of just what has happened and I am happy to say that I think we have come through the initial period in a thoroughly satisfactory manner and I am sure you will be interested in some of the details.

You will be gratified to learn that since November 1, 1941, we have taken in thirty-eight new members and have lost forty-two by death and by resignation and otherwise. This is only a net loss of four members during this hectic period, or less than one percent on the basis of a membership over four hundred. This does not quite tell the story, however, since in common with most other clubs it has been our practice to remit the dues of members who have entered the armed services, and many others who are working for the government in Washington have transferred to a non-resident basis. The resultant loss in income to the Club is approximately $300 per month.

To compensate for this loss in revenue, it appeared advisable to make commensurate overall reductions in our expenses, and this has been done in spite of almost universal individual wage increases. Many consequent curtailments in the services of the Club have been evident to you all and I know have been accepted in the helpful cooperative spirit that was anticipated.

All credit for coming through this eventful year must be given to a loyal and enthusiastic membership as well as to our able and conscientious manager, Emile Campenhout, and his cooperative staff.

Also it [this issue of *The Grosse Pointer*] shows our members and sons of members who have joined our armed forces. I know that you join me in wishing each of these men Godspeed, victory and safe return. Few, if any, clubs have ever shown their roster in individual photographs in this manner and that it was possible for our Club to have this issue was through the earnest cooperation of Com. George Slocum and Leo J. Fitzpatrick.[4]

1943: The deprivations of war

Paging through the yearbook of 1943 tells a story in itself of how the war was affecting the Club and its members. There are no articles describing social events; no descriptions of regattas or cruises; no bowling news. The only reference to dining is a tribute to the manager for "plugging away" and "doing the best he can" with food shortages, ration restrictions, and his staff being commandeered for war jobs or drafted into the service. Almost every advertisement in the book contains a reference to the war.

From that yearbook, one would hardly know the Club was functioning except for two pictures, both from the same party, with just a caption and no accompanying text. The pictures are telling in that all of the men appear to be older and therefore ineligible to serve, and not one person is smiling.

Of course the GPYC did continue with activities for those who remained on the home front, even though not many of them were recorded for posterity. This was the year that the first annual cruise to the Old Club was initiated. In the housekeeping department, a scheduled conversion from coal-fed furnaces to oil heating was completed.

Commodore Ward H. Peck continued the somber tone that defined the year in his annual address to the membership.

> In this year of war, leisure hours for most of our members have been few. Yachting and the many related pleasures which we have enjoyed with such zest and satisfaction in normal times have been secondary to the race with the Axis "to git there fustest with the mostest men"—and weapons.
>
> The going has been uphill—it's been tough—and it isn't over yet, but from all indications we have rounded the bend and are headed for the drive down the stretch. There is no doubt now about the final outcome, and

ROLL OF HO[NOR]

MEMBERS AND SONS OF MEMBERS OF GROSSE P[OINTE]

ENSIGN JOHN L. BARRETT

CORP. JAMES F. BARRET[T]

LIEUT. COMMANDER GEO. W. CHRISTIANSEN

MAJ. FRANK COUZENS

PVT. TORE N. FRANZEN

LIEUT. JAMES M. FRENC[H]

Figure 9. Members and sons of members serving in the armed forces by late 1942. Note Maj. Frank Couzens, left page, second row, second from left, who had been commodore in 1940.

Figure 10. Commodore Ward H. Peck, 1943.

the same old competitive spirit which assures us of victory should be a big factor in hastening a sound prosperity when peace returns.

And even though time for our favorite pastime has been greatly curtailed, the same "will to win" which has characterized our efforts in the great struggle both at home and abroad—appropriately enough—has not only carried this Club along with it, but has brought an even higher degree of success to its other activities during the past year than ever before. We not only have held our own in refilling vacancies in our ranks, which have resulted from the usual causes, but at this writing we have a net gain of thirty members which completely filled our active membership several months ago and the net cash position of the Club shows a great improvement over what it was at the beginning of the year.

To those members of the Club who are in the Armed Forces of our country, in all the far corners of the earth, as well as to the sons and daughters of members who are serving, may they know we are constantly thinking of them—wishing for them the best of luck — victory—and safe return.[5]

Yachtsmen become "Coastie" helpers

In August 1936, the U.S. Coast Guard designated the GPYC as the permanent base of operations for a seventy-five-foot USCG cutter. A USCG cutter remained in the harbor until at least 1943, when a Coast Guard station was established on Belle Isle. Current GPYC director Tim Robson recalls that his uncle Robert Shiels was stationed with the Coast Guard at the GPYC for part of the war and told his nephew that he remembered sleeping on the screened porch, which would have been what is now the Binnacle dining room.

Detroit is located in USCG District Nine, which includes all five Great Lakes plus the St. Lawrence River. District Nine is further divided into smaller areas, Area "H" being comprised of Lake Huron, the St. Clair River, Lake St. Clair, the Detroit River, and the eastern end of Lake Erie, including Toledo.[6]

Photographs of the GPYC harbor from 1942 through 1946 show many powerboats and sailboats with three-foot-high identification numbers on their hulls. This indicated that the boats were available upon request for any duties that the USCG might require of them.[7] Many of these volunteers were from Power Squadrons based at local area yacht clubs. In addition to helping the war effort, volunteering one's boat for duty could mean greater fuel allowances and sanctioned time spent on the lake.

Figure 11. Sailboat in GPYC harbor with three-feet-high identification numbers, indicating owner volunteered his vessel for assisting the USCG in the war effort.

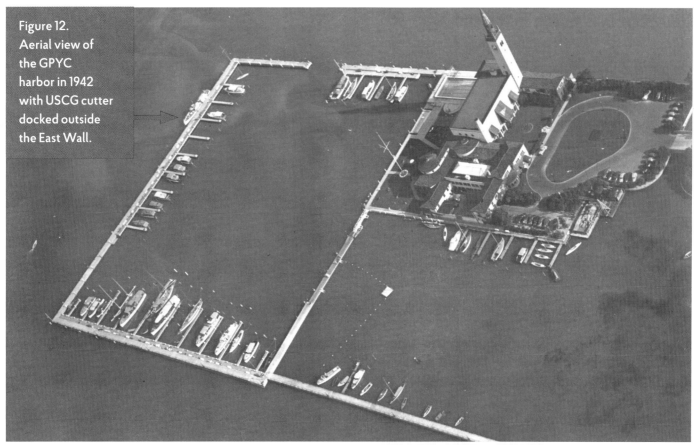

Figure 12. Aerial view of the GPYC harbor in 1942 with USCG cutter docked outside the East Wall.

Some boats in the harbor had the prefix "CGA" attached to their three-foot numbers. These boats were owned and operated by USCG Auxiliary members, who reported for duty on a regular schedule, putting in twenty-four-hour stretches twice a month. During this period, GPYC member Dr. Earl H. Teetzel, who was then a vice commodore in the USCG Auxiliary, served as deputy commander for the Auxiliary in Area "H."

Figure 14. Member Dr. Earl H. Teetzel, wartime deputy commander of Area H for the U.S. Coast Guard Auxiliary. He was also commander of the Detroit Power Squadron from 1938 until the end of the war.

Figure 13. Coast Guardsman Robert Shiels, stationed early in the war at the USCG base located at the GPYC (with sisters Ailine and Ethel Jean). He was assigned to patrol boat duty and slept on the screened porch of the Club, which is now the enclosed Binnacle dining room.

District Nine had 6,512 members of the Auxiliary, who owned a total of 2,122 boats.[6] Civilians who were Auxiliary members performed many of the functions that Coast Guard members would normally perform but were unable to do so because they had other wartime duties. Those duties included protecting the all-important shipping channels with about a dozen well-armed Coast Guard boats patrolling around the clock from Lake Huron through the connecting channels of the St. Clair River, Lake St. Clair, and the Detroit River down to, and including, Lake Erie.

1944: The beginning of the end

By early 1944 the fortunes of war were definitely improving for the Allies. In the winter of 1943 the German army had its first real taste of defeat in Russia. In October, Italy surrendered and switched sides; Mussolini and his remaining loyal Fascist troops had fled north. In the Pacific, U.S. Marines, despite terrible losses, were slowly recapturing territory lost to the Japanese in the early months of the war, while the Navy was winning battles on the sea and in the air.

Meanwhile, the daily operations of the Club were still strained from wartime shortages. Commodore James H. Marks presided over the March 2 board meeting, at which a motion was made and passed to restrict the sale of rationed liquors to the extent deemed necessary in order to conserve the Club's supply. The sale of unrationed liquors was to continue with no restrictions.

Figure 15. Commodore James H. Marks, 1944.

Figure 16. Clark-Wall wedding at GPYC, 1944. Left to right, Lt. Ray Priebe, USN, best man; Marilyn Wall, maid of honor;
Ensign William P. Clark, USN, groom; and Christine Wall, bride. Courtesy member Christine Drummy, daughter of bride and groom.

Figure 17. Future GPYC commodore Lt. George E. Kriese, naval aviator, pictured aboard an aircraft carrier somewhere in the East China Sea, June 1945. Aircraft is an FM-2 Wildcat, U.S. Navy fighter.

But a true feeling of hope was clearly in the air. Pictures from the New Year's Eve party at the Club show a real celebration happening. More happy faces can be seen in photographs from the opening dinner dance, a stag party, and a teen party featuring jukebox music. Several bridal pictures were notable not only for the lovely ladies themselves but for the fact that the grooms were all serving in the armed forces.

The successful landing of Allied troops in Normandy, France, on D-Day, June 6, 1944, had to be even more wonderfully encouraging news for the home front. There were many pictures in the yearbook from the July fourth regatta and anniversary celebration. It is easy to imagine that the feelings of patriotism on that occasion must have been nearly overwhelming. At that point, there were thirty-eight members of the GPYC serving in the armed forces.

1945: Victory

On May 7, 1945, Germany surrendered to the allies. Japan signed the document of surrender on the battleship *Missouri* on September 2. The war was over. The joy must have been enormous, the relief intense. At war's end, forty-one members of the GPYC had served their country in the armed forces of the United States. Commodore C. B. Thomas reflected the feelings of his fellow members, while touting the many improvements to the Club, in his annual address:

Now that total victory has been won, we can look back in retrospect and appreciate all the more what the Grosse Pointe Yacht Club has meant to us during the trying years we have gone through. We can realize now, more than ever, how well it served as a place where we could relax occasionally with our friends so that we might keep on with our daily duties

Figure 18. Commodore C. B. Thomas, 1945.

— working determinedly toward the end we have now achieved.

Of utmost importance has been the sincere, conscientious efforts of our manager, Emile,

and his loyal staff who have worked long hours to overcome almost insurmountable difficulties and make certain that service remained at a high level. I am sure that I am only repeating what each of you feel, in saying that despite war time shortages, our food and service at GPYC remained the finest in the community.

Our board of directors approved an extensive program of improvements to the clubhouse and grounds, many of which have already been completed. Each had the purpose of making the Club a more enjoyable place for each of you.

To mention only a few — there is the new ladies' locker room, an enlarged parking grounds, revamping of our kitchen, important improvements to our harbor and docks, new screening on windows and doors, refurnishing of the ladies' powder room, extensive improvements to the bowling alleys—the latter including the sound-proofing of the ceiling. We have shown a number of these Club improvements in this issue [of *The Grosse Pointer*], knowing that each of you, in seeing them pictured, will have even more pride in your GPYC membership.[8]

Figure 19. Commodore C. B. Thomas, third from right, president of Chrysler Export Corporation, one month after the war in Europe had ended, performing an official government inspection tour of the production capabilities of surviving factories.

1946–1950: Postwar recovery and prosperity

The five year period following the war was the first five years of stability that the Grosse Pointe Yacht Club had experienced since the opening of the clubhouse in 1929. It was a time to celebrate, and by all accounts that was exactly what the membership did. To quote from a 1948 issue of *The Grosse Pointer*, "The Grosse Pointe Yacht Club has a well earned reputation for unusual special parties."[9]

In that particular case they were referring to the Harvest Moon Party, also known as the Harvest Festival. At the 1946 party members posed for pictures with various large farm animals and a tractor, the grand prize of the evening being two cocker spaniel puppies. Just one year later, the grand prize was a one-thousand-pound Hereford steer, and by 1948, the prize list included a power lawnmower, a two-hundred-pound pig, a one-thousand-pound steer, and the grand prize of a new Chevrolet.

The 1949 Harvest Moon Party changed direction and became a two-day carnival, complete with full-sized merry-go-round, a shooting gallery (three hits won a pack of cigarettes), and carnival booths featuring games of skill and strength.

GPYC

Figure 20. Commodore George N. Lilygren, 1946.

Games and parties seemed very popular during this period, and no wonder, considering some of the prizes to be won. The prizes in 1949 included large baskets of food products, a fishing rod, a games table, a pedigreed cocker spaniel, and a television set.

Above, figure 21. In January 1947, Ladies Bridge Night included cocktails, cigarettes, and hats. This photo was taken in the old Grille Room (now the Spinnaker) when murals still graced its walls.

Left, figure 22. Perfect weather allowed the 1946 crowd at the Show Boat Party to enjoy dinner and dancing under the stars.

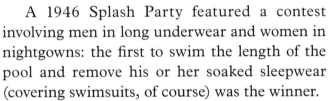

Figure 23. Commodore Robert P. Sherer, 1947.

Figure 24. Commodore Albert P. Teetzel, 1948.

A 1946 Splash Party featured a contest involving men in long underwear and women in nightgowns: the first to swim the length of the pool and remove his or her soaked sleepwear (covering swimsuits, of course) was the winner.

The tradition of the anniversary celebration on July fourth continued, and the 1949 event became very special when July 3 was declared to be "Circus Day." Professional performers arrived in red circus wagons, and the one-ring circus on the lawn featured clowns, trained animal acts, and a wirewalker.

At that time, the Commodore's Ball was held in the spring, but there was also a Directors' Ball, usually in January, to welcome the new directors who were elected at that time of the year.

There were many other parties that appear to be annual traditions, including the Show Boat Party, Father and Son Dinner, Mother and Daughter Luncheon, Stag Dinner, Junior Home-From-College Party, and Ladies' Bridge Party. Highlights from these parties included professional wrestlers at a 1948 Stag Party and boxing matches at a Father and Son Dinner; the Show Boat Party in 1950 featured a short mast

roped to the diving board of the pool that had dollar bills attached to the far end, which guests were encouraged to try to retrieve.

During the postwar period, the Club also continued to remodel, redecorate, and update where necessary. In 1946, the new Trophy Row was unveiled. The trophy cases were created from the "blind windows" that originally were meant to be windows overlooking the indoor swimming pool. When plans changed and the pool became the bowling alley, the windows were bricked over and hung with curtains. The trophy cases were customized to fit those window spaces.

In 1947, a glass block wall was constructed on the south and east sides of the swimming pool as a safety barrier and a windbreaker. The Main Dining Room got a makeover in 1949, with new colors and unusual light fixtures made especially for the Club in New York.

Bowling continued to be a very popular activity. In 1946 a bowling association was formed with the Detroit Boat Club, the Detroit Yacht Club, Bayview Yacht Club, Edison Boat Club, and Wyandotte Boat Club. Their first full bowling season was in 1947, at which time the group of

Figure 25. Commodore John R. Sutton Jr., 1949.

Figure 26. Commodore Clarence E. Bleicher, 1950.

bowling teams officially became the Detroit River Yachting Bowling Association (DRYBA). Issues of *The Grosse Pointer* were always full of bowling news and pictures from games and social events.

Summers were filled with swim meets, sailing regattas, powerboat cruising, and pool activities—in short, all of the things that had been so popular and pleasurable before the war intervened. In the "some things never change" category, the summer 1947 issue of *The Grosse Pointer* contained a bulletin from the house committee regarding reported violations of proper attire between the pool area and the clubhouse, and directed members' attention to "House Rule No. 20" on the subject.

That same issue of The Grosse Pointer featured an invitation from the Old Club for members "...to avail themselves of the Old Club's privileges for a day's outing." It went on to state, "There is no charge for the trip by ferry between the GPYC and the Old Club." GPYC member Bob Hackathorn remembers riding the ferry as a child with his family. He believes the boat's name was *Ojay* and it may have been an old PT boat from World War II, or at least something very

similar. When he tried to confirm the information about the boat with the Old Club, he was told that the club has had two fires since that time and most of their historical records have been lost.

In 1950 the practice of reviewing the fleet began. It was introduced at the Show Boat Party, with Commodore Clarence Bleicher reviewing the fleet from his yacht, *Alma D*, complete with cannon salutes.

In the spring of 1946, Club manager Emile Campenhout resigned to pursue a business venture and was replaced by his former assistant manager, Fred Gebstadt. Campenhout had begun his career with the Club in 1929 as a clubhouse steward.

Issues of *The Grosse Pointer* from these five years show GPYC members playing hard and smiling broadly, perhaps in part trying to make up for the first five years of the decade when playing was not an option and smiles and laughter didn't come easily. It was a decade of the most severe contrasts, and the GPYC, very much used to dealing with adversity, had survived once again and headed into the 1950s with confidence and optimism.

Figure 27. Swimming pool with glass block walls added in 1947 for wind protection.

Above, figure 28. These members appear to have positioned themselves "above the fray" for the 1948 outdoor Show Boat activities. They are seated on the open balcony that is today's enclosed Binnacle dining room.

Above, figure 29. Member William (Bill) Farr came to the 1948 Halloween party dressed as Baby Snooks, a popular radio character in those days. Posing in their whimsical costumes are, left to right, Bill Farr, Mrs. Farr, Mrs. Ray Legg, and Henry Hopkes Jr..

Right, figure 30. The Junior Homecoming party for college students, held during the December holidays in 1948. It was a reunion for "the boys and girls who grew up here [in the Pointes] together." Also invited were "their pals who are a bit younger and are still in school here in Detroit." *(The Grosse Pointer,* 1949, no.1, 19)

Below, figure 31. Left to right, Past Commodores A.P. Teetzel and B.F. Stephenson enjoy a spin on the merry-go-round behind their daughters, Mrs. Kenneth Winslow and Nancy Teetzel at the two-day Harvest Moon Carnival in early September, 1949.

Above, figure 32. The Keno party in November 1949 featured a dazzling array of prizes, including huge food and beverage baskets, a portable grill, a games table, and this television set, won by Irene Franzen, daughter of member Tore Franzen.

Above, figure 33. Smiles and laughter are everywhere at the children's Christmas party, December 1949. In addition to the requisite appearance from Santa, attendees enjoyed a show featuring Montana Frank, California Joe and Pinto the Wonder Horse. It was later reported that while Pinto was awaiting his cue in the Rotunda, "he fortified himself for the performance with a healthy mouthful of evergreens and silvered twigs from the centerpiece." *(The Grosse Pointer,* 1950, no.1, 13)

Figure 34. *My Sweetie*, with "Wild Bill" Cantrell at the helm, driving to victory in the 1949 Gold Cup race. For unlimited hydroplanes, the Gold Cup is the ultimate annual race to win.

The Legend of *My Sweetie*

Sometime in the 1940s, two soon-to-be members of the GPYC decided to build a racing boat together. Ed Schoenherr (commodore, 1964) and Ed Gregory Jr., then young men in their 30s, were best friends who had a passion for speed. After some experience racing smaller boats, their thoughts turned to "going for the gold" — that very prestigious Detroit race, the Gold Cup. Problem: not enough money to build a real contender. When asked for a loan, Ed Gregory's father turned them down; but Ed Schoenherr's father-in-law, Stark Hickey (commodore, 1957) obliged.

World-renowned naval architect John Hacker designed the boat, but was not interested in having his company manufacture a race boat, so the two Eds turned to Les Staudacher, whose wood-working company in Kawkawlin, Michigan, just north of Bay City, specialized in the construction of wooden church pews and prayer stools. Their boat was built over a four-month period in 1948, in great secrecy, so its anticipated high performance could not be easily duplicated. Ed Gregory's son, GPYC member Scott Gregory, said that the boat was to be powered by a 12-cylinder Allison aircraft engine, and that the men spent $700 to buy three of those war surplus engines and another $700 for a forged steel propeller made in Italy.

The grand plan was for the two owners to take turns racing the boat, but after the first race they entered — the Ford Memorial Regatta with Ed Gregory driving — they concluded that they needed a professional driver. They hired veteran auto and boat racer "Wild Bill" Cantrell, who competed in the Indianapolis 500 that year. Bill's first season with the new boat was a disappointment, but the next year, 1949, *My Sweetie*, began chalking up victories. In fact, Cantrell won every race they entered, including the Gold Cup.

That same summer, the international challenge for the Harmsworth Trophy was being held in Detroit, and *My Sweetie*, as the boat was named, with Wild Bill at the wheel, looked to be the most promising defender of the U.S.-held trophy. Fate intervened in those plans, however, according to Ed Schoenherr's son, John (commodore, 1997). The two Eds were quite suddenly summoned to Rose Terrace, home of Anna Dodge, widow of auto magnate and GPYC member Horace Dodge. Mrs. Dodge informed them that she wanted to buy their boat for her son, Horace Jr., and handed them a blank check to fill in their price. Amazed, the two men asked to be excused, and following a hasty conference, they returned the check to Mrs. Dodge in the amount of $25,000. The deal was sealed, and suddenly *My Sweetie* had a new driver, Horace Dodge Jr., driving in the competition for the Harmsworth Trophy.

Once again, fate intervened. Or did it come to the rescue? Horace Jr., then 48, was not a seasoned racer, and his performance in *My Sweetie* did not impress the members of the selection committee, who were naturally hoping for a United States win over the single challenging boat from Canada. Each competing country was allowed to field up to three entry boats, so in addition to *My Sweetie*, two other U.S. boats had already been selected to compete against the highly favored Canadian challenger.

To win the trophy, any entry boat from one country had to place first in two races. On the first race day, *Such Crust* from Detroit took the win, and on the second day, the race was won by *Skip-a-Long* from Lake Tahoe, California, which gave the U.S. the overall win and the Harmsworth Trophy. *My Sweetie*, driven in the first race by Bill Cantrell, led the first lap, but dropped out with mechanical problems. Piloted by Horace Jr. in the second race, she came in third.

John Schoenherr and Scott Gregory said their fathers used the money they received from Anna Dodge to settle all the debts incurred from their foray into boat racing, including repaying the loan from John's grandfather, Stark Hickey. After paying Bill Cantrell and all their boat mechanics for services rendered, they had about $3,000 in profit, which they used, as any self-respecting yachtsman would, to throw a huge party in the Gold Cup Room of the Whittier Hotel on the Detroit River.

Top, figure 35. Left to right, Ed Gregory and Ed Schoenherr, owners of *My Sweetie*, with driver "Wild Bill" Cantrell.

Bottom, figure 36. "In Driver's Seat: Dodge, not Cantrell," reads the headline in the Sports section of *The Detroit News*. The accompanying photo shows driver Bill Cantrell in the boat, former owners Ed Schoenherr and Ed Gregory standing by the boat, and Mrs. Horace E. Dodge with son Horace, standing on the dock to the right, as they take possession of *My Sweetie* ten days before the Harmsworth race.

Figure 37. Member George Bass's 68-foot schooner *Ben Bow* crossing the start line in the 1950 St. Petersburg-to-Havana saltwater classic, USCG Cutter *Nemesis* in foreground. *Ben Bow* finished second and placed fifth.[10]

IMAGE ACKNOWLEDGEMENTS
Chapter Four

1. Detroit Yacht Club
2. GPYC
3. National Archives
4. – 7. GPYC
8. Detroit Yacht Club
9. – 12. GPYC
13. Tim Robson
14. GPYC
15. GPYC
16. Christine Drummy
17. Past Com. George Kriese
18. – 33. GPYC
34. Bill Osborn
35. Past Com. John Schoenherr
36. *The Detroit News*
37. St. Petersburg Yacht Club and photographer Ray Kendall Williams

Figure 1. Thunderheads in the night sky provide a dramatic backdrop to the Grosse Pointe Yacht Club on a summer evening in 1958. Photo by Bob Frye.

By Larry W. Stephenson, M.D. and
Carol Stephenson

1951 through 1960

A decade of renewal

During the 1950s, the United States experienced significant economic growth, particularly in manufacturing and housing construction. In reviewing the Club's history during this period, one senses similar confidence and vitality in the membership that was present in the country as a whole. This would become the first full decade since the 1929 opening of the clubhouse in which the daily operations of the Club would not sustain any major disruptions. Although the United States was once again at war, this time in Korea from 1950 to 1953, it seemed to have no discernable impact on the Club other than a declaration from the board of directors that they would again, as they had during World War II, waive dues for members serving in the armed forces.

A spirit of renewal and revamping seemed to permeate the Club in this decade. In the clubhouse, several rooms were redecorated, four were renamed, and one was reconfigured. The kitchen received a major upgrading. At the February 23, 1951, board meeting, Rear Commodore Anthony Motschall reported on plans for a guardhouse to be built at the main entrance to the property. A guard would be stationed there "preventing trespassers, marauders and uninvited strangers from entering the Club premises." Members were to be issued stickers with the Club burgee for their automobiles in order to be easily identified by the guard.

When the clubhouse first opened in 1929, several rooms were given names that have been changed over the years. In 1951, the room originally known as the Private Dining Room became the

Figure 2. These coasters, with the official twenty-fifth anniversary logo, were given out in 1954 to commemorate the silver anniversary of the clubhouse.

Commodores' Room. The announcement of the name change in the 1951 summer issue of *The Grosse Pointer* reminded members that the room was still available for private functions.

Today's Ballroom was originally called the Club Room, and by the 1950s was referred to as the Main Lounge. It was one of the first rooms to be refurbished in this decade, although not to any great extent. The pride of the room, the Frank Vining Smith painting *Sea Witch*, received a cleaning and frame regilding, and new draperies were hung. A picture of the room from a 1951 issue of *The Grosse Pointer* shows carpeting on both long sides of the room, and the accompanying article reports, "the priceless Austrian carpeting has been expertly repaired." It goes on to note, "this carpeting, purchased abroad in 1928, is now irreplaceable." The tones of aqua and henna in the carpet were to be "adopted as a color continuity

throughout the Club." To this end, the Rotunda was painted, the stone walls restored and, "the ceiling dome brightened by a combination of aqua and henna."[1]

By the end of the decade, the Main Lounge was being referred to in *Grosse Pointer* articles as the Ballroom, but it is unknown when or if this name change was ever officially made.

The room we now know as the Venetian Room was originally the Club Lounge, then the Green Room, presumably because it was painted in some shade of green. In 1951, the carpet in the Green Room was cleaned and repaired at the same time as the carpet in the Main Lounge. It was referred to as a handwoven Austrian rug, which was most likely similar to the Main Lounge carpet. The repair job included, "the reweaving of more than forty holes caused by the carelessness of smokers." A message from the board reads, "Your directors

Figure 3. The Green Room after its 1955 facelift and renaming as the Senza Nome Cocktail Lounge. One year later, in 1956, the name was changed to the Venetian Room.

Figure 4. Commodore J. Edgar Duncan, 1951.

Figure 5. Commodore Paul Marco, 1952.

cannot help but wonder if the members who were so careless at their Club would act similarly in their own homes."[2]

In 1955, a full facelift was deemed to be in order for the Green Room. Grosse Pointe decorator William Austin was awarded the job, and according to the 1955 yearbook, "the transformation of the Green Room has simply been breathtaking." The room was also renamed, and it is very possible that this was necessitated by a change in wall color. It was now known as the Senza Nome Cocktail Lounge, *senza nome* in Italian translating to "without name."[3] It seemed to be a popular name for Italian restaurants then, as it still is today. But just one year later, in June 1956, the name was changed again to the Venetian Room.[4] Perhaps "Senza Nome" was not quite as popular with the membership as it was with Italian restaurant patrons.

The enthusiastic response to the transformationof the Green Room may have been on the directors' minds when they once again contracted with William Austin for a makeover of the Ladies' Card Room, originally known as the Ladies' Library and Bridge Room. In addition to decor changes, new larger windows on the lake side of the room replaced the old smaller windows.

Opposite the windows, large mirrors were hung, framed with draperies to look like windows, which gave, "a feeling of increased space plus a marked increase in day-lighting." The color scheme of geranium and white was said to have been chosen for its harmony with the new decor in the Venetian Room, which gives some idea of that room's new look.[5]

A 1957 issue of *The Grosse Pointer* features a photograph of the redesigned Ladies' Card Room, along with a photo of the newly updated ladies' lavatory next to the Card Room. Another photo shows the transformation of the main entrance to the Club. The accompanying description mentions new steel and glass entry doors, cove lighting in the ceiling, and new carpeting and draperies. Kudos were given to Commodore Mervyn Gaskin, whose company "restored the finish of the standing metal ashtrays in the hallway — without expense to the Club."[6]

At the May 22, 1958, board meeting, Commodore Charles Jacobson suggested giving the Ladies' Card Room yet another new name. He proposed two — the St. Clair Room and the Lakeshore Room — and asked the board to come up with additional ideas, all to be voted upon at the next meeting. The next meeting's vote

Figure 6. Commodore Anthony B. Motschall, 1953.

Figure 7. Commodore Warren H. Farr, 1954.

produced a tie between two of the proposed names. Since one board member was absent, it was agreed that yet another vote would take place at the next meeting. That vote, taken at the July 31 meeting, produced a unanimous vote for the Lakeshore Room, and thus it is today.

A "Tentative Entertainment Schedule for 1959" gives March 7 as the date of the opening of the new Grill Room (present-day Spinnaker).[7] In earlier times, Grill had been spelled Grille, but for some reason the name was altered now to Grill. When the clubhouse first opened in 1929, this room was referred to as the Men's Grille, or sometimes the Men's Restaurant, and in 1938 became known as the Grille Room.

At this point in time, the configuration of the room did not change, but it did get a general revamping along with the rest of the Club's rooms. In 1939, colorful murals had been painted on the walls, but at some later date those murals were covered by paneling. It was most likely during this renovation that the paneling was installed.

Commodore Gaskin's annual report for 1957 mentions his appointment of a future planning committee, which had already begun submitting plans for what would become the most ambitious clubhouse construction project of the decade: an extension and enclosure of the porch on the east side of the building. Plans called for the resulting room to become, "a most attractive cocktail lounge and snack room."[8]

The grand opening of the Lakeview Terrace Lounge was held in April 1960. Apparently there was such a demand for reservations that it became a two-evening affair; both nights were sellouts with nearly six hundred in total attendance. Liberto's Bourbon Street Six from New Orleans alternated with Art Quatro's Orchestra to provide continuous dance music throughout both evenings.[9]

The new room was described in the 1960 summer issue of *The Grosse Pointer* as, "a large rectangular room seventy by twenty-two feet, adjacent to the Ballroom and overlooking Lake St. Clair for its entire length. It not only has the space of the former screened porch but it's longer, and is cantilevered out an additional twelve feet. At one end is a small dance floor; at the center, and looking toward the lake, is a deluxe cocktail lounge bar. The ceiling is a series of deep arches, with thermopane windows from floor to ceiling in the arched sections." Of course, today this room has become the Binnacle dining room.

Figure 8. Steel sheet-piling being driven into the lake-bed to protect the harbor, 1953. Commodore Anthony Motschall, Past Commodore Paul Marco, and Vice Commodore Leonard Jacques look on.

Unfriendly waters

In the early spring of 1952, water levels on Lake St. Clair began to rise. When the water began causing damage in the harbor, a special board meeting was called on March 14 to discuss the problem. Just one week later, on March 21, the first full day of spring, a major nor'easter blew in and pushed the already high water levels well over the docks and into the basement of the clubhouse. Witnesses spoke of waves like ocean breakers. All along the western shoreline of Lake St. Clair, floodwaters reached record levels, and damage from both water and ice was extensive. In addition to flooding the clubhouse basement, water seeped into the Fo'c'sle and under the bowling alleys.[10]

A full damage report estimated that 75 percent of the harbor was unusable. At a special meeting of the board, it was determined that $171,000 would be needed to restore the harbor and install sheet-piling for protection. Overall damage was estimated at $250,000. The board appropriated $35,000 to take the necessary first steps in the repair process and to build a cinder-block wall around the island grounds of the Club.[11]

Next, the board went to the National Bank of Detroit and borrowed $75,000, part of which they designated to paying off the balance of the original debt from 1938 to the Collateral Liquidation Corporation. An attempt was made to borrow additional funds from other banks, but without success. At that point, the board approved a proposal to raise the initiation fee, but that alone would not come close to covering costs. Once again, the Club was facing potential financial peril.[11]

Enter GPYC member and investment banker Paul Moreland, who proposed a plan for an innovative bond offering to the members. The board members liked what they heard and

✦ ✦ ✦

Figure 9. Commodore William O. Kronner, 1955.

instructed Moreland to proceed with working out the details. He enlisted the help of Melvin Huffaker, a fellow member of the Club and an attorney, and together they created the Bond and Consent Assessment Plan to finance the repair operation. The program was a complete success. By year's end, $224,000 in bonds had been subscribed, and just two years after the initial offering, half of the amount of outstanding bonds had been retired.[11]

As part of the harbor repair, twenty-one new catwalks were built and sheet-piling was installed that extended forty-eight inches above the previous concrete seawall. New cinderblock seawall, reinforced with steel rods and concrete, was put in place along the east and north sides of the clubhouse. A similar seawall was built on the south side, from the swimming pool to Lake Shore Road. A steel and concrete bridge replaced the old wooden walkway. As a result of this construction, the capacity of the harbor increased from sixty-one to eighty boat wells.[10, 11]

In a special letter to the membership in 1952, Commodore Paul Marco said the following about the flood and its aftermath:

"This year, when unforeseen flood conditions suddenly endangered the property, your officers and directors were faced with an emergency of a kind not experienced in the quarter of a century since the clubhouse was built. While the most immediate action was imperative, it was realized that any protective measures undertaken in repairing the damage and guarding against recurrence, must be the best and most lasting possible; for the best would be the cheapest—in the long run."[12]

Swimming and bowling

In 1952, the swim team received a big boost when the husband and wife team of Clarence and Betty Pinkston took over coaching duties. Both were Olympic medalists in diving; Clarence won gold and silver in 1920 and two bronze in 1924, and Betty captured gold and silver in 1924 and gold again in 1928.

The GPYC swim team had been languishing in the basement of the Inter-Club circuit before Betty and "Pink" arrived, but by the end of their first full season with the team, the GPYC swimmers had vastly improved in point totals, in

Above, figure 10. This article from the Spring 1952 *Grosse Pointer* welcomes Betty and Clarence Pinkston to the Club as the new swim team coaches. Between the two, they held three gold, two silver, and two bronze Olympic medals in diving.

Figure 11. Left to right: Commodore Farr, Betty and Clarence Pinkston, and member Mel Huffaker. Just four years after the Pinkstons assumed their coaching duties, the GPYC team won the 1956 Michigan Inter-Club Swimming Association (MICSA) championship.

Above, figure 12. Commodore Hickey feigns a "christening" of the new automatic pinsetters with a bottle of champagne, as three enthusiastic bowlers laughingly urge him on.

numbers, and, perhaps most importantly, in enthusiasm. At the 1953 sports dinner, the squad, all on their own, chipped in and presented the Pinkstons with a deep-fat fryer. According to a 1953 *Grosse Pointer* article, "Both Pink and Betty were visibly touched by the tribute and Betty shed a few tears." The team went on to win the Michigan Inter-Club Championship in 1956.[13]

Bowling continued to be a popular pastime for many members. Nearly every issue of *The Grosse Pointer* from this decade has bowling news. There were long lists of scores and averages and action photographs on the lanes. There were men, women, and mixed leagues bowling five nights a week, Monday through Friday; Saturday was Juniors' day. The season culminated every spring with the Bowlers' Jamboree, where cocktails preceded the awards, followed by dinner and dancing. The program took a big step forward in 1956, when automatic pinsetters were installed.[14]

Sailing

A first for the GPYC in sailing occurred in 1952 when *Orient*, a sixty-four-foot cutter belonging to member Paul Smiley, won the Port Huron-to-Mackinac race in the Cruising A class. Paul not only crossed the finish line first, but his corrected time was sufficient to take the win. Although member-owned boats had previously won the race, they had done so representing either the Detroit Yacht Club or Bayview Yacht Club. This was the first time in the history of the race that the winning boat officially represented the Grosse Pointe Yacht Club, flying the GPYC burgee.[15]

That same summer of 1952, the GPYC played host to the sixth annual Luders International Championship regatta. Ten teams from the United States and Bermuda competed, with the trophy going to the Indian Harbor Yacht Club crew from Greenwich, Connecticut.[16]

The silver anniversary year of the GPYC clubhouse saw a record turnout of 170 boats for the annual GPYC Regatta in July 1954. The weather, however, was uncooperative. The wind died and the fleet was stranded out on the lake. By the 7:00 pm deadline, only half the classes had drifted over the finish line; the larger cruising classes were all DNF. Trophy plaques presented to the winners were silver medallions mounted on walnut boards, commemorating the twenty-fifth anniversary.[17]

Unquestionably the most prestigious event of the decade for the Club's sailors was hosting the North American Yacht Racing Union's championship finals in August 1955. The winner of this race would be declared the North American Senior Sailing Champion of the United States and Canada and would capture the historic Mallory Trophy. The trophy itself was a large silver soup tureen that had been presented by Sultan Selim III to the family of Lord Nelson in 1812, expressing the gratitude of Egypt for removal of the threat to that country's security by Lord Nelson's victory on the Nile, commonly known as the Battle of Trafalgar. The trophy was named after Clifford D. Mallory, founder of the NAYRU.[18]

Figure 13. Paul Smiley standing at the helm of *Orient*. This yacht was first to finish and first in corrected time in Cruising A Class in the 1952 Port Huron-to-Mackinac race.

Opposite page, figure 14. The GPYC's seventeenth annual Bluenose Regatta, 1955. Commodore George Slocum initiated the race in 1939 to provide a second annual yachting event at the GPYC. He named it for the cold, blustery weather ordinarily prevalent in late September, when the race is held.

Figure 15. The Mallory Trophy, awarded to the North American Senior Sailing Champion of the United States and Canada.

Figure 16a. Left to right: Yachting committee member Dan Beck looks over the shoulder of Rear Commodore Mervyn Gaskin as he shows off the silver anniversary medallion to members George Cossaboom and Tore Franzen. Cossaboom chaired the 1954 yachting committee and Franzen was GPYC chairman of judges and timers in the annual regatta

GPYC member George C. Cossaboom was general chairman of the championship series. Following the event, at the next annual winter meeting of the NAYRU at the New York Yacht Club, George was singled out by the organization's president, "for the most extraordinary precedent set by the Grosse Pointe [Yacht] Club and the Mallory Race Committee for faultless conduct of the Mallory Cup Series in Detroit."[19]

GPYC sailors finished the decade in style with two 1960 Port-Huron-to-Mackinac wins. Member Aaron Evans won the Class D in his thirty-one-foot boat *Alady*, while member Carter Sales Jr., co-owner of forty-foot *Comanche*, took the Class C race. *Comanche* also won the Class C Chicago-to-Mackinac, and finished fourth in the fleet overall.[20]

The social scene

The 1951 Games Party drew such a large crowd that the Main Lounge (Ballroom), Green Room (Venetian Room) and Main Dining Room were all filled to capacity. Also in 1951, the "Soiree Continental" party, with a French and

Figure 16b. Silver medallion commemorating the twenty-fifth anniversary of the clubhouse. The medallions were mounted on wooden plaques and given to winners in the July 4, 1954, regatta, and may have been given for other purposes as well. When present member Christopher Izzy purchased one of these medallions, he was told by the seller that it had been given to his grandfather in 1954 for being a twenty-five year member of the Club.

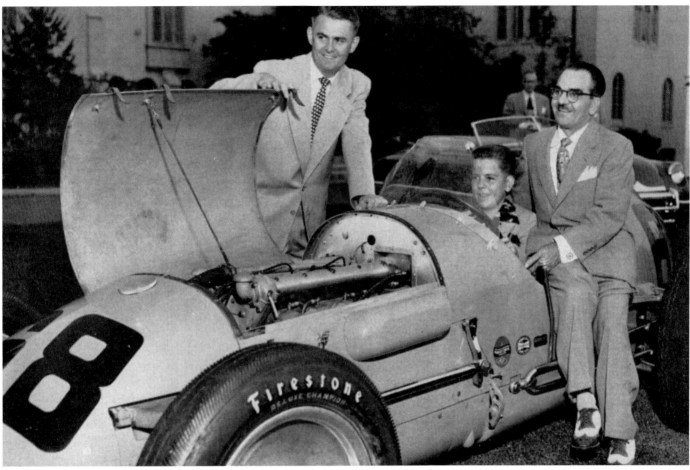

Figure 17. Annual Father and Son day of fun at the GPYC, 1951. Left to right: Detroit Tigers pitcher Teddy Gray, Tommy Chaplow, and his father, Bryan Chaplow. Indianapolis 500 racer owned by member Gene Casaroll.

Figure 18. The star of every showboat party was always the showboat. This showboat from 1956 provided a spectacular background setting for the more than 800 guests who enjoyed dining and dancing under the stars.

Figure 19. Three generations of commodores are represented in this photo. Commodore Stark Hickey, 1957, is seated, holding his granddaughter. Edward Schoenherr, standing far right in second row, would become commodore in 1964. John Schoenherr, standing far right in first row, was commodore in 1997.

Moroccan theme, featured entertainment chairman Rex Regan joining in on the piano with one of the bands to entertain his fellow members.

In 1952, the St. Patrick's Day party had already become the St. Patrick's/ Gay Nineties/ Millionaires party when it was noted that the party date fell on tax deadline day, and Paupers was added to the mix. It thus became the SPGNMP party, shortened to Paupers' party.

The Summer 1955 issue of *The Grosse Pointer* featured a spread of pictures from the Old Fashioned Field Day at the Old Club. Most of the fun seemed to be centered on the egg-throwing event, and especially on the missed catches.

Club history was made in 1958 when Commodore Charles Jacobson's daughter Eleanor made her debut at the Club. It was the first time

a sitting commodore had presented his daughter to society while serving his term.

Beginning in 1952, the first issue of *The Grosse Pointer* for each year published a tentative entertainment schedule. The 1952 schedule ran from March to August, but all subsequent schedules ran from either March or April through December."

During this decade, many parties and events were repeated annually: The Commodore's Ball; Directors' Open House; July Fourth celebration; St. Patrick's Day Party; GPYC Annual Regatta in July; Commodore's Review of the Fleet and Showboat Party in August; Mother and Daughter Luncheon; Father and Son Party; Bowlers' Jamboree; Old Fashioned Field Day (day at the Old Club); Ladies' Bridge Luncheon; Bluenose

GPYC

Figure 20. Commodore Mervyn G. Gaskin, 1956.

Regatta; Thanksgiving Ball; Junior Prom; Children's Christmas Party. Several one-time events also appeared: a "Cinerama" Party at the Music Hall, a Western Party, and an Amateur Play, "1890 Frolics," just to name a few.

Through 1955, excluding the summer months, "Dinner and Dancing" is on the schedule for nearly every Saturday that there was not a specific party. In 1956 and subsequent years it began to appear less often, perhaps because it was becoming more expensive to secure dance bands on a regular basis. It is also interesting to note that on the 1960 schedule the Thanksgiving Ball, which was a black-tie affair, and the Junior Prom are no longer listed, possibly a harbinger of social changes in the wind.

Royalty passes in review

On June 26, 1959, Queen Elizabeth and President Dwight Eisenhower presided over the formal opening of the 2,300-mile St. Lawrence Seaway. To further celebrate the event, the Queen and

Figure 21. Large crowds gathered on both sides of the river in 1959 to view the royal yacht *Britannia* docked at Windsor. Queen Elizabeth II and Prince Philip took part in the inaugural Freedom Festival on July 3, before beginning a cruise of the Great Lakes.

Figure 22. Commodore Stark Hickey, 1957.

Figure 23. Commodore Charles L. Jacobson, 1958.

Prince Philip began a forty-five-day journey on the 415-foot royal yacht *Britannia* through the Great Lakes that would culminate in Chicago. On July 3, the royal couple arrived in Detroit and Windsor just in time to be a part of the inaugural Freedom Festival. Later that day, the *Britannia* sailed up the river and into Lake St. Clair, where pleasure boats were lined all the way up the freighter channel on both sides, presenting a "royal" review. Members of the GPYC who were not out in their boats had a clear view of the magnificent yacht as it steamed past on its Great Lakes journey.

Financial stability

In Commodore Mervyn Gaskin's annual report for 1957, he referenced the ongoing struggle that the GPYC had been engaged in for thirty years with the State of Michigan concerning title to the land upon which the clubhouse stands.[8] Citing the Submerged Land Act, the state refused to grant clear title to the land because the clubhouse was built mostly on land-fill. This was not only a title issue; the dispute also affected the Club's ability to acquire a liquor

license.[21] Commodore Gaskin reported that Past Commodore William Kronner had been able to resolve most of the issues to the benefit of the Club. One year later, in 1957, Commodore Stark Hickey reported in his annual message that the matter had finally been completely resolved. A payment of $30,900 had been made to the state and the title was free and clear.[22]

Commodore Hickey was also able to report that the High Water Disaster Bonds, sold back in 1952 after the water damage to the harbor and clubhouse, were on track to be completely paid off by the end of 1959.[23]

The end of the decade

When Commodore Robert Weber took the helm in 1959, the Club was on solid financial ground, and that is how the decade would end when Commodore William Ternes took over in 1960.

Commodore Weber's message to the membership in 1959 was entitled, "What Is the Grosse Pointe Yacht Club?" He answered his own question, in part, in this way:

Figure 24. Commodore Robert F. Weber, 1959.

Figure 25. Commodore William A. Ternes, 1960.

To some it is land, harbor and building; to others it combines a beautiful park, wherein a masterfully designed building stands, surrounded by a magnificent harbor in which are moored the finest yachts on the Great Lakes. To the members it is a close association of friends, bound together in fellowship.

It is this latter description which provides the answer — for without the close association of friends and the continued flow of fellowship there would be no Club.

I like to think of the Grosse Pointe Yacht Club as a home away from home — a home that complements the home — for within its boundaries you find facilities and services and a dedicated staff to provide that friendly, homelike atmosphere.[24]

Nicely said.

IMAGE ACKNOWLEDGEMENTS
Chapter Five

1. GPYC

2. William Johnston

3. – 16a. GPYC

16b. Christopher Izzy

17. GPYC

18. Past Com. John and Shelley Schoenherr

19. – 20. GPYC

21. *The Windsor Star*

22. – 25. GPYC

Figure 1. *Ticonderoga*, member Bill Brittain's 73-foot ocean-racing ketch was berthed at the GPYC during the summers 1962–1964. Photo by Morris Rosenfeld.

By Thomas M.J. Hathaway

1961 through 1969

Decade of transformation

The 1960s were a time of dramatic change in America, often referred to as the "Swinging Sixties," during which there was a significant cultural shift from the conservative post-war Eisenhower years to the liberal Kennedy New Frontier era. The decade brought new values with the music of the Beatles, the civil rights movement, the reappearance of feminism, the Cuban missile crisis, war in Vietnam, student protests, the first Super Bowl, and more. It culminated with strangely contrasting events like the drug-fueled rock concert at Woodstock and Neil Armstrong's historic walk on the moon. The culture, customs, and membership of the Club were all affected by the change.

If the 1950s were a time of rehabilitation for the Club, the second half of the twentieth century proved in many ways to be years of transformation. The Club, for example, entered the decade as a pleasureboating club and emerged as a renowned sail racing club. Major improvements were made to the harbor, clubhouse, and grounds during this time, and there was strong desire to grow the Club's footprint by acquiring rights to the lake bottom immediately south of Club property.

Like other private clubs of the era, the GPYC was tasked with managing its finances and finding new streams of revenue to promote growth through new member attractions. Over the course of the decade, the Club would see membership grow from 675 to a record 902 members, and the number of boat wells would more than double, from 112 to 237. Each year was marked by progress as Club leadership stewarded assets and adroitly responded to a changing culture while remaining true to founding principles.

For decades, nonboating activities were part of the GPYC experience. In previous years, archery, croquet, bowling, swimming, diving, and shuffleboard had been the popular pastimes. Now, in the 1960s, tennis, paddle tennis, snow, and water skiing were the passions of those with active lifestyles.[1]

The decade saw another change as well: the transition from high-society debutante parties and formal gatherings to more casual, family-oriented occasions. High class was now déclassé; top hats and tuxedos were giving way to "mod" wardrobes with wide lapels and bell-bottom trousers. Side-burns grew longer as hemlines got shorter.

Harbor expansion, ice damage, and tight money

Early in the decade, Club leaders were concerned about the cost of previously approved expansion of the south harbor. But due to cost-cutting and construction efficiencies, the final price of the harbor project was one-third of the anticipated amount, enabling loans that were incurred to be paid on schedule in 1963. An interesting piece of Club history was uncovered during harbor expansion, which briefly stalled the project. Remnants of the old Grosse Pointe Shores municipal pier were discovered when workmen unexpectedly dug into its old pilings, which proved virtually immovable. Those old pilings were so deeply planted that the new ones could not be installed. The fix for the contractors was to build around the area where the pier had been.

Unfortunately during the following winter, ice crushed some of the new pilings, creating a "bulge" in the east wall of the harbor.[2] The protrusion, which was determined not to be a structural problem, is still visible along the east wall at the end of the main pier.

In addition to expansion of the south harbor, Club grounds to the west of the harbor were also enlarged in late 1962 when the Club was able to acquire 2.14 acres of Lake St. Clair bottomland from the State of Michigan. The bottomland was subsequently filled with soil excavated during the expansion. The parking lot and tennis courts occupy the filled area today.

GPYC

Figure 2. Commodore John R. Wilt, 1961.

At the same time, the GPYC was looking to shore up finances. The early 1960s were a time of national economic recession, and private clubs everywhere were looking for ways to retain current members and gain new ones. The GPYC, under Commodore J. Earl Fraser, instituted a new, lower-priced Senior member classification for Active members who had been with the Club for twenty-five years. In addition, a committee was formed to recruit new members. The initiation fee was reduced from $1,500 to $750, which proved to be very successful in attracting new members. In fact, it was so successful that by June 1963 the $1,500 initiation fee had been restored. Later that year, as recruiting efforts began to falter, the fee was reduced to $900. The Club ended the year with 677 members.[3]

That same year, Club leaders briefly pursued the feasibility of consolidating with other clubs, and informal merger meetings were held with the Detroit Boat Club and the Lochmoor Club. Ultimately the membership was consulted, and a decision not to merge was made. There was a firm faith in the future of the Club.

Figure 3. Commodore Paul I. Moreland, 1962.

Figure 4. Commodore J. Earl Fraser, 1963.

Figure 5. Happy trophy winners at the 1967 Bowlers' Jamboree pose in the Rotunda.

Ironically, after years of dealing with record-high lake levels in the 1950s, 1963 saw levels recede to near-record lows. During the winter of 1964, the inner harbor was dredged two feet below its soundings to allow safe passage of vessels in the harbor. At the same time, the Club negotiated a fifty-year lease from the State of Michigan for six additional acres of submerged land for harbor use.[4] In June 1964, the GPYC made the final $6,000 payment on the underwater land it had purchased in 1962 from the State of Michigan, thus acquiring title to it.[5]

Investment in Club facilities continued in 1964 with the refurbishment of the Main Dining Room under the direction of member William Schmidt. Work included new windows, new carpeting, and painting at a cost of $17,500.[6] The grand opening of the magnificent Main Dining Room was a sell-out, and the new look was enthusiastically received by members.

With the expanded number of boat wells in the harbor, Commodore Edward J. Schoenherr over-saw construction of a harbor control tower, which was located on the east lawn's northeast corner and, operated both the drawbridge and swing bridge for the convenience of boaters.[7] And with all boat wells in the harbor occupied, the board authorized the creation of a new T-Dock to accommodate further growth in the boat population.

By mid-decade, signs of growth

Member totals were back up in 1965, and the board again restored the initiation fee to $1,500.[8] The board confidently prepared plans for new dockage in the west harbor and pledged to add fifty new members to address the cost of the investment.

Expansion continued as the board requested a permit from the Village of Grosse Pointe Shores to purchase the land created by harbor-dredging deposits.[9]

In May 1965, owing to union contract demands, the board approved, for the first time, automatic tips and service charges on members' dining bills to ensure proper employee compensation.[10]

The next year, 1966, further capital improvements were made to the clubhouse, grounds, and harbor. Despite a tight budget, the Club

Figure 6. This diagram superimposed on a photo of the GPYC clubhouse and harbor was part of a prospectus sent to members in 1959, seeking their approval for the proposed construction projects. If approved, construction would proceed according to the numbered sequence. Project 1 was the extension and enclosure of the open porch that was completed in 1960 and eventually became the Binnacle. Project 2 provided a new seawall and fifty-two new boat wells. Project 3 added new bottomland area, as did Project 5, which also included another eighty-eight new boat wells. Project 4, a new glass-fronted entrance, was never completed.

constructed two new tennis courts in response to members' requests. Shortly afterward, two more tennis courts were added. Eight new wells on T-Dock and eight new floating wells in the southwest corner of the harbor were constructed, along with a floating ramp for the launching and storing of Club sailboats. New fuel pumps and a pumpout facility were installed, and upgrades were made to provide a better supply of electricity and potable water for the harbor.[9] The harbor now had 194 boat wells, more than 82 of which had been

1961 THROUGH 1969 **115**

Here's what the Project Plan would give us:

PROJECT 4

PROJECT 1

PROJECT 3

PROJECT 2

added since 1960.[11] The Club also leveled and seeded the new fill area parallel to Lake Shore Road that had been created from the western harbor-dredging deposits. Evergreens were planted along the perimeter and are still evident today.

At the end of Commodore John W. Paynter's year in 1966, the membership had grown to 734, the highest total since 1958. That growth continued in 1967 under the stewardship of Commodore Harry J. Chapman, with a board again committed to providing members with an enhanced Club experience by attending to their diverse interests.

In the harbor, 44 new boat wells were constructed because of increased demand, bringing the total count to 241.[12] It was determined that the revenue generated from these new wells would pay for the resulting construction costs of $44,000 over five years. The harbor committee overseeing the expansion program, chaired by William D. Plante, who would become commodore in 1977, developed a new pricing policy for boat wells based on the dimensions of the well, not the size of the boat it contained. Plante's contribution was deemed more equitable to boaters and also provided a more stable stream

Figure 7a. Excavation for the Club's second swimming pool began in May 1969. By June, the pool structure was nearing completion.

Figure 7b. The new pool officially opened on August 3, one month late due to a two-week strike of sheet metal workers and twenty-three days of bad weather. It was dedicated the night before at the Showboat party, where the first swimmers, Commodore James Gagne, Past Commodore John DeHayes, and Vice Commodore Roger Smith were playfully tossed in.

Figure 8. Platform tennis comes to the Club, 1969.

Figure 9. Members Sheldon Veil, left, and Ronald Birgbauer took the men's doubles victory in the first tournament held on the new paddle tennis courts in June 1969.

of revenue to the Club.[13] Past Commodore Plante's pricing policy is in place today. The year also saw the installation of a harbor communications system by Bell Telephone Company that enabled immediate contact with the harbor office from almost anywhere on the docks.[14]

That same year, the last vestige of male chauvinism at the Club manifested itself in the creation of the Tower Room on the third floor of the clubhouse that was designated as a men only retreat. It is now known as the Tower Pub, serving both men and women.[15]

By the end of Commodore Harry Chapman's busy year, the Club had gained an additional 49 members, bringing the total to 783, the highest level in the Club's history, along with a record number of harbor wells.[11]

The 1960s draw to a positive close

The years 1968 and 1969 under Commodores John F. De Hayes and O. James Gagne respectively, were defined in part by a series of much-needed capital improvements. The list of planned projects included 57 new boat wells, two paddle tennis courts, an increased parking area, rebuilding the entry roadway, kitchen renovations, and the purchase of leased land from the Village of Grosse

Pointe Shores. The land was on the north side of the clubhouse underlying the Grill Room (today's Spinnaker), kitchen, Commodores' Room, and Main Dining Room. In addition to this lengthy list, it was determined that there could be no further delay in building a new swimming pool due to significant leakage problems in the old one.[12]

Helping to fund these projects was the welcome continuation of a steady increase in membership. By the end of 1968, the Club roster had reached 795.[16] Summer of 1969 saw the completion of the new pool, along with expanded parking and a new roadway and bridge to the clubhouse. On the day of dedication at the Showboat and Fleet Review, Commodore O. James Gagne said, "This is the proudest moment of my life."[17] The decade ended with a record membership total of 902.[18]

Not just a club — a way of life

Throughout the free-spirited 1960s, the GPYC proved adept at providing unique and entertaining experiences for its members. A steadily expanding menu of activities and programs attracted a collegial mix of young and old. Club functions of all kinds were well attended.

In 1961, Chubby Checker's "Let's Twist Again," Ben E. King's "Stand By Me," and Del

Figure 10. Fleet Review, 1969. Left to right: Commodore and Mrs. O. James Gagne, Vice Commodore and Mrs. Roger K. Smith, Rear Commodore and Mrs. Ralph J. Kliber on the foredeck of Gagne's yacht, *Imperial V.*

Shannon's "Runaway" were top songs on Detroit radio. Rock and roll was unquestionably the music of the time. Club planners, torn by the dilemma of tradition versus trendiness, decided to compromise. The year's biggest theme party therefore became the "Rock and Roar" 1920s party, with the clubhouse decorated as a speakeasy, "rather nostalgic to the oldsters," but still promising to be "rip roariously enjoyable to the younger set." *The Grosse Pointer* magazine noted:

Commodore John R. Wilt was the epitome of sartorial perfection for the golf links in creamy white linen plus fours and high black socks, with two-tone gold shoes. He wore a striped blazer jacket and visored cream-hued cap. Mrs. Wilt was in a flapper dress of pink silk printed in a splashy rose design, and a headache band of maline with rosette at the side.

[Past Commodore] Robert F. Weber soon divested himself of the great raccoon coat in which he arrived; Mrs. Weber was in a flapper dress of pale rose velvet with scalloped hem."[19]

The year 1962 saw a variety of popular social events on the Club calendar. Among them were the Spring into Spring, a reopening party; an Easter Egg Hunt; the Bowlers Jamboree; Club Night at the Opera; the Ladies' Fashion Show; Members' Mixer Party; Fathers and Sons Party; 4th of July Children's Circus and Fireworks Gala; a record-setting Annual Regatta; Boat Hop Night; the Commodore's Review and Showboat; a sold-out Children's Christmas Party; and another full house for the Mardi Gras winter closing party, described as "a blinger!"[20] The once boaters-only Club was now a family-oriented place with a little something to offer nearly every member who passed through the gate.

Figure 11. Commodore Edward J. Schoenherr. 1964.

Figure 12. Commodore Harold E. Cross, M.D., 1965.

A carnival was held at the Club in 1963, complete with the creation of a midway, shooting gallery, gypsy fortune-teller, and live highlights from *Kiss Me Kate*, presented by the Grosse Pointe Community Theatre.[21] Commodore J. Earl Fraser made it a priority during his year to involve more members' children in Club planning and activities through the Teenage Committee. The committee had already planned and hosted three Annual Junior Showboat Parties along with other teen-themed gatherings, and with Commodore Fraser's support, they proudly set a Junior Showboat record that summer with an attendance of nearly five-hundred teens.[22]

Also in 1963, Mrs. George M. Slocum, widow of the Club's seventh commodore (and one of the longest-serving ones), entertained her large circle of friends at a breakfast during the holidays. This holiday breakfast had become an annual tradition at the Club and was enthusiastically attended.[23]

Throughout the sixties, the country was experiencing a social revolution, and slowly but surely, the Club was changing with the times. By 1967, Club members were listening to Aretha Franklin's "Respect," The Mommas & the Poppas' "California Dreaming," and the Beach Boys'

"God Only Knows," which might well have inspired the inaugural Clambake Party. *The Grosse Pointer* reported:

Zingiest, zaniest party ever to hit the Club was the season's opener, a clambake special that filled the staid, old building with laughter and happy faces...

...In the Venetian Room Hank Warren set up a trio that made sounds, while two live go-go girls shivered and shimmied like the front end of a 1934 Ford at 100 mph. They drew an open-mouth[ed] crowd, some of whom sat on the floor in front of the stage riser on which the girls danced...

...Ballroom walls were strung with fishnets, ring buoys and rope. On the tables, candles burned from the tops of old bottles and *(gulp!)* goldfish swam in bowls."[24]

The Clambake Party was designed to celebrate the reopening of the Club after spring cleaning. While attendance was light at that first event, the buzz surrounding it must have captured members' attention, because the following year the party was a sell-out. By 1969, the Clambake was sold out ten days in advance, and attendance was a whopping 538 people. Seafood was abundant

Figure 13. Wearing their aprons and bibs, committee members for the 1967 Clambake party are ready to dive in to the feast. Tables were decorated with live goldfish in bowls.

and extravagant, featuring clams, oysters, crab legs, and whole lobsters. Decorations were more elaborate, with stuffed gulls and lobster traps hung festively around the clubhouse, and nametags were oversized lobster bibs. Fish bowls with live goldfish were given as table favors.[25]

Also in 1967, the Club hosted a Mod Dinner Dance, during which the clubhouse went psychedelic for the night, with women in miniskirts and men in hippie attire. Lighting was turned seductively low and the ceiling was in continuous motion with constantly changing colors and shapes. Attendees danced first to an orchestra, followed by a rock-and-roll band in what was described as a "mod follies, and a mod fashion show."[26] The times were indeed a-changing.

In 1968, more than six-hundred members and guests attended Commodore John DeHayes' formal Commodore's Ball. Later that winter, the clubhouse rocked to music at the first annual Snow Ball, sponsored by the Teenage Committee and attended by more than 300 GPYC teens in

evening attire. "The teens responded so well to the idea of a formal dance that there was talk of making the Junior Showboat Party in August a formal affair."[27]

Figure 14. *The Grosse Pointer* for December 1965 featured these candid pictures from a Roaring '20s party. The photos were taken "simply for beauty" and "would be a credit to any Follies-Bergere line."

Figure 15. GPYC Commodore John R. Wilt modeling at a Club fashion show. His golf ensemble featured a blue Bermuda shorts and a light blue shirt, topped by a roll-brimmed straw hat.

Figure 16. Partygoers at the 1961 Rockin' Roarin' '20s Party. Note member Don McPhails, sixth from right, dressed as a flapper, standing next to member Russ Nutter dressed as Charles Lindbergh.

ROARING FORTIES
By Past Com. Ralph J. Kliber
Excerpted from *The Grosse Pointer,* Winter 1999

Marine artist Jack Gray's painting, "Roaring Forties" in the foyer vividly illustrates the challenge of the sea to the sailing vessels and their crews plying their trade with less glamorous cargoes. As Captain Alan Villiers puts it in, "Men, Ships and the Sea;"

"They sailed the roaring forties with Australian grain or Chilean nitrates in their holds and teenage crews in their forecastles."

What are the *Roaring Forties?* No, not years, but the prevailing, raging westerly winds. The imaginary east-west bands around the girth of the earth as it spins on its north-south axis are "latitudes" — zero at the Equator, 90 degrees at the Poles. The *forty degree north* line runs roughly across the United States from San Francisco to New York City. *Forty degree south* runs from southern Australia, over New Zealand and cuts across the lower part of Chile and Argentina in South America, just above the ever dangerous Cape Horn.

Why *Roaring Forties?* The prevailing westerly winds have the full sweep of the Pacific Ocean until they bang with full force against the Rockies in the north, the Andes in the south. The danger to sailing vessels is obvious, particularly west of southern South America where Cape Horn must be rounded.

The crews of the sailing vessels were dominated by young men. Work aloft in the rigging was dangerous. Death was a common event, as Captain Villiers sadly observes,

"Nowhere is death more painful than at sea. Ashore there are diversions; one forgets. But at sea there is only the little band of men. And when one goes, no one comes to take his place."

May we salute those valiant young men of the sea who braved the *"Roaring Forties"* in sailing vessels, artist Jack Gray who so vividly depicts them, and the late Commodore Mervyn G. Gaskin who donated the painting to the Grosse Pointe Yacht Club in 1965.

Figure 17. This dramatic painting entitled *Roaring Forties,* by Jack Gray, hangs in the clubhouse foyer. Photography by James Dorian.

Figure 18. Bob Sellers, far right, Skipper of the Year, 1965. He is seen here with the Milton O. Cross Memorial Trophy, awarded for his DRYA achievements that year. The trophy was made by Tiffany's and was on display in the GPYC Rotunda.

Putting the "yacht" in GPYC

During the 1960s, the Grosse Pointe Yacht Club was recognized as one of the country's outstanding sail racing clubs. This was due in part to the Club's expanded and improved harbor on Lake St. Clair, but it also was in large part because of a dedicated group of members with a passion for sailing who gave their time and talent to host successful, high-profile regattas.

It began in 1960 when Carter Sales' forty-foot yawl *Comanche* won Class C in both the Port Huron-to-Mackinac race and the Chicago-to-Mackinac race, and Aaron Evans's thirty-one-foot sloop *Alady* won Class D in the Port Huron-to-Mackinac race.[28] In 1961, Commodore John R. Wilt presided over the thirty-second Annual GPYC Regatta, which had a record entry of 198

yachts.[29] But with the rapidly growing interest in sailboating across the area, that record did not stand for long.

It was in 1962 that member Bill Brittain brought the famed seventy-three-foot ocean-racing yacht *Ticonderoga* to the Great Lakes and a berth at the GPYC. The *Ticonderoga* had won every Southern Ocean Racing Association competition, including the Miami-to-Nassau, Tampa Bay-to-Ft. Lauderdale, St. Petersburg-to-Havana and Bermuda-to-Halifax races.[30]

In 1963 two new trophies were initiated, recognizing the growing importance of competitive sailing at the Club, especially among young people. The Commodore Paul I. Moreland Trophy was dedicated as a Beginner's Class Annual Sailing Award to the young sailor who made the

Figure 19. Aaron Evans' *Alady*, 1960 Class D winner of the Port Huron-to-Mackinac race.

Figure 20. *Comanche*, owned by Carter Sales, was the 1960 Class C winner of both the Port Huron-to-Mackinac and the Chicago-to-Mackinac races.

most progress in learning to sail. The Commodore Stark Hickey Junior Sailing Trophy was given annually to the GPYC sailor under age eighteen who won the Junior Sailing Championship.[31]

In 1964, the thirty-fifth anniversary of the clubhouse opening, the Annual Regatta set another all-time record with an entry list of 224 boats.[32] That same year, the Club hosted the prestigious North American Yacht Racing Union's Mallory Cup races. Both racing events were under the watchful eye of member Frank P. McBride Jr., who would become commodore ten years later.

In 1965 the Club received one of its most precious artifacts, a painting by acclaimed marine artist Jack Gray titled *Roaring Forties*. This dramatic piece of marine artwork, which captures the raging fury of the sea in those latitudes, was generously donated by Past Commodore Mervyn G. Gaskin. Commodore Harold Cross gratefully accepted the painting, which is on display in the Club lobby today, stating it would "be an excellent companion piece for several beautiful paintings donated in the early days of GPYC by officers and members."[33]

In 1967 the GPYC was the host club for the National Raven Championships. The event was awarded to the GPYC through the efforts of

Figure 21. Bill Brittain's *Ticonderoga*, built in Quincy, Massachsetts in 1936, was a premier racer on both the Atlantic and Pacific oceans. Brittain owned the boat from 1959 through 1965 and added a number of ocean race wins to its already impressive record. Photo by Morris Rosenfeld.

Figure 22. Commodore John W. Paynter, 1966.

Figure 23. Commodore Harry J. Chapman, 1967.

members Carter Sales Jr. and Robert B. Sellers, who chaired the event. The two men were highly praised by national participants.[34] That year, the Club's Annual Regatta drew the largest fleet of entries in DRYA history with 347 boats.

The 1967 Bluenose Regatta, the Club's final race of the season, had a record participation of 230 yachts.[35] The event heralded the establishment of one of the Club's most coveted sailing trophies, the William P. Fisher Perpetual Memorial Trophy, named in honor of the accomplished industrialist and yachtsman. Designed by member William M. Schmidt, the trophy was donated by members Mrs. John L. Drummy, Ms. Mary V. Fisher, Everett E. Fisher, and Thomas K. Fisher. It is awarded annually to the Class A winner in the Bluenose. The first boat listed on the base of the trophy is *Apache*, which had once been owned by none other than Thomas K. Fisher. That particular year, the boat was campaigned by the legendary W.D. "Toot" Gmeiner, who sailed her to victory for the Detroit Yacht Club.[36]

By 1968, the reputation of the GPYC as a top-notch yacht racing club was firmly in place:

Grosse Pointe Yacht Club's pre-eminent position in Detroit and Great Lakes yachting has been brought into greater focus as it moves into its 1968 season… The schedule is the greatest, the most glorious in the Club's long history…

No layout on fresh water can match the ideal setting, facilities and waters of the GPYC…

The aggressive and receptive attitude of the GPYC towards sailing also will bring greater rewards in the sport this season. For the first time in the history of Lake St. Clair sailing, skippers from Australia, Canada, France, England, Italy, Sweden, Norway, and Denmark will be guests of the GPYC. This will come during the national Tempest class championships, followed by the world's international series in this class the first two weeks in September.

Another first to add prestige to the GPYC will be the holding of the Great Lakes Yacht Racing Union Richardson Cup series of match races in Cal 40s. There is no dressier, more ceremonious, and dignified event in Great Lakes yachting than the Richardson.[37]

This was a one-design race, where the identically rigged boats were supplied by the race committee and the sailors crewing were the only variable. Thomas K. Fisher and his son, Thomas K. Fisher Jr., went on to win the Richardson trophy in 1968 and 1969 for the GPYC. It was the first time sailors from the Detroit area had won the event since 1932. As Great Lakes champions, the Fishers were invited to represent the area in the Congressional Cup Series in Long Beach, California. The GPYC had achieved national status as a racing yacht club.[37]

Figure 24. Thomas K. Fisher's Cal-40, *Conquest*, circa 1967. Cal-40s became popular during the 1960s, so much so that they eventually had their own start time in the weekly DRYA races. Tom Fisher became known for always having a uniformly dressed crew. At some point, his crew wore the orange pants pictured here, and they subsequently became the signature attire of a Tom Fisher crew.

Figure 25. The Cal-40 Fisher crew being presented with the Richardson Cup, GPYC Ballroom, 1969. Thomas K. Fisher is far left, standing next to his son, Thomas K. Fisher Jr. Along with their blazers, the crew is sporting their signature orange pants. The Richardson Cup is visible to the left of Thomas Fisher Sr.

Figure 26. In the background of this photo of an unidentified children's event is the harbor control tower that was built in 1964, used exclusively to open and close the harbor bridges. The harbormaster's office was a small free-standing building adjacent to the east side of the Commodores' Room. Fuel pumps were located on T-dock.

Figure 27. An aerial view of the harbor in 1969. A comparison with the diagram published in 1959 (fig. 6, p. 114) indicating proposed projects shows that projects two, three, and five were completed as planned. The harbor control tower is not visible in this photograph.

Figure 28. Commodore John F. DeHayes, 1968.

Figure 29. Commodore O. James Gagne, 1969.

The 1960s were an exciting and prolific time in the history of the GPYC. In less than a decade, the Club had managed to enlarge its harbor, enhance its clubhouse and grounds, attract a vibrant, growing membership, and provide it with an enviable array of sporting, social, dining and entertainment offerings. As 1969 ended and the decade of the 1970s began, members were living well and enjoying the benefits of a more relaxed and greatly diversified Club experience. And yet, for all the change, the GPYC remained true to its traditions of elegance and gentility. It was still a place where one could escape the pressures of a world in constant transition and reconnect with certain timeless fundamentals.

IMAGE ACKNOWLEDGEMENTS
Chapter Six

1. Mystic Seaport archives

2. – 9. GPYC

10. Mrs. James O. Gagne

11. – 16. GPYC

17. Jim Dorian

18. – 20. GPYC

21. Mystic Seaport archives

22. – 23. GPYC

24. – 25. Thomas K. Fisher Family

26. Past Com. John and Shelley Schoenherr

27. – 29. GPYC

Figure 1. GPYC member Jerry Girschner handles the throttles as daughter Kristyl pilots the *Kristyl Lady* to a Detroit River speed record for women of 73.692 miles per hour on June 2, 1978. The GPYC burgee is painted on the hull, crossed with a flag bearing their sponsor's logo.

By Thomas M. J. Hathaway

1970 through 1980

An era of consolidation and renewal

The 1970s started with a robust 902 members of the Grosse Pointe Yacht Club enjoying world-class facilities and a burgeoning array of sports and entertainment options. However, when the economic and social upheaval of the 1960s began to unravel in the early 1970s, the Club, along with the country, would feel the pain. The Kent State shootings, Watergate, the resignation of President Richard Nixon, stagflation in the Carter administration with interest rates accelerating to as high as twenty percent, and the Organization of Petroleum Exporting Countries (OPEC) oil embargoes, which led to gas rationing, all contributed to unease and uncertainty throughout the country. Michigan's economy was additionally burdened when Detroit automakers were suddenly threatened by the rapidly growing popularity of foreign competitors. The resulting economic conditions eventually led to a severe recession in the mid-1970s. Disposable income, for the first time in years, was on the decline.

For private clubs, the decade came to be defined by economic challenge, and the GPYC was no exception. The Club was suddenly faced with a significant decline in membership. In 1970, total membership reached a high-water mark of 902; by 1974, Active membership had declined to 470 from 549 in 1970.[1,2] Given the reduction in the number of members int all classifications, as well as members' spending at the Club,

Girl zooms to record in powerboat

By JOE DOWDALL
News Staff Writer

A petite brunet and a stopwatch quieted down the haunts of boatmen from Sindbad's up to the Shipping Channel yesterday.

Kristyl Girschner kept her dad's 27-foot Magnum, "Kristyl Lady," as straight as a bullet with its two 410-horsepower engines wide open to set a Detroit River speed record for women at 73.692 miles per hour.

The occasion was the Lake St. Clair Offshore Powerboat Racing Association's speed trials to open the Spirit of Detroit Regatta.

Kristyl's speed topped the 70 m.p.h. runs made 50 years ago by Marion Barbara Castairs in her British Harmsworth Trophy challengers, Estelle II and Estelle

Figure 2. Fifty years earlier, on the Detroit River, Marion Barbara Carstairs had set the women's record at 70 mph in her British Harmsworth Trophy challengers *Estelle II* and *Estelle IV*.

Figure 3. Left to right: Commodore and Mrs. George Beard, Vice Commodore and Mrs. Harold De Orlow, and Rear Commodore and Mrs. William Plante on the foredeck of member C.M. (Marce) Verbiest's 106-foot motor yacht *Helene*. The *Helene* had been built in 1927 for member Charles Sorensen.

In September 1976, Commodore Harold S. De Orlow and the board hired Peter Behr as Club manager to improve operations. As a result, positive changes were made in cost control and in member services areas.[4]

In 1977, the Club held a general membership meeting, which resulted in two landmark decisions. A reclassification of membership categories added, for the first time, Class A and B Social memberships. The articles of iIncorporation were amended to add a special assessment, not to exceed monthly dues, for one month each year. The first assessment was implemented in May 1977 for badly needed repairs, replacements, and improvements.[5]

These critical changes, along with slowly improving economic conditions in the Detroit area, led to a turnaround in Club membership and its economic health. By 1979, harbor wells, which had been fully occupied at the beginning of the decade but had experienced vacancies throughout the intervening years, were again completely filled, and total membership once again surpassed nine hundred. The Club had weathered a decade of ups and downs, demonstrating once again the resilience of Club leadership and membership. A highlight of the 1979 fiftieth anniversary of the opening of the clubhouse was Commodore Sheldon F. Hall's announcement that two hundred new members had joined the Club. That was especially welcome news in that it allowed the Club to significantly reduce its debt and avoid a special assessment.[6]

the board began to propose and enact a variety of solutions. To attract new members, initiation fees were reduced from $2,000 to $1,500. Dues in all categories were increased to provide more operating capital. One-of-a-kind theme parties were organized with the hope of attracting increased member participation. Perhaps with a certain amount of foresight, Commodore Ralph J. Kliber and the board had, in 1971, instituted a minimum expenditure policy for Club members. Their goal was to generate more revenue from required member use.

Although the Club had spent a good deal of money addressing historic high water levels in 1973, by April 1974, Commodore Frank P. McBride and the board authorized borrowing up to $200,000 to finance a series of delayed improvements that included significant roof and general facility repairs. Dues were again increased in November 1975, and an additional $75,000 was borrowed.[2, 3]

The GPYC becomes a yachting leader

The 1960s had ended with the Club competing for the top spot in the Detroit River Yachting Association (DRYA) standings, and the 1970s saw the continuation of that ascent. With the harbor expansion completed under future commodore William D. Plante's sage analysis and direction in the 1960s, the Club's sailing fleet also grew in size and capability. As George E. Van, internationally known yachting writer for the *Detroit Times* and *Detroit News*, noted in 1970:

It was like the spring flight of birds as the biggest fleet in the history of the Grosse Pointe Yacht Club made its 1970 landing in more than three hundred berths in the enlarged harbors. It's a magnificent fleet of sail and power that festoons the clubhouse and the grounds. It's a fleet that embellishes and completes the setting of America's most beautiful yacht club. More than ever this season, the GPYC dominates the yachting picture on Lake St. Clair. The compelling beauty of this boating setup makes the GPYC known internationally.[7]

The 1970s began with the Club boasting some of the most prestigious vessels on the Great Lakes, including Frank C. Piku's 54-foot Marauder *Al-Di-La III*; Carter W. Sales Jr.'s 40-foot sloop *Manitou*, the former Royal Canadian Yacht Club winner of the Canada's Cup; Thomas K. Fisher's 53-foot *Gypsy*; J. Alfred (Skip) Grow's 35-foot *Red Wing*; Past Commodore Jim Gagne's 63-foot cruiser *Imperial; V,* C. M.(Marce) Verbiest's 106-foot *Helene*; Arthur G. Sherman Jr.'s 90-foot *Maradon*; and Walter Schreiber's 81-foot *Opal-M.*

Carter Sales Jr.'s *Manitou* proved the overall winner of the forty-first summer regatta in 1970, while the Club finished one through four in Class A with Frank Piku's *Al-Di-La III*, Tom Fisher's *Gypsy*, and Norbert H. Hollerbach's *Belle Aurore* following. *Gypsy* won the final race of the DRYA season, the Club's Bluenose, the stormiest race of the season. Twenty-one boats failed to finish, with one sinking, one losing a mast, and one damaged below the water line but hauled out before sinking.[8]

But the Club's 1970 sailing season also experienced a big loss. Carter W. Sales Jr., one of the most decorated and accomplished sailors of the DRYA, was posthumously honored as Class A Champion of the DRYA. His beloved boat *Manitou* was named Boat of the Year by the Cruising Club of Detroit. Sales' eleven straight victories in 1969 may never be duplicated. As George Van described it:

There's a gap in the fleet at the GPYC. And it's a big one. *Manitou*, the Canada's Cup queen[,] is gone. More, so is Carter Sales, Jr. He came ashore after the tough GPYC Bluenose race and a few days later, he left us. And ever since, all the good guys in the sailing gang, all over the land, have been trying to adjust to his going… The Regatta guns will continue to boom and, for some of us, there will be a hollow sound in the echoes. A new crop of young skippers will hit the starting line. And the bevy of talent that has emerged at the GPYC recently forecasts future winners.[9]

In other notable sailing action, Howard Boston won the Port Huron-to-Mackinac Class D with his 33-foot Ranger, *Long Ranger*. The rest of the GPYC fleet endured the vagaries of Great Lakes racing and showed well in all other classes but failed to take another top spot.[10] Tom Fisher's *Gypsy* fared better in ocean racing as he captured the Ft. Lauderdale-to-Charleston ocean race.

Figure 4. Member Tom K. Fisher's 53-foot *Gypsy* sailing a Port Huron-to-Mackinac race. Note the crew member in the rigging, furiously clearing a jib sheet carried aloft on the spinnaker pole.

Figure 5. Sixty-one-foot *Sassy*, owned by member "Dutch" Schmidt, first-to-finish in both the Port Huron-to-Mackinac and Chicago-to-Mackinac races, 1972.

In 1971, GPYC entries dominated and took ten out of the first thirteen places in the DRYA. That included the first four rankings: *Manitou, Gypsy, Al-Di-La III* and *Belle Aurore*.[11] But 1972 was the year the Club served notice on the sailing community that it had arrived:

> This will be remembered as the year E. Russell (Dutch) Schmidt came out of nowhere as he busted into the yachting picture with his wonderful *Sassy* and was first to finish in both Mackinac races from Port Huron and Chicago. Never before had a blow boat carrying the burgee of the Grosse Pointe Yacht Club led the fleet into Mackinac Island's crowded harbor in these two great fresh water sailing classics.[12]

That same year, the GPYC had twenty-eight boats starting in the Port Huron-to-Mackinac race and five starters in the Chicago-to-Mackinac. Member Don McQueen's *Sundance* captured a first in Class B in the Port Huron race.

It was also in 1972 that the United States challenged the Royal Canadian Yacht Club in Toronto for the Canada's Cup, which was first raced in 1896. Don McQueen's *Sundance* and Dave Gamble and Frank Piku's *Aggressive* both battled Bayview Yacht Club's *Dynamite* for the right to be the U.S. challenger. After a summer-long series of trial observation races, eight selection finals were raced, with *Dynamite* ultimately winning and becoming the U.S. challenger. She went on to win the Canada's Cup over RCYC defender *Mirage* for the first U.S. victory in eighteen years, bringing the Cup to Lake St. Clair for the first time.[13]

The following year was another outstanding sailing season at the Club:

> Nineteen seventy-three will be remembered as the year the Grosse Pointe Yacht Club put it all together, as the saying goes, and carried off a most challenging schedule of boat races that gave the Club the greatest year in its

Figure 6. *Aggressive*, owned by members Frank Piku and Dave Gambe, in trials with BYC's *Dynamite* to determine who would represent the United States in the race for the Canada's Cup.

Figure 7. Member John Rummel skippered *Morning Star* to many victories throughout the 1970s.

history. The Club was the nerve center of yacht racing all season. The trials and final running of the Great Lakes Yacht Racing Union for the Richardson Cup match race sailing championship, and the Finn Nationals for the one-design title, drew participants and officials from the country's yachting centers, again putting the Club in national focus.[14]

"Dutch" Schmidt's 61-foot sloop *Sassy* beat a record fleet of 227 boats sailing in winds gusting above forty miles per hour to win the Bluenose in record-setting time, winning Class A and taking the overall prize, the William P. Fisher Memorial Trophy.[15] Brothers John and Mike Hughes won Class C with *Notre Dame du Lac* (the former BYC *Dynamite*) and Norbert Hollerbach's *Belle Aurore* won in the G-1 Class and was also the season class champion. Dr. Gerald Murphy's *Dazy II* and Roy Barbier's *Roulette* finished one-two for the season in the DRYA Class A standings, with *Sassy* not participating in enough races to qualify for the championship. Frank Piku's and Dave Gamble's *Aggressive* was the DRYA Class B champion.[16]

The GPYC greeted the 1974 sailing season with much anticipation:

> The Grosse Pointe Yacht Club makes a bigger splash in boating news as the years roll on... the big guy himself, E. R. (Dutch) Schmidt, had just brought in *Sassy* to her well. The blue-hull sixty-one-footer had been on the seas, away from the Club since last September, racing on the East Coast and in Florida waters... *Sassy* was among the leaders in all six of the SORC races last winter.[17]

The Grosse Pointer reported that the GPYC would be competing that year with the biggest sailing fleet in its history. Some of the biggest boats with the most promise for victory included Roy Barbier's *Roulette*, John Rummel's *Morningstar*, Bob Thoreson's *Valkyrie*, Don McQueen's *Sundance*, and *Aggressive*, owned by Frank Piku and Dave Gamble.[17]

And what a year it was as *Aggressive* brought home the *Coppa d'Europa* (European Cup) by winning the world two-ton sailing championship in Italy:

> Lake St. Clair yachtsmen rejoiced with pride in other years as their sailing queens brought home honors as winners racing in outside waters. As great as these exploits have been—successes that excited and thrilled all of us who love blowboats—none was greater than the saga of *Aggressive* in winning the world's two-ton sailing championship as she swept the international series in the Mediterranean sea off San Remo, Italy, in September.

> *Aggressive*'s owners, Dave Gamble and Frank Piku, flew the burgee of GPYC as the skippers and an indomitable crew put their Club in the world yacht racing spotlight. And world attention will be drawn to our Club next summer when Gamble and Piku defend their

Figure 7. GPYC Commodore George Beard presents John Burkard, skipper of BYC's *Ricochet*, the Coppa d'Europa for winning the two-ton world championship. The GPYC was host to the international race in 1975.

Figure 9. *Black Majic*, owned by member John Rummel, in the 1979 St. Petersburg-to-Havana race. They were second in and finished second in the IOR class.

championship against Italian, French, and other European two-ton skippers and the best from South America and this country. The series is scheduled to begin June 29. Our Bob Sellers, as chairman of the world two-ton championship, will have the full force of the GPYC organization supporting this prestigious yachting event. The world series will be preceded by the North American two-ton championships, beginning in mid-June and sponsored by our neighbor club to the north, Great Lakes Yacht Club.[17]

The year 1975 was naturally dubbed the summer of the two-tons. The term referred to a class of sailboats, all around the forty-foot range.

But the spotlight this summer will be on the races and matches of the two-ton sloops in the North American, World, and Canada's Cup events. This is the hot class and it will be an international focus as all of the top designers, particularly the younger ones, bid for fame and glory with the latest creations from their drawing board.[18]

As the sailing world focused on Lake St. Clair that summer, Bayview Yacht Club's *Ricochet* edged out *Aggressive II* to win the world two-ton championship.

In the Port Huron-to-Mackinac race, GPYC boats and skippers were again prominent:

At the top will be "the little giant killer" of the Great Lakes. This is *Aggressive II*, the thirty-seven-footer owned by Frank Piku and Dave Gamble and a tough crew... *Aggressive II* not only won honors in Class B, but polished off the greatest fleet ever to sail in a long distance race in fresh water when she took overall honors in Bayview Yacht Club's fifty-first annual Mackinac Island race. An armada of three hundred three boats started up Lake Huron and two hundred ninety-eight finished at Mackinac Island. Thirty were from the GPYC.[19]

Norbert Hollerbach's *Belle Aurore* took Class G honors with Robert Yuhn's *Windtime* placing second.

Figure 10. Commodore Roger K. Smith, 1970.

On the first June weekend in 1980, the Detroit Yacht Club sponsored a regatta with a start line at the GPYC and the finish line at the DYC. It became a real test of skill for the one hundred ninety-three entries in seventeen classes, battling winds of twenty to thirty knots. GPYC boats in the NA40 Class took the top three spots: Steve Perry's *Sensation* was first, Lyndon Lattie's *Frangipani* came in second, and Don McQueen's *Sundance* was third. In July, Don McQueen sailed *Sundance* to another Class C first in the Bayview Mackinac race, while Bob Thoreson took first in Class E on *Valkyrie*.

With Ted Hood and Ted Turner defending the America's Cup throughout the 1970s, sail racing had captured the American imagination. Nowhere was the passion more in evidence than on Lake St. Clair with the Club's impressive lineup of champion skippers and legendary boats.

A ride on the wild side

In 1973 the GPYC became actively involved in the creation of the Lake St. Clair Offshore Racing Association and assisted in its first two major races held off the Club's east wall; Jerry Girschner, A. P. (Pete) Smith, and George Blake were on the organizational committee. Participating

Club members were encouraged to paint the GPYC burgee on their hulls. Member Wallace G. "Wally" Harper won both of those races with his 27-foot Magnum offshore racer *Li'l Smidgen*. Harper also raced his boat in Florida that year, where he became the national high-point champion in the Production class, as well as the high-point driver for Lakes Erie and St. Clair and Driver of the Year winner for Ohio.[20]

The Club continued to host offshore power-boat races throughout the decade. In 1975, Pete Smith won Class Four with his 27-foot Magnum *Wolverine* and became high-point boat of the season in his class.

Member Jerry Girschner and daughter Kristyl Girschner raced together in several offshore races in the early 1970s. Kristyl later raced on her own, and on June 2, 1978, she broke the women's speed record on the Detroit River, posting a speed of 73.692 miles per hour. She went on to win several offshore races in the following years.

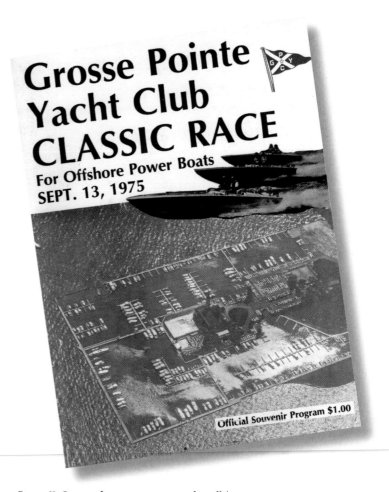

Grosse Pointe Yacht Club CLASSIC RACE
For Offshore Power Boats
SEPT. 13, 1975

Official Souvenir Program $1.00

Figure 11. Cover of souvenir program for offshore powerboat race sponsored by the GPYC in 1975.

Figure 12a, top. The Club revs up for offshore powerboat racing, with member Wally Harper piloting his 27-foot Magnum *Li'l Smidgen*.

Figure 12b, bottom. Another 27-foot Magnum, *Wolverine*, owned and skippered by member Pete Smith.

Figure 13. Member Wally Harper, 1973 high-point national champion in the offshore powerboat production class.

Figure 14. Member Pete Smith, winner of several offshore powerboat races in both Michigan and Florida.

Figure 15. *Kristyl Lady* crewmembers, left to right: Mark Shankin, navigator and riding mechanic; Kristyl Girschner, pilot; member Jerry Girschner, throttleman.

Figure 16. Warren Winstanley's Mardi Gras Party, 1971. Left, swinging his partner, is sheik Harry Tennyson; the king of diamonds on the right is Commodore Ralph Kliber. Perhaps if the three costumed Muses (middle) would suddenly burst into a bump-and-grind, the clown would not look so forlorn.

Oh what fun they had!

Following the ambitious capital improvement programs of the 1960s, Commodore Roger K. Smith wanted to focus on members' individual needs and interests. He proposed moving the tennis courts further west on the property to improve parking availability and recommended building a stairway to the Terrace Lounge on the lake side of the Rotunda for member convenience.

Commodore Smith's vision found support in Warren O. Winstanley, who joined the Club in 1970 and became the entertainment chairman under Commodore Ralph J. Kliber in 1971. Winstanley was a commercial photographer, working primarily in the automobile industry, whose work took him around the world. He also did work for Universal Studios in Hollywood, which enabled him to secure some of the most exotic props for his magnificent theme party decorations. Commodore Kliber's friend Jack Thompkins, a vice president of American Airlines, and Club member Wayne Long, of Long Transportation Company, made arrangements with the Club to transport the props and other equipment brought in from California for the extraordinary weekend parties at no charge to the Club.[21] And thus the Winstanley entertainment era began.

Winstanley was the mastermind behind some of the GPYC's most fantastic and memorable theme parties and galas. "There's only one way to decorate for a party—and that's all the way," Winstanley said in an interview for *The Grosse Pointer*.

Figure 17. A Night at Maude's, *à la* Warren Winstanley, February 10, 1971. John Griffin (left) and "Maude," Joann (Mrs. James) Fisher, wearing a dress that actress Joan Blondell wore in the movie "Maude." The dress, along with required insurance, came to the party from Hollywood, arrangements courtesy of Mr. Winstanley.s

Figure 18. When Warren Winstanley planned a party, he wanted the whole world — or at least the whole Club — to know about it. A derelict boat was requisitioned and mannequins were sent aloft to publicize this South Seas Islands party in 1971.

Winstanley had creativity and a flair for the dramatic and spectacular, as well as the ability to execute his grand plans down to the last exacting detail," said Past Commodore Ralph Kliber, who was commodore in 1971, one of Winstanley's halcyon years. "He was a perfectionist. Often Warren would begin decorating for a party on Friday afternoon. He'd work all night constructing props and sets and special effects. He'd continue all day Saturday, then go home, shower, and come back to enjoy the party.[22]

His first "production" was labeled the Tinseltown Thing. An aerial spotlight circling in the sky welcomed guest "celebrities." Winstanley's vintage Bentley was parked in the front circle, and sitting on the top was a female mannequin holding a glass of champagne. Inside the Club, movie projectors had been placed on two elevated platforms in the Ballroom, cranking out old movies onto screens throughout the evening.[23]

The success of the Tinseltown party was quickly followed by the Shipwreck Affair, a South Sea Islands party. Winstanley bought a rotting boat hull from Jefferson Beach Marina, cut it in half, and placed it on the circular lawn in front of the Club to look like a sinking ship. He ran square-rigged sails up the flagpole, dressed mannequins in sailor outfits, and sat them astride the tops of the sails. A bamboo hut on stilts was constructed in the center of the Ballroom, rising to enclose the Ballroom chandelier. Waitresses wore grass skirts, and background noises of jungle sounds, birdcalls, and animal screams played over the public address system.[24]

For his Elizabethan Feast, he sent an invitation to Queen Elizabeth II, who declined but sent her representative, British Consul General I. R. MacGregor, and his wife. A bridge was constructed over an artificial moat at the Club's entrance. The doorman was dressed in chain mail, and many guests appeared in rented sixteenth-century medieval costumes. Spears, shields, battleaxes, and real boars' heads on platters were the period decorations, and knives were the only utensils provided for the meal. A harpist, a trio, and "serving wenches" all sported medieval

★ ★ ★

GPYC

Figure 19. Commodore Ralph J. Kliber, 1971.

costumes rented from a Hollywood movie studio. Hundreds of candles were burning in wrought-iron candelabra as the commodore rose to toast HRH Queen Elizabeth II.[25]

The annual Clambake had been initiated in the mid-1960s to popular acclaim, but the Winstanley touch brought it to another level. Guests entered the Club via a wooden "plank" to receive their lobster aprons imprinted with their first names. The three Muses in the Rotunda became fisherwomen dressed in yellow slickers and carrying lobster traps. Clams and oysters were served in a clam café, which had a smoking chimney created with dry ice. The Ballroom sported a mermaid on a pole and arches of kerosene lanterns, and table centerpieces were live take-home goldfish in bowls. The wait staff wore seamen's caps, bandannas, turtleneck sweaters, and black skirts or pants. In the Venetian Room, two go-go mermaids performed throughout the evening in a giant lobster trap. Music was provided for the sellout crowd by a New Orleans jazz band.[26]

Figure 20. Party of the year: 45th annual Commodore's Review. with Count Basie's Orchestra for dancing, 1974.

Figure 22. Commodore Frank McBride and Count Basie at the 45th annual Commodore's Review, 1974.

Figure 23. Commodore Curtis Carmichael, 1972, proudly sporting a shirt that says it all.

Figure 23. With burgees tacked to their sweaters, the Fashion Show planners play cheerleaders, 1973. Left to right: Joann Fisher, Barb Kirk, Lore Girschner, Clare Westcott, Bette Savage, Barb Lozeller, and Joan Knies.

The Mardi Gras party saw four hundred partygoers enter the foyer to find a trash-filled, boarded-up alley simulating the entrance to the Court of the Two Sisters restaurant in New Orleans. An arbor with live grapes filled the Rotunda for the costumed southern ladies and gentlemen, and in the Dining Room the pillars were transformed to plaster decaying over brick, with Spanish moss hanging from wrought iron between the pillars. The Ballroom featured a setting of New Orleans buildings, and the bar resembled the famous Pat O'Brien's bar, complete with old-fashioned ceiling fans and serving its signature New Orleans "hurricane" drink. Members and guests were treated to a Creole-style dinner with a dessert of flaming Bananas Foster.[27]

Winstanley clearly went to great lengths to set the stage, so to speak.[28, 29] After his term as entertainment chairman ended, the "Winstanley touch" may have departed, but his successors attempted to continue the grand themes and intriguing decorations through most of the 1970s despite the frustrations of the economic downturn.

Commodore Curtis C. Carmichael's year featured Splashdown '72, where two hundred fifty young people gathered on the East Lawn for an outdoor dancing party and a costume-themed Oktoberfest. A series of gourmet dinners with a new Club wine list was implemented under Commodore George M. Cooper's administration. American Bandstand '74, a party billed as a 1950s and 1960s party with period dress, where waitresses wore car hop costumes with roller skates and members came attired in prom dresses, cheerleader uniforms, letter sweaters, saddle shoes, white socks, and black leather jackets, was one of the more unique parties during Commodore Frank P. McBride Jr.'s year.[30] A Lumberjack Pancake Supper, complete with costumes, provided a style contrast to the unique Progressive Dinner Party between the Club, the Lochmoor Club, and the DAC during Commodore George L. Beard's 1975 term.

The U.S. bicentennial year of 1976, under Commodore Harold S. De Orlow, featured a GPYC Dance Class with Latin, waltz, foxtrot, swing, and polka dances being taught along with the hustle and the bump. That year, a new

Figure 24. Commodore Curtis C. Carmichael, 1972.

Figure 25. Commodore George M. Cooper, 1973.

concept in member entertainment was instituted with the GPYC Dinner Theatre, featuring Neil Simon's "Plaza Suite," which Commodore De Orlow proclaimed was one of the best events to come to the Club in years. That 1976 season was highlighted with the arrival of the Norwegian 205-foot sailing vessel *Christian Radich* in Detroit after the bicentennial Tall Ship extravaganza in New York. Commodore De Orlow joined other Club officers for a reception on the vessel.[31]

A sumptuous Seafood-a-Rama, which would have turned even the great seafood purveyor Joe Muer green with envy, was a smashing success and inaugurated an annual seafood tasting during Commodore William D. Plante's year in 1977.[32]

By 1978, Commodore James L. Taylor Sr.'s year, membership was on the upswing, and in 1979, Commodore Sheldon F. Hall and the board planned and implemented a series of member events to commemorate the fiftieth anniversary of the formal opening of the clubhouse on July 4, 1929. As in 1929, the fiftieth anniversary commemoration included a huge barbeque luncheon, ceremonial speeches, and a fifty-gun salute. Swimming exhibitions were reminiscent of a similar show fifty years earlier, and the evening ended with a formal dance.[33]

The 1979 Fleet Review came close to being rained out, but in 1980 Mother Nature dug in her heels and actually made it happen. About 4:00 PM, after several inches of intermittent rain had fallen, the review was officially canceled and rescheduled for Labor Day weekend. Amazingly, Fleet Review for 1980 was nearly rained out altogether, as ominous rain clouds, stiff winds, and choppy waters greeted boaters on the rescheduled day of the review. But even though the threatening weather prevented some boats from participating, the review went off with enthusiasm and ended just as the rain began.

One of the highlights of the 1980 social season that did not suffer from bad weather was a progressive dinner with the Grosse Pointe Hunt Club. Members enjoyed cocktails and hors d'oeuvres at the Hunt Club then "progressed" to the Yacht Club for dinner and dancing.

★ ★ ★

★ ★ ★

GPYC

Figure 26. Commodore Frank P. McBride Jr., 1974.

GPYC

figure 27. Commodore George L. Beard, 1975.

Figure 28. Left to right: Nancy Georgi, Stephanie Smith, Kristin Strong, and Meg Maghielse receive their award for the eight-and-under freestyle relay at the Club's Junior Sportspersons' Brunch.

The Republican National Convention came to Detroit in 1980, and some prominent people were seen at the GPYC during the event. CBS newsmen Walter Cronkite, Dan Rather, and their wives enjoyed Sunday Brunch, while ABC threw a party for their delegation of newscasters and crew, which included Barbara Walters.

Member activities and attractions in the 1970s

Throughout the 1970s, bowling continued to be a popular Club activity. The Club hosted tournaments, members participated in outside tournaments, and the popular annual Chicago Yacht Club rivalry continued. Other popular sports at the Club included ballet exercise classes, ice skating on a rink built on the East Lawn, and paddle tennis.[34] The Club sponsored an interclub paddle tennis tournament in 1975, with thirty-two teams from throughout the metropolitan area participating.[35]

Tennis continued to be popular at the Club, no doubt inspired by the professional success of the likes of Chris Evert, Billie Jean King, Jimmy Connors, and Bjorn Borg. The Club built two new tennis courts in 1973 to accommodate that popularity.[36] There is little doubt that the 1973 nationally televised "Battle of the Sexes," the tennis matches between Billie Jean King and Bobby Riggs, inspired a similar battle over the Fourth of July festivities in 1980. Lucy Gorski, 1979 GPYC singles champion, took on men's champion Milt Hoffman. Lucy had the ladies cheering after winning the first set, but Milt came back to take the second and third sets for the win.

The children of members enjoyed many sporting activities, from the emerging competitive swimming team to bowling, junior sailing, skiing, and tennis. The swim team, under coach Tom Teetaert, set six new records in the MICSA final event at the Country Club of Detroit in July 1980, as they captured the championship. Future commodore Kevin B. Granger scored a double by participating on the winning Sears Midwestern Series Junior Championship sailing team in 1970 and earning a Junior Bowler Championship in 1971.[37]

Figure 29. Commodore Harold S. De Orlow, 1976.

The 1970s also saw further Club facility improvements in several areas. The Lakeview Terrace Lounge was completely redecorated, transforming it from a cocktail lounge to a "warm folksy, pub-like room where the most is made of mellow dark woods and rich color."[38] A ship's figurehead was added to the bar in the middle of the room to give it a nautical theme. During the Club's winter shutdown in 1974, the former Grill Room became the Spinnaker, a bit less formal, nautical-themed dining area. During the remodeling, the original fireplace was uncovered, repaired, and returned to operating condition.[39] The wooden Spinnaker sign that still graces the room was made by Past Commodore George Beard at Jerry Girschner's pattern shop.[40]

In response to increased boat traffic, a new harbormaster's tower was built, along with a spiral staircase to access it from the docks south of the swimming pool. It was dedicated on July 4, 1974, and remained in use until the present one was built in 1993–94.[41]

The economic turmoil of the 1970s was certainly felt at the Club, but the GPYC did what virtually every other club in the country had to

Figure 30. Commodore William D. Plante, 1977.

Figure 31. Commodore James L. Taylor Sr., 1978.

do at that time: it tapped into the creative resources of its diverse membership to find ways to survive economically. And those members responded. As a result of their due diligence, members continued to engage in world-class sailing, boating, and championship athletic events while enjoying some of the most original and extravagant member parties ever experienced at the Club. All in all, not a bad position to be in as the 1980s began.

Figure 32. 1974: The new harbormaster tower came complete with steel spiral staircase. This building would be replaced in 1994 with the current structure.

Figure 32. Commodore Sheldon F. Hall, 1979.

Figure 33. Commodore Paul A. Eagan, 1980.

IMAGE ACKNOWLEDGEMENTS
Chapter Seven

1. Kristyl Girshner

2. Ibid

3. GPYC

4. Tomas K. Fisher, Jr.

5. Karl Schmidt.

6. GPYC

7. John Rummel

8. GPYC

9. John Rummel

10. – 12a. and b. GPYC

13. Kristyl Girshner

14. Richard Smith

15. Kristyl Girshner

16. – 17. GPYC

18. John and Shelley Schoenher

19. – 34. GPYC

Figure 1. First in and first overall; Member "Dutch" Schmidt's *Sassy* tops the field in the 1984 Port Huron-to-Mackinac race.

By Larry W. Stephenson, M.D.
and Carol Stephenson

1981 through 1989

Financial breathing room

With the election of President Ronald Reagan in November 1980, it was hoped that the effects of high inflation in the late 1970s would begin to ease. At the January 15, 1981, board meeting, reports seemed to indicate that previous financial pressures on the Club were beginning to recede. Through the first months of 1981, optimism at the Club, along with the rest of the country, rose steadily until midsummer, when the economy took another unexpected downturn. Fortunately this turned out to be more of a dip than a plunge, and things were once again on the right track by mid-1982. At the end of that year, the Club was running in the black, and the board felt that the Club's financial position was strong enough to support the purchase of a $100,000 certificate of deposit as an investment in the future.[1]

An important and very welcome financial milestone occurred in 1984 when the Club, for the first time in its history, became debt free.[2] Back in 1969, a second mortgage had been taken out to finance an expansion of the harbor and construction of a swimming pool. At a September party that drew 350 attendees, Commodore John Woodle lit the fire to consume an oversized reproduction of that mortgage. Several past commodores made a grand entrance on an antique fire truck and a fireworks display wowed the crowd.

Figure 2. Bayview Yacht Club, sponsor of the Port Huron-to-Mackinac race, issues gold medals to every crew member of the winning boat in each class. *Sassy's* crew members would receive one of these medals in 1987, as they did in 1984.

1981: Bubbling, paddling, and remodeling

The compressors and hoses for the first bubbling program in the GPYC harbor were installed in the late fall of 1980. Air that was pumped into the wells under and around the boats would keep the water from freezing and allow boats to remain in the harbor through the winter months and, in effect, year-round. Apparently enough interest had been expressed by boating members to make this project seem feasible. The program's security was highly touted. Docks were brightly lit and boats were constantly monitored by TV cameras that transmitted images to screens located in the bowling area. The bubbling was geared primarily to sailboats, and, indeed, the spring of 1981 found twenty-three sailboats and two powerboats had successfully weathered the winter in the harbor without any mishaps.[3] Bubbling remained a popular alternative to dry winter storage throughout the 1980s.

The February 1981 issue of *The Grosse Pointer* reported that the paddle tennis courts had been refurbished. A new deck had been built that connected the two areas of play, and the trailer that members used for warming up between games had been moved closer to the courts.

Figure 3. Happy Echlin puts some muscle into her paddle tennis swing on the way to winning the 1982 mixed championship with her husband, Lew.

⋆ ⋆ ⋆

GPYC

Figure 4. Commodore James D. Mitchell, 1981.

Could those improvements have been the reason why the men's GPYC paddle tennis team was undefeated in its last three matches and, at that point, in second place in the men's suburban league?

In his message to the members in the April issue of *The Grosse Pointer*, Commodore James Mitchell reported that the remodeling of the Commodores' Room was completed, new food refrigeration coolers had been installed in the kitchen, and the modernization of the ladies' locker room was on track to be completed by the beginning of the swim season.

On June 30, the 137-foot *Pride of Baltimore* sailed into the GPYC harbor for a two-day stay. The ship, belonging to the city of Baltimore, was an authentic reproduction of a U.S. Navy fighting ship from the War of 1812. Members were allowed to go aboard for a tour during her stay. As a point of interest, five years later, while sailing just north of Puerto Rico, the ship encountered a squall delivering eighty-knot winds. She capsized and sank, taking three crew members with her. Eight crew members were rescued.

1982: A historic flagpole finds a new home at the GPYC

In May, citing overuse of the Club's facilities, Commodore George Kriese and the board felt it necessary to cap the membership at nine hundred. Outside parties were also curtailed, as they were interfering with Club usage by members.

A most unusual regatta took place at the GPYC on June 2, 1982. Member and auto racing devotee Joe Schulte masterminded the event, pairing boats and crews from GPYC, Bayview Yacht Club, and Crescent Sail Club with members of Formula One race teams. The teams were in town for the running of the inaugural Detroit Grand Prix, and since most of them came in from Europe, they arrived early in the week. What better way to adjust to the time change than racing on the water.

Sixteen NA-40s participated: GPYC member John Martin's *Tortue* with the Arrow race team aboard finished first, while members Don and Greg McQueen's *Sundance* came in third with the Marlboro-McLaren team. The event was received so well and generated such good publicity that it was repeated for the next four years, with ever greater participation of race crews and even some

Figure 5. The historic Dodge flagpole being moved by barge from Rose Terrace in Grosse Pointe Farms to the Grosse Pointe Yacht Club.

Figure 6. Formula One Grand Prix drivers take time from racing on the streets of Detroit to become part of the crew of racing sailboats on Lake St. Clair during the third annual Detroit Grand Prix race week.

★ ★ ★

Figure 7. Commodore George E. Kriese, 1982.

drivers. Following the 1986 regatta, Mr. Schulte moved to New York, and without its chairman, the event unfortunately ended.

It was in 1982 that the present nautical flag-staff was erected on the island in front of the Club. The center pole was a gift to the Club from Anna Ray "Yvonne" Ranger in memory of her deceased grandmother, Anna Thompson Dodge.

The pole was originally located at Rose Terrace, the Dodge estate in Grosse Pointe Farms, where it was used primarily as a flagpole.

Early photographs show that a lamp had been mounted about thirty feet up from the base of the flagpole, and from the 1920s through the 1950s it also served as the rear range light for a dredged channel leading from the main shipping channel in Lake St. Clair to the dock that accommodated the Horace Dodge yacht, the 258-foot *Delphine*.

The pole was transported by barge to its new home at the Club so the restoration and conversion to a nautical "mast" with a gaff and yardarm could begin. Vice Commodore Roy Barbier, who spearheaded the project, remarked, "The pole is a unique one because of its expensive type of construction. I don't think anyone would be able to buy one like it today." He went on to say, "We had to have the top 9.5 feet cut off and replaced because it suffered extensive lightning damage. Its total height is now 112.5 feet. A 12-inch bronze ball mounted on the pole's top has been refinished. It was covered with fiberglass and a coat of Awlgrip paint by former member Jerry Girschner."[4]

Formal dedication of the flagstaff was set for the following spring during ceremonies celebrating Memorial Day and the official opening of the harbor for the season.

1983: The Club gives the nod to the ladies

Some needed attention was given to the harbor in 1983. Damaged steel sheet piling in the southwest corner was replaced, as were worn cables on the drawbridge. Upgraded electric

Figure 8. Welcome to aerobic dance class: Mary Brieden, wife of member Brian Brieden, leads her group through a series of twists, turns, kicks, and stretches to the sound of music in the Club's Ballroom.

Figure 9. Jane Kay (Nugent), the first woman invited to become a member in the Club's first gender-neutral membership category, Social. Photo from the 1978 yearbook.

The changing status of GPYC women

By Carol Stephenson

There are no surviving bylaws from the Club's formation in 1914, but bylaws from the major reorganization in 1926 do not mention female members in any category. This would be in keeping with the times, as private clubs in those days were routinely restricted to male membership, with nary a thought given, by men or even by most women, to having it otherwise.

That being said, what do we make of the four women's names appearing on membership rosters between 1927 and 1930? Board minutes for July 22, 1927, give a list of proposed Active members who were unanimously elected at that meeting, and on the list was the name Mercy J. Hayes. On April 9, 1928, Elizabeth H. Stevenson was elected to membership, and Mrs. Percy W. Grose became a member on July 19, 1929. At a September 29, 1930, board meeting, thirteen members were assigned the task of soliciting much-needed funds from fellow Club members to keep the Club operational. On the list of members to be solicited was Anna E. Kresge.

Recalling the fact that the clubhouse was being constructed in the years 1928 and 1929, and the fact that new members were being recruited in earnest at that time, it is safe to assume that these women were prominent members of the community and had the means to pay the initiation fee, which had reached $3,300 by January 1929. In the Columbia University Catalogue of 1926-1927 there is a Miss Mercy J. Hayes listed as a trustee of the Teachers College; her address is given as 301 American State Bank Building in Detroit. Percy W. Grose was a prominent Detroit attorney who was alive and well when his wife was elected to membership. Sebastian Kresge, the five-and-dime store magnate, was married to his first wife Anna Elizabeth Harvey from 1897 to 1924 when they divorced. They had five children, daughter Anna Elizabeth being the last. Either one could have been the Anna E. Kresge on the list. No information could be found about Elizabeth Stevenson.

The obvious question is what was their status as women members? Because there would be no mention in the bylaws of any women in any membership category until several years later, did that mean these women were treated as equals by their fellow gentlemen members? Considering the times, it is highly unlikely. It had only been since 1920, through ratification of the Nineteenth Amendment, that women were allowed to vote. Given the fact that it was not until 1983 when GPYC bylaws were issued that specifically granted women the rights to vote and hold office, it seems a logical conclusion that these early women members did not have those privileges then, nor did they probably expect them. One might even go so far as to speculate that these four women may have been quite proud to be a part of a group that would normally have been available to men only.

During the Great Depression when membership was rapidly dropping, there is no record of any women joining the Club. The first female membership category that we know of was established in the reopening and reorganizational year of 1938. According to the new bylaws, Active Class A members had the right to vote, hold office, transfer membership, had an interest in Club property and assets, and had the right to participate in the distribution of said property and assets upon dissolution. The widow of an Active Class A member was given lifetime entitlement to the same privileges with the exceptions of voting and holding office. There was no mention of privileges for women members in any other membership category.

The two exceptions of voting and holding office continued when bylaws issued on September 1, 1952, stated that the widow of a Class B member was now able to apply for membership, but as with Class A widows, there were no voting or office-holding privileges nor "any voice in the government of the Club." Annual dues were to be fixed by the board. This "special Widow membership" was also extended to widows of Class A and Class B members who had died prior to September 1, 1952, upon application to and approval of the board. These bylaws stated that a widow's membership would automatically terminate upon her remarriage.

The bylaws published in the 1964 yearbook set specific rules for several new categories of membership extended to women. Intermediate members, both men and women, were classified as those between the ages of twenty-one and thirty-eight. They could not vote, hold office, nor have any interest in Club property or assets. Upon reaching age thirty-eight, they would be eligible for Active membership. The difference? Lady Active members still could not vote or hold office.

Lady Active members were eligible to become Lady Senior members if they could make it through twenty-five years of Lady Active membership. There was no application fee, and dues would be the same as those for Widow members. There were two other categories for women members mentioned in these bylaws. Upon the death of a Life Member, his widow could become a Lady Life member, exempt from all dues. Non-Resident membership was defined and Lady Non-Resident members are included in the overall definition. Both men and women could become resident members and apply for membership in any category for which they were eligible.

And now we come to 1977. The membership classifications in the bylaws published in the yearbook no longer show the Active class divided into A and B. At some point during that year, the board must have voted to establish the Social membership category, because it was in that year that the first woman was invited to join the Club as a Social member, not a LADY Social member. For the first time in Club history, a membership category had been established that was officially gender neutral.

That first breakthrough member was Jane Kay, now Jane Kay Nugent. At the time, Jane was a vice president at Detroit Edison and a member of the company's Senior Management Committee, as well as a member of The Detroit Club, the Detroit Athletic Club, and the Edison Boat Club. Jane laughs when she recalls being approached by a prominent Club member asking her to join the Club in a new membership category that had just been created for both men and women. The board, he said, was looking for a "safe" woman to become the first female Social member of the Club. Jane says that over the years, as she was wont to speak her mind on Club issues of interest to her, she often wondered if she was still considered "safe."

As stated in this chapter, in 1983 Lady Active and Lady Senior Active members were finally given voting privileges and became eligible to hold office. In 2010, the GPYC elected its first woman commodore, Mary Treder Lang. Today there are no more membership categories with the prefix of Lady. When it comes to gender, the GPYC has walked tall into the twenty-first century.

Figure 10. Miss Jane Kay's Social membership acceptance letter from 1977.

service with meters was installed on Bridge and Hickory Docks, with plans calling for the same installation to Moby Dock. New purchases included an aluminum workboat with a seventy-horsepower outboard and tow bars to assist in the Junior Sailing and Race programs, as well as two electric golf carts for fast delivery of food and beverages.

The Fourth of July celebration was enhanced by the presence of the Detroit Concert Band, which performed for about 350 members. Protocol chairperson Justin "Judd" Moran was quoted as saying, "It was successful beyond our

Figure 11. The 1983 Stag Night had a record crowd. Shown here are honorary chairman, member Bryan "Chappie" Chaplow (*left*), with all-pro former Green Bay Packer and Detroit Lion Ron Kramer. Kramer was an all-American football star at the University of Michigan.

Figure 12. Marlene Boll gets set for a long court shot in the suspense-packed 1983 southeast division championship.

★ ★ ★

GPYC

Figure 13. Commodore Roy E. Barbier, 1983.

dreams, so much so that we ran out of food." As a grand finale, Commodore Roy Barbier personally conducted Sousa's "Stars and Stripes Forever." According to the August *Grosse Pointer*, "Commodore Barbier's musical prowess is not new. It goes back to when he sang on the old Ford Family Radio Hour."

On October 4, what was to become the first annual car show was held on the front lawn. It was billed as the '84 Car Show, with fourteen member-dealers previewing their new 1984 models. By the end of the evening, dealers were already talking about the following year's show and bringing in some classic cars to add a splash of color to the mix.

In 1983 the Lakeview Terrace Lounge, which had opened to great fanfare in 1960, was completely stripped and remodeled into what we know today as the Binnacle Dining Room. According to Commodore Barbier, the layout of the room had been considered problematic for quite some time. "The bar was not arranged properly for the narrow type of room it serviced," he said. He continued, "By moving the bar to the far end, we've created lots of extra space, and it doesn't interfere with the waiters serving the members." The Binnacle was debuted at the November 2 annual election.

At a special membership meeting on December 6, female members were given full voting rights. Lady Active and Lady Senior Active members were now welcome to attend annual meetings and vote for board members and were eligible to become board members or Club officers. Further, a female member who married was no longer terminated until her new husband became a member; the membership could now remain in the wife's name. To the board's credit, these changes were unanimously approved.[5]

1984: Plans take shape to expand our "architectural jewel"

As the 1984 boating season opened, the harbor committee was pleased to announce that every well was assigned, with sixteen floaters and a waiting list. However, the winter had not been kind to the east seawall. Damage had been caused when severe winds blew ice into and over the wall, and repairs were required. The upgrading of the electrical service, including the new meters,

Figure 14. Attending the GPYC's 1984 annual ladies luncheon were Chris, Kim, and Debbie Van Elslander. As the event closes, the three compare notes on the day's festivities.

continued. Two new aluminum harbor boats replaced the old wooden "slugs." Harbor committee member Larry Baluch surveyed and charted the entire harbor and measured the water depths. He also numbered, color-coded, and charted the more than one thousand pilings in the harbor for future ease in repair and replacement.

Construction began in early June on a new and more upscale gatehouse. Club Manager Lindy Mills said, "The overall objective was to create an entry into our Club that was in keeping with both the original architecture and the beauty of our Club here." A bathroom was installed at the rear of the new structure for the tennis players. The gatehouse was expected to be operational by early September.[6]

On June 21, the swim team posted its fiftieth consecutive win in the Michigan Inter-Club Swimming Association (MICSA), beating the Country Club of Detroit. Swimmers and their supporters proudly hoisted a sign reading, "Fifty is Nifty!" Junior sailors also had a reason to be proud when it was announced that the GPYC Junior Sailing program had the largest enrollment in the entire state.

The Port Huron-to-Mackinac race in July saw GPYC member E. Russell "Dutch" Schmidt's brand-new 78-foot sailboat *Sassy* take both the overall win and the corrected win in the IOR-A class. As she crossed the finish line at Mackinac Island on Sunday at 11:30 PM, she shattered the old Cove Island course record by nearly four hours. The following week, in the Chicago-to-Mackinac, she was once again first over the finish line, at 11:14 PM on Sunday, but corrected time put her back to fifth place.[7]

On August 3, the historic presidential yacht *Sequoia* docked at the GPYC for two days. She was sailing the Great Lakes as part of a preservation fund-raising tour and particularly wished to thank members of the Club who had donated $5,000 or more to the effort. Beginning with Herbert Hoover, eight presidents had used the yacht. During World War II, President Franklin Roosevelt held war strategy sessions onboard with British prime minister Winston Churchill. President John Kennedy celebrated his

Figure 15. Presidential yacht USS *Sequoia* visits the Grosse Pointe Yacht Club in August 1984.

Figure 16. Member Charles "Charlie" Davis enjoying a tour of the USS *Sequoia* at the GPYC guest dock.

last birthday on the yacht. Crew members happily gave GPYC members tours of the historic vessel, and before she left to continue her journey, Commodore John Woodle presented the captain with a GPYC burgee to add to the ship's collection.

The second annual auto show was held in September, featuring the 1985 models, plus some beautiful antique and collectible vehicles. Voice synthesizers warning of open doors, low fuel, and unfastened seat belts were a big hit with the crowd. Over four hundred members and guests were present to stroll the grounds and view the show.

At the end of the year, incoming Commodore James Daoust reported to the membership that plans were being considered for a major renovation of the north wing of the clubhouse, including the kitchen, the Spinnaker, the ladies' room off the main lobby, the coat room, and the chair and storage room for the Dining Room and Ballroom. He said that the house and forward planning committees had been meeting with an architect for over six months and plans for the project would be presented in the near future.

Figure 17. An early phase of the extensive North Wing Project on a winter day in 1986.

Plans for this renovation had actually started a few years earlier as simply a kitchen remodeling and expansion. John Boll was rear commodore in 1984 and chairman of the planning committee. Committee members included past commodores Ralph Kliber and George Kriese, and directors Ted Smith and Fred Schriever, who would each become commodore. Boll explained that the kitchen had originally been built to accommodate three hundred members, and those same facilities were now expected to serve a membership that was three times that size. Health department officials were threatening to close the kitchen if necessary improvements were not made in a timely fashion.[8] When the planning committee added the expanded membership numbers to the equation, it became apparent that it would behoove the board to consider an expansion of more than just the kitchen. This is what eventually became known as the North Wing Project.

One of the architectural firms that toured the club during this time was Smith, Hinchman & Grylls Associates of Detroit. In an article in the

Figure 18. Detail of the copper rain conductors on the Grosse Pointe Yacht Club clubhouse.

September *Grosse Pointer*, the firm's president, Philip J. Meathe, praised the clubhouse: "It's a landmark. You couldn't replace it today." He was very impressed by the beautiful proportions, the many examples of symmetry, and the meticulous attention to detail. For example, he pointed out the rain conductors on the exterior walls. The conductor boxes have a raised wreath design and are attached to the walls with specially shaped anchors, not merely run-of-the-mill bolts.

Meathe was puzzled by the elaborate details of the clubhouse's south wall and speculated that an entrance may have been planned for the area. Although none of Guy Lowell's plans have survived, one preliminary sketch from Henry and Richmond did show a door centered beneath the windows in what is now the Venetian Room, which was never built. In the same article, Merv Gaskin, GPYC commodore in 1956, talked about the original construction of the clubhouse. In 1927, when construction began, he was not yet a member but was chief engineer for the firm that supplied the structural steel. He recalled several parts of the preliminary design being scrapped. "There were supposed to be apartments above the ballroom," he said. "An elevator was supposed to go up to those rooms. Neither the rooms nor the elevator [was] installed."

The article ended with a quote from Meathe. Speaking of future remodeling, he warned, "Any money invested should not be invested on a stopgap measure. Do it right," he said, "because we've got a jewel here — an architectural jewel."

1985: It was a very good year

The winter of 1985 saw the harbor bubbling program continue to expand. Then in its fourth year, forty-nine of the fifty available wells were occupied, up from thirty-five the previous year.

In forming committees for the year, Commodore Daoust noted that there had been a noticeable increase in members under age thirty-five, particularly in the Junior classification (sons and daughters of members). Therefore, the recommendation was made to form a new committee to serve the needs of this group, which was called the "under thirty-five committee" until formalization was complete.

GPYC

Figure 19. Commodore John C. Woodle, 1984.

Figure 20. Welcoming attendees to the 1985 annual Sportsman's Night is a giant Alaskan brown bear with event chair, Past Commodore Frank McBride, who stood six-foot-four inces tall.

Figure 21. Commodore James R. Daoust, 1985.

In mid-January, members received a real gourmet treat when chef Jeff Gabriel, a U.S. Culinary Olympic gold medal winner, invited four other Olympians to join him in creating a very special seven-course meal at the Club. With proper wines carefully chosen to complement each course, the lucky diners all agreed that the dinner was a real *tour de force*.

In the July issue of *The Grosse Pointer*, Commodore Daoust thanked the membership for the generous outpouring of contributions to purchase bollards and chains to line and light the driveway. More than eighty members subscribed.

The swim team continued its winning ways, garnering its sixtieth consecutive MICSA win with a victory over the Birmingham Athletic Club. Although it may have been a bit premature, the Club had already rented a plane, which flew above the pool area following the win, trailing a sign that read, "The Yacht Is Hot... #60."

Arguably the most important event of the year took place on September 13, when the ground-breaking ceremony was held for the new north wing. Commodore Daoust reported that the long-range planning committee, under the chairman-

ship of Vice Commodore John Boll, had worked tirelessly for two years to make the project a reality. The kitchen was to receive a much-needed expansion and upgrade of facilities. A more adequate bar would be built in the Spinnaker, and more dining space would be added by developing the area behind the fireplace. A new service elevator was to be installed that would be available to members and guests confined to wheelchairs. The following Easter was the goal for completion.

The North Wing Project was the most significant and costly construction project the board had approved since the completion of the clubhouse in 1929. Since the Club had finally become debt free in 1984, there was some concern as to how the membership would feel about taking on this new debt. Therefore, before final approval was given, the board presented the plans and the budget to the membership, and they overwhelmingly gave their consent.[2]

At the annual meeting on November 11, good news prevailed as members were told that the harbor was at full capacity, membership was at an all-time high of 950, with a waiting list, and finances were healthy and running in the black. The $1,200,000 renovation of the north wing was reported to be ahead of schedule and still within budget. The only financial news to dim the evening was that profit margins in both the clubhouse and the harbor were down. In the harbor, this was due to the increased cost of repairs resulting from high water levels. For the Club, insurance rates increased by $100,000, mostly attributed to liability costs resulting from the serving of liquor.

1986: The north wing opens, and the water is up

The February 1986 *Grosse Pointer* detailed renovation project progress, which was still on schedule to open on Easter Sunday. Work had actually begun shortly after the groundbreaking the previous September, but major construction did not begin until January 6. The Dining Room was originally considered for inclusion in the project, but the board decided to wait until the following fall in case there were unforeseen cost overruns.

An interesting discovery was made when the paneling in the Spinnaker was removed: hand-painted murals were on the walls. The paintings had been done when the Spinnaker, then known as the Grille Room, was remodeled in 1939. The scenes depicted men and women, wearing fashions from that era, participating in typical Club activities. The murals had been covered with paneling, most likely in the 1959 renovation of the room. Every effort was made to preserve the murals in some way, but in the end it could not be done. The new configuration of the Spinnaker made it impossible.

Past Commodore Daoust later commented, "It was a shame they couldn't have been saved."[9] (See chapter three for photographs of some of these murals.)

With the Club being completely closed for three months, some other area clubs generously made their facilities available to members. A GPYC Super Bowl party was held at the Lochmoor Club and a Valentine's Day dinner dance attracted 150 members to the DAC.

Then came the big day: Easter Sunday, March 30. Just twenty-four hours earlier, carpet was still being installed and board members and wives were helping out with the final sweeping, dusting, and polishing. The opening and Easter Brunch went off without a hitch, but the true grand opening did not occur until two weeks later, on Sunday, April 13. The crowd, estimated to be about six hundred, enjoyed hors d'oeuvres as they toured the kitchen and sipped complimentary champagne in the Spinnaker.

Before boating season began, the Club announced that a new system for well assignments would be put in place. In essence this meant that boat owners would no longer have to reapply every year for their wells. Annual bills would be sent out to each member who had used a well in the previous year; if a member did not pay the bill, that well would become available to other members on a waiting list. Also new in the harbor was a two-way radio system to enable communication between the harbormaster and the dock hands. When the harbor officially opened on Memorial Day, brand-new flags were raised, courtesy of protocol chair James Acheson.

Water levels in Lake St. Clair had been rising over the previous several years, but in 1986 the monthly levels broke all records that the Army Corps of Engineers had been keeping since 1918.

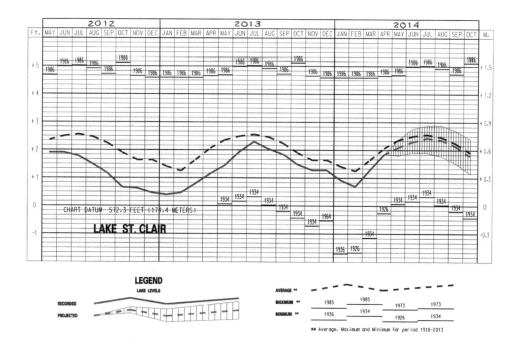

Figure 22. U.S. Army Corps of Engineers' chart of Lake St. Clair monthly water levels for years 2012, 2013 and 2014. The blue-dash line shows average lake levels over several decades; the red line is actual lake levels over the same time period. The shaded red portion is predicted 2014 levels. Highlighted above in yellow are recorded high-water levels for 1986, showing the marked contrast of that record-setting year to each of the three years of 2012–2014.

Figure 23. Long hours and hard work preserved the Club's heritage in *A Beacon of Tradition: The Complete History of Grosse Pointe Yacht Club*. This forty-nine-page monograph was published in 1986. Shown here are the heritage committee members (*left to right*): Past Commodores John DeHayes, Ralph Kliber, and Roger Smith, Margie Reins Smith, Past Commodore Paul Moreland, and Jim Gallagher.

In January, the level was already 2.5 feet above the monthly average, and it slowly increased until it was 3 feet above average in October. Back in 1952 the board had done their job well when they did not skimp on the harbor renovation necessitated by high-water damage that year. In spite of the damage that was being caused to homes all along Lake Shore Road, especially when strong winds blew out of the east or northeast, the harbor remained in service throughout the season. The docks, however, did require elevated platforms to remain usable, and the pipes that brought water and electricity to the docks had to be raised.

The clubhouse, unfortunately, was another story. In a taped interview, Commodore Fred Schriever remembered that water came through the outer door of the Fo'c'sle and seeped through the walls. He recalled that four inches of new concrete had to be poured onto the floor of the entire lower level to keep the floor from buckling. Water began coming in through the drainage system as well, which required extensive maintenance.[8]

All this emergency work required the board to approve a new assessment to supplement dues income. The membership had just absorbed an assessment for the North Wing Project, which they had approved. Commodore John Boll said later that the unforeseen circumstances of this assessment, coming so soon after the previous one, angered many members and made them rather suspicious of its necessity.[8]

In June, the fifth and what would become the final Grand Prix Regatta was held, with the Ligier team aboard GPYC member Roland Tindle's boat *Assail*, taking the win.

In August, Past Commodore Ralph Kliber received the first copy of *A Beacon of Tradition: The History of Grosse Pointe Yacht Club*. Commodore Kliber had headed the heritage committee that oversaw the book's publication from start to finish. The forty-nine-page book chronicled the Club's history from its founding over seventy years earlier. Member-artist Paul Gillian, whose rendering of the clubhouse appeared on the back cover, was said to have ensured that the painting was accurate down to the number of individual panes in the windows.

The Main Dining Room finally received its makeover and opened on September 5. In writing about the opening, Commodore Boll noted:

Although the board approved 'The Dining Room' concept, the decision as to whether the room remains available for member use on Friday and Saturday evenings or reverts to private party use, will be determined by you. I encourage you to make 'The Dining Room' a part of your weekend dining enjoyment and entertainment.

'The Dining Room' activity will be monitored monthly to see if member participation warrants its continuation in this capacity. After six months, the board will evaluate the experience and make its decision as to the future of 'The Dining Room.' We've brought 'The Dining Room' back to you — now it's in your hands.

In the fall, the front circle received some new landscaping to accommodate a seventeenth-century British naval cannon, a custom-crafted reproduction of a ship's anchor, and a fife rail with brass belaying pins surrounding the flagpole. On old sailing ships, the belaying pins for the rigging were attached to the fife rail.

The cannon had been purchased from a home in Marblehead, Massachusetts. Since the cannon was no longer functional, member Robert Rehmann bored out the end so a sixteen-gauge blank starting cannon could be implanted. Member Jerry Girschner made a styrofoam model of the anchor, and a friend of board member Fred Schriever, Paul Barrow, who was not a member but donated his services anyway, cast the anchor. The final touch was the fife rail that was built to exacting detail. Upon the project's completion, Commodore Boll remarked, "I think it says a lot about the Club when it's so well liked that even non-members want to donate to it."

In early November, GPYC member Bob Kaiser clinched the world championship of off-shore powerboat racing by scoring two second-place finishes and a first in the final competition of the season in Key West, Florida. During the final race, the 160-mile course was shortened to 130 miles due to treacherous wave heights measuring eight to ten feet. Bob and his throttle-man, Errol Lanier, collected points by placing in every race of the season.[10]

1987: A big year on the lake and a new Club manager

In January, the world competition for DN class iceboats was held on Anchor Bay in Lake St. Clair. DN stands for *Detroit News*, which had created the racing series for these one-man iceboats back in the 1930s, and thus the DN designation was attached to the iceboats themselves. The inter-national competition drew participants from the United States, West Germany, Austria, Poland, Denmark, Sweden, and Canada. Greg Smith, son of GPYC Past Commodore Roger Smith, captured fourth place, and in the North American competition that directly followed, he took second.[11]

On July 12, the GPYC experienced a fire caused by overheated electrical transformers in the basement. It was later confirmed that the overheating was a result of the unusually high outdoor temperatures that had occurred that day. Although a great deal of wiring was destroyed, the Club's electricity was temporarily restored within six hours, thus avoiding most food spoilage. Within thirty-two hours, the electricity was operating as usual.

By mid-July, the swim team had pushed its streak of consecutive MICSA victories to an impressive seventy-two.

Out on Lake Huron, in a national offshore powerboat race, member Bob Kaiser set a new world speed record in his 38-foot Cougar

Figure 24. Greg Smith, in his DN Class iceboat, placed fourth in the international competition held on Lake St. Clair in 1987. The following day, in the national competition, he took second place.

Figure 25. Bob Kaiser goes airborne over the waters of Lake Huron as he powers his 38-foot Cougar catamaran *ACR Systems* to a world average speed record of 108.643 MPH over the 162-mile course.

Figure 26. Member Bob Kaiser, offshore powerboat champion, 1986 and 1987.

catamaran, attaining an average course speed of 108.643 miles per hour during the 162-mile race. He went on to win the 1987 National Offshore Championship with the title US-1 Champion and was also the year's Pro Series national champion.

At the end of July, there was an exchange rendezvous with the Catawba Island Club (CIC). The two clubs had not had reciprocity for at least ten years, and this was an attempt to reverse that situation. The weekend event saw twenty-nine boats from the GPYC cruise to Catawba, while twenty-eight CIC boats docked in the GPYC harbor. The success of the rendezvous was clear when CIC indicated it wanted to make it an annual affair.

Two Club boats took top honors in the sixty-third annual Port Huron-to-Mackinac race. Member E. Russell "Dutch" Schmidt's 78-foot *Sassy*, with sons Russ and Karl aboard, captured first overall in the IOR class. Member Steve Gagne, owner of *Triumph*, collected first place in IMS-1 and IMS overall.

July continued to be a big month for the GPYC when a new general manager was welcomed to the Club. John "Jack" Sullivan came to the GPYC from the Nakoma Golf Club in Madison, Wisconsin, where he had been manager for twelve years. Outgoing general manager Lindy Mills, who had resigned his position, helped welcome Jack to the Club at a special reception on July 19.

In the October *Grosse Pointer*, Commodore Robert Yuhn reported that the board was considering moving ahead with plans to refurbish the Ballroom in the coming year.

1988: The most successful financial year in Club history

In late January, the social year began with a new twist to the popular Sportsman's Stag Night party. In response to members' requests, there was a sit-down dinner instead of a buffet and a featured speaker from the sports world. Red Wings coach Jacques Demers spoke to a recep-

Figure 27. Manager Jack Sullivan takes the helm of GPYC in July 1987.

tive crowd of 350 gentlemen diners in the Ballroom. The talk and the evening were so well received that Red Wings Night would become an annual event at the Club.

Figure 28. Member Steve Gagne's C&C 61-foot *Triumph* captured first place, IMS-l and IMS overall in the 1987 Port Huron-to-Mackinac race.

Red Wings Night

By William Jennings, DDS

The Red Wings Night idea started in 1987 after a letter was received by the board from member Mike Murray suggesting that an event with a guest speaker and a nice sit-down dinner was needed so members could entertain friends and clients easily. We agreed with his suggestion and I offered to chair the event. The challenge was attracting someone with an honorarium that would allow the event to be financially viable. I contacted Bill Jamieson, a friend and the PR director of the Red Wings, and he agreed to help.

The first Red Wings Night was January 28, 1988. Red Wings Coach Jacques Demers was the speaker, accompanied by his assistant coaches and several players and staff. Prior to dinner, there was an opportunity to meet the players, get autographs, bid on silent auction items, and collect door prizes. After dinner, the group took questions from the audience and some stayed later to mingle with the guests. A live auction of autographed Red Wings paraphernalia was also part of the fun.

The format was a big hit, and the Red Wings dinner sold out every year. It was a great complement to Commodore Frank

Figure 29. Red Wings Coach Jacques Demers.

Under the watchful eye of Commodore Theodore "Ted" Smith and the board, workers and craftsmen entered the GPYC in February and began a major facelift of the Ballroom. The room was painted, new draperies were hung, carpeting was replaced, light fixtures were cleaned and polished, and air conditioning was installed. Soundproofing panels that lined the walls were deemed an ineffective eyesore and were removed.[12] The fireplace was given a marbleized paint treatment and the windows and trim were glazed to simulate stone. Member D. J. Kennedy, a celebrated local interior designer who headed the project, said, "In essence, we were trying to bring the room back to look as it originally did, and to highlight more of the fine detail work throughout this huge, elegant space."

The Venetian Room and Lakeshore Room also received some attention. The Venetian Room was replastered and new moldings were installed. The fireplace received the same marbleizing treatment as in the Ballroom and the furniture in both the Venetian and Lakeshore rooms was reupholstered.

In May, artist and swimming co-chair Shelley Schoenherr dove right in, figuratively speaking, to the bottom of the (empty) pool and painted a seven-foot-high and nine-foot-long GPYC burgee. It took the better part of four

Figure 30. Member Ken Meade's 44-foot *Renegade* was the overall winner of the 1989 Chicago-to-Mackinac Island race and also took first in the IOR division.

days to complete and had to be done in plenty of time for the pool to be filled and ready for use on Memorial Day weekend. Shelley confided that she, husband John, and co-chairs Christine and Mike Kirchner were inspired by a Budweiser beer commercial in which the company logo was painted on the bottom of a swimming pool.[13]

Fourth of July activities took on a special meaning, as this was the fiftieth anniversary of the reopening of the Club in 1938. On a day blessed with perfect weather, 758 people enjoyed the outdoor family barbecue, while another 202 diners ate indoors. The day was capped with a champagne toast led by Commodore Smith, a fifty-gun salute provided by Vice Commodore Fred Schriever, using special miniature cannons, and the traditional fireworks display.

The swim team made GPYC history, winning the MICSA finals for the fourth straight year and remaining undefeated in regular dual meets for four consecutive years. After winning the finals, swimmers donned T-shirts with the slogan "Winning Isn't Everything... Just a Tradition."

Even though there was frustratingly slow air in the Port Huron-to-Mackinac race in July, GPYC members Ed Palm and George Gerow, co-owners of *Fast Company*, managed to take first place in the IOR-C class. The boat, a Bruce Farr 37 Sloop, also placed second in the IOR-2 class in the Chicago-to-Mackinac race.

McBride's Sportsmen's Night, (aka Stag Night) and both were held for many years. In addition to Coach Demers, coaches Bryan Murray, Scotty Bowman, Dave Lewis, and Mike Babcock, several Red Wing players, Zamboni driver Al Sobotka, and current GPYC member and long time team equipment manager Paul Boyer were all speakers at these dinners.

The honorarium came from the auction proceeds and a percentage of the ticket sales. It began as a donation to the speaker's favorite charity, but for many years the money went to the Konstantinov/Mnatsakanov Fund after the terrible accident in 1997 in which both players were seriously injured. Over the nearly twenty years that Red Wings Night was held, several thousand dollars were donated. As a thank you, the GPYC gave courtesy memberships for the year following the dinner to the participating Red Wings, cementing the Club's relationship with the Wings. Over time some of the Red Wings have become Club members.

I enjoyed being master of ceremonies over the years and the fact that GPYC Red Wings fans had an opportunity to interact with so many people in the Red Wings organization. It was a fun night for members and their families and friends and gave the Club a financially successful event in the slow winter months.

Figure 31. Shelley Schoenherr takes time to proudly pose with the Club burgee she painted on the bottom of the swimming pool.

★ ★ ★

Figure 32. Commodore John A. Boll Sr., 1986.

★ ★ ★

Figure 33. Commodore Robert E. Yuhn, 1987.

In September, board members traveled by train to the Royal Canadian Yacht Club in Toronto for the annual directors' cruise. Not only did they have dinner with the officers and directors of the club, but they were in the spectators' gallery for the second race of the Canada's Cup competition.[12] The Cup had been held by the Canadians for thirteen years. GPYC member Ken Meade and his partner and skipper, John Uznis, representing Bayview Yacht Club in their boat aptly named *The Challenge 88*, went on to win the series in the seventh race, proudly bringing the Cup back to the United States.

Paddle tennis players were delighted when the old wooden courts built in 1965 were torn down in August and replaced with new aluminum courts. They featured heaters underneath the playing surface to keep them free of ice and snow.

In November, a much-needed dredging was planned for the harbor and permits were requested to remodel the T-dock to make twelve new wells available.

In the December issue of *The Grosse Pointer*, Commodore Fred Schriever began his inaugural message with these gratifying words: "As every member who reads the Club's financial report or attended the annual meeting knows, the Grosse Pointe Yacht Club has just completed the most successful year in its entire history."

1989: The eighties end on a high note

The year began with requests for permits to begin construction of a warming and viewing house to be built between the new paddle tennis courts. Up to this point, a trailer had always been parked in the vicinity to give players a place to warm up between sets. It was hoped that the project would be finished before the end of the season. In fact, it was stalled by government regulations, but once these were waived by the state, construction began and the facility was ready for the fall season.

The harbor, according to Commodore Fred Schriever, looked like "there is some sort of winter boating season in Michigan. A record number of boats, seventy-two, are being bubbled there this year."[14] The dredging that had been planned for late fall was delayed by bad weather but was projected to be completed well before the official opening of the harbor. Permit requests for

Figure 34. Commodore Theodore H. Smith, 1988.

Figure 35. Commodore Fred E. Schriever, 1989.

remodeling the T-dock finally came through, but for eleven instead of twelve new wells. The planned construction also included moving the sailing center to the southeast corner of the harbor to make room for several new boat docks. The project was completed in time for the summer season.

The redecorated Binnacle Dining Room opened on March 4. The board had approved the project going forward because it had become the most popular dining area in the Club.

In the April *Grosse Pointer*, Commodore Schriever reported the following:

> The last group of new wells that the Club is building for Grosse Pointe Shores on the north wall will soon be finished. Over the past three years, the Club has developed sixty-one wells there for the Village. You will recall that in 1987 we agreed to do this work in exchange for permanent rights to wells one to twenty-eight and all the wells south of the center line of the T-dock. For many years, the Club leased all of the wells in our harbor north of the clubhouse from Grosse Pointe Shores. When our lease expired three years ago, we were able to negotiate the agreement with them that will soon be concluded.

The GPYC swim team ended the 1980s with yet another undefeated season. They won their fifth straight MICSA championship and recorded their eighty-third consecutive dual-meet victory.

On August 12, the sixtieth annual Fleet Review went off flawlessly under sunny skies. Commodore Schriever reviewed the fleet from—what else—a sixty-year old boat, the 96-foot *Electra*, owned by member Fred Ruffner.

It was also in August that an Australian boat, *Antipodean*, made a brief stop in the GPYC harbor. She was owned by the president of Oceanfast, the company that built her, based in Perth, Australia. He and his crew of five were sailing the Great Lakes as part of a fifteen-month tour of the United States. What made her so unique was that her sister ship, *Never Say Never*, was featured in the James Bond movie of the same name.

The automatic pinsetters in the bowling alleys were rebuilt and updated. New bowling manager David Sill also screened and recoated the lanes with urethane and repainted the gutters, walls, and scoring area. Commodore Schriever assured bowlers that further improvements were planned for future years as funds became available.

Figure 36. *Challenge 88*, co-owned by member Ken Meade, wins the Canada Cup in 1988, bringing it back to the United States after many years of residing at the Royal Canadian Yacht Club.

As 1989 drew to a close, membership stood at just over one thousand with a waiting list. In a November article in *The Grosse Pointer*, Commodore Schriever reflected on some of the accomplishments of the year, which he attributed mostly to the continuing financial stability of the Club. A few of the items on his list that haven't already been mentioned were the installation of 220-volt electrical service at the Guest Dock, the development of a new dining area on the pool deck, the acquisition of six new sailboats for the Club's fleet, new carpet in the men's and boys' locker rooms, a new pool heater, and continued progress toward a complete rewiring of the entire clubhouse.[15]

Figure 37. GPYC members gather on the slopes of Sun Valley, Idaho, for a group photo on the annual ski trip to the western United States, 1989. Pictured are couples, left to right: Past Com. Fred and Pat Schriever, Past Com. Jim and Julie Mitchell, Don and Betty Savage, Bill and Ingrid Mortimer, and Past Com. Bob and Jackie Thoreson.

IMAGE ACKNOWLEDGEMENTS
Chapter Eight

1. Karl Schmidt
2. Jim Dorian
3. – 5. GPYC
6. Joseph Schulte
7. – 9. GPYC
10. Jane Kay Nugent
11. – 15. GPYC
16. Charles Davis
17. GPYC
18. Jim Dorian

19. – 21. GPYC
22. USACE
23. – 24. GPYC
s25. – 26. Bob Kaiser
27. GPYC
28. Steve Gagne
29. – 30. GPYC
36. Tuppy Gravel
37. GPYC

Figure 1. 1992: Coach Fred Michalik, center, flanked by assistant coaches Anna Francis, center-left, and Jim Bellanca, center-right, pose with the GPYC swim team following their 103rd consecutive dual meet victory and eighth consecutive MICSA championship. Coach Michalik and his predecessor, Tom Teetaert, get full credit for guiding the team through this unprecedented string of victories.

By Elizabeth S. Rader and
Past Com. Robert L. Rader Jr.

1990 through 1999

The 1990s will be remembered as a time when technology moved to the forefront of everyday life on this planet. The cellular phone, the Internet, and people's ability to obtain information instantaneously changed the quality of life and human interaction forever. The decade saw unrest and uneasiness—in politics and the economy. The Gulf War began. Bill Clinton became the forty-second president of the United States, and Monica Lewinsky became a household name. We learned that terrorism could hit home with the 1993 car bombing of the World Trade Center in New York City and the 1995 bombing of the Alfred P. Murrah Federal Building in downtown Oklahoma City. We became aware of the loss of innocence with the massacre of students at Columbine High School in Colorado. We concerned ourselves about "Mad Cow Disease;" were riveted by the twists and turns of the O. J. Simpson trial; mourned the loss of Diana, the "People's Princess;" and John F. Kennedy Jr.; and ended the decade in widespread fear of the world crashing to a standstill as a result of the "Y2K millennium bug."

Under the bubble, however, life was much less tumultuous. At the Club, the 1980s ended in a healthy economic upsurge that carried over to the 1990s, with the decade leading up to the year 2000 showing promising growth and stability. The 1990s were unique, as this period signified

Figure 2. This medal with blue ribbon was won by GPYC swimmer Brennan Schoenherr during the 1992 MICSA swim finals held at the Country Club of Detroit. Brennan was competing in the boys age 15–16 backstroke event, which he won in record-setting time. The old record stood for twelve years. The GPYC team went on to take the overall win.

the end, not only of a century, but also of a millennium. It would not be all smooth sailing, however, as the decade would ultimately reveal some uncertainty in the economy, some unforeseen Club expenditures, and, by the end of the decade, growing tension between the GPYC and some residents in the community over the topic of harbor expansion.

Not atypical of any other period throughout the Club's history, the Yacht Club can be characterized during this time as a coordinated machine comprised of a talented and experienced team: a board of directors, management, membership, and staff. During this decade, considerable effort was put forth by all parties to maintain and improve the Club's programs and facilities while respecting tradition and closely monitoring finances. All eyes were focused on maintaining the Grosse Pointe Yacht Club's status among the finest clubs in the nation for future generations of members.

1990: "A year of refinement"

In 1990, Tymon C. Totte, DDS, took the helm as commodore of the Grosse Pointe Yacht Club. His mantra was to have the following twelve months constitute a "year of refinement." Totte hit the ground running, adding eight new committees, including bylaws & rules, security &

★ ★ ★

Figure 3. Commodore Tymon C. Totte, D.D.S. 1990.

safety, parking, energy, special events, *The Grosse Pointer* magazine, strategic planning, and winter bubbling.[1] Membership was strong and the harbor was full, with a waiting list of members wanting to berth their boat at the Club.

GPYC sporting teams were busy on the sailing and swimming circuits. The Club added six new Optimist boats to its sailing fleet in 1990 and, in its inaugural experience with these tiny vessels, hosted an Opti national seminar on Memorial Day weekend. The new boats were used by the Junior Sailing program for its youngest sailors, the Novice fleet, ages nine to ten. A couple of years later, in 1993, the Club added the J-22 to its fleet in an ongoing effort to build its instructional, recreational, and racing programs. At 22.5 feet in length with a self-bailing cockpit and room for four to six sailors, the J-22 was easy for junior and adult sailors to handle.

The Grosse Pointe Yacht Club Swim Team started the decade by breaking a MICSA record for most consecutive wins at Finals with five, and winning their 88th consecutive dual meet. A couple of years later, on Wednesday, July 1, 1992, the GPYC swim team achieved an unheard-of

Figure 4. Member John Stevens skippers his *Sprint III* and crew in an early practice for the 1990 Port Huron-to-Mackinac race, which he had won in the past.

accomplishment: their 100th consecutive MICSA dual meet victory. They would go on to surpass that later the same year by stretching their win streak to 103 and a record eight consecutive MICSA championships.

Committee members came up with a new format for Fleet Review Weekend, beginning with Friday night's Harbor Lights Night. Commodore Totte credits the idea of Harbor Lights Night to a number of nostalgic childhood memories. He was very close to his uncle, GPYC commodore John R. Wilt (1961), and lived with him for two years when his own father was serving in the military. Totte fondly recalls the beautifully decorated "Show Boat" events in previous years at the Yacht Club. This memory, coupled with memories of Venetian Night at the Detroit Yacht Club and family Christmases at Islamorada, Florida, featuring fishing boats with their outriggers resplendent in lights, precipitated the idea of implementing something similar at the GPYC. In celebration of Fleet Review, it was the committee's goal to have the entire harbor aglow in white lights for the enjoyment of members as well as passersby on Lake Shore Road.[2] In addition, in a break from tradition, Commodore

Totte decided on an in-harbor review to eliminate the weather element out on the lake. The Club's officers reviewed the GPYC fleet aboard Bob Thoreson's boat, *Valkyrie*. Totte fondly recalls Fleet Review weekend as the most memorable event of his year.

As a *Grande Dame* of yacht clubs, the GPYC's facilities require ongoing maintenance to keep her shipshape. During the 1990s, the Club saw completion of several major projects, as well as the preparation and groundwork for many others. The decade began with harbor painting, refurbishing of the men's and ladies' restrooms, and renovation of the Commodores' Room. It soon became apparent that Totte's "year of refinement" would evolve into a year of repairs as the Club's thirty-year-old fuel tanks required replacement, a retaining wall on the north side of the Club needed repair, and the harbor required dredging as a result of low lake levels.

On the social scene, members were concerned about health issues related to secondhand smoke. They wrote letters to board members and management in an effort to abolish smoking in the Club's restaurants and bars. The matter was referred to the facilities committee for a review of

Figure 5. Junior tennis players pose with Club pro Steve Story, completing his first season at the GPYC in 1990. The group celebrated by throwing a pizza party.

the Club's smoking policy. Club management and committee members worked hard to appease both sides, reviewing the possibilities of implementing no-smoking areas in the Binnacle, Spinnaker, and Main Dining Room and installing a smoke purification system in the respective dining rooms. Additional efforts included removing the cigarette machine from the Club's property, eliminating ashtrays on tables in the dining rooms unless requested, and posting "Thank you for not smoking" signs to encourage members and guests to refrain from smoking in the Club's dining rooms.

In 1990, the family of Commodore J. Earl Fraser (1963) presented a "deed of gift" establishing a Distinguished Member of the Year trophy donated in his memory. This trophy continues to be awarded annually "to a non-director member in recognition of outstanding and distinguished contribution and service to the GPYC in time and talent. The recipient is to be selected by the board of directors and may or may not be a current boat owner, and is to be designated 'Distinguished Member of the Year.'"[3]

Throughout the decade, the Club hosted celebrities from the sports and entertainment worlds. The yachtsman's committee hosted several prominent figures from the world of sailing, including Gary Jobson, a world-class sailor; analyst, and statistician on *Courageous* and *Defender*; Dennis Connor, skipper of *Stars & Stripes*; John Bertrand, strategist on *Stars & Stripes* and former Olympic sailor; and Buddy Melges, skipper of *America3*, a successful defender of the America's Cup. Melges thrilled members by bringing the America's Cup Trophy on his visit to the Club. On June 9, 1992, a crowd of 250 GPYC members and guests were on hand to meet Buddy and view the world's oldest sporting trophy.

Celebrities who visited the Club in the 1990s were not just from the world of sports. Nolan Miller, the fashion designer best known for creating the glamorous clothes worn by the stars of popular television shows *Dynasty* and *Charlie's Angels*, visited the GPYC in conjunction with his visit to Detroit for the North American Auto Show and the launch of a new ready-to-wear collection

Figure 6. In 1990, GPYC members were watching the popular TV show, *Dynasty*, known for the elegant fashions worn by the leading ladies. Designer Nolan Miller brought some of those *chic* creations to the Club while he was in town dressing models for the North American International Auto Show. Mr. Miller poses here with two of the models.

at Jacobson's department stores. A highlight of the evening was his presentation of sixty-four of his high-fashion, over-the-top designs. The GPYC ladies also hosted columnist and radio personality Shirley Eder. Eder entertained GPYC members and guests with her behind-the-scenes observations of Hollywood at a spring ladies' luncheon on March 11, 1993.

During the 1990s, representatives from the Detroit Red Wings, including coaches and players, were the guests of honor at Winter Stag Nights. These events typically drew crowds in excess of three hundred, which featured speeches, a question-and-answer session, and an opportunity to mingle with the players and obtain autographs and photos. GPYC's Eighth Annual Red Wings Night scored a record-breaking attendance of 380 members and guests on

March 14, 1996. That year's party featured Coach and General Manager Scotty Bowman, Assistant Coach Dave Lewis, PR Director Bill Jamieson, Assistant PR Director Paul Boyer, Announcer Ken Kal, Building Director Al Sabotka, Players' Captain Steve Yzerman, and Chris Osgood and Kris Draper. Guests received Red Wings pennants for collecting autographs. A silent and live auction featured jerseys and hockey sticks signed by the Red Wings. Throughout the cocktail hour, players signed autographs. After dinner, Coach Bowman offered insights into the team and the NHL. Afterward, the Red Wings and staff answered questions and signed more autographs. "The evening originated eight years ago in response to a member's request," recalled Dr. Bill Jennings, who was a board member at the time and served as chairperson of the event. "The first Red Wings Night featured Jacques Demers as speaker and was an immediate success, building to this year's unprecedented attendance."[4]

A big part of any yacht club is its rendezvous events—winter and summer. The Club's first annual Florida Winter Party was held at Lighthouse Point Yacht Club on Friday, February 16, 1990, with more than eighty members in attendance. New in 1990 was the addition of a family outing by boat to the Old Club on Harsens Island. In 1991, the rendezvous program grew to include a dinner cruise program, co-organized by the social committee, whereby the GPYC fleet visited local area waterfront restaurants for dinner on several Mondays throughout the summer. The Club's boating rendezvous schedule also expanded to include more adventurous destinations such as Okeechobee Lodge in the North Channel.

1991: Expect the unexpected

In 1991, Commodore Tom Ogden, one of the youngest commodores in Club history, celebrated his forty-second birthday at his Commodore's Ball on December 1, 1990. Every commodore seems to have a goal or two for his or her year, and 1991 was no exception. Ogden's motto for the year was "Work hard—play hard." He noted, "If each person moving up the commodores' chairs improves the Club just a little bit more than when

★ ★ ★

GPYC

Figure 7. Commodore Thomas D. Ogden, 1991.

he found it, then the Club continues to progress and improve."[5] In spite of some trying issues on the national and international fronts due to a recession and the Persian Gulf War, the GPYC showed strength in terms of membership, programs, facilities, and financial performance. The year saw the completion of a number of large projects, including the renovation of the Bowling Center. In addition, the board approved funding ($250,000) for the modernization of Shoreline Docks 1–17 and renovation of the seawall adjacent to those wells. Located on the north side of the Club, outside the Commodores' Room and the kitchen, the old "Garbage Dock" was one of the original retaining walls installed in 1928–29, when the clubhouse and grounds were first built. Because it was suspected that erosion was causing soil from the Club's grounds to "leak" into the harbor, a diver was sent down to inspect the walls. Commodore Ogden recalls the diver took a rod and poked it into different areas to check the integrity of the structure. He found areas of erosion here and there but then came across one spot where he poked and the rod went

Figure 8. Under the direction of second-year Sailing Master Pat Barry, 1991 junior sailors take a break from their workout for a little fun. New additions to the fleet that year included six new Optis, two Lasers and this powerboat.

all the way through, revealing a significant problem. To fix this, heavy-duty sheet pile and diagonal braces were driven down into the lake bottom to support the walls. Aboveground, holes were drilled in the sidewalk and a significant amount of concrete was pumped into them. As Ogden recalls, "We realized then that maybe we were closer to losing that side of the clubhouse than we ever imagined." He said that if you walk along that sidewalk today, you can still see the series of holes that were drilled.[6] Along with the wall repair, docks and walkways contiguous to these walls were renovated and modernized. A landscaping program continued in front of the clubhouse and adjacent to areas of the harbor that were renovated, and the main entry, lobby, and Rotunda of the clubhouse were redecorated. Even the valet house received a new coat of paint to better coordinate with the Club's architecture.

The year 1991 witnessed many firsts for the GPYC. The first female officer of the Club, Deanne Buono, was selected as powerboat fleet captain. Dee was very active at the Club, having joined as an Intermediate member in 1973, a single parent with four children. Later, as the owner of a 36-foot Chris Craft, she is thought to

have been the first female Active member with a boat docked in the harbor. In her role as fleet captain, Dee spearheaded the committee for Friday night activities on the weekend of Fleet Review, organizing the decorating committee, barbeque, and antique boat show.[7] Other firsts in 1991 included the introduction of a Junior

Figure 9. Competitors and friends, Ed Shaw, first-place finish in the NA 40 class, and Sonny Tindle, second-place finish in the NA 40 class, display their flags at the Annual Regatta Awards Dinner.

Boating Safety Course, which was well received by members. In addition, Chef Mike Green took first place in an international ice-carving competition, representing the United States in Russia. Bertram owners also gathered for a first-ever Great Lakes Bertram Rendezvous at the Club, which saw thirty Bertram powerboats and their owners attend from various home ports around Lake St. Clair and Lake Erie.

Late in his term, Commodore Ogden suffered a heart attack that forced him to temporarily cut back on his time at the Club. Vice Commodore Charles Stumb ran the board meetings in his absence. Out of respect for Tom and the office of commodore, the vice commodore refused to sit in the commodore's chair until it was his turn at the helm.[8]

1992: "We are all just part of a bigger picture—the finest yacht club around"

Commodore Charles "Charlie" Stumb faced the challenge of a slowing economy coupled with a need to provide higher levels of member services at a reasonable cost. Only a few months into the year, it was necessary to deal with a rogue ice floe

that damaged sixty feet of the East Wall and ripped out electrical wiring. At the same time, work continued on both a strategic plan and a master plan—documents designed to provide direction for the Club and its facilities well into the future. As part of its ongoing assessment of Club needs, the board undertook a thorough review of the harbor facilities, as well as the clubhouse and grounds. A prominent consulting firm was retained to explore options for the harbor—from upgrading the utilities and docks to total renovation. Another firm was engaged to do the same for

Figure 10. Matt Kirchner displays his winning form in the breaststroke.

Figure 11. Brennan Schoenherr gets a powerful start in the backstroke during a MICSA meet against Birmingham Athletic Club. The overall win for GPYC became number one hundred in consecutive dual-meet victories for the team.

Figure 12. Amanda Hanley awaits her turn on the starting block.

Figure 13. Thirty-six boats from all over North America participated in the 1992 International Star Class North American Championship, hosted by the GPYC. Following the race, Commodore Stumb received a letter from one of the jury members stating in part, " Having been involved in world championship regattas in many countries, three Olympics and six America's Cups, I can recall none that exceeded the excellence of your event."

Figure 14. Commodore Charles E. Stumb Jr., 1992.

Figure 15. Some of the people who contributed to the success of the prestigious Star Class championship event held at the GPYC were, left to right, Mr. and Mrs. Oliver Moore from *Yachting Magazine,* ESPN Commentator Gary Jobson, Patty Corona, and Club Regatta Chairman Ed Palm.

Figure 16. A GPYC weekend ski trip to Boyne Mountain in 1993 brought out this group of junior skiers hoping to pick up a few pointers at the Boyne ski school.

the clubhouse and facilities; to assist in the preparation of a master plan for improvements. Items under consideration included terrace dining and a snack bar, offices for swimming, tennis, sailing, harbor and administrative functions, locker rooms, and handicap access to the Club. As with all capital projects, the goal was to make improvements that would enhance enjoyment of the Club.[9]

One of the many highlights this year was the continued success of the GPYC Swim Team. The Club's talented swimmers continued on a roll, celebrating one hundred consecutive MICSA dual-meet victories by defeating the Birmingham Athletic Club. Past Commodore Stumb fondly recalls the team tossing him into the pool after the big win. The GPYC Swim Team continued on to win the balance of its dual meets, finishing the season undefeated with an amazing record of 103 consecutive dual-meet victories and its eighth consecutive MICSA championship.[10]

The Club's sailors also had much to brag about, as the 1992 GPYC Junior Sailing team exceeded all previous GPYC records by winning eight awards at the 1992 Grosse Pointe Club Regatta in June. Winning sailors were spread among all three classes of competition. Later in the year, GPYC played host to more than one hundred of the world's finest sailors during September 10–18 for the International Star Class North American Championships. Considered one of sailing's most prestigious events, this regatta was the first world-class sailing event hosted by the Club in twenty years.[11]

Later, in December of that year, the Club introduced a new publication to the membership titled *The Mast*. Formatted as a monthly newsletter, it was produced in-house and designed to replace the use of fliers to alert members to upcoming events. It was part of an ongoing effort to provide better-quality communication to members.

★ ★ ★

Figure 17. Commodore Herold "Mac" Deason, 1993.

As his year drew to a close, Stumb recalled that he and his wife, Patty, had decided in the very beginning that they would have fun and not take things too seriously. "The year passed quickly and we realized that we were only a part of the bigger picture—the finest Yacht Club around."[8]

1993: Membership matters

At the GPYC, members expect top-notch service with an array of quality programs at a fair price. This appeared to be a challenging task in 1993 as the Club confronted an aging infrastructure and a stagnant economy, but plans for major renovations to the east end of the Club were already well underway. Under the command of Commodore Herold "Mac" Deason, followed by Commodore J. James Morrow, the Club entered into a two-phase, two-year upgrade of the east side of the Club. Phase one consisted of a total renovation of the Pool Terrace dining area. It included demolition of the area now known as the Harborside Grill, which at the time was not much more than a wooden snack shack. It was upgraded to the existing structure and complemented by a full commercial kitchen along with outdoor seating. Upstairs, the area now known as the Binnacle Terrace was constructed, offering members open-air dining and an unparalleled view of the harbor and lake. Construction of the Pool Terrace dining facility and the Binnacle deck were the major renovation projects of the year.

Throughout the year, Deason worked with the Pointe Club (members forty years of age and under) in an effort to revitalize their activities. He also called upon the membership committee to establish a "Social C" category in an effort to mitigate the cost of membership for young people who were not eligible for Junior membership. Subsequently, a recommendation was made by the committee to establish a new category of membership for those aged twenty-one to thirty-five who were not sons or daughters of current members. It provided dues credit to enable these members, when their age permitted, to move directly into Social A membership without paying additional fees. The board motioned and approved to adopt this recommendation subject to amendment of the bylaws by the membership at the annual meeting.[12]

Figure 18. Harbormaster Dave Jordan stands in the rubble of the former Grog Shop. No turning back now! Construction on the new Grog Shop and harbormaster's office was about to begin.

Figure 19. Commodore J. James Morrow Jr., 1994.

The GPYC Swim Team experienced its first loss of a dual meet in eighteen years in 1993 after accumulating 103 victories and eight consecutive MICSA championships.

1994: "Being commodore is about giving back"

Midway through the decade, membership was strong and the Club was financially stable. Pending challenges threatened this stability, however, as tax-law changes, "barrier-free access" rules, and a barrage of other legislation impacted the Club. Although the clubhouse and grounds remained in good condition, it was becoming more and more evident that the aging harbor required significant attention. Commodore Morrow advised the membership that a committee had been commissioned the prior year and was in the process of planning what needed to be done to the harbor and the best way to put it in place. The process would be laborious and complex as it would need to consider state DNR regulations, local permitting and leases, harbor utilization, finances, and member expectations.

Figure 20. GPYC organizers of the 1994 MICSA tournament gave the event a "bell tower" theme. Committee member Shelley Schoenherr put her artistic skills to work, creating an eight-foot comic replica of the campanile she named "Tommy Tower." Ever the good sport, then-Treasurer Mark Weber agreed to don the tower and walk around the event greeting visitors. Pictured here with wife Judy, Past Com. Weber still talks about how miserable he was inside the costume in the July heat.

Concurrently, phase two of the east clubhouse renovation project was underway, involving the expansion and renovation of the locker rooms, Grog Shop, and harbor offices, as well as barrier-free access to the south side of the Club. The new and expanded Grog Shop and harbor offices would now include offices for the harbormaster and staff, sailing master, and swim coach so that they could have a bird's-eye view of their domain.[13] Barrier-free access on the south side of the Club included construction of a terraced ramp to the pool deck and an exterior elevator to the upper levels of the south side of the Club, accessing the Binnacle, Ballroom, and accounting offices, with the potential of going to the third floor at some point in the future. The project was finished in time for the boating season and brought significant enhancements to harbor operations. This two-year, two-phase, $2 million project was completed on time, with the funding of the project coming from cash from operations.[14]

The Club experienced another busy year in 1994, in particular because it hosted the 14th annual MICSA finals, July 30–31. Past Commodore Ted Smith, who co-chaired the event in 1982, served as general chairman of the event: "I'm particularly close to this event because I swam in the MICSA meets in the late 1940s and early 1950s when there were only six clubs in the association."[15] Bill Storen (who would become commodore in 1999) and his wife, Julie, who co-chaired the event with a team of more than two hundred volunteers, were credited with the championship coming off as one of the best ever, with nearly three thousand swimmers and their families in attendance at the Club each day.

The Club's Junior Sailing Program had a great year in 1994. The team journeyed to the prestigious Oyster Bay Racing Clinic in New York in May, and Club teams competed in six local DRYA regattas, U.S. Sailing events, and numerous off-lake regatta trips. GPYC sailors were also extremely competitive in local events, taking second place in the DRYA Club Championships, the team's best finish in more than five years. The season was highlighted with

Figure 21. Commodore Robert E. Thoreson, 1995.

GPYC hosting the Optimist Dinghy Great Lakes Championship and concluded with seven GPYC sailors participating in the Canadian and North American Championships in Optis and Lasers at Kingston, Ontario, in late August.[16]

With a full harbor and boaters on a wait list for a well assignment, the harbor committee, in conjunction with the board of directors, proposed and ultimately adopted a harbor-utilization plan. The plan provided a formula for well application, mandating that in order to apply for a specific well, the eligible boat (length including bow pulpit and swim platform multiplied by beam width) should displace at least 75 percent of the usable space in the well.

Past Commodore Morrow recalls an interesting story from the year regarding the assignment of member numbers. He reports Commodore Mark Weber used to tell stories about his father, who was member number 30 and also the thirtieth commodore of the Club. It seemed that in the Club's earlier days, commodores were given a member number that corresponded to their number as commodore. During Commodore Morrow's year, it was

Figure 22. Inspired by a personal emergency at sea, Dr. Jim McCarty organized the first GPYC Boat-Handling for Mates course in 1995. Aboard each volunteered boat, participants learned maneuvering techniques, radio calls, and docking skills. Pictured here, front row, left to right, are students Judy Weber, Rene Cornillie, Linda Schaden, Linda Lloyd, and Kim Bill. Volunteer instructors, left to right, Tom Campau and Jim McCarty, are behind. This would be the first in a series of similar events at the GPYC.

suggested the Club return to this practice, and the board of directors proposed and approved its reinstitution. So today, when a commodore takes office, he or she receives a new member number that corresponds with their numerical order in the succession of commodores.[14]

Summarizing his year, Morrow concludes, "I would tell you that being commodore is about giving something back. It's about providing some value to the Club. If I had to look for legacy, perhaps it would not be the fact that I was commodore, but more the fact that we've been involved in the Yachtsman's Committee and that we've been able to generate funding to build a world-class sailing program and provide some true value to the young people in the Club and to the yachting community as a total."[14]

1995: The new Tower Pub—friends, food, and spirits

In 1995, the membership was advised of the urgent need to repair and upgrade the Club's harbor. After sixty-five years, it was sorely outdated, with boat well proportions that were incompatible with modern, wider-beam boats. Both the electrical service and water pressure were insufficient, and the telephone system was outdated. Aesthetically, the harbor was unattractive. Commodore Robert Thoreson

Figure 23. In October 1995, the newly designed Tower Pub opened its doors to members twenty-one years and older as a casual bar and eating area. Three committee members who helped to guide the project from paper to reality are pictured here, left to right: Past Commodores Jim Morrow, Mark Weber and John DeWald

Figure 24. The Club's fanciest watering hole, the third-floor Tower Pub, opened in 1995 with a reception for the many members/donors who helped make it a reality. Occupying space that was previously underutilized, the Pub offered a beautiful wood bar, a fireplace, and a spectacular view of the lake. Half-hulls of members' boats decorated the paneled walls, and still do.

announced that a five-year reconstruction program was an attainable goal, with the hope that a section of the harbor could be started by the following fall.[17] Results of a member survey the preceding spring had indicated that the harbor was a major concern, with a majority of members believing it needed substantial work.

Several house projects were also initiated that year, including the installation of new carpet in the Ballroom, a new front entrance walkway, and new windows in the Fo'c'sle that were true to their original design. Also, the doors in the Main Dining Room kitchen were replaced to match the other Dining Room doors.

In 1995 the Club offered for the first time a Mates' Boat-Handling Course under the direction of the powerboat committee. More than forty-five female participants turned out for what, afterward, many called a "life-changing day." Active member and powerboat owner Lynne De Grande set the tone. She assured the aspiring boat pilots, "[You] have more ability than you realize." The class was divided into eight teams of students, who were assigned to GPYC member boats. Students and instructors immediately put to sea; each student learned how to handle a relatively large boat (30–40 feet in length) in open water, then how to maneuver it back into the harbor and alongside a dock.[18]

Out of a member survey the preceding spring, the idea of the Tower Pub was born, as more than 50 percent of respondents indicated they would use the Club more if there was a casual place to gather. At the time, the tower room was essentially just an open, underutilized space for training and instructional sessions and was not easily accessible. It was decided the space could become a casual bar, separate from the other dining areas, that members could reach without going through the main entrance of the club-house. One of the big proponents of the Tower Pub at the time was influential board member Ed Connelly. As Past Commodore Sloane Barbour recalls, "We were in a board meeting, and we had been talking and talking and talking about it, so all of a sudden he (Connelly) gets out his check-book and throws a $20,000 check in the middle of the table, and he looks around the table and says, 'Okay, guys, let's get serious.' That got everybody's attention."[19] This marked the birth of a Special Gifts fund. Spearheaded by Connelly and Past Commodore John DeWald, and with the support of many members, the Tower Pub project attracted member donations of nearly $180,000 and became a new place in the club-house for members to relax and enjoy. The Pub opened with a reception for sponsors on October 25, 1995. The room provided members with a comfortable setting in a casual atmosphere with spectacular views of the harbor and Lake St. Clair. Open to members and guests over age twenty-one, it was the first smoke-free bar in the Grosse Pointes.[20]

In 1995, the board moved to relax the dress code, making both the Binnacle and Spinnaker casual through Labor Day. This was based on the over-whelmingly positive response to the casual dress code that had been in effect in the Binnacle on a trial basis.

Figure 25. Commodore Sloane R. Barbour Jr., 1996.

1996: Laying the foundation for growth

In 1965, Sloane Barbour, sponsored by former board member Bud Greiner, joined the GPYC and also sailed in his first Mackinac race. Thirty-one years later he would rise to become commodore of the Grosse Pointe Yacht Club. Barbour also earned the title "Old Goat," having sailed in more than twenty-five Mackinac races. His grandfather had been commodore of the Toledo Yacht Club in 1928. As Sloane recalls, "1996 was the year the board really got serious about the harbor. With the help of two past commodores, Ted Smith and Fred Schriever, we put together a program to

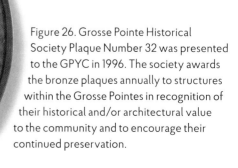

Figure 26. Grosse Pointe Historical Society Plaque Number 32 was presented to the GPYC in 1996. The society awards the bronze plaques annually to structures within the Grosse Pointes in recognition of their historical and/or architectural value to the community and to encourage their continued preservation.

start redoing the harbor. Battleship Row was close to falling in at the time. The tiebacks were broken, so we thought we would start with repairing them. We had a committee that was very ambitious and said, 'while we repair that, let's repair the wall along the parking lot and redo all those wells'—so that's where it all started. We broke ground the year I was just going out of office as commodore and it was completed later that winter."[19]

In 1996, the Grosse Pointe Yacht Club received an historical site designation by the Grosse Pointe Historical Society. The Club was awarded a bronze plaque in recognition of the historical and architectural value of the property to the community.

An updated proposal for the development of a health and fitness facility in the area of the Club that used to house the ladies' locker room was presented to the board. It was suggested that a health club, along with restroom facilities at the tennis courts, be integrated into the Club's five-year plan.

Spring shutdown this year revealed a number of problems and challenges as age continued to take a toll on some of the Club's facilities. Numerous repairs had to be made to the lift bridge and the swimming pool. The pool had developed a number of leaks, and it became apparent that additional repairs would be necessary through-out the summer. Treasurer Jim Anderson recommended that a complete assessment of the swimming pool be conducted in the fall, with an *ad hoc* committee established to assess its long-term needs. In the meantime, the harbor remained a focal point. At a special meeting with the membership in March, the recently formed Strategic Harbor Renovation Group presented a multiple-phase plan for the redesign and improvement of the facilities and services in the GPYC harbor. It was projected that the majority of phase one of the renovation would be absorbed out-of-pocket, with any remaining costs covered by construction financing. Phase two was to include Club, Battleship Row, and Lakeside docks, including utilities and associated parking modifications. The cost of phase two was projected to be $1.2 million.[21]

Figure 27. Commodore John H. Schoenherr, 1997.

The second in a series of harbor renovation update meetings was held May 9 for the benefit of Club members. Harbor renovation committee co-chairs Dwight Labadie and Jim Anderson presented final plans for redevelopment of the southwest harbor along with a financial analysis of the renovation process and a Q&A session for members. Analysis and discussion focused on financial options to pay for the renovation, and a determination was made as to what features of the new harbor would best benefit boaters. Several considerations and scenarios were presented. The renovation committee favored a financial approach that involved a combination of increased operating efficiency, investment income, and modest increases in initiation and well fees, together with short-term construction financing. No votes were taken that evening, but a recommendation was made to proceed with the renovation of the southwest harbor, beginning in fall 1996. The project would start with seawall replacement and dredging, followed by construction of new twenty-foot-wide slips and new docks with adequate electricity for water, pump-out, telephone, cable TV, and bubblers. It was anticipated that construction would proceed through fall and winter 1996–97, and if the work proceeded on schedule, completion was anticipated in spring 1997. Alternative dock construction materials, including treated wood, recycled plastic, and existing concrete, were displayed on the north side of the clubhouse near Tee Dock for testing and member evaluation.[22]

A new pricing policy for the fuel dock was implemented in spring 1996. Designed to provide GPYC boaters with marine fuel prices among the lowest in the area, the new policy increased the discount per gallon to all members and granted an additional discount to well-eligible members on weekdays. In addition, in an effort to improve its fueling service to members, the Club added a second diesel pump and expanded the fuel dock to include Well #157. With credit going to the Harbor Utilization Policy, the Club boasted a full harbor. To accommodate this pleasant problem, additional harbor staff was hired to maintain the appearance of the docks and to offer dockside delivery and boat washing services to members.

Past Commodore Barbour recalls that of the year's several projects, two in particular stand out: the separation of the Club's sewage and waste water pipes and the aforementioned harbor renovation. In an interview, Barbour joked that he will be forever remembered as the "Sewer Commodore." He recounts the project's estimated price tag of $250,000; it came in close to budget, and the Club was able to write a check for it. He recalls the start of the long-awaited harbor renovation project as a second highlight.[19]

1997: The "number-one yacht club in the nation"

Incoming commodore John Schoenherr's personal history at the Club went back generations. His grandfather, Stark Hickey, was commodore in 1957; his father, Edward Schoenherr, was commodore in 1964, making John the only third-generation commodore in the Club's history. Upholding a family tradition, the Schoenherrs' children grew up at the Club and participated in the sailing and swimming programs. Son Brennan still holds a MICSA record from 1992.[23]

In February 1997, *Club Leaders Forum* named the GPYC as America's top yacht club. Thousands of general managers and club presidents from across the country were surveyed and asked to identify the most highly regarded private clubs in the United States. The group nominated and ranked clubs based on ten criteria: history of excellence, quality of membership, condition of facilities, caliber of professional staff, enlightened

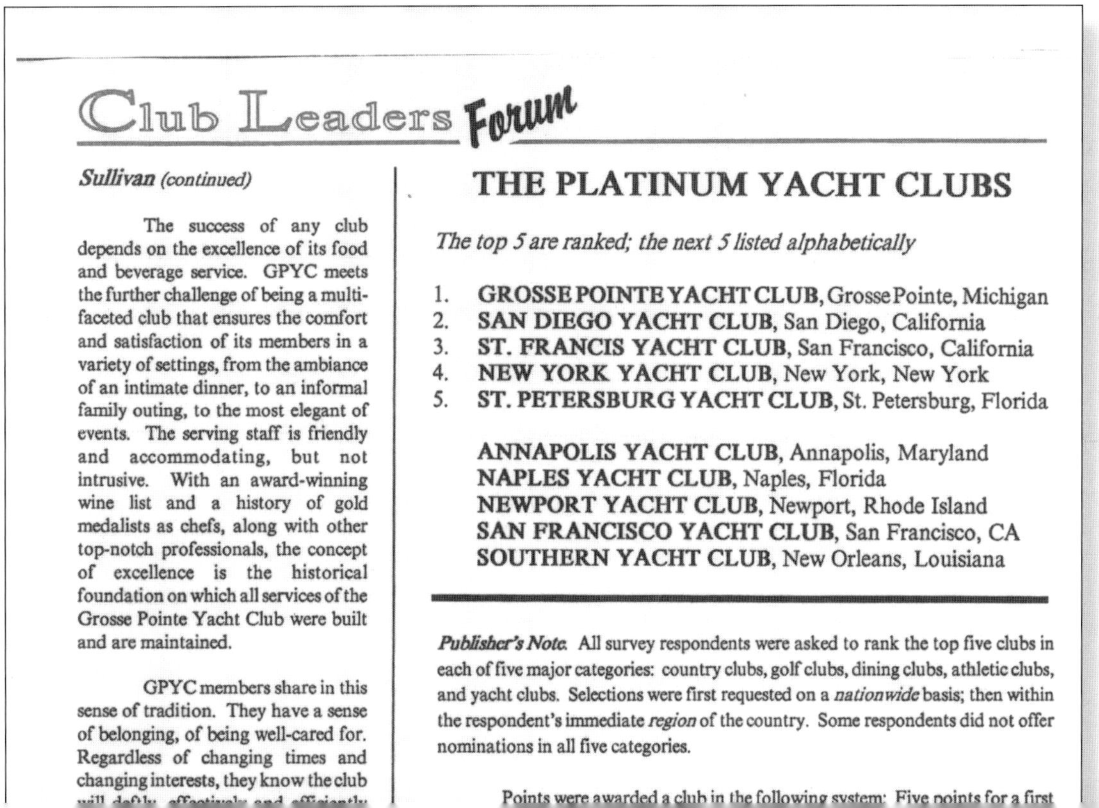

Figure 28. *Club Leaders Forum* announced its first club rankings in 1997. Club managers and presidents from across the country were polled, and when the votes were tallied, the Grosse Pointe Yacht Club was named the finest yacht club in the country.

Club Leaders *Forum*

Sullivan (*continued*)

The success of any club depends on the excellence of its food and beverage service. GPYC meets the further challenge of being a multi-faceted club that ensures the comfort and satisfaction of its members in a variety of settings, from the ambiance of an intimate dinner, to an informal family outing, to the most elegant of events. The serving staff is friendly and accommodating, but not intrusive. With an award-winning wine list and a history of gold medalists as chefs, along with other top-notch professionals, the concept of excellence is the historical foundation on which all services of the Grosse Pointe Yacht Club were built and are maintained.

GPYC members share in this sense of tradition. They have a sense of belonging, of being well-cared for. Regardless of changing times and changing interests, they know the club will deftly, effectively and efficiently

THE PLATINUM YACHT CLUBS

The top 5 are ranked; the next 5 listed alphabetically

1. **GROSSE POINTE YACHT CLUB**, Grosse Pointe, Michigan
2. **SAN DIEGO YACHT CLUB**, San Diego, California
3. **ST. FRANCIS YACHT CLUB**, San Francisco, California
4. **NEW YORK YACHT CLUB**, New York, New York
5. **ST. PETERSBURG YACHT CLUB**, St. Petersburg, Florida

ANNAPOLIS YACHT CLUB, Annapolis, Maryland
NAPLES YACHT CLUB, Naples, Florida
NEWPORT YACHT CLUB, Newport, Rhode Island
SAN FRANCISCO YACHT CLUB, San Francisco, CA
SOUTHERN YACHT CLUB, New Orleans, Louisiana

Publisher's Note. All survey respondents were asked to rank the top five clubs in each of five major categories: country clubs, golf clubs, dining clubs, athletic clubs, and yacht clubs. Selections were first requested on a *nationwide* basis; then within the respondent's immediate *region* of the country. Some respondents did not offer nominations in all five categories.

Points were awarded a club in the following system: Five points for a first

Figure 29. This donated Sea Ray Bowrider was the grand raffle prize at the Annual Yachtsmen's Day event in May 1997. Tickets sold raised over $20,000, a record amount for the Yachtsmen's Fund. Pictured here are the proud winners, then-board member Jim Anderson and wife Patti. Jim would become commodore in 2000.

and consistent governance, adaptability to changing times, member devotion to their club's distinctive culture, spirit of generosity in the community, prudent fiscal management, and a universal acknowledgment of greatness.[24] When the rankings were tallied, the Grosse Pointe Yacht Club was ranked number one among all yacht clubs. Retaining this elite ranking as one of the top three yacht clubs in the United States since the award's inception in 1997 continues to bring great honor to the Grosse Pointe Yacht Club and its membership. Members and staff alike consider the perpetuation of this ranking and maintenance of excellence an ongoing mission.

In 1997, harbor renovation remained at the top of the Club's agenda. Up until the swimming pool project six years later, it was arguably the biggest renovation project undertaken at the Club. The challenge was how to do it on a timely basis with as little disruption to boat owners as possible. To facilitate this, the harbor renovation committee and engineering committee met every Thursday morning for a year. Meetings with the contractors

would last two to three hours to make sure the renovation was going as planned. Phase one was finished on time and within budget; what resulted was a beautifully renovated portion of the harbor. The new four-foot-wide docks would be home to twenty-eight boats in the 50- to 75-foot range. Constructed of galvanized steel and concrete for durability with wood trim for looks, the docks were approximately one foot wider than the previous ones. Upgraded electrical service was added with power pedestals capable of supplying 240-volt, 100-amp service to each dock to accommodate larger boats. Green belts were planted to hide plumbing and electrical components and to set the dock areas apart from the newly paved parking lot.[25]

Being the grand old lady she is, the Club requires continual investment in the maintenance and refurbishment of facilities, grounds, and equipment. The engineering committee was tasked with surveying the Club to identify structural problems that might be anticipated and to come up with a proactive schedule for

Figure 30. The flagship of the 1997 Fleet Review was the 106-foot yacht, *Helene*. This beautiful lady of the lake was originally built in 1927 for GPYC member Charles Sorensen.

Figure 31. Above, GPYC swimmers had another big year in 1997 when they upset favored Great Oaks Country Club to win their nineteenth MICSA dual meet title. Members of the victorious Eight-and-Under Mixed Medley Relay are, left to right, Julie Zaranek, Elyse Krausmann, Michael Cytacki and Amy Wren Miller.

Figure 32. Left, On the podium for GPYC, proudly receiving their medals for the Girls' Championship 200-Meter Medley Relay are , left to right, Erica Stock, Ashley Wenk, Kammy Miller and Megan Zaranek.

upkeep of the facility. In the meantime, the house committee inventoried every room in the Club to determine whether there was a need for painting or other maintenance. Furniture was also inventoried and evaluated as to whether repair or replacement was needed. It was decided that a good rule of thumb would be to refresh or redo each room every seven years to ensure that equipment and furnishings would be well maintained. Developing a look-ahead plan for repairs and renovations would also enable the Club to budget accordingly and help minimize any unplanned expenditures. Through the combined efforts of both of these committees, a full appraisal of the facilities, along with a five-year plan, was completed the following year.[26] This would provide future boards with a framework to ensure continuity of effort and direction.

Support remained strong for the development of a health facility at the Club, and the board remained committed to continue studying this project.

The house and finance committees also began working together to explore the concepts of special gift and endowment funds to further provide for the financial security of the Club.

The Club's sporting teams continued to excel as Pat Barry and the Junior Sailors came in second in the DRYA racing program, while Fred Michalik put the swim team back on top by winning its fifteenth MICSA finals title and ninetenth dual meet title since the league was formed in 1940. The Club's swim program now boasted more dual meet and league championship titles than any other club in the history of MICSA.[27]

1998: Another legacy fulfilled

Like his predecessor, Commodore Mark Weber grew up at the Club in the 1950s. Mark is a second-generation commodore; his father, Robert F. Weber, was commodore in 1959. In the December 1997 *Grosse Pointer*, Commodore Weber called upon the board of directors, members, and staff to join him in affirming the Club's core values as a private yacht club and continuing the emphasis on strategic and visionary planning, on harbor renovation, and on enhancing the value of membership.

GPYC

Figure 33 Commodore Mark R. Weber, 1998.

As in recent years, the harbor continued to be the topic *du jour*. The harbor renovation committee presented three sound reasons for redoing the walls of the harbor, with old age as the most immediate and primary concern. The sea-wall defining the outer harbor shared by the GPYC and Grosse Pointe Shores dated back to 1929 when the clubhouse was first built. The oldest section of this seawall, along the north side of the harbor, was badly eroded. Underwater inspections had shown that many of the steel sheers were badly corroded and, in some instances, did not make contact with the lake bottom. Second, a majority of wells in the outer harbor were built prior to the 1980s and were now too narrow for the wider-profile boats they now had to contain. This resulted in a shortage of wells in the popular 35- to 45-foot range. Third, the State DEQ (Department of Environmental Quality) has specific guidelines that determine how wide fairways must be in relation to the size of the boat wells they adjoin. By definition, most of the fairways in the old portion of the GPYC harbor were too narrow. The planning and permitting

Figure 34. In 1998, GPYC directors and fleet officers were invited to experience a day's cruise aboard the nuclear submarine *USS Michigan* out of Bremerton, Washington. The delegation pictured here accepted the invitation, left to right, Jim Anderson, Bruce Fralick, Jim McCarty, Carl Rashid, Mark Weber, Dennis Andrus, Curt Neumann, and Jim Ramsey. When the story appeared in *The Grosse Pointer*, the group made it clear that they had paid for the trip themselves, lest members begin to ask for an audit.

Figure 35. Member John Mager offered the use of his 95-foot yacht, *More Toys for Us*, as the flagship for the 1998 Fleet Review. Commodore Mark Weber graciously accepted.

Figure 36. A piece of history found a home at the GPYC when the iceboat *French Boy* was restored and donated to the Club by member Sybil Jacques, shown here, widow of member Leonard Jacques. The boat, now displayed on the wall of the Fo'c'sle Room, had been owned by the Club's fourth commodore, John French, and sailed by his sons in the 1920s.

process remained ongoing in an effort to make the proposed new harbor a reality. However, all signs indicated harbor renovation would be a long-term process. In the meantime, a number of needed improvements were completed in the spring to the plumbing, telephone, and electrical systems in the harbor. Hickory, Moby, and Bridge Docks received upgrades that included new 220-volt/50-amp and 120-volt/30-amp electrical power, water lines, telephone service, and cable TV service. Wood risers were added to Moby and Hickory docks owing to the high water levels. In addition, the remainder of the harbor received a general sprucing up, including PVC cladding around steel pilings, anti-seagull caps on the tops of all pilings, and "No Wake" signs posted at the harbor entrance.[28]

The archives committee had been established the prior year by Commodore Schoenherr to help preserve the history of the Club. The brainchild of his wife, Shelley Schoenherr, and first chaired by Mary Huebner, the committee presented a proposal to the board to preserve the Club's historic documents. This would require the purchase of fireproof cabinetry and suitable display cases. The cabinets would contain original documents, and the display cases would contain duplicates that could be viewed by members. In an effort to preserve many of the stories and memories from bygone days, past commodores were also interviewed and video-recorded. On May 21, 1999, the archives commitee sponsored a brunch that featured the inauguration of the archives cabinet, located in

Figure 37. This is the first cabinet purchased by the Club in 1999 that was to be used exclusively for archival material. Presently located in the Venetian Room, it features displays of historically significant memorabilia, much of which has been donated by Club members.

Figure 38. Commodore William J. Storen, 1999.

the Venetian Room, which now houses numerous historical items, including valuable early photographs and other memorabilia, donated by many Club members.[29] Of note was a gift from GPYC member Sybil Jacques in the form of a wooden iceboat that was originally owned by John French, GPYC commodore from 1926 to 1931. Built in 1920, *French Boy* is a museum-quality piece that can be found on display in the Fo'c'sle.[30]

As in prior years, the membership committee continued to urge the Club to move forward with the establishment of a health facility.

1999: The quest for harbor modernization

William "Bill" Storen became commodore of the GPYC in 1999. His goals were to continue to develop Club activities that enhanced family values and to maintain a high level of member satisfaction. He recalled that the Club was blessed with mostly "calm waters" during his tenure; the economy was good and membership was growing. The membership committee also was very active in its efforts to bring in new members. Storen credits fellow Past Commodore Jim Ramsey for spearheading the implementation of membership

surveys to determine what members liked and disliked about the Club and its services, with the goal of continued improvement.[31]

An endowment fund proposal was presented to the board in 1999 with the endorsement of the finance committee. Many challenges still existed with regard to the establishment of a tax-exempt fund at the Club, but the proposal was seen as a starting point. It was developed with the assistance and professional guidance of the law firm of Butzel Long. The board recommended that the endowment board be comprised of seven members including three current GPYC board members. The proposal was to be studied and then submitted for approval at the February board meeting.[32]

After a great deal of hard work by members under the leadership of Vice Commodore Jim Anderson, the harbor renovation plan was ready for implementation. The plans called for modernizing and expanding the harbor, subject to Grosse Pointe Shores Village Council approval, to accommodate new, wider boats and fairway requirements.

Figure 39. The Sensenbrenner mansion "Tamagami," located on the shores of Lake Winnebago near Neenah, Wisconsin, before it was demolished in the late 1970s.

The Tamagami Door
By Carol E. Stephenson

It's the secret door. It's almost always locked, and there are GPYC members who are unaware of its existence. But wine vault tenants and those who have dined in the wine cellar know it well. It's the wonderful old oak door that guards the entrance to the wine cellar and wine vault room.

The door originally belonged to the late Frank J. Sensenbrenner, who headed Kimberly-Clark Corporation for over twenty-five years as it grew from a small Wisconsin paper mill to the world-class paper products manufacturer that made "Kleenex" a household word. His forty-four-room Tudor-style mansion stood on the shores of Lake Winnebago, near Neenah, Wisconsin. Construction of the mansion began in 1926 and took three years to complete. In its time, it was considered the most imposing private home in the state. The owner called his home *Tamagami*, a local Indian word meaning "home of the chief."

The house was spectacular, with a slate roof from Normandy, France, a staircase of hand-carved Mankato stone, and a leaded glass window from floor to ceiling overlooking the lake. In the basement were a huge wine cellar, a billiard room, and a movie projection room.

When Sensenbrenner died in 1952, he left the estate to Marquette University in Milwaukee. For several years the home was utilized for conferences and retreats, but when upkeep became too expensive, the mansion was torn down in the late 1970s and everything that could be salvaged was sold. The father of GPYC member Dr. Larry Stephenson purchased several items, including two beautiful old doors and a small leaded glass window, which he subsequently gifted to his son.

In 1999, Assistant Manager Mary McLaurin, was supervising construction of the wine cellar. Dr. Stephenson was also involved as one of the founders of the wine vault program. He still owned one of the doors, and when he offered to donate it, Mary enthusiastically agreed that it would be a stunning entry to the cellar. The door was covered in paint and had to be cut down to fit the space, but once it was refinished and the hardware polished, it was clear that it was worth the effort.

The next time you are in the Fo'c'sle, take a peek around the corner and check out the beautiful old door that once graced a stately Wisconsin mansion. A piece of *Tamagami* has found a home at the GPYC.

Figure 40. Assistant Manager Mary McLaurin, right, explains the details of the wine vault program to new vault owners Heidi and Jon Whiteman. The launch of the member wine vault program was held in conjunction with the grand opening of the wine cellar, October 17, 1999.

Figure 41. Looking at the splendid restoration of the door to the wine cellar, it is hard to imagine that someone once covered such beautiful wood with thick layers of paint.

Figure 42. Fleet Captain John Mager hosted the commodore/past commodores, fleet officers, and board members aboard his yacht *More Toys for Us* at the annual Fleet Review in 1999. The yacht served as the flagship for the review.

Also during this time, Commodore Storen and his predecessor, Past Commodore Mark Weber, collaborated closely on renovating the Fo'c'sle room and the bowling alley because collectively those projects cost more money than was available in a single year's budget. To accomplish the project, capital funds from Past Commodore Weber's year and those allocated for Commodore Storen's year were combined, enabling the two officers to complete a project that would make the Club a better place.[31]

Later in the year, Commodore Storen developed a medical issue that came to be known as "commodore-itis:" a heart problem. Storen preferred to call it a "speed bump," although it necessitated open-heart surgery. Commodore Storen's cardiologist, member Dr. Brian Litch, arranged for his surgery to be performed by fellow member Dr. David Martin. Within a week, Storen was back at the Club cheering the swim team at a meet.

A review of the goals and objectives established at the beginning of the year showed that harbor modernization was front and center, as was the need for long-term capital planning. A list of priorities was given to the engineering committee for review, which included replacing the swimming pool, upgrading the tennis courts, purchasing a backup generator, and upgrading the HVAC system. Work continued with an architect on developing plans for a health facility, a 6,000-square-foot building located adjacent to the tennis courts, at an approximate cost of $1.2 million.[32] In addition, the strategic planning committee was tasked with updating the Club's strategic plan based on the 1998 membership survey.

In 1999, a group of Grosse Pointe Shores residents called NYCE (Neighbors Concerned about Yacht Club Expansion) filed suit and halted a proposed addition to the Grosse Pointe Yacht Club harbor. These lakefront property owners cited concerns about the plan from an aesthetic and environmental standpoint. A subsequent vote of Shores residents to approve the joint application by the Village and the Grosse Pointe Yacht Club to work together toward harbor renovation was narrowly defeated. As a result, the Yacht Club and the Village of Grosse Pointe Shores worked independently to restore the shared harbor, with the GPYC board resigned to renovating the harbor within its existing footprint.

Figure 44. Another first-place finish for *Saturn* in the Cruising B Class, 1999 Port Huron-to-Mackinac. Owner/member Wally Tsuha, left, and his crew were getting used to collecting first- place flags.

Figure 43. The crew of *Big Kahuna*, owned by member Jim Tepel, proudly dispays the PHRF C Class flag they received for their first-place finish in the Port Huron-to-Mackinac race, 1999.

Figure 45. Summer of 1999 saw the GPYC hosting the top twenty high school teams from around the nation competing for the High School National Sailing Championship. In this photo, Flying Juniors jockey for position at the starting line.

Also in 1999, the quality of Grosse Pointe Yacht Club's sailing program was recognized by the DRYA, as once again the Club was awarded the Jack Sutton Award for Outstanding Junior Sailing Program for the fourth time in five years. This award recognizes the best DRYA program each year.

GPYC unveiled a newly built wine cellar at a grand opening on October 17, 1999. Construction of the new cellar was paid for through the sale of member wine vaults for vintage storage. The project was led by members Ed Shaw, Dr. Larry and Carol Stephenson, Club Manager Jack Sullivan, and Assistant Manager Mary McLaurin. The cellar not only provided state-of-the-art storage for both Club wine and members' private stock, it also became a great venue for private dinner parties for up to eight people.

The use of cellular phones in the clubhouse was discussed. It was determined that their use in the dining rooms was offensive and it was strongly suggested that members refrain from using them while in any of the Club's dining areas.

Late in the year, at the November annual meeting, James A. Anderson became commodore of the Grosse Pointe Yacht Club. His "to-do" list for the coming year was long and ambitious. As the Club prepared to enter the next millennium, it was apparent that in spite of the challenges of an aging infrastructure and a softening economy, the Grosse Pointe Yacht Club was prepared to stay the course and face whatever storms might lie ahead.

Figure 46. Looking eastward along the south harbor fairway.

Figure 47. Past Commodores Sloane Barbour, Ted Smith, Fred Schriever, John Boll, John DeHayes, Frank McBride, Ralph Kliber, and Mark Weber listen attentively as Fleet Chaplain Father Al Hillebrand blesses the fleet, May 1999.

IMAGE ACKNOWLEDGEMENTS
Chapter Nine

1. Fred Michalik
2. Brennan Schoenherr
3. – 19. GPYC
20. Charlie Davis
21. – 25. GPYC
26. Jim Dorian
27. GPYC
28. *Club Leaders Forum*
29. – 35. GPYC
36. – 37. Jim Dorian

38. GPYC
39. Larry Stephenson
40. GPYC
40. – 41b. Michele Penoyer GPYC photographer
42. Tom Kliber
43. – 45. GPYC
46. Jim Dorian
47. Tom Kliber
48. Jim Dorian

Figure 48. "Room at the mark!" the start of the 1998 Bluenose Regatta.

Figure 1. Members got their first look at the new swimming pool complex via this artist's drawing, which was included in a flyer providing information and also seeking member input for the project. The drawing contains one significant difference from the completed facility: Windows at the base of the pool deck to accommodate meeting rooms that never fully materialized.

By Past Com. James L. Ramsey.

CHAPTER TEN

2000 through 2010

A new millennium and the promise of continued success

Contrary to scenarios of gloom and doom painted by Y2K prophets, the twenty-first century rolled into the Grosse Pointe Yacht Club much the way it did all over the world—joyously and raucously, without electronic meltdowns or global calamity. At midnight, during a festive New Year's Eve party in the Club Ballroom, Commodore James A. Anderson raised his glass, wishing happiness and good fortune for all in the century ahead. The decade of the 1990s had been one of unprecedented prosperity. There was reason to be optimistic.

2000: Let those good times keep on coming

I have long felt that what is good for the Grosse Pointe Yacht Club is good for my community, Grosse Pointe Shores, and the greater Grosse Pointes. I can't imagine Grosse Pointe without the Grosse Pointe Yacht Club. I can't imagine Lake Shore Road without the Grosse Pointe Yacht Club being the prominent feature of that road.

My mother gave me a lot of pieces of advice in short sound bytes that played an important role for me as commodore. I remember when we were deliberating what to do about the swimming pool and, on another occasion, voting on a plan for the harbor: In both of those situations, what came to mind was my mother's quote: 'If you are going to eat a frog, don't look at it too long.' So when you have a problem and you are debating it, don't debate it too long. Just get on with it, make your decision, eat the frog, and go forward.

—Commodore James A. Anderson

The year 2000 arrived with excitement for the future, tempered with sadness for what had come and gone forever. The decade ahead would be filled with its own share of excitement and sadness.

Business began on a bullish note.

Despite wars in Iraq and Yugoslavia, the American economy enjoyed unprecedented growth in the 1990s. Personal income had doubled during the decade, and the Grosse Pointe Yacht Club had prospered accordingly. By 2000, membership totals approached 1,200; monthly Club financials showed record profits; the membership committee welcomed a steady stream of new-member prospects every few weeks; and demand for larger wells for bigger boats in the Club harbor was at an all-time high. The Club was on a roll.

Good times encourage positive thinking. One of Commodore Anderson's first steps was to launch an ambitious strategic plan to guide the Club through the coming decade and beyond. Unlike so many strategic plans that are long on aspiration and short on direction, Anderson's plan gave detailed strategies for achieving specific objectives. He believed that if the GPYC were to continue to fulfill its mission as "a premier yacht club, among the finest in North America," it needed a detailed road map that not only

Figure 2. Commodore James A. Anderson welcomes in the new millennium.

Figure 3. The way it might be. An artist's rendering of an ambitious new harbor proposal with a much-expanded footprint, larger slips, broader fairways and numerous new amenities. After much passionate campaigning for and against the project, including a lawsuit filed by a small group of neighborhood dissidents, Grosse Pointe Shores residents voted not to work with the Club to pursue its completion.

★ ★ ★

Figure 4. Commodore James A. Anderson, 2000.

Figure 5. The new and relocated men's and ladies' restrooms threw some people an embarrassing curve at first.

identified the destination but also showed how to get there. The plan, with its five-year outlook, was adopted and signed by the board of directors as a show of commitment. And while the goals and strategies would be adjusted as circumstances changed, it was clear that strategic planning would be a high-priority item for Club leadership going forward.

Two key elements of the "Anderson Plan" were a larger and significantly upgraded boat harbor and a new swimming complex. Plans for the new harbor had hit a snag earlier when a small group of Grosse Pointe Shores residents organized NYCE (Neighbors Concerned about Yacht Club Expansion), suing the Club over the expanded size of the project. The lawsuit was eventually dismissed without prejudice in 2001, but it did put harbor expansion on hold as planners returned to the drawing board.

Even so, the Club underwent a series of major improvements that year: 11,000 cubic yards dredged from the harbor to counter low lake levels, $300,000 in electrical upgrades to the docks, a new computer system for the clubhouse, and a complete refurbishment of the lobby and

foyer. In seeming support of its progressive attitude, the GPYC was, for the second consecutive three-year time period, named by a nationwide survey of club managers and presidents as the number one yacht club in America, ranking it above such storied places as the San Diego Yacht Club, St. Francis Yacht Club, and New York Yacht Club. The Club was also named the number one private club in the state, ahead of Oakland Hills, the Detroit Athletic Club, and the Country Club of Detroit.[2]

It was some year.

2001: Oops! Wrong water closet

A light but noteworthy moment in Club history occurred when the men's and ladies' restrooms "changed places" during the 2001 lobby makeover. As built in 1929, the men's room was adjacent to

Figure 6. Unlimited raceboat *Miss Tubby's Submarines* wins the Gold Cup in 2001.

Figure 7. The winning boat proudly wore the GPYC burgee through-out the race weekend.

Figure 8. GPYC Manager Jack Sullivan, left, boat promoter Jim Dorian, boat owner Laurie Jones, and Commodore John DeWald pose with the Gold Cup trophy.

what is now the Spinnaker Room, but at that time was the Men's Grill Room, making it convenient for the gentlemen frequenting that part of the Club. Larger than the ladies' room, it boasted nearly a dozen urinals along one wall—way more than needed to satisfy the calls of nature. On the other hand, the original ladies' powder room, located near the stairs to the Rotunda, was too small, and uncomfortable lines formed during large events.

At that point, the house committee asked, "Why not switch the two?" After all, the men didn't need all that room and the ladies would appreciate the added space. Consequently, under Commodore John DeWald's watch, the decision was made to transpose the two. Unfortunately, the power of habit being what it is, some members

forgot about the change. Oblivious to new signage, they walked through a familiar door—into the wrong room. It caused more than a few beet-red faces until members became accustomed to the new arrangement.

The year 2001 also saw the installation of a computerized scoring system in the bowling alley and the first installation of cellular phone transmitters in the Bell Tower that would provide additional income to the Club. (The Bell Tower, one of the highest structures in the Pointes, is an excellent location for such equipment.)

Down on the Detroit River that summer, the hydroplane *Miss Tubby's Submarines* wearing the GPYC burgee won the Gold Cup race. According to Club Manager Jack Sullivan, "A woman who owned a hydroplane raceboat contacted a friend

210

Figure 9. Commodore John E. De Wald, 2001.

Ernie Dossin and *Miss Pepsi*

Ernie Dossin, longtime member of the GPYC, died in 1996 at the age of 80. In 2001, Ernie, his father Russell, and two uncles, Roy and Walter, were posthumously inducted into the Unlimited Hydroplane Hall of Fame. The four men were honored for their years of hydroplane sponsorship that produced many wins and several National High Point Championships for their boats. Ernie also traveled with the teams through all their racing years, serving as crew manager and family representative while continuing to fulfill his duties in the family business. His son, GPYC member Doug Dossin, says, "He was a hands-on team manager and at any race site he could be seen covered in grease from making adjustments on the boat."

The Dossin family came to hydroplane racing through their business, which started in 1898 when Ernest J. Dossin sold freshly grated horseradish from a horse-drawn cart. The product line of Dossin's Food Products expanded over time, and in 1936 the company was awarded the Pepsi Cola franchise for the State of Michigan and northern Ohio.

of the Club to see if we would be interested in being the boat's club sponsor. I said sure, put our burgee on the boat and I'll speak with Commodore DeWald. That would be pretty neat. Well, the boat won the Gold Cup, the oldest boat race in history. The boat and her crew came to the Yacht Club that Sunday after the races. We bought them all drinks and dinner. The boat was displayed in front of the Club for the members to see. We got some very fun, favorable press as a result."

Excessively high water bills were noted that year and new metering equipment was installed to assess the problem.

The most troubling news had to do with the economy. Warnings were rampant about a downturn in the nation's economic health. According to a number of indicators, the glory days of the previous decade would soon come to an end.

Financial warnings or not, the Club's aging aluminum swimming pool was deteriorating quickly and action needed to be taken. A swimming pool development sub-committee was formed, and under the leadership of board member Bob Kay, a series of information and input sessions were held with the membership as plans for the new pool were developed.

Figure 10. Club member Ernie Dossin holding the Gold Cup, right, with driver Chuck Thompson.

Figure 11. *Miss Pepsi*, owned by the Dossin family, at speed on the Detroit River. She was one of a number of Gold Cup racers campaigned by the family.

The Dossins saw hydroplane racing as a public relations vehicle for promoting their business, and in 1946 they leased a boat for one race, the President's Cup in Washington, D.C., named *Pepsi Cola III*. In 1947 they bought a boat that had been built in 1938, reconfigured it so it could accept a surplus WWII Allison airplane engine and named it *Miss Peps V. Peps V* was so named because, for a brief period of time, the American Powerboat Association ruled that boats would not be allowed to have commercial products as names. The Dossins left off the "i," but cleverly brought a curlicue from the "P" around to the end, so the eye would still see Pepsi in the name. The "V," or five, was added because at the time, a bottle of Pepsi sold for five cents. *Peps V* was raced by Danny Foster, also a Hall of Fame inductee, and won several major races, including the 1947 Gold Cup and National High Point Championship.

The first *Miss Pepsi* was built in 1948, and the second, and final, *Miss Pepsi* was built in 1950 by Les

Staudacher from a John Hacker design. The latter was a three-step hydroplane with twin 12-cylinder engines placed nose-to-nose. Between 1950 and 1952, she had nine wins, and took the National High-Point Championship in 1951 and 1952. After sitting out the 1953 and 1954 seasons, she raced again in 1955 and 1956 before retiring. Driver Chuck Thompson would also be destined for the Hall of Fame.

Following their years in boat racing, the Dossin family made a significant contribution to the city of Detroit when the Dossin Great Lakes Museum on Belle Isle became a reality. The museum was devoted to, and continues to be, a premiere resource for Great Lakes history. The final *Miss Pepsi* was brought to the museum and placed in a specially constructed building next to the main building.

Present at the dedication ceremony in 1963, along with many members of the Dossin family, were driver Chuck Thompson and builder Les Staudacher.

■=✖=■

2002: God rest Queen Mum

This was an eventful year—around the world, in outer space, and at the Club.

In retaliation for the horrific September 11, 2001, terrorist attacks, the United States invaded Afghanistan in what would become our nation's most prolonged military conflict.

In England, Queen Mother Elizabeth, affectionately known as "Mum," passed away at age 101. Her daughter, Princess Margaret, predeceased her earlier that same year at age 71.

On Mars, significant traces of what appeared to be ice—life-giving water—were found by the *Mars Odyssey* space probe.

At the Club, the second-longest-serving general manager, Jack Sullivan, announced his departure, ending fifteen years on the job. He was replaced by Mike Mooney, former general manager of the Detroit and Annapolis Yacht Clubs.

The Binnacle dining room, which began as an open-air porch, received a major remodeling—the most ambitious redo since it was first enclosed in the 1950s. Club member and decorator D. J. Kennedy transformed its casual ambience—a kind term for worn and shabby—into a place of luxury, with dark woodwork, hanging chandeliers, and high-end tapestries.

On July 4 the *Mariner*, a bronze sculpture depicting a heroic captain at the helm of a sailing ship, was dedicated in the courtyard. Donated by Past Commodore John Boll and his wife, Marlene, the sculpture would form the focal point of a formal garden that would greet members and guests. At this same ceremony, the bell in the Club tower, which hadn't rung in decades, pealed out ship's time, thanks to its new electronic striker mechanism.

Farewell old swimming pool; bring on the new

Plans for a new swimming pool had been set in motion two years earlier by then-Commodore Jim Anderson, who appointed a committee to study the project. The shortcomings of the old pool quickly became apparent: it was too shallow at the deep end to allow the safe use of a diving board and too shallow at the other end to permit full underwater turns by competitive swimmers. The pool was also too narrow, with room for only five swimming lanes. In addition, there was limited deck space for sunbathers and no wading place for toddlers.

A new swimming pool complex could solve all of these problems and give members amenities

Figure 12. Commodore Carl Rashid pulls the chain connected to the plug that begins draining the old swimming pool for the last time. It was both a sad and happy moment.

Figure 13. Past Commodore John A. and Marlene Boll and Grace and Commodore Carl Rashid at the dedication of *The Mariner*.

unmatched by those of any facility in the area. It would also be the largest capital expenditure in Club history. According to Commodore Carl Rashid Jr., "As commodore, one of the first initiatives I undertook was to form three task forces: a swimming pool task force, a harbor renovation task force, and a capital funding task force. I did that primarily because all three were in committee at the time, and none of them seemed to be moving very fast. I thought if we were really going to get this pool [project] going, as we should, we needed a task force. The purpose was to get people together who have the

knowledge and expertise, including our outside consultants, to allow them to think out of the box, to meet as frequently as they had to meet, to get the project on target."

Construction of the Club's third outdoor swimming pool officially began on a Sunday afternoon in September under the watch of Commodore Rashid. A party was organized. Revelers raised their voices in disharmony to a song titled "Kiss the Pool Goodbye," written for the occasion by member Bill Frost. Past Commodore Ralph Kliber, who had presided over the building of the second swimming pool, was

Figure 14. Commodore Carl Rashid Jr., 2002.

on hand dressed as King Neptune. At the appointed moment, Commodore Rashid gave the word and the plug in the old pool was pulled.

As the water level began to drop, a number of members felt compelled to jump in for one last sentimental dip. Above the laughter, a few members began singing "Auld Lang Syne" and were soon joined by others. Amid the gaiety, there was the sad realization that this was truly an end, not just a beginning. The next day, work crews began demolition. Days later, the old pool was gone.

The new swimming pool takes shape

Construction now began in earnest. A huge barge was brought into the harbor and positioned on the north side of the clubhouse where Shoreline dock normally stood. The barge was secured, then filled with water to bring it level with the Club break-wall. Steel ramps were welded into place, connecting the barge with the shore and creating a roadway that heavy equipment could use to access the construction site.

The excavation process was not easy. The land on which the Club was built is mostly fill, a good portion of which turned out to be industrial spoil. Shovels uncovered pieces of old buildings: steel window casings, stairwells, plumbing, and the like. Some thought that what was being unearthed was actually part of the old Hudson Motor Company, but no pieces of Hudson automobiles were discovered. (In fact, that building was demolished in 1961, long after the fill at the Yacht Club was put in place.)

As the dig descended below lake level, water began pouring into the excavation. To deal with the water and the unsteady soil surrounding the excavation, steel sheeting was driven deep into the ground, forming a dam to keep the excavation from becoming a premature swimming pool. Dam or not, large pumps were still needed to keep up with peripheral leakage. In earlier times the pumps would have simply returned the unwanted water to the lake — but not in an environmentally conscious twenty-first century. Every gallon pumped out of the site had to be fed into massive filtration equipment towed into position by 18-wheelers. The water that emerged from the filtering process was clean as tap water, but it still could not be returned to the lake. Instead it had to be hauled to the City of Detroit and disposed of by the Water and Sewage Department.

With the arrival of fall, the Club changed command and the project came under the watch of Commodore James Ramsey. He hoped that construction would be aided by a mild winter like the ones that preceded it. His wish was not to be granted.

2003: The ice cometh

The winter of 2003 brought heavy snow and plunging temperatures that besieged work crews and equipment. As the frigid weeks wore on, diners in the Binnacle looked out in dismay at a huge, ugly hole in the ground surrounded by hills of frozen dirt. *We're spending how much on—this?*

Progress was slow, but by late winter the time had come to pour the concrete that would form the swimming pool structure. It would be an act of incredible industrial choreography: one hundred truckloads of concrete made the trip up the Club drive and across the deck of the barge to the excavation.

Figure 15. Construction of the new swimming pool took place in 2003 during one of the harshest winters in recent history. What began as a huge, watery hole in the ground gradually evolved into a grid of steel-reinforced concrete surrounding the pool basin. At one point, someone remarked that it looked like the foundation for a high-rise office building.

Figure 16. Commodore James L. Ramsey, 2003

Spring arrived on March 21 without any letup in the cold. The construction crews pressed on, knowing they were behind schedule to meet the May 31 grand opening. Days of rain followed the snow. Memorial Day came and went; the official opening of the swimming pool was reset to the July 4 weekend.

Finally, by the end of June, the swimming pool complex neared completion. Commodore Ramsey remembered watching the new pool filling with fresh water and the finishing touches being put on the surrounding sundeck. Just then, member George Milidrag's 131-foot mega-yacht, *Princess Tina*, arrived in the harbor, back from its winter stay in Florida. The yacht's arrival was pure coincidence, but for Ramsey it felt like a sign of affirmation: the new pool complex, with all its headaches and delays, its time and cost overruns, was at last done, and done well: the pool had eight lanes, each 25 meters in length, with water depth ranging from 4 to 12 feet; there was a one-meter diving board; also a water fountain. A kiddies' wading pool rounded out the complex. The Grosse Pointe Yacht Club would be a better place for it.

Something we saw during my year was a little disturbing, but it tells you something about the changing nature of this club and maybe other clubs—that, for the first time, our Social members surpassed our Active members in total. I took it as a sign that building the pool was a good thing, that we are a yacht club first and foremost, but we can never overlook the fact that we are also a family club and that we have to appeal to a greater diversity of tastes and values than just boating. It isn't enough anymore to have just a dock and boat wells and maybe some fuel pumps. You really have to be a full-service club, at least when you're the Grosse Pointe Yacht Club.

One of my favorite stories about the Club has to do with the first time I ever saw it. I was six years old. World War II had just ended, and I was riding in the car with my mother, out Lake Shore, looking at this beautiful body of water and asking her if that was the ocean. Lo and behold, along the horizon appeared this incredible cathedral-like structure with a steeple jutting into the sky. I had never seen a building that grand before, and I asked her, 'Mom, does a king live there ?' Well, as we all know, mothers are truthful about all things. She looked me squarely in the eye and said, 'Yes.' — Commodore James L. Ramsey

And now the bill ...

Building the new swimming pool was one thing; paying for it was another. The task of servicing long-term debt would fall to subsequent boards into the next decade.

The new pool had originally been budgeted at a cost of $4 million, with a mid-course adjustment to $5 million. The final, as-built cost was $6 million, to be financed over ten years. To service the debt, the board of directors approved a $750 annual assessment for Active and Social members, with smaller assessments for other classes of membership. Thus, everyone in the Club was asked to help pay for the new pool over the following five years. Hardly anyone was happy about it, but it had to be done.

Figure 17. The finished simming pool complex took no time in connecting with young and old, swimmers and sun worshippers alike.

Even with the assessment, the Club would have to cut expenses and find new sources of revenue to pay for the project. An influx of new members was needed, but the economy was beginning to experience a downturn. An alternative plan was called for. It was now belt-tightening time at the Grosse Pointe Yacht Club.

The situation was even more difficult because of an unexpected decline in membership that had begun several years earlier when Commodore Rashid discovered that nearly one hundred of the Club's Junior and Intermediate members were incorrectly classified. The members in question should have been fleeted-up to Social and Active status years earlier but had not been because of a clerical error. The mistake cost the Club tens of thousands of dollars in dues income. It also put the Club in the uncomfortable position of asking these members to immediately fleet-up and pay a portion of what was considered their unpaid dues. When confronted, many of the members resigned.

Figure 18. The GPYC's own *Ship to Shore Cookbook*, with recipes supplied exclusively by members.

Figure 19. One of many spectacular weather displays seen at the Club, caused by endless combinations of temperature, sunlight, and water.

As a result, the Club did not recoup the lost dues money and lost scores of younger members as well.

The year 2003 has been described in retrospect as "The Perfect Storm," recalling the chilling book and movie of the same name. And in some ways it was. As board members assembled for a meeting, they were informed that the United States was again at war with Iraq over allegations of weapons of mass destruction.

Adding to the turmoil, the U.S. economy went into a long-anticipated slide, bringing unemployment, business failures, and frequent use of the "R"-word: Recession. At the Club, another "R"-word prevailed: Resignations.

But amid the gloom, there were also bright spots.

On the eve of Fleet Review Weekend 2003, a massive power outage paralyzed the eastern half of the United States, plunging southeastern Michigan and the Club into darkness on the eve of the Club's biggest social event. The review was immediately postponed until the following weekend. Still, GPYC members had no electricity at home and were unable to put gasoline in their cars. In response, Club chefs set up an outdoor barbecue and dispensed food and cold beverages to hungry members. Meanwhile, Harbor Master Alex Turner used the pumps at the Gas Dock (connected to an emergency generator) to fill containers so that members could get gas for their cars.

Then there was the East Lawn. As the new swimming pool neared completion, it became apparent that the Club's long-neglected East Lawn, which adjoins the pool deck on the north and east, was going to look like a sore thumb next to the new construction. But there was no money in the budget for new grass, much less landscaping. Then a member had the idea of selling personalized brick pavers to members. The idea soon expanded beyond bricks, allowing members to put their names everywhere on the East Lawn rejuvenation project: on flower beds, sculptures, park benches, and shrubbery. The plan was a success. Members stepped up to donate, and their purchases enabled the creation of the garden-like setting that is the East Lawn today. It was one more example of Club *esprit de corps* overcoming adversity.

And for the third straight time, with rankings being voted in three-year intervals, the GPYC was named the top yacht club in America.

2004: The clubhouse turns 75

While much of the nation's attention was focused on the upcoming presidential race between George W. Bush and John Kerry, members were hard at work planning the 75th anniversary celebration for the GPYC clubhouse. Commodore Ted Huebner and his wife, Mary, were determined to make the occasion a memorable one, and they had dozens of volunteers to assist them. The event was scheduled for the July 4 weekend, just as it had been in 1929 when the clubhouse first opened. The anniversary of the opening of the clubhouse was significant because, in the eyes of some, that Grand Opening was the true beginning of the GPYC.

To mark the occasion, a 75th anniversary history book was published, chronicling the Club from its roots to 2004. And while GPYC histories had been compiled at various milestones in the Club's history — at twenty-five and fifty-five years, for example — the 75th anniversary book broke new ground with the detail and depth of its coverage.

The celebration party, too, was noteworthy. There was an official tribute from the State of Michigan signed by the governor, a baseball game between members and staff, a Celtic bagpiper band supplying music, an antique boat show, and a huge fireworks display. There was

Figure 20. General Manager Mike Mooney, left, and Past Commodore Sloane Barbour, center, welcome America's Cup winner Dennis Conner.

Figure 21. A large spotlight was used to project the Club logo on the tower during the 75th clubhouse anniversary celebration.

Figure 22. A commemorative fountain was graciously given to the Club at the 75th anniversary of the clubhouse by Dr. James and Suzanne Acheson.

Figure 23. The Club's second history book was published in honor of the occasion. It focused primarily on the years between 1929, when the clubhouse was completed, and 2004.

even a pie-eating contest, with the commodore himself going face down in a plate of banana cream goodness to celebrate the occasion. And of course throughout the weekend, there were copious amounts of food and drink, enjoyed by all. The party ended with the dedication of a commemorative 75th anniversary fountain, donated by member Dr. James Acheson, which resides just inside the front gate of the Club.

Behind the festivities, however, there was serious work going on.

In response to surveys showing member concern about the quality and consistency of food at the Club, a new head chef, Rob Carney, was hired from the Annapolis Yacht Club, where he had worked with manager Mike Mooney. Carney's assignment was twofold: provide a dining experience that would make GPYC the quintessential place to dine in the Grosse Pointes and improve the Club kitchen's financial performance.

At the same time, Club management was given a tough mandate to cut expenses and improve operating efficiency while not compromising programs and services to the members. A goal was set to raise the membership total back to 850 to offset declines in the roster in previous years.

Figure 25. Commodore W. Theodore Huebner, 2004.

Plans were also approved to install a permanent bar in one of the gazebos on the new pool deck. The temporary bar that began as an experiment the previous year proved to be a hit. At very little cost, a real poolside bar with electricity, refrigeration, and mood lighting looked as though it could be a profitable attraction in the summer.

Moreover, members seemed to be responding favorably to the new chef's innovative Eastern Shore style of cooking. Food and beverage losses were beginning to slow, and diner satisfaction scores were improving. In the Club dining rooms at least, things were looking up.

2005: Incentives, fitness, and debate

In an effort to increase Active membership, the Club introduced an incentive program for Social B and C members that allowed them to fleet up to Active without the traditional transfer fee. It was the first in what would become a series of initiatives proposed by the membership committee over the coming years to attract and retain members while the economy was in the doldrums.

Figure 24. Commodore Ted and Mary Huebner dressed up in Prohibition-era attire to recall the Roaring Twenties.

Figure 26. Commodore Bruce Fralick and his bridge officers salute the fleet during the 2005 Review Weekend.

Averse to discounts, board members shifted their focus to an onsite health and fitness center. According to reports, potential new members had frequently mentioned this as a critical make-or -break factor in deciding whether to join the Club. Club leaders had for many years discussed the idea of a fitness center somewhere on Club grounds to give health-conscious members a place to work out. The problem was, no one seemed to be able to agree on the location and scope of such a facility. Some wanted it inside the clubhouse, with minimal equipment and overhead expense. Others argued that such a center should have its own dedicated building, separate from the club-house, so that ladies, *sans* makeup, could run in, do their daily workout, and get on with their day. Still other advocates asserted that a premiere yacht club should have a state-of-the-art facility with top-of-the-line health equipment and professional staff.

Unfortunately, as Commodore Bruce Fralick observed, there was no money for such an under-taking—even a modest one, for that matter.

As the debate wore on, the subject shifted to a back burner, as it had in the past.

Figure 27. Chef Robert Carney arrives from the Annapolis Yacht Club as the new head of Food and Beverage at the Club.

Figure 28. Commodore Bruce E. Fralick, 2005.

Improvement in the kitchen; harbor discussion continues

One topic that provoked no controversy in 2005 was the presence of the new head chef, Robert Carney. After just one year on the job, he was having a positive impact on the Club's *à la carte* dining business. Food and beverage income was up and members were returning to the dining rooms. It was beginning to appear that it might just be possible for a private club (contrary to the opinion of many club experts) to actually make money from its restaurants.

The harbor, as the Club's most reliable source of profit, was under constant discussion at this time. Since expanding the footprint of the harbor was no longer on the table, there was considerable debate as to how to maximize the existing space for the benefit of boats and boaters.

Yet another harbor plan, showing new dock configurations by yet another architectural planning firm, was brought forward for discussion.

One issue of consideration in any new GPYC harbor design was the presence—or absence—of a second entrance. There were a number of factors favoring the second entrance, which would be located in the East Wall and protected by a parallel stone breakwater. On the positive side, the entrance would eliminate the need for the drawbridge—a constant source of concern because of reliability and convenience issues—and streamline boat traffic in the east end of the harbor. On the other hand, the entrance would be costly—at least $1 million, perhaps $2 million—to construct.

The debate continued as Commodore Robert Kay took the helm.

2006: The Club fills in after Hurricane Katrina

When one of the deadliest hurricanes in U.S. history slammed into the Gulf Coast in August 2005, it claimed the Southern Yacht Club in New Orleans, the intended host of the 2006 U.S. Youth Sailing Championship (USYSC). Although the SYC would rebuild over time, the damage to the clubhouse and harbor was so severe that there was no way the event could be

Figure 29. "I paid how much for this?" Member Dr. Larry Stephenson hangs on for dear life in a Jersey Skiff race on the Detroit River during Gold Cup weekend. His ride was purchased at a Gold Cup fund-raiser held at the GPYC. The doctor's boat won the skiff race.

Figure 30. The Up North Rendezvous took place on Drummond Island in 2003, with two of the Club's largest yachts participating: Elena Ford's *Unity,* left, and George Milidrag's *Princess Tina.*

Figure 31. The remainder of Bailey's Drummond Island harbor was also filled with GPYC boats during the rendezvous.

held there in the near future. An alternative venue was needed — and found — at the Grosse Pointe Yacht Club.

Earlier, the GPYC had applied to host the USYSC regatta, but the nod had been given to the Louisiana club. In the wake of Katrina, the U.S. Sailing Committee called the GPYC to ask whether the Club would now host the event. The board considered the request but was reluctant to commit because the time needed to plan and organize a national regatta, hosting 100 boats and 150 sailors from all over the country, was so short. Moreover, the Club had already committed to host the MICSA finals and the Mallory Cup sailing competition for high school students from around the Midwest that same summer. Attempting to stage three major events in the same time frame could be asking for trouble. In the end, the GPYC sailing committee stepped forward and agreed to host the regatta. Board members crossed their fingers and gave their consent. The Mallory Cup would be contended in May; the USYSC event would happen in late June; and the MICSA finals would follow in late July. It was a daunting task in the middle of the Club's busiest

Figure 32. Commodore Robert J. Kay, 2006.

season. But all three competitions came off flawlessly that summer because once again, as they had so often in the past, members stepped up to volunteer their help.

Figure 33. When Hurricane Katrina devastated large areas of the deep south, the 2006 U.S. Youth Sailing Championship was hastily moved from New Orleans to the GPYC. Despite short notice, the event turned out to be a great success.

Meanwhile, Commodore Kay found time to implement an idea he had been considering before he took office: a series of one-on-one sessions with members who had something to say to the commodore. Commodore Kay made himself available in the manager's office from 6:00 to 7:00 pm every Wednesday. Members were invited to come in and say whatever was on their mind. In retrospect, Kay admitted he didn't know what he might be confronted with during those first sessions—anger, threats, impossible demands, perhaps. But that was not the case. The vast majority of the members who took him up on his offer to talk wanted to do exactly that — talk. They sat down, expressed themselves, frequently offered constructive ideas, and then shook hands, wishing him the best.

One day at a time

Otherwise, 2006 was a year like many others in the life of the Club, with an agenda of issues large and small that needed to be addressed to ensure the day-to-day functioning of the organization. And if it is true that just showing up

is a measure of greatness, so too is attention to detail — to the unheralded tasks that accrue into significance over time. GPYC records are filled with such meaningful trifles: a new oven for the kitchen, wallpaper for a locker room, dredging in the harbor, weed control, sewage system repairs. The willingness of the Club's governors, managers, and employees to deal with these mundane challenges underscores the fact that the true measure of a premiere yacht club is not so much in the elegance of its trappings or the glitter of its historic events but rather in the way it goes to work each day.

The first Wake-Up Wednesday was held in fall 2006, featuring a talk, usually by an invited member, on some aspect of his or her career or business. It was the beginning of a series of informative Wednesday morning get-togethers that remain a popular feature of the Club at this writing.

Last but not least that year, the board resolved to end the member assessment for the swimming pool by the following year and to pay off the balance of the loan inside the allotted ten-year

Figure 34. Fleet Review Weekend 2006 featured outdoor movies for the kids.

Figure 35. An Otsego Ski Weekend wouldn't be complete without a hike to Beaver Cabin for rest and refreshment.

time frame. It would require fiscal discipline of the highest order. The directors were bound and determined to achieve their goal.

And once again, for the fourth straight three-year interval and despite adverse times, the Club was voted in an independent survey as the top yacht club in the country.

2007: Letting the light shine in

I see a club that has survived and will continue to survive. It's no secret that we built up a good, solid rainy day fund some years ago, and it's still there. Even though we've been through some tough economic times in the last three or four years, we have not had to dip into it. That's through a series of good boards and good management, and I think we're in a position to go forward. We have had a couple of real good surveys [of the membership], and the board is looking at how they can implement them.
—Commodore J. Dennis Andrus

One important issue that had come before the board in 2006 was the replacement of the glass in the Ballroom windows. The three twenty-foot-high windows were one of the most striking features of the Ballroom's gothic revival architecture. But time had taken its toll on these intricately shaped structures since they had been installed more than seventy-five years earlier. The wood frames—no fewer than sixty of them—were rotted to the point where there was little more than layers of paint holding them together, and they were constantly leaking air in and out of the clubhouse. From a safety standpoint, it was only a matter of time before a strong wind might blow the panes of glass completely out—or worse yet, in.

Finding a craftsman who could restore the frames and replace the glass was a task that fell to member Don Endres, who served on the engineering committee. Endres knew of professional woodworker Mark Jarrett. Jarrett would build the new windows in his shop, using

Figure 36. Commodore J. Dennis Andrus, 2007

modern insulated glass with low-e coating. Then he would bring them to the Club and raise them into position on scaffolding erected onsite. The job would take several months and cost more than $150,000. Despite a tight capital budget, the go-ahead was given. The work was performed flawlessly, on time and on budget. The new windows were finished just in time for the spring start-up. Commodore Andrus, who presided during the project, recalls that when the old windows were being removed, a Prohibition-era pint whiskey bottle was found behind one of the frames where it had been stashed for over seventy-five years. And yes, it was empty.

Another item of discussion at the board table that year was the idea of an affiliation between the GPYC and another club, or clubs, in the area. The issue had come to light in an article published in a club management magazine. The article contended that in order to satisfy the diverse demands of potential new members, private clubs should consider alliances with other clubs that enable them to offer a wider variety of attractions such as golf, indoor tennis, equestrian sports, or fitness facilities. Under that scenario, a given club would not need to invest hundreds of thousands of dollars to create, say, an indoor swimming pool but instead "share" one at another club that was so equipped.

The article also indicated that it was not necessary for two clubs to merge and compromise their identities. In theory, the two clubs would form a cooperative effort that, for very few dollars invested, would allow them to broaden their palette of programs and services and become more attractive to potential members.

It so happened there were two clubs in the Grosse Pointes that might be ripe for such an affiliation. The clubs in question (which will remain anonymous) were contacted to see if there was any interest on their part. There was. Several exploratory sessions were held. But discussions soon stalled, and that was the end of it, for the time being.

In the meantime, the Club was continuing to explore the idea of a health and fitness center of its own somewhere on Club grounds. A feasibility study was approved and funds were set aside to create a plan for the facility if the study indicated that the board should proceed.

Elsewhere, plans to renovate the harbor in partnership with the Village of Grosse Pointe Shores were put on hold. Approval for the second harbor entrance — once the Club decided it actually wanted the entrance — would have to come from the State Department of Environmental Quality (DEQ), and the application process would take time. Moreover, even optimistic estimates put the cost of a totally renovated harbor at nearly $10 million. Until the economy recovered, and until membership totals returned to 1990s levels, an all-new harbor for the Club was not in the cards.

2008: New East Wall dockage and a new general manager

Instead, emphasis this year would be on dredging to make the old harbor sufficiently deep during periods of low lake levels. In addition, a plan was brought forward to reconfigure the wells along the East Wall to accommodate yachts of

Figure 37. Restoring the intricate windows in the Ballroom was a meticulous process.

GPYC

Figure 39. Commodore David E. Martin, M.D., 2008

Figure 38 The completed Ballroom windows overlooking the courtyard behind *The Mariner*.

one hundred feet or more. The move would make the GPYC harbor one of the few "big boat" harbors on the eastern Great Lakes. The consensus was that the presence of prestigious large yachts in the harbor—along with the revenue they would generate—would be good for the Club. The board, under Commodore David Martin, M.D. resolved to move forward with the idea.

Earlier that year, General Manager Mike Mooney announced his resignation. He decided to return to the East Coast to supervise construction of a new high-end yacht club and then become its manager. The search for a new manager began immediately. It ended several months later with the selection of Thomas G. Trainor CCM who previously managed the Detroit Yacht Club (DYC), just as Mike Mooney had. Mr. Trainor would be the Club's twelfth general manager.

The ever-popular Club bowling lanes which had undergone a major rebuild in 1999, were again in need of attention. But in a cash-tight environment, there were no funds available for the task. In response, seven members who were keen bowling enthusiasts pledged more than $35,000 to have the lanes refinished.

The Club continued to note unusually high water bills from the Shores Village. The bills were totally out of line with what was known about the Club's historic water consumption. The Club hired an independent engineer to analyze and evaluate the situation.

Meanwhile, the membership committee, under the leadership of members Cathy Champion, Marita Grobbel, and Peter Gleason, was hard at work trying to find ways to attract new members. Responding to their promotional efforts, 75 new members joined the Club in 2008.

That same year, the country was hit by the worst financial crisis since the Great Depression. It was triggered by the fall of investment banking giant Lehman Brothers. More banks followed suit, and soon Wall Street was in free fall.

In Detroit, auto production slowed drastically. General Motors and Chrysler were hemorrhaging money and would eventually need a federal bailout to survive bankruptcy. Soon the recession in southeastern Michigan was more severe than in

Figure 40. General Manager Thomas G. Trainor CCM arrives at GPYC in 2008.

Figure 41. The clubhouse standing proud and tall over a bevy of new boats being displayed during Yachtsmen's Weekend.

Figure 42. The crew aboard Steven Nadeau's *Brandilee* scrambles to weather during the Bluenose Regatta.

any region of the nation. Private clubs in the region were in survival mode, cutting hours, reducing staff, discounting initiations, and hunkering down.

Through it all, however, GPYC managed to maintain its composure.

The annual GPYC Yachtsmen's Weekend, which had grown over twenty years to become one of the largest in-the-water spring boat shows in Southeast Michigan, changed its name to the Great Lakes Boating Festival. And even though area boat dealers were hard-hit by the recession, in 2008 the festival expanded into a three-day event and offered a host of new attractions, including wine tastings, art exhibits, and educational seminars for first mates. The rebranded boat show managed to raise over $110,000 that May weekend, with proceeds going to the Junior Sailing Program.

In other waters, the Club's annual "Up North" rendezvous took place for the first time at the new state harbor at St. Ignace, nearly three hundred miles to the north. Despite the economy and the high cost of marine fuel, the event was well attended. The group of GPYC boaters who traditionally cruised the northern waters of the Great Lakes in the summer was unfazed. St. Ignace would be one more on a list of Club cruising destinations that included the North Channel, Mackinac Island, Cheboygan, Drummond Island, Traverse City, and Charlevoix.

2009: Honoring those who served

Just before taking office in November 2008, Commodore James "Jimmy" Taylor Jr. acted on a conviction he held through much of his life: Respect for veterans in the service of their country. Pulling together a group of members with military experience, he organized the Club's first Veterans' Recognition Brunch. Invitations were sent to members and their friends and families to gather at the Club and share a few hours of appreciation for military veterans. All branches of the U.S. military were welcome. The

Figure 43. Commodore James L. Taylor Jr., 2009.

inaugural event was held on Sunday, November 9, prior to Veterans' Day. The Ballroom was patriotically decorated for the occasion; World War II–era music played over the sound system; and mess tables of GI "chow" were prepared by the kitchen. Afterward, veterans wearing red carnations were invited to share stories from their service experience. The brunch was an over-

whelming success. An encore event was held the following year. Thanks to Commodore Taylor, the Veterans' Recognition Brunch is now a regular part of the Club calendar.

Like the commodores and boards that preceded them, Commodore Taylor and his board were deeply concerned with keeping the Club afloat by cutting costs and finding ways to keep and attract members. A ten-year cash projection by member and economic analyst Dick Bania indicated that the Club needed to cut costs by $230,000 that year, and efforts were being made to achieve that goal.

The board also decided to reorganize the membership committee by creating three subcommittees within it: retention, recruitment, and employee feedback. In addition, the committee created Member Appreciation Week, and another subcommittee was formed to personally call resigning members. The committee's task was not to convince the member to reconsider but to determine the real reason for the resignation. In the end, after a number of calls, the group concluded the problem wasn't the Club—it was the economy.

Amid all the economic turmoil, however, Fleet Review Weekend in August that year was festive and well attended. A Club tradition returned with the "Showboat," a barge decorated to resemble a riverboat that was brought into the

Figure 44. The first Veterans' Brunch was organized at the Club in 2009 by Commodore Jimmy Taylor Jr. It is now an annual event.

Figure 45. Rear Commodore Bob Rader, member Tony Soave, and Commodore Jimmy Taylor Jr. enjoy the view from Mr. Soave's motor yacht *Mallard,* flagship for Fleet Review 2009.

Figure 46. Member Dr. Larry Stephenson, Past Commodore Jim Anderson, board member Bob Joslyn, and Past Commodore Jim Ramsey pay a visit to the 1,013-foot freighter *Paul R. Tregurtha* as it unloads at St. Clair, Michigan. The *Tregurtha* is known as "Queen of the Lakes" because she is the longest of the Great Lakes thousand-footers and has the best guest accommodations.

Figure 47. "It fits!" Member Dr. Gary Bill's spouse, Kim, tries on a Ferrari during the annual Auto Preview.

Figure 48. Members proudly show their colors before a U-M/MSU football game.

harbor for the occasion. The showboat had been a center of attention at Fleet Reviews in bygone years, in part because there was a female mannequin in the wheelhouse that did not appear to be clothed. The showboat that arrived for the 2009 celebration was devoid of any mannequin, dressed or otherwise.

The Club election that fall produced a tie between two candidates for the board. A coin toss decided who would be admitted. Member John Seago won the toss over Blaise Klenow and became the new board member. Later the following year,

a vacancy occurred on the board and Mr. Klenow was appointed to fill the slot. Two months afterward, he won election to the board and today (2014) he is rear commodore of the Club.

And for the fifth straight time, GPYC was voted by the Club Leaders Forum the finest yacht club in America—a distinction the Club would hold for fifteen consecutive years. (For a better understanding of the selection/election process conducted by Club Leaders Forum, please refer to endnote 1 on page 429.)

Figure 49. The bowling center underwent a major refurbishment in 2005 — one of many upgrades since the first alleys were installed in 1940.

Figure 50. The Lakeshore Room was completely redecorated in 2010 as part of a regular plan of maintenance and renewal.

Figure 51. GPYC members during a Club Rendezvous in front of the Crew's Nest at Put-In-Bay.

2010: Lady at the helm; fine art on the walls

My advice to future commodores is to stay the course and [to] build camaraderie among your team that goes beyond the board of directors to the spouses and past commodores because there is a wealth of history there. You are the captain of the ship, and it is up to you to guide it [along] the right course. You have one year to do that after many years of planning leading up to it… and know that it is a full-time job in itself.

—Past Commodore Mary Treder Lang

The first woman to govern the GPYC took office in late 2009 when Mary Treder Lang was elected commodore.

An accountant by trade, Treder Lang focused her efforts on continuing to preserve the financial health of the Club. A subcommittee was established, headed by Secretary William Vogel, to develop a plan of action should the recession continue indefinitely. A long-range capital expenditure plan for the Club looking out to 2017 was also created. And to make the transition to the chairs easier for incoming flag officers, the order of treasurer and secretary was reversed so that the newest officer would serve as secretary instead of treasurer. Under the new plan, James N. Martin, who had served as treasurer the previous year, would now serve a second term as club treasurer. Martin, now commodore (in 2014), is the only officer in recent history to serve twice as treasurer and never as secretary.

To preserve the viability of the Club's revenue-producing rooms, the board approved a long-overdue renovation of the Lakeshore Room. Interior designer and member Elisabeth Meda coordinated and supervised the project.

Figure 52. Ladies Book Club members gather for a talk by local author Margaret Carroll as part of their regular get-togethers.

Figure 53. Commodore Mary Treder Lang, 2010.

With continuing focus on membership, a new member marketing initiative, "Mission Possible," was unveiled. Its goal: 48 new members. Under the program, new Active and Social members would be able to defer payment of their initiation fee for twelve months with no service fee. The reasoning was simple: get new members in the door. Once in, they will want to stay. After twelve months, it was hoped, the recession would begin to ease.

However, despite everyone's efforts, the inflow of new members could not offset the attrition, and membership at the Club dropped below the 800 mark.

Several months earlier, talks were restarted with a club in the area about a possible "shared services" agreement to see if such an affiliation might be of mutual benefit.

Discussions also continued with a private consulting firm to analyze what the Club should be doing to meet future expectations of members and prospects. The focus of their study would be the clubhouse, to determine what new features and attractions might be developed there. In the meantime, a long-range planning committee of

Club members had been at work on a parallel path. Two topics of special interest were a health and fitness center to attract new members and a redesigned bar in the Spinnaker Room that would "wow" patrons and generate added business. The two planning groups would compare notes and coordinate efforts.

The year drew to a close on a positive note with the confirmation that the Club's already impressive collection of artwork would grow considerably with the addition of nautical paintings on long-term loan at no charge from the Dossin Great Lakes Museum. The paintings, primarily of sailing ships done by historically significant marine artists, would hang in prominent locations throughout the clubhouse, enhancing its yacht club decor.

And so the first decade of the new millennium came to an end, with a leaner Grosse Pointe Yacht Club persevering despite hard times. The period was a sobering one for Club members and staff alike. But what had come out of it was a new sense of financial discipline, together with operating efficiencies that probably would never have happened without the challenge of adversity.

Figure 54. Olympic sailing team member Carrie Howe, winner of collegiate, national, and international sailing competitions, learned the early skills of her sport at the Club. She was named 2008 Yachtsman of the Year for her achievements.

Figure 55. Lightning flashes behind the clubhouse on a summer evening.

IMAGE ACKNOWLEDGEMENTS
Chapter Ten

1. – 4. GPYC

5. Jim Dorian

6. – 8. Greg Campbell

9. GPYC

10. – 11. Courtesy of the Detroit Historical Society

12. – 13. Tom Kliber

14. GPYC

15. Jim Dorian

16. GPYC

17. Shelley G. Schoenherr

18. Greg Campbell, Cynthia Naughton

19. Tom Kliber

20. GPYC

21. Shelley G. Schoenherr.

22. GPYC

23. Jim Dorian

24. – 25. GPYC

26. Tom Kliber

27. GPYC photographer Michele Penoyer

28. GPYC

29. Larry Stephenson

30.– 32. GPYC

33. GPYC photographer Michele Penoyer

34. Tom Kliber

35. – 37. GPYC

38. GPYC photographer Michele Penoyer

39. GPYC

40. – 42. Jim Dorian

43. GPYC

44. GPYC photographer Michele Penoyer

45. Mandy Wegner

46. *Tregurtha's* captain Tom McMullen

47. Jim Dorian

48. GPYC

49. GPYC photographer Michele Penoyer

50. Jim Dorian

51. GPYC

52. GPYC photographer Michele Penoyer

53. – 54. GPYC

55. Tom Kliber

Figure 1. A spectacular pyrotechnic display lit up the night sky in honor of the Club's centennial year. The salvos blasted and boomed for over thirty minutes.

By Past Com. James L. Ramsey.

2011 through 2014

2011: A new decade brings new optimism

As the economy goes, so goes the Grosse Pointe Yacht Club.

Signs that the U.S. recession was beginning to move in a positive direction had begun the previous year. Retail sales showed modest gains as far back as the fall of 2009. In Michigan, automobile production was beginning to increase. At GPYC, debt dropped below the $1 million mark for the first time in six years. The Club was on track to be debt-free the following year.

For incoming Commodore Robert L. Rader Jr., that was encouraging news. A previous survey of the membership had shown high levels of satisfaction with most aspects of the Club, but also pointed out areas of needed improvement. It was time to tweak the Club's strategic plan to put the facility in alignment with future needs. In an improving economic climate, a yacht club with just the right features and amenities could be highly compelling to potential members.

With the urging of a private consulting firm, ambitious proposals were brought forward that would make sweeping changes at the Club, including a health and fitness facility, an expanded bar in the Spinnaker Room, and even hotel rooms inside the Clubhouse. In the end, the board looked at the proposals, weighed the cost estimates, and concluded that the harbor was still the Club's number-one priority. If major funds were to be spent anywhere, it would be there.

While planners worked to agree on a new harbor configuration, other less ponderous projects received the go-ahead. In keeping with a systematic redecorating plan, the Venetian Room underwent a complete renovation: new oak paneling, carpet, drapes, and furniture. Even the large Flemish oil painting on the wall was refurbished. Approval was also given to begin

Figure 2. The Venetian Room received a sparkling refurbishing in 2011 as part of a rigorous house committee plan to maintain and upgrade the clubhouse.

Figure 3. Expanding the popular Gazebo Bar and Deck gave patrons an improved view of the harbor and lake.

★ ★ ★

GPYC

Figure 4. Commodore Robert L. Rader Jr., 2011.

expansion of the Gazebo Bar on the Pool Deck. The Gazebo Bar had proven to be an increasingly popular warm weather destination with members. The bar's only problem was that it had limited seating, so the decision was made to expand the Pool Deck and increase the seating capacity to three hundred-sixty degrees around the bar. When completed, it would give members a much-improved place to congregate, with a sweeping view overlooking the harbor and lake.

Outdoor parties are deeply embedded in the Club's DNA, no matter what the season. The first "Winter Blast" party was held outdoors, at night, on the East Lawn that February, and despite temperatures in the teens, attendance exceeded all expectations. The event featured an ice bar, skating rink, fire pits, live entertainment and, of course, cold drinks. The Winter Blast would become a regular event on the Club's social calendar from that evening on.

The remainder of 2011 was notable for several occurrences.

On their way up north in their boat, members Dean and Diane Petitprin, together with guests Marita Grobbel and Past Commodore Dennis Andrus, plucked a downed pilot from the waters of Lake Huron. The victim had kept himself afloat without a life preserver for over seventeen hours after his airplane had run out of fuel and gone down several miles from shore off Port Sanilac. The victim's strength was almost at an end when the Petitprins spotted him. Their prompt action undoubtedly saved his life. They were named "Yachtsmen of the Year" at the Annual Meeting.

Ryan Seago, nineteen-year-old son of member Dr. John Seago, skippered his way to three first-place finishes in winning the Bayview NOOD Regatta that summer. Also, GPYC junior sailors distinguished themselves at the Junior Olympic Sailing Regatta hosted by the GPYC, winning the Open BIC and Collegiate 420 classes. Coming back after a run of hard luck in previous years, GPYC swimmers took fourth place at the 2011 MICSA Finals. And the Pointe Club, a club within the Club for younger members under age forty-five, was reorganized this year.

2012: An unpleasant discovery, followed by a pleasant turn of events

The decision to rebuild the south half of the East Wall of the harbor came to fruition under the watch of Commodore Ronald A. Schaupeter — and not a moment too soon. As work crews removed the decking, they discovered that the infrastructure — a network of steel rods and beams reinforcing the inner and outer side-walls — was badly deteriorated. The seawalls themselves, the only barrier to the lake, were in danger of collapse. Heavy wave action or impact from ice floes could cause a catastrophic breach in the structure, putting the entire harbor in jeopardy.

And so, before the new "big boat" wells along this part of the harbor could be constructed, the seawall itself would have to be replaced at an estimated cost of $800,000. This unwelcome expense would be in addition to the cost of the new enlarged wells, which had been already budgeted at $400,000. It was not the kind of news Club leaders wanted to hear, especially since they were hoping to free the Club of debt the following year. Now they would have to borrow additional money to address the East Wall problem.

But as the saying goes, When the going gets tough, the tough go partying.

In late March, a gala "gangster get-together" was held to cast off the winter doldrums and welcome members back to the Club after the annual shutdown. The theme of this year's event was "The Commodore's Speakeasy," a Prohibition -era-style party that had members dressing up like gangsters and molls in dark suits and flapper-style dresses. A password had to be whispered through a steel door before attendees were admitted to the Ballroom, which had been

Figure 5. The first "Winter Blast" party, held outdoors in February 2011, was so popular it became an annual Club event.

Figure 6. The "Blast" extended inside as well. Here, partygoers find respite from the chill in the warmth of the clubhouse.

converted to look like a blind pig. Once inside, guys and dolls were invited to play blackjack, roulette, or craps, sip a little "illegal" booze and dance to music from the 1920s and '30s. The evening was judged a welcome success.

Despite the East Wall difficulty, there were positive events as the year unfolded.

Efforts were underway to reform the Club's contested election process and convert it to a "slate," or uncontested format, in which members would not have to run against each other for a seat on the board. The downside of a slate process, of course, is that it limits a member's right to vote. But for years many eligible members had declined to run for

Figure 7. They saved a life at sea. Left to right: Skipper Erik Krueger, members Dean and Diane Petitprin, Marita Grobbel, and Past Commodore Dennis Andrus.

Figure 8. Commodore Ron Schaupeter gets arrested at his own Prohibition-era party that welcomed members back to the Club after the spring shutdown. The charge? Bootlegging. It was a spoof, of course.

election to the board out of fear of losing, and the pool of qualified board candidates had shrunk to a dangerously low level. In September 2012, at a special meeting of voting members, it was decided after spirited debate to try the uncontested election process for a period of three years and then revisit the issue.

At a meeting with officials of Grosse Pointe Shores, the Club presented information showing that we had been incorrectly overcharged for water for a considerable number of years. Shores officials, acting in good faith, agreed that independent arbitrators should represent both sides in an effort to resolve the problem. In June, the Shores agreed to a settlement of $400,000, to be repaid to the Club in sixteen annual installments of $25,000.

Also on the positive side, the Club's food and beverage operation showed a profit for the first time in twenty-five years: $43,000 in the black. Our popular chef, Robert Carney, had accomplished the near- impossible. Under his recommendation, a new attraction was added to the Gazebo Deck: an

Figure 9. Commodore Ronald A. Schaupeter, 2012.

Figure 10. Tennis starts young at GPYC. Assistant tennis pro Dan Amato instructs a group of members' children.

Figure 11. Chef Robert "Rob" Carney quickly made his culinary mark on the Club. He left us way too young.

outdoor pizza oven. The oven was an immediate hit, dispensing far more pizzas than expected in the first month of operation.

Adding to the good news, the Club's investment portfolio in September showed a healthy 9.1 percent gain, year to date.

In the meantime, repair work on the East Wall was successfully completed. The new structure was stronger than ever, and the job was completed on time and slightly under budget. Repairs to the crumbling moat bridge leading to the clubhouse were also completed without disruption to the flow of traffic. A loan was transacted to cover the cost of both projects.

Last, but not least, new, enlarged slips along the East Wall were completed. Ninety-five feet long and 27 feet wide, they offered unprecedented accommodation for large yachts on the Great Lakes. In seeming affirmation of the decision to build them, the first customer was a transient 101-foot yacht that took on 4,000 gallons of fuel.

Figure 12. Enlarged boat wells along a portion of the East Wall made the Club a haven for large yachts, one of very few on the eastern Great Lakes.

The year had its tragic side, as well. On November 3, Chef Robert Carney died of a heart attack at age fifty-one. Perhaps more than any other individual in recent memory, Carney had helped turn a critical part of the Club in a positive direction.

2013: National regatta earns Club high praise; a new harbor plan is offered

Keeping with tradition, Commodore Schaupeter handed the helm of the Club to incoming Commodore William C. Vogel at the annual meeting of the Club in November 2012.

With low water levels persisting throughout the Great Lakes, the go-ahead was given for additional dredging inside the harbor. An estimated 4,500 cubic yards of soil would be removed.

A winter seminar on iceboating, conducted by then-GPYC Sailing Director Ron Sherry, himself a seven-time iceboating world champion, enjoyed good attendance. Sherry had three iceboats on display in the clubhouse to add dramatic emphasis to the occasion. Although the evening was very much about the present, it recalled for many the Club's earliest days when iceboats ruled frozen Lake St. Clair in the winter. The vintage iceboat *French Boy*, which adorns a wall in the Fo'c'sle, also serves as a reminder of the era.

An "Edible Michigan" party was held this year. Conceived by Commodore Bill and Sue Vogel, it featured a six-course menu utilizing predominantly Michigan-made and-grown products such as whitefish, trout, and jams made from thimbleberries that grow along the shores of Lake Superior. Wine pairings indigenous to northern Michigan vineyards were offered, along with a selection of beers and ales from Michigan micro-breweries.

Two members were awarded high professional honors this year. Member Robert Joslyn was named Attorney of the Year by a vote of his peers, and Past Commodore John Boll was hailed an Outstanding Business Leader by Northwood Institute.

The largest sailing event ever held at the Club took place this year. The USODA (Opti) National Championship showcased three hundred-twenty sailors, ages eight to fifteen, from seven different countries, competing in identical 7-foot, 9-inch

Figure 13. Commodore William C. Vogel Jr., 2013.

Figure 14. Sailing Director Ron Sherry, preparing for a Club seminar on iceboating. Sherry himself was a North American and world champion iceboater.

Figure 15. Optis, Optis, Optis everywhere. The fleet of dinghies line up for the start of the 2013 USODA National Championship. It was the largest fleet of entries in the history of GPYC. The event was a tremendous success.

dinghies known as "Optis." The Opti class is the largest sailing class in the world and serves as a training ground for future Olympic sailors. The event brought over a thousand visitors to the Club each day. They were joined by two hundred fifty volunteers, many of whom were GPYC members.

During a week of competitive sailing that began with two hundred sixty Optis launched in slightly over twenty minutes, the GPYC kitchen turned out more than three thousand breakfasts and nine hundred-ten banquet dinners.

When it was over, kudos began pouring in from USODA officials, competitors, and their families who said it was the best organized, smoothest-running and most hospitable Opti Nationals they attended. Commodore Vogel beamed with pride, as did regatta chair and Past Commodore Jim Morrow. Then-Secretary Blaise Klenow served as regatta co-chair, along with board member Sean Schotthoefer.

After a rigorous search process, David Daniot was selected executive chef of the Club. He was the hands-down choice after the field of candidates was narrowed to two finalists, each of whom was asked to prepare an *à la carte* dinner for two groups of thirty members. The members sampled the two chefs' offerings and voted with their palates. Daniot's cuisine was the unanimous favorite. He began work at the Club in February 2013.

A new design proposal for the harbor was submitted by board member Graham Korneffel. The Korneffel plan regained some of the slips that were lost in earlier layouts, but also required moving the current lift bridge further to the north. It was decided that the proposal would be shown to the membership for comment later in the year. Meanwhile, plans for the health and fitness center were put on indefinite hold for budgetary reasons.

Plans to have the clubhouse officially declared a historical site were completed. The application to the state was ready for submission.

As the year drew to a close, members were given their first look at the new plan for the harbor. With a cost estimate of $9 to 10 million, it was explained that the makeover could be done in three phases to ease the financial impact on the Club. Much discussion was focused on moving the lift bridge to accommodate the new layout, a task that would cost approximately $1million. Once again, the question was raised whether the plan should allow for a second entrance in the East Wall. True to form, some members were strong proponents while others vehemently opposed the idea. There was also concern about the new plan reducing the size of the Guest Dock along the East Lawn to provide additional wells for member boats. The presentation ended with a promise to consider member feedback and get back to everyone in the new year.

Figure 16. Competitors' ages ranged from eight to fifteen. They came from all over the country, some from abroad, to race at the Club.

Going from modern to an eighty-five-year-old traditional

By Bruce Bradley

Shirley and I joined the Grosse Pointe Yacht Club in 1996, and in 1999 bought a new cruising sailboat, a 38-foot Beneteau, *Ode To Joy*. Over the next eleven years we sailed out of our home port at the GPYC. We cruised all the Great Lakes (except lake Ontario), sailed DRYA races and eight Port Huron-to-Mackinac races, and did many day sails on Lake St. Clair. While most of our sailing was cruising and day sailing, we did enjoy racing, especially the Mackinac races with our family-based crew.

During the summer of 2010 we sailed/ motored to our summer house on Cape Cod through Lake Erie, the Erie Canal, Hudson River, New York Harbor, Long Island Sound, Narragansett Bay, and along the southern Rhode Island and Massachusetts coast. (A narrative of the trip was published in the late fall 2010 and winter 2011 issues of The Grosse Pointer). During the summers of 2011 and 2012 we cruised the New England Coast, which included a month spent exploring the coast of Maine. Our final trip in Ode To Joy was a cruise to the Bahamas in the fall of 2012 and winter of 2013 via the Intra-coastal Waterway to West Palm Beach, Florida, and across the Gulf Stream.

Figure 17. The Bradleys' previous sailboat, *Ode to Joy*.

Back to the Future

I began my sailing career as a child on Long Island Sound, day sailing on a 19-foot John Alden-designed "Sloop Sakonnet" and cruising on my grandfather's 44-foot Herreshoff, a Fishers Island 31, named *Procyon*. Our family frequently cruised the New England coast on *Procyon*, creating wonderful memories and a love for big-boat sailing and cruising. I vividly recall my father and grandfather talking at length about the beautiful design and workmanship of Herreshoff, how well the boat sailed, its perfect balance and ability to handle the chop off the New England coast, especially Buzzards Bay.

Procyon was designed by Sidney DeWolf Herreshoff under the watchful eye of his father, "Cap'n Nat," and was built by the Herreshoff Manufacturing Company, Bristol, Rhode Island, in 1929. The boat was the sixth hull of fourteen boats in its class, which were built mostly for residents of Fishers Island, New York. In those days the size of the boat was usually described by its waterline length, which is 31 feet; thus the class was named "Fishers Island 31."

My Grandfather reluctantly sold *Procyon* in 1959 to a sailor and author at the well-known yacht design firm of Sparkman Stevens, Francis L. Kinney. I have always had an interest in

Figure 18. Their current pride and joy: eighty-five-year-old *Procyon*. Photo by Morris Rosenfeld.

Procyon and over the last several years I developed a growing interest in finding her. During the summer of 2012 I had the opportunity to sail on another sister-ship, Kestrel. After a great sail that lived up to everything said about the "Fishers Island 31s," I asked the museum if they could locate *Procyon*. They discovered her about three miles from our summer home on Cape Cod, and for sale by Ballentine's Boat Shop, which is highly regarded for restoration of classic and antique boats. She was in good condition with stunning brightwork, original teak deck and mast, and a well-preserved hull. Fate was knocking; I bought her!

After fourteen wonderful years sailing *Ode to Joy* with all its modern cruising amenities, we put her up for sale.

The story of *Procyon* is about much more than finding my grandfather's boat. It is about going back from the modern to the classic boat and discovering that the basics of sailing without modern technology can be very rewarding. Especially significant is the excellent performance of the old designs. *Procyon* is a very fast boat.

When I grew up sailing we had no electronics other than an RDF (radio direction finder). We had ice for refrigeration and battery power only for lights and engine starter. Navigation tools were a hand-bearing compass, parallel rules, dividers, navigation books with tables (tides, currents, etc.) paper charts, and our noses. We also had no roller furling, used a mechanical windlass for hauling up the anchor and had a sounding line for water depth. We had running back stays and steered with a tiller. Yet, all in all, we managed to get along quite well.

We spent our first sailing season with *Procyon* (August and September 2013) learning the boat, which is much longer and heavier than the Beneteau, has more sail area, is steered with a tiller, has running back stays and is faster. We found *Procyon* to be just as easy to sail, if not easier, since she has a self-tending, club-footed jib, is beautifully balanced, has wide teak decks, and has better visibility from the cockpit. Shirley and I can handle her comfortably. The previous owner would often sail single-handed in the right weather. *Procyon* is much more challenging in heavy winds since the mainsail has a large sail area and reefing is done by traditional slab reefing. With a little experience, we were able to master heavy weather fairly well. Setting the sails and furling require more effort than the modern rig. The large main is furled on the boom and demands effort to haul up; but I can still do it, thanks to a good winch and workouts with my physical trainer. The jib is hanked on to the head-stay and furled on the club boom. Hauling up the jib requires very little effort as it is relatively small. This extra effort is a small price to pay for such a magnificent sailing boat. With her deep-vee hull,

Figure 19. Left to right: Members Shirley and Bruce Bradley with Bruce's sister, Christie Mauro. Bruce is holding the first-place award *Procyon* received at the 2014 Mystic Seaport Museum antique boat show.

long forefoot keel and weight, she handles the heavy choppy seas of Buzzards Bay far better than any fin keel boat. She points higher than our Beneteau and sails fast, consistently sailing over eight knots in moderate-to-heavy breeze and over seven knots to windward.

We did learn of a new hazard, though. Often, while out sailing, we would notice many other boats sailing toward us on near collision courses. It turned out that we were the subject of many "photo-ops" and, of course, loved it.

We had our first overnight shakedown cruise over Labor Day Weekend, 2013, when we joined the Barrington Yacht Club cruise at Cuttyhunk Island, a day sail from our home on Cape Cod. We had another couple aboard, and the accommodations worked out very well for the two couples. We were warmly received by many old friends who enjoyed having a classic boat join the fleet.

My philosophy on equipping and maintaining the boat is, first and foremost, to maintain its historical and classic integrity. As much as possible, everything that is visible should reflect the appearance and functionality of the original design. Updated features that are not easily seen, but make sailing more enjoyable and safer, include

a modern diesel engine, hot and cold pressurized water, refrigeration unit in the icebox, automatic bilge pump, and a small Garmin GPS, which includes depth and speed, mounted on a lever that is only visible when it swings into the companionway when underway. We have been able to maintain the interior in its original configuration and have only replaced cushions and worn-out plumbing fixtures. The exterior is also original with only slight modifications to the running back stays, new cockpit cushions, and a much-improved full-batten mainsail. We even replaced the need for an autopilot with a simple system to "lash" the tiller for those long straight runs and for tending to other tasks. This is often not necessary since the boat is so well balanced the heading can be controlled by the set of the sails alone.

Our second season of owning and sailing a classic Herreshoff, the summer of 2014, brought many new experiences. The first major event was a family reunion with my siblings and cousins who sailed on *Procyon* many years ago when it belonged to my grandfather. It was a wonderful way to bring the family back together. We began racing in a weekly evening sailing series where we met other area sailors as both crew and competitors. We had no trouble finding crew to sail on our classic, and won our first race. We joined the nearby Buzzards Yacht Club, a small informal club with great sailing programs and were able to participate in their PHRF race series. We cruised to Mystic Seaport Museum (three days each way) to participate as an exhibit in their annual Classic and Antique Boat Rendezvous. We were pleased to be given the prize for the best restored sailboat over 40 feet. At the end of the summer we cruised to the Herreshoff Museum in Bristol, Rhode Island, (where she was originally built in 1929) for their annual regatta. It was a great summer!

I suppose that owning an eighty-five-year-old classic sailboat is a step back in time —which, of course, it is. But it also represents a huge leap forward in the enjoyment of sailing, family, and friends. In that respect, it is something of a time machine that allows us to select the past, present, or future anytime we step aboard.

2014: The centennial year arrives; let the celebration begin

When James N. Martin became commodore of the GPYC in November 2013, he did not need a crystal ball to see what was ahead of him. In addition to maintaining the financial stability of the Club and keeping it viable to its members, governance was now faced with the additional task of celebrating the Club's one-hundredth birthday. The lion's share of that responsibility would fall directly to the commodore. And while anyone with unlimited funds can throw a big party, funds in this case were not unlimited, the Club being very much in post-recession recovery mode. Moreover, this was to be a year-long celebration — how does someone sustain a party for twelve months?

The event would require a mixture of planning, good taste, and adroit timing, not to mention fiscal responsibility. Commodore Martin was undaunted. A planning committee had been quietly at work for months, and now it was time to set the year in motion. While many events were on the schedule, the committee determined that the big centennial celebration would take place August 14-17, 2014, during Fleet Review Weekend, traditionally the largest social event of the summer.

By good fortune, Club researchers working on this history book had discovered the existence of an early burgee that pre-dated the present design. The old burgee was a "swallowtail" in shape, with a white field, blue cross, and red letters. It was learned that the burgee had been adopted shortly after the Club's founding and had served as its official insignia for over a decade. It was a major find: The original burgee, paired with the present-day blue and red pennant, would become the logo for the 2014 centennial year. Throughout the year, the centennial logo turned up everywhere at the Club — on literature, clothing, glassware, even trash receptacles.

As the writing of this book progressed, many wonderful old photos were collected for inclusion. Eight of them were enlarged and displayed around the clubhouse, generating curiosity as well as excitement about what would be revealed of our Club's historical roots.

Figure 20. Commodore James N. Martin, 2014.

Figure 21. The old and new burgees were flown together to celebrate the centennial year. Visitors often think the U.S. ensign is improperly displayed at the Club, since it is flown below the Club burgee. But the GPYC flagpole is actually a mast, rigged with a gaff which is considered a place of honor on a ship. The burgee therefore flies from the top of the mast, while the larger flag, or ensign, flies from the gaff just below it.

The centennial celebration

The opening salvo of the centennial year was the Commodore's Ball, always a festive occasion, and this year all the more so with the centennial squarely in mind. One of the highlights of the evening was a proclamation from the State of Michigan recognizing the Club for its one hundred years of significant presence in the Grosse Pointe community. The document was signed by Governor Rick Snyder and presented by Ania Bieciuk, who was appointed to represent the State.

That winter will be remembered as one of the most severe in decades, as plunging temperatures and heavy snowfall punished the region for weeks on end. Ironically, the inclement weather at the

Figure 22A. The Club's inaugural Member Business Showcase gave GPYC business people the opportunity to show their wares to fellow members.

Figure 22B. Display tables representing the various businesses were arranged in the Ballroom and Main Dining Room. The atmosphere was cordial, relaxed, and successful. A second event was held the following year.

close of January provided the perfect setting for the Club's fourth annual Winter Blast, a party held outdoors inside a tent on the east lawn that featured an ice bar topped with an ice luge, lively music, and of course plenty of liquid refreshment to ward off the chill.

The party carried over to the inside the clubhouse with bowling competitions between GPYC and DAC members, who are traditionally invited to attend. The featured cuisine of the evening was, appropriately, comfort food — in particular, mac and cheese — that was made to order with exotic toppings and served in the Fo'c'sle. Attendance at the event this year was a record-breaker, with over three hundred stalwart partygoers defying the elements.

In February, the Club debuted its first-ever Member Business Showcase, an event that allowed GPYC business people to personally present their products and services to their fellow members. Businesses were on display in the Main Dining Room and the Ballroom, enabling members to order a cocktail and stroll the tables where the various companies were represented. What seemed to amaze everyone was the professional diversity of GPYC members. The range of member offerings extended from banks and law firms to energy-saving industrial lighting, fine jewelry, home restoration, and plumbing and heating. The event was judged to be extremely successful by both representatives and attendees, and a second event was planned for 2015.

A cold winter gave way to a resoundingly cold spring, but members' thoughts were still fixed on the upcoming boating season and a summer of centennial celebration. Eventually the thaw came, and by June the GPYC harbor again filled with boats.

That same month, there was good news concerning Past Commodore David Martin, M.D. who had moved from the Grosse Pointe area to head up cardiovascular surgery at Borgess Medical Center in Kalamazoo, Michigan. Consumer Reports had named Borgess as one of the top fifteen hospitals in the U.S. for heart surgery. The announcement was a tribute to the presence of Dr. Martin, whose professionalism was a key factor in the hospital's selection.

Figure 23. The GPYC harbor, despite its age, is arguably the Club's defining feature and most certainly its critical asset. It is to the Yacht Club what a golf course is to a country club, and is therefore an endless topic of discussion. During the centennial celebration, the docks and their resident boats were the scene of many planned and impromptu get-togethers.

Summer rendezvous are always popular, but the Up North Rendezvous in early August was particularly noteworthy as forty-seven GPYC boats made their way to Mackinac Island for the annual Club get-together. Perfect weather prevailed during the event, and one hundred ninety-six boaters got an insider's look at the Governor's Mansion during a cocktail reception that was held in honor of the centennial year of the Club. The rendezvous was said to be one of the most successful in recent memory.

Fleet Review and dinner dance

The highly anticipated centennial party began on Thursday, August 14, the first official day of Fleet Review Weekend, with the traditional dressing of ships and docks. The theme for decorators was "The Great Gatsby," and boat owners were encouraged to break out white lights and flapper-era costumes to evoke the Roaring Twenties. Of course once the decorating was

complete, the mood was too enticing to resist, and an unofficial pre-Harbor Lights Night dock party ensued.

The next night, Friday the 15th, was a party for everyone, not just boaters. Out on the East Lawn, there were games galore to entertain the kids, while adults could stroll the docks, chat with friends, and

Figure 24. Left to right: Carole Bania, flapper Shannon Andrus, and Amy Schaden share a toast during the "Great Gatsby" party on Harbor Lights Night with Commodore Jim Martin and wife Louann.

Figure 25. If anyone should wonder what all the celebrating was about on Fleet Review Weekend, this cake said it all. Like the ceremonial wedding cake, it was cut up and shared by members as a wish for continued good fortune.

take in the lights, sights, sounds, and decorations everywhere. In true Club fashion, there was plenty of food and liquid refreshment at the ready. At 10:00 p.m., the first of the fireworks salvos went off, turning heads skyward and soon drawing Oohs and Aahs of appreciation from the crowd. It was a spectacular aerial show, one of the biggest in recent history. Traffic along Lake Shore Road slowed to a near stop during the bombardment, and when it was over more than a half-hour later, hundreds of horns from cars and boats honked in mutual appreciation.

It was Commodore Jim Martin's goal for the one hundredth anniversary celebration to have one hundred boats participate in the Fleet Review. That turned out to be a tall order, but even so, sixty-seven boats participated in the review.

The review over, many members retired to clean up and change for the swanky dinner dance to follow, held inside a large tent on the East Lawn.

The cool temperatures, which were typical of the summer of 2014, prevailed this evening, keeping partygoers comfortable. After cocktails and hors d'oeuvres, diners settled in for one of the Club's trademark banquet suppers.

At a break in the festivities, Commodore Martin focused his remarks on the hundred-year journey of the Club through time. After commending his wife Louann for her extraordinary work during the centennial year, he turned his attention to the Club. "This has been a memorable day in a memorable week in a memorable year," he said. "I want to salute everyone — members, staff, and guests — who made it possible. And above all, on this, our hundredth anniversary, I salute the Grosse Pointe Yacht Club."

Our founding fathers would have enjoyed being there.

And perhaps some of them were.

Figure 26. The Club harbor is an impressive place any-time the boats are in; but on Fleet Review Weekend, it is simply magic.

Figure 27.

Figure 30.

Figure 28.

Figure 31.

Figure 29.

Figure 32.

Figure 27. Kids are never bored during Harbor Lights Night.

Figure 28. Left to right: Molly Perkins, Ellie Groustra, Julia Gebeck, and Alicia Bonahoom sample the chocolate fountain.

Figure 29. Past Commodores George Kriese and John DeWald enjoy a relaxed moment aboard the flagship during the review.

Figure 30. A salute to the boats from the commodore and his lady.

Figure 31. Mrs. Rene Hansemann's yacht, *Resolute*, made an impressive sight as she passed in review.

Figure 32. Past Commodore Ron and Priscilla Schaupeter show 'em how it's done on the dance floor.

Figure 33. Left to right: Past Commodore Bob and Susan Kay with Denise and Alex Miller.

Figure 33.

Connecting with our birthplace

In late August, board members and spouses paid a visit to the place where it all began, the summer home of the Club's first commodore, George Marsh. Hosting the visit were the home's present owners, Mr. and Mrs. Robert Roney, who provided tours of the main floor where the founding meetings of the fledgling Grosse Pointe Yacht Club were held in 1913 and 1914. An architect by profession, Roney resisted the temptation to modernize the structure, and the layout and decor are remarkably similar to the way they would have been in Commodore Marsh's day. The original wood wall paneling, taken from the old, demolished St. Paul's Church rectory, was still proudly in evidence. In those quasi-original surroundings, it was not hard to feel the presence of George Marsh, welcoming that group of gentlemen to his home on December 3, 1913, and getting down to the business of establishing a new yacht club.

Later, at a cocktail party on the home's lakeside front lawn, Mr. Roney, an avid sailor now in his eighties, gave an entertaining talk on the history of the place, noting that he and his wife, Dorothy, are only the second owners. He bought the home from George Marsh's estate in 1961 and has lived there ever since. Those in attendance departed with a keen sense of appreciation for how the Club came to be.

The "other" *Sea Witch*

At a reception in the Ballroom on September 3, directly below the spectacular painting of the *Sea Witch*, GPYC members and guests applauded as another *Sea Witch* was unveiled. The "other" *Sea Witch*, done on a much smaller scale, was also painted by Frank Vining Smith at the behest of our third commodore, John H. French.

John H. French was serving as commodore, with his 124-foot yacht *Siele* docked in the harbor, when the clubhouse had its grand opening on July 4, 1929. He had earlier commissioned the large *Sea Witch* canvas, which he presented as a gift to the Club on that occasion. But apparently adhering to the *caveat emptor* principle, the commodore asked to see a smaller version of what Mr. Smith would be painting before giving his final approval.

Figure 34. Left to right: Past Commodore Jim Ramsey, Robert and Dorothy Roney, and Dr. Larry Stephenson gather at the Roneys' Lake Shore home, originally owned by the Club's first commodore, R. George Marsh. When research clearly revealed the Marsh home was where the founding meetings of the Club took place, the Roneys kindly offered to host a centennial celebration party.

Figure 35. Robert Roney addresses board members and wives on the lawn of the birthplace of the Club. Mr. Roney is an accomplished sailor himself and a recipient of the Great Lakes Cruising Club's prestigious Admiral Bayfield Award for circumnavigation of all five Great Lakes in his sailboat *Godspeed*. By pleasant coincidence, the award was presented at GPYC.

Figure 36. Conrad "Duke" Williams tells the story of the miniature *Sea Witch* to a group of interested members. Mr. Williams, who resides in New Orleans, generously loaned his painting to the Club for the centennial celebration.

Backman-Schmitt family: the one-hundred-year connection

Ignatius and Wilfred Backman joined the fledgling Grosse Pointe Yacht Club in 1914. On the first page of chapter one is a photo of the original membership card issued to Ignatius in 1914. Page four of the same chapter shows Ignatius and Wilfred receiving awards for their ice-boat racing skills. Their younger brother, Alonzo Backman, joined the Club in 1927.

As the Club celebrated its centennial year, the Backman family continued to be represented. Joe Schmitt, member since 2001, is the grandson of Alonzo and Adelaide Backman. Joe and wife Susan have twin daughters who became legacy members in 2005. Elizabeth and her husband, Carl Rashid III, son of Past Commodore Carl Rashid Jr., were once members, and Allison and husband James LaFranca continue to be GPYC members.

Figure 37.

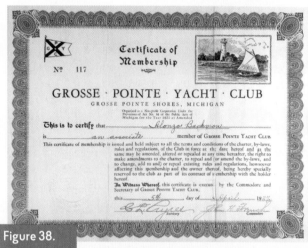

Figure 38.

Figure 37. Top right: Adelaide and Alonzo Backman, grandparents of member Joe Schmitt, shown with fellow GPYC members and iceboat racers.

Figure 38. Middle right: Alonzo's certificate of membership in the GPYC, which he joined in 1927.

Figure 39. Three generations of the Schmitt family today. Joe Schmitt, seated center with wife Susan, is a direct descendant of the Backmans.

Figure 40. Commodore Kevin B. Granger, 2015.

Figure 41. Commodore Granger takes the helm of the Club as it enters its second century.

This smaller version of *Sea Witch* now graces the home of Commodore French's great grandson, Conrad "Duke" Williams III. Mr. Williams, a prominent New Orleans attorney, told the audience that the painting had traveled with him throughout his years of service in the U.S. Navy before he settled permanently in New Orleans. He pointed out a small amount of damage to one of the corners, which was incurred during Hurricane Katrina.

Mr. Williams then related the story of how his painting came to the Club. He recalled receiving an email from an unknown address and luckily, before relegating it to the junk file, he read it. The email was from member Dr. Larry Stephenson, who was chairing the centennial book project, and was part of his quest to discover what had happened to the model for the *Sea Witch* painting. Not only did Mr. Williams own the painting, he graciously offered to send it to the Club for display at his own expense.

As this book goes to press, Club members are still enjoying the "other" *Sea Witch* on display in the Ballroom. And those who happen to be down in the Fo'c'sle are treated to another legacy from the French family mounted on the wall, the beautifully restored iceboat *French Boy* that once belonged to the French family.

Admittance to the National Register

The Club notched a historic milestone on September 19, 2014, when word was received that its application to the National Register of Historic Places had been approved. It meant that the GPYC clubhouse was now officially recognized by the State of Michigan and the Federal Government as historically significant and would be added to their official list of structures deemed historically important and worthy of preservation. It was a fitting affirmation of the Club's one-hundredth birthday. A plaque commemorating the honor will soon be unveiled at the Club.

Where to from here?

On November 14, 2014, at a brief meeting of the board after the Club's annual dinner meeting, Commodore James Martin passed the helm of the Club to incoming Commodore Kevin B. Granger. Newly selected board member Brian Fish joined four returning incumbents, Jason Grobbel, Graham

Korneffel, Joe Schaden, and Sean Schothoefer, completing the Club's cast of twelve directors. That group would govern the Club through the year 2015, and beyond the scope of this chronicle.

As the Club's new commodore, it was surely a poignant moment for Kevin Granger, a time of optimism and excitement, tempered with perhaps a tinge of apprehension. An investment manager by profession, Granger made a frequent habit of looking ahead; and he knew what was on the horizon. His job, among other challenges, would be to lead the Grosse Pointe Yacht Club into the next century of its existence. But Granger was confident. He knew he had the support of his board, and that together they had a solid strategy in the form of the Club's strategic plan, a living document that had been created to help guide the Club nearly fifteen years earlier. Over time, Club planners had modified the plan to keep it in sync with changing tastes and demands, but the document still stood as the bible of what the Grosse Pointe Yacht Club aspired to be and also served as a roadmap for getting there. Fundamental to the present plan was a set of core values representing everything the Club holds sacred. They are:

• Excellence
• Integrity
• Respect for the Club's heritage and traditions
• Civility and mutual respect
• Friendship and camaraderie
• Family orientation
• Financial prudence
• Community
• Fun
• Transparency, engagement, and responsiveness in governance and management
• Willingness to change

With those guiding virtues in mind, the commodore and board vowed to address an issue that had been under discussion for decades: a new harbor. It would be the costliest undertaking since the clubhouse was constructed eighty-five years ago, and money was still tight from the recent recession. But the time had come to get the project out of the talking phase and into reality. The new harbor would be leadership's number-one priority in the coming year. Construction could begin as soon as fall 2015.

Figure 42. Chef David Daniot beams with pride after winning a silver medal at Luxembourg.

Meanwhile, another major project demanded attention: a health and fitness center. Research consistently showed that a fitness facility was a high-priority item with new and prospective members; not having one could become a competitive disadvantage. A fitness center would therefore have to be part of the planning process. Commodore Granger made it his goal to put a fitness facility plan and a financial strategy in place during his year.

Just as the calendar year was coming to an end, the Club received good news from Europe. Executive Chef David Daniot had won a coveted silver medal at the elite Villeroy and Boch Culinary World Cup in Luxembourg. To qualify for the event, Daniot had to compete against a thousand other chefs; once he made the cut, his

Figure 43. Commodore Kevin and Julie Granger at the Commodore's Ball, December 6, 2014.

work was judged by a jury of fifty-five master chefs. When the competition was over, Chef Daniot placed twenty-fifth out of one hundred eighty-four culinary competitors, worldwide. The award was undoubtedly satisfying for the chef, who had faced a demanding environment at the Club after the death of his popular predecessor. Winning the silver medal not only validated his credentials as a world-class chef, it also reinforced the Club's reputation as a great dining destination.

With that, the centennial year 2014 drew to a close. In many respects, it was a year much like the ninety-nine that preceded it: with struggles, setbacks, advances, challenges, achievements, fellowship, laughter, good times, and — as always

— questions. Will there be a new harbor? What about a health and fitness center? What will the economy do? What do members want? What will the future demand?

Through it all, the Club has sailed straight and true, acclaimed as one of the finest yacht clubs in America. How? By being true to what she has always been: a haven from the everyday; a signature landmark to her community; and, rising above a horizontal landscape, a refreshing reminder of the verticality of life.

Will there be a Grosse Pointe Yacht Club one hundred years from now? God willing, with vision and tenacity, there always will be.

IMAGE ACKNOWLEDGEMENTS
Chapter Eleven

1. Tom Kliber

2. Jim Dorian

3. – 16. GPYC, Michele Penoyer

17. – 19. Bruce Bradley

20. GPYC

21. – 25. GPYC, Michele Penoyer

26. Tom Kliber

27. – 35. GPYC

36. Jim Dorian

37. – 39. Schmitt family

40. – 43. GPYC

44. Tom Kliber

PART II

Figure 1. *Saramar III* owned by Charles T. Fisher.

Early members and their boats

By Larry W. Stephenson, M.D., and Ross B. Stone

Introduction

In researching the formative years of the Grosse Pointe Yacht Club, it became apparent that learning who the early members were and the types of boats they owned would provide a very distinct impression of the Club and what it must have been like to be a member in those days. We therefore set out to identify some of those early GPYC members, along with their boats. In this case, "early" is defined as members who joined between the years 1914 and 1941. Members are listed by name, with a few facts about them and the name and type of boat or boats they owned. Obtaining the information was time-consuming and tedious because only a single member roster is known to exist between

1914 and 1939. Only twice did we locate other sources listing some of the members along with their boats. One of those was a newspaper article about the grand opening of the clubhouse on July 4, 1929, which named nine boats, along with the names of their owners, that were in the harbor that day. The other source was from July 1938 when the Club reopened, listing seventeen boats in the harbor, fifteen of which were named and their owners identified.

Inclusion in this article required not only information about the member beyond their name, but also about the boat they owned. In some cases, high-profile members were identified but no information could be found about any boat they might have owned. In other cases, we found the names of a few members who owned sizeable boats, but no further information about them. Those conditions precluded these members from being mentioned in this article.

Information about high-profile members and large yachts tended to be easier to find going back some seven to ten decades, so what is contained herein is likely skewed in that direction. Due in part to the limited amount of available information, we arbitrarily stopped at fifty-seven members, as we felt this was a reasonable number to tell the story. The number represents somewhat less than ten percent of the membership during the designated time period.

Among these selected fifty-seven members whose boats were part of the GPYC fleet, we found there were six yachts over 200 feet in length and another twenty-three between 100 and 200 feet in length. Many of these yacht owners were early captains of the automotive industry. Since this was a period of such rapid growth and prosperity in Detroit's history, it seems likely that very few other yacht clubs at that time could have claimed a fleet of motor yachts equal in size and number to that of the GPYC. The largest yachts could not be kept in the Club harbor. Some were anchored in the Detroit River.

The late George Van, noted newspaper columnist,covered yachting activities in the Detroit metro area for many years. Below is an excerpt from an article in the Old Club 1872–1972 Centennial Album in which he describes the relatively brief era of the mega yachts owned locally.

The comparatively small craft of the club's [Old Club] early years steadily increased in size, peaking in the period from the turn of the century [1900] up into the mid-thirties. That's when the Internal Revenue Tax Collector determined the size of every boat, and the luxurious queens of this great era gradually disappeared.

There was a magnificent fleet of these lovely ladies in our waters before they were eliminated by the depression. All were around 150 to 250 feet long with tall ornamental spars, clipper bows and veranda-like stern decks. Many of them anchored off The Old Club. They were too big to come into the docks, and guests were brought ashore in launches.

The local fleet included Phil Fletcher's *Winyah*; the *Hiawatha,* owned by one of the Newberrys (or was it a Buhl?), Dodge's *Nokomis* and the three sister ships, the 243-footers [235-225 footers] — Fred Fisher's *Nakhoda*, Alfred Sloan's *Rene* and Walter O. Briggs' *Cambriona*.

So it is likely that the Great Depression, along with increasing taxation, particularly the establishment of the personal income tax and its rate increases during the 1920s and 1930s, caused a steep decrease in the number of yachts that exceeded 150 feet at the GPYC.

Several boats in this list were requisitioned by the United States Military for duty in World Wars I and II, while two more, having been sold to Canadians, were requisitioned by the British Military. The service of these boats to their countries is duly noted.

Members and Their Boats

1. **Alger, Russell A., Jr.** — joined 1925/26. Logging and lumber business in Michigan and Canada; major stockholder and vice president of Packard Motor Company; financial backer of the Wright Brothers' airplane manufacturing company.

   Laurentian, 150 ft., motor yacht
   Winchester, 225 ft., motor yacht
   Builder BIW, 1916
   WWI U.S. Navy, *USS Winchester*,
   (Sp 156)
   WWII Canadian Navy, *HMCS Renard*
   Reveler, 247 ft., motor yacht
   Builder Friedrich Krupp, Germaniawerft, Germany, 1929
   WWII *USS Beaumont. Reveler* was built for Alger, but he died in 1930 before taking delivery.

2. **Rear Com. Alger, Russell A. III** — joined 1932. Son of Russell A. Jr.; stockbroker; GPYC rear commodore 1934.

   Baccarat, 46 ft., sailboat
   Builder / Designer Russell J. Pouliot, Detroit, Michigan, 1933.
   Baccarat won the Port Huron-to-Mackinac race in the years 1933-1936 and was the Class B winner of the 650-mile race from New London, Connecticut, to Bermuda in 1934.

3. **Allmand, John T.** — joined 1939. Helped organize Fisher Body Corporation and served in numerous positions with the company, including vice president.

   Janna II, 65 ft., motor yacht
   Builder Smith and Williams, 1925

4. **Barthel, Otto F.** — joined 1923 or earlier. Nationally prominent patent attorney; served on numerous local and national powerboat and sailboat race committees; commodore of Detroit Yacht Club, 1906, 1925.
Dolphin, 32 ft., sailboat

5. **Bennett, Harry** — joined 1939. Ex-navy deep-sea diver and boxer; in charge of Ford Motor Company Service Department, which handled the company's internal security.
Esthar, 75 ft., motor yacht

6. **Bliss, Haskell** — joined 1941. Director of sales, Nash Motor Company (automotive manufacturer), then vice president, Nash Kelvinator Corporation.
Maid Marion, 109 ft., motor yacht
Builder New York Yacht Launch and Engine Company, 1936

7. **Bodman, Henry E.** — joined 1940. Chairman of the board, National Bank of Detroit.
Brilliant, 61 ft., sailboat
Builder Sparkman and Stevens, Nevin's Yachts
Red Head, 60 ft., sailboat
Builder Robert Jacob Shipyard (RJS), New York, 1936

8. **Bonbright, Carl W.** — joined 1929. Manufacturer and financier.
Bonnie II, 58 ft., motor yacht

9. **Breech, Ernest R.** — joined 1940. President, North American Aviation Corp.; chairman of the board, Ford Motor Company.
Breech's Boy, 29 ft., cabin cruiser

10. **Briggs, Walter O.** — joined 1928. Founder and president, Briggs Manufacturing Company; owner of Detroit Tigers baseball team and Tiger stadium (Briggs stadium).
Janie III, 118 ft., motor yacht
Builder Consolidated Shipbuilding Corp., 1925
Cambriona, 225 ft., motor yacht
Builder P and J, Wilmington, Delaware
WWII U.S. Navy *USS Crystal* (PY-25)

11. **Broderick, David F.** — joined 1939. Insurance broker and owner of 33-story Broderick Tower, Detroit.
Phween, 75 ft., motor yacht
Builder Wells/Chance Markle, 1928

12. **Rear Com. Bush, Charles T.** — joined 1927. President of Strelinger Company, Detroit, major supplier of heavy machinery and cable to industry in Michigan and surrounding states; manufacturer of Little Giant marine engines.
Helchabro, 55 ft., motor yacht

13. **Coffin, Howard** — joined 1926. Co-founder, Hudson Motor Car Company; chairman of the board, National Air Transport Company (forerunner of United Airlines); major land developer on Georgia's east coast; known to have entertained Presidents Calvin Coolidge and Herbert Hoover, as well as pilot Charles Lindburgh at his estate on Sapelo Island; developed Sea Island where he built and owned The Cloisters Hotel (The Cloisters).
Zapala, 124 ft., motor yacht
Builder Luders Marine Construction, Stamford, Connecticut, 1927
WWII U.S. Navy patrol boat

14. **Connolly, William F.** — joined 1928. Judge, Recorders Court of Detroit.
Noremac, 55 ft. (estimated length), motor yacht

15. **Com. Couzens, Frank** — joined 1938. General contractor; Detroit mayor; founder and chairman of the board, Wabeek Bank.
Junior, 22 ft., speedboat
Marlan C, 53 ft., motor yacht
Builder Chris Craft, Algonac, Michigan

16. **Currie, Thomas E.** — joined 1927. General contractor; owner of lumber-yard and mill.
Banty II, 47 ft., motor yacht

17. **Dodge, Horace E.** — joined before 1920. Co-founder, Dodge Brothers Company, which manufactured components, cars and trucks.

    Hornet, 96 ft., motor yacht
    Built 1905

    Hornet II, 99 ft., motor yacht
    Built 1910

    Nokomis, 149 ft., motor yacht
    Builder P and J, 1913
    WWI *USS Kwasid*

    Caroline, 187 ft., steam motor yacht
    Builder P and J, 1914
    Name changed to *Delphine*, 1919

    Nokomis II, 243 ft., steam motor yacht
    Builder P and J, 1917
    WWI *USS Nokomis* (sp-609)
    WWII *USS Nokomis* (yt-142)

    Delphine, 258 ft., motor yacht
    Builder Great Lakes Engineering Company, Detroit, Michigan, 1921
    Horace Dodge visited the yacht almost daily during its construction. He died unexpectedly at age 52 in December 1920, a few months before its completion. At the time, it was the largest private yacht in the United States. His widow, Anna, kept it as a memorial to her late husband and used the Dodge mansion, Rose Terrace in Grosse Pointe Farms, as its homeport until the 1960s. It typically had a crew of 54. Recently she underwent a $60 million restoration and is berthed at the Port of Monte Carlo, Monaco.
    WWII U.S. Navy *USS Dauntless*, used exclusively by Admiral Ernest King, Chief of Naval Operations.

    Speedboats
    Lotus, 40 ft.
    Hornet, 40 ft.

    Commuter Yachts Used to commute from home to work.
    Delphine, 45 ft. Builder Elco Company, New York, 1914
    Anna D, 53 ft.
    Built Milwaukee, Wisconsin
    *Boats co-owned with his brother John

18. **Fisher, Alfred** — joined 1928. One of seven Fisher brothers of Fisher Body Corporation.

    Alma F, 88 ft., motor yacht
    Builder Defoe Shipbuilding, Bay City, Michigan (DSB), 1928
    WWII U.S. Navy patrol boat

    Alma F, 75 ft., motor yacht
    Builder DSB, 1938

19. **Fisher, Charles T.** — joined 1927. Co-founder, Fisher Body Corporation.

    Saramar II, 106 ft., motor yacht
    Builder RJS, 1927
    WWII U.S. Navy(YP-556)

    Saramar III, 153 ft., motor yacht
    Builder DSB, 1930
    WWII *HMCS Husky*

20. **Fisher, Frederick J.** — joined 1928. Oldest of Fisher brothers and co-founder of Fisher Body Corporation as well as president and chairman of the board.

    Nakhoda, 235 ft., motor yacht (A model of this yacht is displayed in the Commodores' Room)
    Builder P and J, 1929
    WWII U.S. Navy *USS Zircon* (PY-16) . During the latter portion of the war she served as the secondary flagship for the Commander-in-Chief of the U.S. Atlantic fleet.

21. **Fisher, Lawrence D** — joined 1927. One of the seven Fisher brothers.

    Margaret II, 62 ft., motor yacht
    Builder P and J, 1925

    Margaret III, 106 ft., motor yacht
    Builder P and J, 1927

    Dol-lar, 64 ft., motor yacht
    Builder Fisher Boat Works, Detroit, Michigan, 1940

22. **Fisher, William** — joined 1929. One of the seven Fisher brothers.

    Laura M XI, 106 ft., motor yacht
    Builder P and J, New York, 1928

23. **Com. Ford, Edsel B.** — joined 1926. President of Ford Motor Company; son of company founder Henry Ford and wife Clara.

    Greyhound, 58 ft., motor yacht

    Acadia, 65 ft., motor yacht

    Marlin, 51 ft., motor yacht

    Buckeye, 40 ft., motor yacht

    Buckeye, 64 ft., sailboat

    Onika, 125 ft., motor yacht
    Builder P and J, 1930

    Sialia, initially 202-foot motor yacht, later lengthened to 223 ft.
    Builder P and J, 1914
    Most sources indicate Edsel's father Henry to be *Sialia's* owner, while other sources, including Lloyds' Register of American Yachts 1930, list Edsel Ford as the sole owner. So the two Fords may have had some arrangement between them regarding this yacht's ownership
    WWI U.S. Navy *USS Sialia* (SP 543)
    WWII U.S. Navy *USS Coral Sea* (PY-15)

    Speedboats

    Acadia II, 21 ft.

    Teaser, 40 ft.

    Typhoon, 40 ft. (A model of this boat is displayed in the Binnacle dining room.)

    *Race Boats

    Goldfish

    999

    Greyhound Jr.

    Wood Fish

    Miss Dearborn, built as a race boat, but due to rule change, used as a test boat.

    *In most cases these race boats were piloted by Edsel Ford.

24. **Ford, John B. "JB" Jr.** — joined 1926 or before. Chairman of the board, Wyandotte Chemicals Corp.

    Royono, 97 ft., motor yacht
    Builder DBS, 1928

    Hiawatha, 85 ft., motor yacht
    Builder Consolidated, 1924

    Royono II, 52 ft., sailboat
    Builder Fisher Boatworks, Detroit, Michigan; designer John Alden

    Royono III, 71 ft., sailboat
    Builder Herreshoff Manufacturing Company, Bristol, Rhode Island, 1936; designer John Alden
    First to finish Chicago-Mackinac race 1946–1949

25. **French, George Russell** — joined 1929. Banker; son of Com. John H. French.

    French Boy, 45 ft., sailboat (NY 32)
    Builder Sparkman and Stephens, 1936

26. **Com. French, John H.** — joined 1926. Banker and industrialist.

    Siele, 124 ft., motor yacht
    Builder P and J, 1926
    WWII *USS Aquamarine* (PYC-7)

27. **Jacobs, Clare,** — joined 1938. President, Jacobs Manufacturing; Olympic medalist (pole vaulting).

    Revelry, 44 ft., sailboat

    Falcon, 45 ft., sailboat (NY 32)

    Sea Jay, 42 ft., motor yacht

28. **Jacobs, Rex** — joined 1929. President, Jacobs Manufacturing (before brother Clare).

    Francis J II, 50 ft., motor yacht

29. **Com. Jewett, Harry** — joined before 1917. President, Paige-Detroit Automobile Company.

    Madonna, 68 ft., motor yacht

30. **Joy, Richard** — joined 1929. Bank president and president of several companies; early investor in Packard Motor Car Company.
Rainbow II, 54 ft., motor yacht
Builder RJS, NY 1923
Rainbow III, 62 ft., motor yacht
Builder RJS, 1926

31. **Judson, Ross** — joined 1927. Founder and president, Continental Motors.
Conoco, 150 ft., motor yacht
Builder DSB, 1927
Conoco, 165 ft., motor yacht
Builder Lawley and Sons, 1929
Trudione, 190 ft., motor yacht
Name changed to *Seventeen* in December 1930
Builder BIW, 1930
WWII U.S. Navy *USS Carnelian* (PY 19)

32. **Vice Com. Keller, K.T.** — joined 1928. President, Chrysler Corp.; GPYC vice commodore 1938 and 1939.
Robark, 83 ft., motor yacht
Builder DSB, 1929
Tideover, 40 ft., motor yacht
Built 1937

33. **Kettering, Charles** — joined 1930. Vice president General Motors; chief of GM Research Laboratories; commodore of Detroit Yacht Club 1934.
Olive K, 97 ft., motor yacht
Builder DSB, 1928
Olive K, 165 ft., motor yacht
Builder DSB, 1929

34. **Knudsen, William S.** — joined 1929. President, General Motors.
Naiad, 60 ft., motoryacht

35. **Macauley, Edward F.** — joined 1939. Chief of design, Packard Motor Car Company; son of member and longtime Packard president Alvan Macauley.
Margaret II, 65 ft., motor yacht
Builder Great Lakes Boat Works, 1923

36. **Com. Marsh, R. George** — joined 1914. President, Marsh Manufacturing Company.
Miss Grosse Pointe (initially *Princess of Grosse Pointe*), 45 ft., motor yacht
Builder Joe Paulet, 1915

37. **Mott, Charles S.** — joined 1929. Co-founder of General Motors; became GM's largest stockholder.
Boat (boat's name unavailable) Huckins Fairform Flyer, 32 ft., cabin cruiser

38. **Mulford, Ora J**. — joined 1928. Owner of Grey Marine, major manufacturer of marine engines.
Viking, 96 ft., motor yacht
This yacht was originally Horace Dodge's *Hornet*, which Mulford renamed *Viking*. In 1915 he replaced the steam engines with two Grey Marine Engines and renamed it again, this time as *Greyling III*.

39. **Com. Murphy, Charles Hayward** — joined 1927. Member of boards of directors at several Detroit institutions.
Althea, 51 ft., motor yacht
Builder Long Island NY, 1907
WWI U.S. Navy (SP-218)
Althea, 106 ft., motor yacht
Builder BIW, 1930

40. **Oakman, Robert** — joined 1927. Real estate developer.
Mamie-O, 101 ft., motor yacht
Builder Great Lakes Engineering Works, Detroit, Michigan, 1927
WWII U.S. Navy patrol boat

41. **Petzold, William A. "Skipper"** — joined 1927. Chief legal counsel and secretary-treasurer of J.L. Hudson and Co., once the nation's second largest department store.
   Josephine, 43 ft., ketch
   Designer John Alden, 1923
   Josephine II, 54 ft., yawl
   Builder, Reed-Cook Marine Construction, Boothbay Harbor, Maine, 1927; designer, John Alden
   Josephine III, 64 ft., sailboat
   Detroit, 25 ft., motorboat
   Chi-Bi-Ev, 37 ft., motorboat

42. **Phelps, George H**. — joined 1927. Owner of prominent national advertising agency and radio station WGH; commodore, Detroit Yacht Club, 1930.
   Skylark III, 94 ft., motor yacht

43. **Com. Pierson, H. Lynn** — joined 1938. Attorney and president, Detroit Harvester Company.
   Picaron II, 36 ft., motor yacht

44. **Rands, William C.** — joined 1928. Founder and president of Rands Manufacturing Company.
   Rosewill, 80 ft., motor yacht
   Builder, DSB, 1926
   Rosewill II, 120 ft., motor yacht
   Builder, DSB, 1931

45. **Sales, Murray W.** — joined 1929. Manufacturer of plumbing supplies.
   Sea Sales III, 78 ft., motor yacht
   Builder DSB, 1928

46. **Com. Scherer, Robert P.** — joined 1940. Son of Dr. Otto Scherer, a 1914 founding member of GPYC. Com. Robert Scherer invented the rotary die encapsulation machine in 1933, which revolutionized the encapsulation field for pharmaceuticals. He soon founded the R.P. Scherer Corporation, which quickly became a world leader in producing capsules for various types of medicines.
   Good Humor, 25 ft., speedboat (Later kept a boat at the GPYC named *Capsule*)

47. **Schlotman, Joseph Bernard** — joined 1927. President of Universal Products Co.; member of the Emory Low Ford family, co-founder of Wyandotte Chemicals Corp.
   Stellaris, 187 ft., motor yacht (previously owned by Horace Dodge)
   Builder P and J, 1914

48. **Shelden, Alger** — joined 1926. Investment banker and private investor; commodore, Bayview Yacht Club, 1930 and 1931; chairman, Grosse Pointe Club, 1948 and 1949; responsible for establishing a USCG base in the Detroit area, at the GPYC, in 1936; U.S. Navy, WWII; founding president, Grosse Pointe War Memorial, 1946.
   Trident, 56 ft., sailboat
   Designer John Alden
   First place, 1930 and 1931 Port Huron-to-Mackinac race
   Strathbelle, 87 ft., motor yacht
   Builder Burger Boat Company, Manitowoc, Wisconsin

49. **Com. Slocum, George M.** — joined 1914. Founder and publisher of two successful publications; *The Michigan Business Farmer* and *Automotive News*.
   Spray II, 40 ft., motor yacht
   Builder Chris Craft, Algonac, Michigan

50. **Vice Com. Sorensen, Charles** — joined 1929. Vice president, Ford Motor Company and one of the company's three directors along with Henry and Edsel Ford. Served as vice commodore of GPYC in 1932 and 1933 and commodore of the Detroit Yacht Club in 1927.
   Helene, 106 ft., steam motor yacht
   Builder, DBW, 1927
   Helene II, 146 ft., motor yacht
   Builder BIW, 1930
   White Cloud, 60 ft., sailboat
   Icarus, 80 ft., schooner

51. Com. Stephenson, Burnette F. — joined 1927. Major real estate developer in Detroit and Tampa-St. Petersburg, Florida.
Anona, 117 ft., motor yacht
Builder George Lawley and Sons, Boston 1904.

52. Stroh, John W. — joined 1926. President, Stroh Brewing Company.
Snapshot, 35 ft., speedboat
Zipper II, 43 ft., commuter yacht
Souris, 65 ft. (estimated), motor yacht

53. Vice Com. Torrey, M.D., Harry Norton — joined 1927. Surgeon; member of Emory Low Ford family, co-founder of Wyandotte Chemical Corp.
Tamarack V, 50 ft., motor yacht
Builder Gar Wood, Algonac, MI, 1928.

54. Trendle, George W. — joined 1938. Part-owner and producer of nationally broadcasted radio shows: The Lone Ranger, The Green Hornet and Sergeant Preston of the Yukon.
Boat (name unknown) 16 ft., catboat-type sailboat, kept in the GPYC harbor

55. Vincent, Col. Jesse G. — joined 1929. Vice president and chief engineer, Packard Motor Car Company. He initially became famous for designing the WWI V-12 Liberty aircraft engine.
Clarinda, 71 ft., motor yacht
Builder DSB, 1926.

56. Com. Woodall, Herbert J. — joined 1926. President of Woodall Manufacturing Company.
Heavy Moon III, 54 ft., motor yacht

57. Zeder, Frederick M. — joined 1932. Chief engineer, Chrysler Corporation.
Pridomar, 75 ft., motor yacht
Builder DSB, 1929.

Yacht/Boat Builder Abbreviations:
1. BIW: Bath Iron Works, Bath, Maine
2. DSB: Defoe Shipbuilding, Bay City, Michigan, originally Defoe Boat and Motor Works
3. P and J: Pusey and Jones, Wilmington, Delaware
4. RJS: Robert Jacob Shipyard, City Island, New York In 1946 bought by Consolidated Ship Building, Morris Heights, New York

Main Sources
Lloyd's Register of American Yachts, 1921-1947 editions

Construction lists of all boats built by the following were obtained via the internet: Defoe Shipbuilding, Bay City, Michigan; Pusey and Jones, Wilmington, Delaware; Robert Jacob Shipyard, City Island, New York.

"The Dodge Fleet of Lake St. Clair" by John F. Polacsek, *Tonnancour; Life in Grosse Pointe and Along the Shore of Lake St. Clair*, Volume I, edited by Arthur M. Woodford Omnigraphics, Detroit, Michigan, 1994.

"Yachts of the Auto Barons," by John E. Polacsek, *Tonnancour*; Vol. II, Omnigraphics, Detroit, Michigan, 1996.

Yachts in a Hurry: An Illustrated History of the Great Commuter Yachts, by C. Philip Moore, W.W. Norton and Company, New York, New York., 1994

The Steam Yacht Delphine and Other Stories, by Jay Ottinger, Sailor's Snug Harbor, Sea Level, North Carolina, 1994.

Figure 2. *Baccarat* owned by Rear Com. Russell A. Alger III.

Figure 3. *Royono III* owned by John B. Ford Jr. (photo by Morris Rosenfeld)

Figure 4. *French Boy* owned by Com. John H. French family.

Figure 5. *Cambriona* owned by Walter O. Briggs.

Figure 6. *Zapala* owned by Howard Coffin.

Figure 7. President Calvin Coolidge and Mrs. Coolidge on the after deck of Howard Coffin's motor yacht *Zapala* near
Sapelo Island, Georgia, 1927.

Figure 8. *Nokomis II* owned by Horace E. Dodge.

Figure 9. *Delphine* owned by Horace E. Dodge.

Figure 10. *Nakhoda* owned by Frederick J. Fisher.

Figure 11. *Onika* owned by Com. Edsel B. Ford.

Figure 12. *Siele* owned by Com. John H. French.

Figure 13. *Olive K* owned by Charles Kettering.

Figure 14. *Naiad* owned by William S. Knudsen.

Figure 15. *Althea* owned by Com. Charles Hayward Murphy.

Figure 16. *Rosewill II* owned by W.C. Rands.

Figure 17. *Helene II* owned by Vice Com. Charles Sorensen.

Figure 18. *Anona* owned by Com. Burnette F. Stephenson.

Image Acknowledgements

1. Thomas K. Fisher Jr.
2. Detroit Yacht Club
3. Grosse Pointe Club
4.–5. Detroit Yacht Club
6.-7. Mystic Seaport Museum

8. Hagley Museum Digital Archives
9. Jay Ottinger
10.–12. Hagley Museum Digital Archives

13. Detroit Yacht Club
14. K. Peter Knudsen
15.–17. Detroit Yacht Club
18. Detroit Publishing Co.

Figure 1. A young Gordon M. Buehrig, car designer extraordinaire, at his drawing board before he penned the lengendary Cord 810.

Our Proud Automotive Connection
GPYC members who were auto industry pioneers

By Past Com. James L. Ramsey

There has always been a symbiotic relationship between cars and boats — and of course between car people and boat people — largely because the early car companies regularly supplied boat builders with engines to power their products, and still do. Out of this mutual relationship came an under-standing of, and affection for the water. In the case of Detroit, as many as one hundred twenty-five fledgling car companies once resided here. It was only natural for the leaders of the more successful enterprises to escape the cares of industry by joining a yacht club devoted to the enjoyment of boats and the water. So it was that a number of individuals who

played pioneering roles in the growth of the automobile industry were also members of the young Grosse Pointe Yacht Club.

Following is an alphabetical list of many of the automotive celebrities who were early GPYC members, along with some of their automotive accomplishments.

Russell A. Alger Jr., son of Russell A. Sr., who was Governor of Michigan, a U.S. Senator, and Secretary of War under President William McKinley. Like his father, Russell Jr. enjoyed tremendous success in the Michigan lumber business and became an energetic entrepreneur.

Figure 2. Russell A. Alger Jr.

Figure 3. Clarence W. Avery

Figure 4. Ernest R. Breech.

One of his early investments was the Ohio Automobile Company, founded by two brothers with the last name of Packard. Alger became a major stockholder and vice president of the company. Together with another large investor, Henry Joy, Alger Jr. succeeded in moving the company from Ohio to Detroit and renamed it Packard Motor Company. The rest, of course, is history.

Mr. Alger fell from a horse while pursuing hounds at the Detroit Country Club. He was paralyzed and died in 1930 at age fifty-seven. His son, Russell A. Alger III, served GPYC as a member of the board of directors and rear commodore in 1934.

Clarence W. Avery was a driving force behind Henry Ford's moving assembly line and was president and chairman of auto body supplier Murray Corporation. A teacher at heart, Mr. Avery was introduced to Henry Ford by one of his students, who happened to be Ford's son, Edsel. In addition to helping develop the moving assembly line, which put Ford Motor Company into ascendency, Avery was also instrumental in developing the Henry Ford Trade School. Avery left Ford in 1927 to join Murray Body Corporation, a near-bankrupt manufacturer of automobile bodies. His organizational skills brought a dramatic turnaround at Murray, and he quickly advanced to president, then chairman.

It is worth noting that Mr. Avery was one of the first automotive executives to work with the UAW to address employee grievances. He joined the Club in 1931 as a Class B, or Social member, and was inducted into the Automotive Hall of Fame in 1990.

Ernest R. Breech, chairman of the board at Ford Motor Company, was Henry Ford II's top executive in the years following World War II. Mr. Breech made a significant contribution to Ford Motor Company by reorganizing and restructuring it to meet modern post-war America. Mr. Breech's presence is said to have paved the way for the "Whiz Kids," a team of ten brainy former Army Air Force officers, including Robert S. McNamara, "Tex" Thornton and Arjay Miller, who brought cost accountability and operational efficiency to the company. Although little is known about Mr. Breech's affection for boats, he did enjoy the distinction of having a Great Lakes freighter named for him. The 626-foot *Ernest R. Breech* was part of the Ford Fleet and sailed under that name for many years. Breech joined GPYC in 1940 and remained a member until he left the area to lead Trans-World Airlines (TWA). He succeeded in revitalizing the airline and guided it to financial stability, just as he had done at Ford Motor Company.

Walter O. Briggs began as a laborer in the railroad industry and ended up owning Briggs Manufacturing Corp., Briggs Stadium, and the

Figure 5. Walter O. Briggs.

Figure 6. Gordon M. Buehrig.

Detroit Tigers. Briggs' early expertise was in railroad car upholstery, which landed him a job as head of the upholstery department at the B.F. Everitt Co., an automotive supplier. While there, he rose to vice president and then president. In 1910, when owner Barney Everitt decided to liquidate the company to build his own auto-mobile, Briggs bought it and proceeded to land a large order for Ford automobile bodies. Soon Briggs Manufacturing Co., as it was now named, was supplying bodies to Chrysler, Stutz, Packard, Pierce-Arrow, and Lincoln. Along the way, Briggs acquired the prestigious body design firm Le Baron which, in the days before carmakers had their own styling departments, gave him the ability to create automobile bodies with superior looks. Over time, Chrysler became Briggs' predominant customer and in 1953 purchased his U.S. car body operation. The deal included twelve factories and thirty thousand employees. Walter Briggs joined the Club in 1928, the same year he founded the Detroit Zoo. His Briggs Stadium was later renamed Tiger Stadium. He died in 1952.

Resource: Wikipedia; Coachbuilt.com

Gordon M. Buehrig, car designer extraordinaire, spent the early part of his career at Packard, GM and Stutz, learning the business and showing himself to be a major talent. But it was at three small specialty carmakers where he created

his most revered designs. Mr. Buehrig was lured from Stutz, where he was chief designer, by Duesenberg, where he penned the breathtaking Model "S." From there, he moved to Auburn, where he shaped the iconic Boattail Speedster (its rear deck was shaped like the overturned bow of a boat). His crowning achievement, however, was the low-slung front-wheel-drive Cord 810, which in 1935 featured a coffin-shaped hood, folding hidden headlamps, and slotted chrome wheels. The car was recognized by the Museum of Modern Art for its originality. Mr. Buehrig joined the GPYC in 1972 and remained a member until his death in 1990. His surviving spouse, Kathryn "Kay" frequently arrived at the Club in her mint Cord 810 sedan until her passing in 2012.

Resource: Wikipedia; New York Times obituary

Walter F. Carey founded Commercial Carriers in 1934 and grew it into the nation's largest transporter of new automobiles.

He also established Commercial Barge Lines, which coordinated shipping on inland waterways with shipping by truck, creating the world's leading water carrier of motor vehicles.

While serving as president of the American Trucking Association during the 1950s, Carey observed that during the short span of fifty years, the trucking industry had grown to become America's second largest employer. Carey himself had contributed greatly to that growth.

Figure 7. Walter F. Carey.

Figure 8. Horace E. Dodge.

Following his service to the ATA, Carey continued to serve industry as president of the United States Chamber of Commerce in the 1960s. Mr. Carey joined the Club in 1942 and was admitted to the Automotive Hall of Fame in 1981.

The Dodge brothers — Horace E., and John F. Although John Dodge was not a GPYC member and not nearly the yachting enthusiast his brother was, they are listed collectively here because the two brothers were inseparable in business, in life, and even death, both ironically dying the same year, 1920. Together, they founded Dodge Brothers Company, a hugely successful manufacturer of automotive components — transmissions, axles, frames, engines, etc. — that supplied Ransom E. Olds and his Olds(mobile) Motor Works. The Dodges also provided much of the early financing, engineering, and hardware for Ford Motor Company, and when their cash-short customer paid them in stock, they became Ford's largest stockholder. When Henry Ford hit pay-dirt with the revolutionary Model T, the Dodges became fabulously wealthy and went on to build cars and trucks branded with their own name. During World War I, the Dodge Company produced significant quantities of cars, trucks, and armament for the Allies. Dodge Brothers Trucks and Cars became part of Chrys-

ler Corporation in 1928. Horace Dodge was an avid boater who owned a string of motor launches, followed by progressively larger yachts. The Dodge brothers also founded their own marine division, which, under Horace Dodge Jr., built the Dodge Watercar, a successful line of speedboats.

The last of the Dodge yachts, *Delphine*, had the distinction of being the largest private yacht in America. Horace Dodge died just three months before the completion of his dream boat, but his widow Anna stepped up in his place. Not only did she oversee its final construction, she had a 3,000-foot channel dug so it could be docked in front of their home, Rose Terrace, in Grosse Pointe Farms. *Delphine* was a familiar sight there until the early 1960s when it was sold to an out-of-state buyer.

Documents showing exactly when Horace joined the Club are not available — only that he was listed as a member both by Club records and Clarence Burton. But given the date of his death when the Club was only six years old, Horace Dodge Sr. can be considered an important member of the GPYC in its formative years.

Reference: Grosse Pointe Historical Society; "The Dodge Family and the Grosse Pointes" by Michael W. Skinner; "The Dodge Fleet of Lake St. Clair" by John Polasek; Clarence Burton, "Detroit and Wayne County, 1922."

Figure 9. Fisher brothers from left; Alfred L, Lawrence P., Charles T., Fredrick J., William A., Howard A., and Edward F.

The Fisher brothers — Fred J., Charles T., William A., Lawrence P., Edward F., and Alfred J. — were all early members of the Club. Fred and Charles, the oldest of the six, founded the Fisher Body Company in 1908 and soon brought their siblings into the business. By 1916, the Fisher brothers' company had become the industry's largest supplier of automobile bodies. Fisher Body built bodies for Ford, Chalmers, Buick, Cadillac, Chevrolet, Hudson, Oldsmobile, and Packard, among others. In 1919, they sold sixty percent of their company to General Motors, making them all extremely wealthy. Seven years later, they sold the remaining forty percent to GM, and Fisher Body became an in-house coachbuilder to the corporation. Five of the six brothers became GM vice presidents and also served on the board of directors. The six joined the Club between 1927 and 1928 and were the owners of a number of grandiose yachts. The last of the brothers left GM in the mid-1940s to pursue other interests, among them construction of the Fisher Building in the Detroit New Center area.

Resource: Wikipedia; historicdetroit.org

Com. Edsel B. Ford I. was the son of the founder of Ford Motor Company and president of Ford Motor Company from 1919 to his death in 1943. Although he was overshadowed and often overruled in that capacity by his demanding father,

Henry I, Edsel Ford nevertheless brought many significant advancements to the company and its products. Edsel was a proponent of style in automobiles, while his conservative father was not. The younger Ford prevailed to give the new Model A a look that makes it popular to this day and equipped it with breakthrough features such as double-action shock absorbers, safety-glass windshield and eventually a V-8 engine. He also persuaded his father to adopt a luxury brand by buying the troubled Lincoln Motor Company and personally inspired the look of the now-classic pre-war Lincoln Continental. Edsel was particularly fond of boats, especially fast ones, and even drove in several Gold Cup races in the 1930s. He joined the Club in 1926. The only child of Henry and Clara Ford died of cancer at age forty-nine.

Harvey C. Fruehauf was born in 1893, the son of Fruehauf Trailer Company founder August Fruehauf, a blacksmith who built his first autom tive-drawn trailer in 1914 for a local lumber merchant who wanted to transport his private boat. The resulting "semi-trailer" was so successful, the merchant ordered several similar trailers from Fruehauf for hauling lumber. They, too, exceeded expectations. Word of August Fruehauf's prowess as a builder of high-quality trailers spread quickly. As orders poured in,

Figure 10. Edsel B. Ford I.

Figure 11. Harvey C. Fruehauf.

Figure 12. George M. Holly.

Harvey joined his father's growing business in 1915 as the full-time bookkeeper. The Fruehauf Trailer Company was incorporated in 1918 with August as president and son Harvey as vice president and general manager.

In 1929, with the retirement of his father, Harvey Fruehauf took charge of what had risen to become America's preeminent trailer builder. Although the company continued to grow under his leadership, Fruehauf himself became embroiled in a controversial dispute with the National Labor Relations Board for failure to comply with the Wagner Act while trying to keep his company union-free. Fruehauf received only a reprimand for his actions, and the Fruehauf Trailer Corporation enjoyed continued growth and prosperity during the post-Depression 1940s, becoming the largest trailer manufacturer in the world. During that era, the name Fruehauf adorned car and truck trailers of every size and description, and the Fruehauf Corporation was regarded as one of the icons of the American transportation industry.

Mr. Fruehauf served as president of the company until 1949 and remained as chairman of the board until 1953 when he retired during a control dispute with his younger brother. He joined the Club in 1938 or 1939 along with his brothers Harry and Roy, who also served in senior positions. He remained a member until his death in 1968.

George M. Holley founded the Holley Motor Company in 1899 to produce motorcycles and engines. George was the chief engineer and designer in the organization, setting speed records and winning races while brother Earl promoted and managed the business.

But it was the carburetor that put the name Holley on the map. The Holley Carburetor Company produced carburetors for the famed Curved-Dash Oldsmobile, eventually becoming the leading carburetor supplier to Ford, Pierce-Arrow, Winton, and Buick.

From there, the company expanded into carburetion for aircraft and marine engines, subsequently becoming the world's largest independent manufacturer of carburetors. The Holley brand name ratcheted to even greater prominence during the 1960s as a supplier of high-performance carburetors for muscle and race cars.

George Holley joined the Club as an Active member in 1929, and was admitted to the Automotive Hall of Fame in 1995. He died in 1963.

Robert C. Hupp was one of the founding members who met in 1914 to lay the groundwork for the Grosse Pointe Yacht Club. He was elected a director of the Club that same year. Seven years earlier, after gaining valuable experience at Oldsmobile and Ford, he had founded his own

Figure 13. Robert C. Hupp.

Figure 14. Com. Harry M. Jewett.

Figure 15. K.T. Keller.

automobile company, the Hupp Motor Company, which rolled out its first production Hupmobile in 1909 and enjoyed immediate success. Hupp's claim to fame was that he was the first carmaker in the U.S. to use all-steel bodies, a feature that made the Hupmobile structurally strong — and popular. Moreover, Hupp was a skilled promoter who staged several endurance runs, including an around-the-world drive that gained notoriety for his products. Hupp himself left the company in 1911 after a dispute with his financial backers over his aggressive investment philosophy. He attempted to start a number of automobile companies afterward, but none achieved the success of his original motor company. Even without Mr. Hupp, the Hupmobile became a respected nameplate that remained in production for thirty years.

Com. Harry M. Jewett was president of the Paige-Detroit Motor Car Company, which produced popular Paige-Detroit automobiles in the early part of the twentieth century and later, in 1922, introduced a lower-cost brand bearing Mr. Jewett's name. The Jewett "Six" remained in production until 1926 when the company was sold to the Graham Brothers who eventually changed the brand name from Paige-Detroit to their own. A noteworthy feature of the Jewett car was an amulet, or charm, that was attached to the dashboard at the request of Mr. Jewett's wife,

who was a spiritualist. She believed it would keep occupants safe from evil. Although it is not certain which year Mr. Jewett joined the Club, by 1917 or earlier he became vice commodore and served as the Club's second commodore from 1919 to 1925. The handsome white-frame home he built and lived in along Lake Shore Road is presently owned by GPYC members Mr. and Mrs. Robert Liggett.

K.T. Keller was the former master mechanic who became Walter P. Chrysler's right-hand man. A lifelong pragmatist, he favored substance and value over styling. Mr. Keller assumed leadership of Chrysler when Walter P. retired in the middle of the Depression. Prior to that, he had successfully overseen the integration of Dodge Division into Chrysler's corporate infrastructure. (Chrysler had purchased Dodge in 1928, eight years after the deaths of the Dodge Brothers.) Keller's firm hand managed to keep the company afloat through the worst of the 1930s, and as World War II loomed, he was the first of the automotive chiefs to voluntarily convert his factories to military production. Under Keller, Chrysler eventually produced more than twenty-five thousand Pershing and Sherman tanks during the war years. Keller's standout performance on behalf of the war effort earned the admiration of President Harry Truman who, in 1950, asked him to leave

Figure 16. Charles F. Kettering.

Figure 17. William S. Knudsen.

Chrysler and put the U.S. Missile Program back on track. Mr. Keller obliged and once again succeeded. Keller joined the Club in December 1928 and was elected to the board of directors in 1930. He remained on the board before and after the Club reopened in 1938 and was one of the driving forces behind its reformation. He served as first vice commodore under George Slocum during 1938 and 1939. An avid fisherman, Keller spent his spare hours at the Club aboard his various boats. One was named named *Rellek*, which is "Keller" spelled backwards.

Charles F. Kettering, aka "Boss Ket," was a prolific automotive inventor for whom the term "genius" would be something of an understatement. Among his noteworthy inventions were the electric starter, leaded "ethyl" gasoline, practical electric lighting for cars and freon gas for air conditioning. In all, Kettering was the holder of more than one hundred eighty-six U.S. patents and was a leading developer of lightweight 2-stroke diesel engines for trucks, locomotives, and other heavy equipment. Perhaps his largest creation was Dayton Engineering Laboratories Company, which was shortened to the acronym DELCO, and became the electronics division of General Motors. He also helped found the Sloan-Kettering Cancer Center in New York. Mr. Kettering served as vice president of research for

GM for twenty-seven years. He joined the Yacht Club in 1930 and was elected to the board of directors shortly after. C.F. Kettering owned several major yachts, which are listed in a separate article.

William S. Knudsen, a Danish-born immigrant, who beame a powerful and accomplished industrialist. He held senior positions at Ford Motor Company and General Motors before becoming president of GM in 1937. Mr. Knudsen's expertise was in mass production, specifically assembly line efficiency, and his talents propelled him to titles of influence at both companies. During World War II, he was commissioned by the Roosevelt Administration as a Lieutenant General in the Army to lead U.S. war materiel production. He was the only civilian in the country to initially attain such a high rank. Mr. Knudsen was the father of Semon "Bunkie" Knudsen, who was a senior executive at GM before becoming president of Ford Motor Company. The senior Knudsen was a member of GPYC from 1929 until his death in 1948.

Alvan Macauley Sr. was born James Alvan Macauley, although he never used his first name. Mr. Macaulay came to Packard Motor Company in 1910 as the general manager to succeed president Henry Joy, who was retiring in 1916. As president, Macaulay moved decisively to establish Packard as an engineering leader among

Figure 18. Alvan Macauley Sr.

Figure 19. Charles S. Mott.

American luxury carmakers. He promoted technological guru Jesse Vincent to chief engineer, and Packard soon launched its legendary "twin-six" V-12 engine. In the eyes of many, the V-12 leapfrogged Packard ahead of Cadillac as the top American production automobile. When the Depression hit, Macaulay acted wisely again by introducing a line of middle-priced cars, the Packard 120s, that sold in volume compared to bigger, more expensive Packard models. The "junior-model" 120s, as they were called, along with government contracts for aircraft engines, kept the company healthy from the mid-1930s through the end of World War II. Like other industrial captains, Mr. Macaulay and his family lived in a beautiful Cotswald-inspired home along Lake Shore Road, designed by Albert Kahn. Little is known about his boating interests, except that Packard supplied legendary boat racer Gar Wood with engines and worked closely with him in their development. Later, in World War II, Packard provided a version of these engines to the U.S. Government for use in PT Boats, each of which used three of them. Mr. Macaulay became a GPYC member in 1929 and was elected to the board of directors later that year.

Charles S. Mott, businessman, philanthropist, and twice mayor of Flint, Michigan, was one of the founding partners in General Motors and

served on its board of directors for sixty years until his death in 1973. Mr. Mott's career began in New Jersey in the family bicycle wheel business, which expanded to making wheels for automobiles. In 1907, the company moved to Flint, Michigan, to be close to the automobile business. It prospered there and eventually became the country's leading supplier of automobile axles. Mott twice sold halves of his company to General Motors in return for GM stock, which made him incredibly wealthy. By the time World War II broke out, he was General Motors' largest stockholder.

Mr. Mott used much of his immense wealth for the good of others. In 1926, he established the Charles Stewart Mott Foundation; his gifts of money and stock soon made it one of the largest philanthropic organizations in the nation. He also provided the funding for C.S. Mott Children's Hospital, which is part of the University of Michigan Medical Complex in Ann Arbor and is nationally recognized for its pediatric services. Mr. Mott joined the Club in 1929.

Resource: Wikipedia; Encyclopedia Britannica

Ora J. Mulford joined forces with banker/investor David Gray and in 1905 founded the Gray Marine Motor Co. Gray engines soon found favor with boat builders and even carmakers, and the company produced as many as seven

Figure 20. Ora J. Mulford.

Figure 21. Charles E. Sorensen.

thousand gas and diesel engines a year before World War I. By 1920, however, the lure of the automobile business had become irresistible to Mr. Gray, and he decided to back the creation of a new automobile called the Gray that would be produced by the marine engine company. Diversification must not have set well with Mr. Mulford, because within several years he used his investment in the company to purchase sole ownership of Gray Marine Engine Division. It was a very smart move on his part. The Gray automobile was unsuccessful and the Gray Motor Corporation went out of business in 1926. Gray Marine Division, on the other hand, continued to prosper, largely by converting car engines for marine use and then rebranding them as Gray-marines. Mulford became a GPYC member in 1928. As pleasure boats soared in popularity in the post-World War II era, so did Graymarine engines. To settle Mr. Mulford's estate when he died in 1944, Gray Marine Motor Co. became a subsidiary of Continental Motors. Graymarine engines were produced until 1967.

Resource: Wikipedia; Gas Engine Magazine — A Brief History of Gray Marine Engines by Max F. Homfeld; Discuss Detroit: Old Car Factories — 12.

Charles E. Sorensen was a Danish-born immigrant who met Henry Ford I before Ford's rise to eminence and went to work for him in 1905, beginning a career that spanned four decades and three generations of the Ford family. He worked as a patternmaker, engineer, production manager, and eventually vice president and director of Ford Motor Company. During his early years with the company, it was Mr. Sorensen who, along with three other men, is credited with being the father of the modern moving assembly line. Prior to that, cars were built in a stationary position, with parts being brought to the chassis for installation. To prove his idea, Sorensen towed a chassis from one end of the Ford Piquette Plant to the other with a rope over his shoulder; and as the chassis moved along, parts were added to it. The practice drastically improved the speed and cost of assembly and in turn revolutionized not only Ford Motor Company but the entire automobile industry. In 1928, Mr. Sorensen became one of Ford's three U.S. directors, alongside Henry Ford I and Edsel Ford. When World War II erupted, Sorensen became Ford's director of production, responsible for building mass quantities of Jeeps, aircraft engines and B-24 bombers. The B-24 was arguably his piece de resistance, as it was Sorensen who was responsible for designing the

Figure 22. Col. Jesse G. Vincent.

Figure 23. Charles E. Wilson.

Figure 24. Fred M. Zeder.

vast Willow Run Assembly Plant where the B-24 Liberator bomber was made. Plagued by staggering start-up problems, Willow Run was never able to achieve its goal of building one bomber every hour, but by the end of the war its production output was still impressive, turning out approximately eighteen to twenty airplanes per day. (A typically good assembly time in the aircraft industry was one plane per day in the early part of the war.) Along the way, Mr. Sorensen is said to have been something of a mentor to a young Henry Ford II, but the two apparently did not always see eye to eye, especially over early production problems at the Willow Run Plant. When Henry II, who at age twenty-four took over the company from his grandfather in 1943, Charles Sorensen resigned. He went on to become president of Willys-Overland, which was renamed Kaiser Jeep and eventually absorbed by American Motors Corporation. Mr. Sorensen joined the GPYC in 1927, became a board member in 1931, and was elected vice commodore the same year. He was an avid yachtsman whose 60-foot sailboat *White Cloud* won the Chicago-to-Mackinac Race in 1942. One of Sorensen's motor yachts named *Helene* was still a familiar sight on area waters as recently as a decade ago. Well past her prime, she still floats sadly but defiantly in a channel off the Detroit River that is reserved for derelict craft.

Col. Jesse G. Vincent was Packard's legendary chief engineer, a title he held despite lack of formal engineering training, for nearly thirty years after joining Packard in 1912.

When the U.S. entered World War I, Vincent became a major in the U.S. Army and was responsible for designing the iconic V-12 Liberty aircraft engine, a feat that is said to have taken just five days. The war ended before the Liberty engine could be fully implemented as an aerial weapon, but surplus versions quickly found their way into high-performance speedboats and race cars. Vincent himself beat heavily favored Gar Wood to win the 1922 Gold Cup in a Liberty-powered boat that for the first time publically wore the name Chris Craft. Several years afterward, in 1929, Vincent joined the Grosse Pointe Yacht Club as an Active member. He remained a member until 1951.

Mr. Vincent is also remembered for creating the Packard Twin-Six, an engine with twelve cylinders that quickly advanced Packard past the eight-cylinder Cadillac at the top of the luxury car market. Vincent put his stamp on almost every Packard built between the wars and was instrumental in elevating the Packard brand to preeminence among American automobiles.

Sadly, Packard's cachet declined during the postwar period, and Vincent, who retired in 1946, lived to see the company shut its doors in 1958.

He died four years later. An official State marker at the old Packard Proving Grounds is dedicated in his honor, calling him "America's Master Motor Builder."

Charles E. Wilson, aka "C.E." or "Engine Charlie," is arguably the most powerful automotive figure to have held membership at the Club. His meteoric career began in 1910 at Westinghouse Electric, where he designed that company's first automotive electric starter motor. C.E. Wilson left Westinghouse in 1919 for Remy Electric, a subsidiary of General Motors that subsequently became the Delco-Remy Corporation.

Wilson was a gifted engineer and a dynamic manager, rising rapidly through the ranks at GM to become vice president in 1928, and executive vice president in 1939. Wilson was elected president of General Motors in January 1941 after William Knudsen resigned all his connections with GM in order that he might accept the invitation of President Roosevelt to direct industrial production in the National Defense Program. Wilson served in that capacity until 1953, when President Dwight Eisenhower invited him to join his cabinet as U.S. Secretary of Defense, which he accepted.

Despite his many contributions to industry and government, Charles E. Wilson's greatest claim to fame was a quote that was incorrectly attributed to him. In testimony before Congress prior to his confirmation as Secretary of Defense, he was misquoted as saying, "What is good for General Motors is good for the country." It was an expression of supreme arrogance that would dog him for the rest of his life. In reality what he said was, "For years I thought that what was good for our country was good for General Motors, and vice-versa."

But the real measure of the man was not so much what he said but what he did. Before becoming Secretary of Defense, to avoid any suggestion of conflict of interest, Mr. Wilson divested his considerable shareholdings in General Motors, a decision that cost him over one million dollars at the time. Moreover, he left a position that paid him a salary of $600,000 a year, plus millions more in stock options, for a job that paid just $22,500 annually.

Mr. Wilson joined the GPYC in 1929, along with an influx of powerful business leaders who became members with the opening of the clubhouse, and remained a member until at least 1935. He passed away peacefully in his sleep in 1961.

Fred M. Zeder was perhaps singlehandedly responsible for the creation of Chrysler Corporation. After earning a Bachelor's degree in mechanical engineering from the University of Michigan and serving an apprenticeship at Allis-Chalmers, Zeder went to work for the fledgling E.M.F. automobile company as head of their body design laboratory. When financially-ailing E.M.F. was bought by Studebaker, Fred Zeder went with them and in 1914 became Studebaker's head engineer. He was twenty-eight years old. When Studebaker experienced its own financial troubles, Zeder hired two precocious friends, Carl Breer and Owen Skelton, to create an all-new Studebaker. They became known as "The Three Musketeers" for their brilliance. The Three Musketeers were subsequently recruited by Walter Chrysler to join him at Willys-Overland Co. and become the nucleus of their engineering department with Zeder as chief engineer. Then, when Walter Chrysler left Willys to revive the failing Maxwell Motor Co., the trio went with him. There they designed an outstanding new car called the Chrysler. But when Chrysler announced his intention to sell the design to Studebaker, Fred Zeder went into revolt. He angrily threatened to burn every one of the Chrysler's plans if the deal was made. If the Chrysler automobile was going to be produced, it would have to be built as a Chrysler. Walter Chrysler relented. The offer to Studebaker was withdrawn, and when Chrysler Motor Corp. was founded in 1925, Fred Zeder was named vice president of engineering. Two years later, he became a director of Chrysler Corporation and served as vice chairman of the board from 1935 to 1957. Mr. Zeder was described as a "dynamic, forceful, enthusiastic and sincere man, with an outgoing, even flamboyant personality." He was said to be a brilliant automotive engineer and a natural-born salesman. He became a GPYC member in 1932. Zeder, Carl Breer and Owen Skelton, all GPYC members and known as the "Three Musketeers," were each inducted into the Automotive Hall of Fame.

Resource: Wikipedia; allpar.com

Automotive Hall of Fame honorees who were members of the GPYC

Name	Inducted
Avery, Clarence W.	1990
Breech, Ernest R.	1979
Breer, Carl	1976
Buehrig, Gordon M.	2000
Carey, Walter F.	1981
Dodge, Horace E	1981
Fisher, Alfred J.	1995
Fisher, Charles T.	1995
Fisher, Edward F.	1995
Fisher, Fred J.	1995
Fisher, Lawrence P.	1995
Fisher, William A.	1995
Ford, Edsel B.	1968
Holley, George M. Sr.	1995
Keller, K. T.	1971
Kettering, Charles F.	1967
Knudsen, William S.	1968
Mott, Charles S.	1973
Skelton, Owen R.	2002
Sorensen, Charles E.	2001
Vincent, Jesse G.	1971
Wilson, Charles E.	1969
Zeder, Fred M.	1998

IMAGE ACKNOWLEDGEMENTS

1. Automotive Hall of Fame

2. Grosse Pointe War Memorial

3.–4. Automotive Hall of Fame

5. Detroit Public Library

6.–9. Automotive Hall of Fame

10. Benson Ford Research Center

11. GPYC

12. Automotive Hall of Fame

13. Wayne State University

14. Detroit Public Library

15.–17. Automotive Hall of Fame

18. Detroit Public Library

19. Automotive Hall of Fame

20. Detroit Public Library

21.–23. Automotive Hall of Fame

24.–25. Detroit Public Library

Figure 25. From left to right, Charles E. Sorensen, Past Vice Commodore of GPYC; Lieutenant General William S. Knudsen, GPYC; member; and GPYC Past Commodore Edsel B. Ford. Photo taken at Willow Run Ford Motor Company bomber plant June 12, 1942.

Figure 1. *Miss England III* was put on display in the GPYC harbor some days before the race was run. The boat had been shipped across the Atlantic to the East Coast and then transported to Lake St. Clair, possibly by the barge on which it is cradled.

The 1932 Harmsworth Race and the GPYC

by Larry W. Stephenson, M.D.

The Harmsworth Cup, formally known as the British International Trophy for Motor Boats, was the powerboat equivalent of the America's Cup sailing trophy during the latter half of the 1920s and early 1930s. It was commissioned in 1903 by Sir Alfred Harmsworth, owner of the *London Daily Mail*. As with the America's Cup, a country holding the Harmsworth Cup defended it only when challenged by another country.

The 1932 Harmsworth Cup Race was likely the biggest sporting event in Grosse Pointe history. Headlines of *The Grosse Pointe Review*, the forerunner of the *Grosse Pointe News*, read, "Eyes of the World Centered Here as Harmsworth Races are Held." Races were scheduled Saturday, September 3rd through Tuesday, September 6th. The races for the Harmsworth Cup were the main event and scheduled for Saturday, Monday, and Tuesday if a third race was necessary.

The Grosse Pointe Review stated, "Hundreds of thousands of spectators are expected to be in attendance," and this appeal was on the front page: "Boy Scouts notice! Grosse Pointe scouts are requested to report at the Neighborhood Club Friday evening at 7:30 p.m. to receive instructions for duty at the boat races." Because of the heavy traffic expected for the weekend, Lake Shore Road from Fisher Road to Nine Mile Road was closed at 6 p.m. Friday. Instructions were given to motorists for getting around the Grosse Pointes during the days of the races, and where to park. Rowboats were available at the Village Pier at 5 a.m. on race days, renting for $1 per day. It would take renters about twenty minutes to row to the course viewing area.

The race was under the authority of the Yachtsmen's Association of America and the Royal Motor Yacht Club. The yacht clubs represented were the Detroit Yacht Club and the Sussex Motor Yacht

Club. The GPYC contributed funds to help under-write the cost of the race, and thirteen members served on one or more of the race's governing bodies.[1] GPYC member Otto F. Barthel was chief race official representing the United States via the Yachtsmen's Association of America.

The layout of the course had the boats racing past the Club's East Wall and making their first turn just north of the clubhouse grounds. Because of this strategic location, the GPYC was heavily utilized by race officials and members of the press, and hosted plenty of eager spectators as well. The harbor was used for docking numerous boats involved with the race.

Back in 1920, England held the Harmsworth Cup when Gar Wood crossed the Atlantic, representing the U.S., to challenge. *Miss America I* won that race and Wood successfully defended the Cup in 1921, 1926, 1928, 1929 and 1930. Those races were held on the Detroit River with the course extending from the Belle Isle Bridge north-ward past Belle Isle. But since 1903, average speeds had increased from 19.53 mph to 85.86 mph, and when a significant accident occurred during the 1931 British challenge, it was determined that the Belle Isle course was no longer appropriate for the increased speeds. On the second day of racing, in the first turn of the first lap, *Miss England II*, piloted by English sports-man Kaye Don, skidded sideways, causing the stern to fill with water, then flipped over and sank. Fortunately, Kaye Don and his two mechanics were tossed from the boat and uninjured.

Kaye Don had won the first heat of that race, and in the second heat where the wreck occurred, both Kaye Don and Gar Wood, driving *Miss America IX*, were disqualified for going over the starting line before the gun, so the third boat in the race, *Mrs. America VIII*, driven by George Wood, Gar's younger brother, won the heat. Since the Harmsworth rules state that the country winning the first two of three races wins the Cup, and the British boat was now unable to compete in the third race, the Harmsworth trophy remained in the United States.

A British challenge was issued once again in 1932, with driver Kaye Don returning to pilot his new boat, *Miss England III*. Her hull length was 35 feet, with a total weight 10,500 pounds. She was powered by two V-12, supercharged V-12 Rolls-Royce aviation engines, with 4,400 total horsepower. Her crew consisted of a pilot and mechanic. *Miss England III* was fast. She had just set a new world speedboat record of 119.81 mph on July 18, 1932, eclipsing the record of 111.712 mph set by Wood the previous March in his old *Miss America IX*.

Gar Wood would be driving *Miss America X*, 38 feet long, weighing 14,000 pounds and powered by four supercharged Packard V-12 aircraft engines, total horsepower 6,400. Wood was forced to build a boat that could contain four-Packard engines because the two Rolls-Royce engines in the British boat were capable of producing over 2,000 horsepower each, and the Packards were then capable of only 1,400 horse-power. Wood's boat also had a crew of two, driver and mechanic, Orlin Johnson. Since *Miss America X* was assembled and in the test phase only days before the race, no attempt could be made to determine its top speed. Wood's plan was likely to run it just fast enough to beat the British boat.

Garfield Arthur "Gar" Wood, who stood five feet six inches and weighed one hundred thirty pounds, was born in 1880 into a family of thirteen children. He became a successful businessman after inventing a hydraulic lift for unloading coal from trucks. He also produced Gar Wood truck bodies and garbage trucks, and over time became a wealthy man. In 1916, he began racing boats, and in 1920 set a world speed record of 74.80 mph on the Detroit River. He won North America's prestigious Gold Cup powerboat race five straight times between 1917 and 1926 and, beginning in 1920, had won several Harmsworth races. In 1921 he became Commodore of the Detroit Yacht Club.

Kaye Ernest Donsky, aka Kaye Don, was born in 1891 in Dublin, Ireland. He started racing motorcycles in 1912. During World War I he was a pilot in the Royal Flying Corps. After the war, in 1921, he began racing cars. He set many class records and attempted on one occasion to set a world speed record in a vehicle built by the Sunbeam Car Company called "Silver Bullet," with an engine producing 4,000 horsepower. In 1931, he became the driver of the race boat *Miss England II* when her former pilot, Sir Henry Seagrave, was killed.

The new site chosen for the 1932 race was Lake St. Clair. The oval-shaped course was expanded from five to seven nautical miles in length, with two straightaways of three miles each and turns at each end. The course extended from just north of the Grosse Pointe ("Little") Club to approximately one hundred yards north of the Grosse Pointe Yacht Club, with straightaways parallel to Lake Shore Road. The racers would run in a clockwise direction and the start-finish line was abeam of the Grosse Pointe Farms Pier Park. Each heat would be five laps totaling thirty-five miles.

The first race was scheduled for seven o'clock Saturday morning because race officials thought the water on Lake St. Clair would be smoother at sunrise rather than later in the day. *Miss America X* was being kept at Gar Wood's boathouse next to his home on the Detroit River a few miles from the racecourse. *Miss England III* was being kept in Henry Joy's boathouse on Lake St. Clair, about two hundred yards from the start-finish line.

At five o'clock that morning there was a cold rain coming down, and in the darkness, lights from an estimated one thousand boats could be seen "moving in an almost endless string toward a common goal, the Harmsworth Course."[2] The boats, most fully loaded with spectators, were all sizes, from canoes and rowboats to sailboats, cruisers and yachts. When dawn broke, the boats could be seen anchored around the rim of the back straightaway and at each turn. The shoreline was said to be "banked solid with humanity for miles"[3] despite the cold September rain. Bonfires along the shore were helping to keep people warm. Clearly the Harmsworth Regatta, which was free to watch, was a pleasant diversion for the crowd from the Great Depression, which was in one of its worst years.

There were whitecaps on the lake. *Miss England III* arrived first at the race site, being towed from Joy's boathouse. The rain stopped briefly, and the spectators could see the brilliant white race boat with bold red letters on its side next to the image of a Union Jack. Kaye Don and his mechanic stood confidently in the boat's cockpit as the boat was being towed. At exactly 6:55 a.m., the five-minute warning cannon was fired and the mighty Rolls-Royce engines were started. The English boat began to circle the course. At about the time the one-minute cannon was fired, the far-off rumble of engines could be heard in the direction of the Detroit River. Soon *Miss America X* could be seen charging into view through the gray morning haze, throwing a wake of white spray. Although the four-engine Boeing B-17 bomber was then a thing of the future, the noise from Wood's four engines probably sounded very much like one as his boat approached the racecourse.

When the starting cannon was fired, both boats were well off the mark, poorly timing their run to the starting line. This may have been due to the fact that the last time Don and Wood raced against each other in the second heat of the 1931 Harmsworth, both were disqualified for jumping the gun on the start. This time, Don crossed the starting line about fifteen seconds after the starting gun was fired and Wood about five seconds after Don. They had two miles to cover to get to the Grosse Pointe Yacht Club turn, with Don in the lead. At the end of the first lap, Don was forty seconds in the lead. He was running with his throttles wide open, Wood was having problems with his boat in the rough water. From the time they left the boathouse, they could tell the boat was out of balance, and early in the race the boat was handling poorly, swerving from side to side. Just as that problem seemed to miraculously subside, a bigger, more immediate problem occurred — a gas pipe broke when Wood opened the throttles, which soaked him in gasoline. Wood's throttle man/mechanic Orlin Johnson reached into the engine compartment in an attempt to fix the problem. As it turned out, fuel was spraying from a broken overflow pipe beside Wood. When Johnson realized what the problem was, he cut back further on the throttles. Wood knew if he pulled open the throttles again, the engines were in danger of backfiring and he might become a human torch — or the boat could blow to pieces.

Meanwhile, Don's lead increased. Wood decided "to hell with the [gasoline] benzol," and gave Johnson the signal to open the throttles.[4] Johnson did as he was told, and luckily the engines did not backfire. By the time *Miss England III* completed the third lap, *Miss America X* was now only ten seconds behind. Don, seeing Wood closing on him, decided to jam his foot down on the accelerator. The throttle control to the port engine jerked loose, crippling the engine. Don's speed dropped to 80 mph. When the boats approached the committee boat signaling the start of the fifth and final lap, Johnson nailed the throttles and they shot past Don. They completed the lap, ending the thirty-five-mile race with Wood three minutes, or more than two miles, ahead of *Miss England III*.

Don passed the finish line and headed for the Joy boathouse, then started calling wildly for a tow, because his boat was sinking. The stern was very low in the water. *Miss England III* made it to the boathouse, was bailed out, and strung up in its cradle so repairs could be made. Wood's boat also underwent needed repairs over the next day and a half.

On Monday the lake was rougher than Saturday. *Miss England III* lost one of its engines due to a broken piston only a mile into the first lap, and pushed on for a few more laps with one of its engines spewing smoke and flames, finally pulling off the racecourse. Just then, the second engine quit. Once again, the Harmsworth Cup belonged to the United States. Wood and everyone else seemed disappointed with *Miss England III*'s mechanical problems during both heats, which prevented a more dramatic showdown.

Three weeks later, on the St. Clair River, Wood and Johnson set a new world speed record just north of Algonac where a measured mile was laid out. *Miss America X* made an upstream run and a downstream run, the two runs averaging 124.86 mph. Perhaps as a result of the 1932 Harmsworth, Wood decided to show the world that *Miss England III*, which had been the world speed record holder going into that race, would probably not have won the 1932 Harmsworth, even without mechanical problems.

Acknowledgements

1. Joel Stone, Senior Curator, Detroit Historical Society for supplying images and other material related to the race.

2. Conan E. "Pat" Fisher, director of the Algonac-Clay Historical Museum for a personal tour of the museum as it related to Gar Wood and the 1932 Harmsworth Race.

3. Ed Theisen, past commodore and historian of the Detroit Yacht Club, for making himself available to answer this author's numerous questions about the 1932 race.

4. Joe Schulte and Doug Dossin, for providing historical information and for editorial comments and advice on the preparation of this manuscript.

References

1. W.D. Edenburn, Facts and Figures of the British International Trophy (four page pamphlet reprinted) published by the Detroit Yacht Club *Mainsheet* and was available shortly before the 1932 Harmwaorth Race.

1. J. Lee Barrett, *Speedboat Kings*, (Hardscrabble Books, Berrien Springs, Michigan, 1986), 121.

2. Ibid, 122.

3. Ibid, 126.

4. A. J. Muntz, At the Ragged Edge, (Scribewerx, Edmunds, Washington, 2013), 119–131.

Figure 2. GPYC courtesy card for entry to the Club grounds during race days. This card, stamped "employee," was apparently required even by GPYC employees for admittance.

Figure 3. The International Harmsworth Ball was held during race week at the GPYC. In this photo, taken in the Main Dining Room, Commodore C. Hayward Murphy, left, and Gar Wood, second left, admire a large cake made in the shape of *Miss America X*. The lovely ladies and the third gentleman are unidentified.

Figure 4. On race days, Lake Shore Road was closed to traffic from Fisher Road to Nine Mile Road. This photo appears to have been taken at Fisher Road looking north, where crowds of people are proceeding up the road to the shoreline viewing area.

Figure 5. Blustery weather did not deter the countless thousands of spectators from the excitement of the race that was attracting "the eyes of the world." Lake Shore Road was a virtual sea of humanity.

Figure 6. The first race was scheduled Saturday morning at 7:00 am, so a large crowd was already gathered well before sunrise.

Figure 7. Gar Wood, left, and Kaye Don, right, photographed at the Detroit Yacht Club on August 24, 1932, ten days before the first race.

Figure 8. Boats of all shapes and sizes lined the straightaways and both turns. This aerial view shows them anchored along the back (east) straightaway.

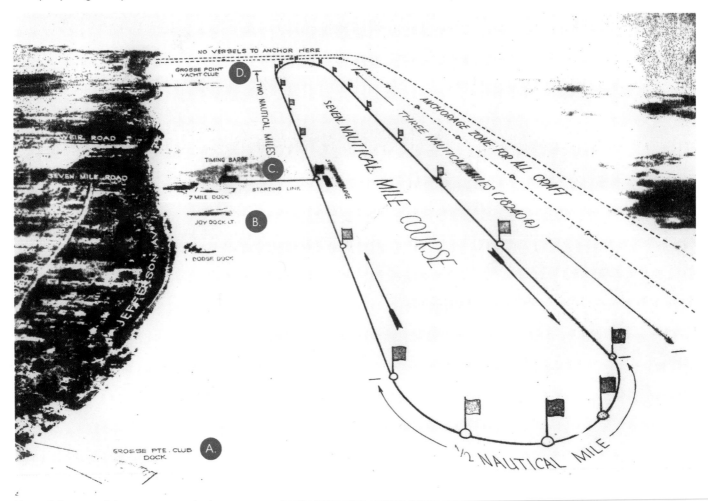

Figure 9. Diagram of the seven nautical mile racecourse. A is the Grosse Pointe Club; B is the Joy Boathouse; C is the starting line, directly east of the Grosse Pointe Farms Pier Park; D is the GPYC.

Figure 10. Kaye Don and his mechanic stand on the bow of their boat, next to the breakwater of the Joy boathouse (now the Crescent Sail Yacht Club), *Miss England III's* home port during the race.

Figure 11. The start of the first race, with *Miss England III*, right, getting the jump on *Miss America X*. The barge in the foreground is carrying race officials.

Figure 12. Gar Wood's *Miss America X*, most likely being photographed from the air.

Figure 13. Kaye Don pushes the throttle to top speed.

Figure 14. The crowd must have been holding its collective breath when it looked as if *Miss England III* would carry the day.

Figure 15. In the first race, Gar Wood shot past Kaye Don at the start of the fifth and final lap to take the lead and the eventual win.

Image Acknowledgements

1. Percell Siniff/Dorothy Jewett family.

2. Joe Schaden

3.–6. The Dossin Family Collection

7. Detroit Historical Society

8. The Dossin Family Collection

9.–11. Detroit Historical Society

12. Jim Dorian

13. Conan E. Fisher

14.–15. Detroit Historical Society

Figure 1. Artist Rick Ford's painting depicts, from left to right, the ice yachts *Deuce IV*, *Ferdinand the Bull*, and *The Flying Dutchman* on Lake Winnebago near Oshkosh, Wisconsin, circa the mid-1940s.

GPYC and championship ice yacht racing

The Stuart International Ice Yacht Trophy and the Hearst International Challenge Cup

By Larry W. Stephenson, M.D., and Carol E. Stephenson

Page thirty-nine of the spring 1947 issue of *The Grosse Pointer* displays photographs of two iceboats. They recall an era when "ice yachts," some exceeding 50 feet in length, were frequently seen skimming across the frozen waters of Lake St. Clair, either joyriding with passengers or locked in fierce sail-to-sail competition for some prestigious racing trophy. Both photos are historically significant in that one of the iceboats already held the title of World Champion, while the other would become World Champion two years later. The iceboats, along with their two owners and skippers in these photos, once called the Grosse Pointe Yacht Club home.[1]

According to the first caption, *Ferdinand the Bull* was owned by GPYC member Rex Jacobs and skippered by George Hendrie. She held the title of World Champion by virtue of having won the Stuart International Ice Yacht Trophy every year from 1940 to 1947. The second photograph depicts *Deuce IV*, a serious contender for the Stuart Trophy that was owned by GPYC member Clare Jacobs and skippered that year by Joe Snay. *Deuce IV* would go on to capture the Stuart Trophy in 1949.

Since iceboating was such an integral part of the early years of our Club, it seems logical that perhaps we should know something about the sport and the members who embraced it.

Rex and Clare Jacobs

Brothers Rex and Clare Jacobs, along with a third brother, Fred, founded the F.L. Jacobs Company, a manufacturing company that supplied components for the auto industry and built machines for well-known companies such as Coca Cola. During World War II, the company was heavily engaged in the production of military war materials. Fred, Rex, and Clare, in succession, served as the company's president.

Rex joined the GPYC in 1929, while the other two brothers joined around the time the Club reopened in 1938. They were all sailors and owned various types of sail and powerboats over the years. Clare was an exceptionally gifted athlete, winning a bronze medal for pole-vaulting in the 1908 Olympics held in London, England. The following year he set a world indoor pole-vaulting record, which stood for the next three years. In sailing, he was known to be a fierce competitor and raced a number of sailboats he owned, the most noted being *Revelry and Falcon*. Rex was somewhat limited in his sailing stamina due to chronic shortness of breath. As a soldier in World War I, he had sustained significant lung damage from poisonous gas.

Clare and Rex also owned iceboats. The two iceboats pictured in the 1947 *Grosse Pointer* were large racing iceboats exceeding 40 feet in length, requiring a two-man crew. Clare owned and usually raced on *Deuce IV*, while Rex's *Ferdinand the Bull* was skippered by George Hendrie, who was also a co-owner of the boat.

Figure 2. Three generations of iceboaters: Left to right, Clare Jacobs, son John, and John Jr. (Jack). Jack is sitting in *Seabiscuit II*, a Skeeter Class iceboat, sometime around 1947.

Figure 3. Rex Jacobs, brother of Clare, photographed around 1946. Rex was co-owner, with George Hendrie, of *Ferdinand the Bull.*

George Hendrie

George Hendrie was part owner of the Macoid Corporation, a company that manufactured components for the auto industry, and was president of the company for many years. His grandfather, also George Hendrie, was born in Glasgow, Scotland, and immigrated to Detroit in 1859 at age twenty-four, where he eventually acquired a number of local streetcar companies as well as other major businesses. Detroit historian Clarence Burton referred to him as the "Father of Detroit Street Railways."[2]

George Hendrie and his brother William joined the GPYC in early 1914 at ages seventeen and nineteen respectively, making them part of the Club's founding members. Club records from 1914 point to George as being one of the best iceboat racers in the Club; records from the 1920s indicate that George, along with a gentleman by the name of Joe Snay, were the membership's top iceboat racers in those years. Both served on the Club's race committee.

Eventually George became a part of the iceboating group that dropped their Club memberships in the years 1929-30 and did not return when the Club reopened in 1938. (See Chapter Two for more discussion of this subject.) In a recent conversation, George's son, George Jr., suggested a possible reason for the iceboaters not returning to the Club. In the same year the GPYC reopened, 1938, the Detroit Ice Yacht Club (DIYC) was formed specifically for iceboat racers. The group organized races for all the different categories of iceboats on Lake St. Clair. George Jr. also recalled that by 1938 the epicenter of iceboating on the lake had shifted from the Grosse Pointes to an area further north in L'Anse Creuse Bay, just south of what is now Lake St. Clair Metropark. Iceboaters found that the ice routinely formed earlier and stayed later in this location than in the area of the Pointes. George Jr. was himself an avid iceboat racer and at one point served as commodore of the DIYC.

Figure 4. George Hendrie, circa the 1940s. George was an early member of the Grosse Pointe Yacht Club, joining in 1914 and becoming one of its most prominent iceboat racers.

Figure 5. The Stuart International Ice Yacht Trophy. The first race for the trophy was held in 1904, and by the 1940s it was arguably the most coveted trophy for iceboaters.

Figure 6. Joe Snay piloting his iceboat, *Gossoon II*.

Joseph W. Snay

Joe Snay was considered an outstanding sailor and iceboat racer in his day. When a win was important to a sailboat owner, Joe was often hired on as crew. It is not known exactly when he joined the GPYC, but Club records show that he served on the race committee during the 1920s and that he was among the group of iceboaters who left the Club in 1929-30 and did not return. He owned and raced a Class A iceboat, name *Gossoon II*.

Joe owned a tavern on the northeast corner of Mack Avenue and Manor Street, which was a popular place for sailors and iceboaters to meet, share a drink or two and play tabletop shuffleboard. For many years, Joe was a Trustee for the Village of Grosse Pointe Farms. He ran twice, unsuccessfully, for Village President.

The Stuart International Ice Yacht Trophy and the Hearst International Challenge Cup

In 1903, F. A. Stuart, owner of a pharmaceutical company in Marshall, Michigan, donated a trophy for an international iceboat competition that was planned for the early winter months of that year.[3] The Kalamazoo Ice Yacht Club (now Gull Lake Ice Yacht Club) was charged with organizing the competition and setting the rules. Ice yacht clubs from the U. S. and Canada were notified of the competition, which was to take place on nearby Gull Lake. Unfortunately, the weather that winter was so unfavorable it forced the postponement of the event to the following year.[3]

Back in those days, iceboats and steam locomotives were recognized as the fastest man-piloted objects on earth. It was claimed that iceboats had exceeded speeds of 100 mph, which generated a great deal of public interest and excitement. Newspaper and magazine coverage of iceboat racing was extensive.[3] Probably for that very reason, newspaper publisher and U.S. Congressman William Randolph Hearst sent a telegram to the commodore of the KIYC, offering to donate a second trophy for the 1904 event.[3] The trophy was to be named the Hearst International Challenge Cup and the KIYC was given the option to define the series of races for the Cup competition.

The inaugural race finally took place in 1904. Ice yacht clubs from Michigan, Wisconsin, Illinois, Ohio, the East Coast and Canada were invited to compete. The Stuart Trophy competition included boats with a sail area greater than 450 square feet, while those with 450 square feet or less would compete for the Hearst Cup. Separate events were held for each award competition. Two buoys were set two miles apart and boats were required to round each buoy five times for a total of twenty miles per race, the winner being the first to win three out of five races.

Wolverine from the KIYC was the first winner of the Stuart trophy. Theoretically, the greater the sail area, the faster the boat; *Wolverine* had a sail area of 800 square feet and was said to be the second largest ice racing yacht in the world. The headline of the Kalamazoo Morning Gazette for Sunday, March 13, 1904, was "*Wolverine* Breaks the World's Record." The accompanying article said, in part, "The spider-bodied flyers at Gull Lake displayed their supremacy of the world in international championship racing and shattered the fastest records ever posted by an Erie, Hudson River or New Jersey club." The Hearst Cup was won by *Hilo*, also from the KIYC.

The first of these two trophies to be won by a Detroit area challenger was the Hearst Cup. In March of 1928, Joseph B. Lodge from the GPYC took the Cup in *Deuce II*. Lodge, a nephew of Detroit mayor John Lodge and first cousin to famed aviator Charles Lindbergh, had joined the GPYC in 1926.[4] In 1938, Joseph Lodge won the Hearst Cup again, and also became the first Detroit area winner of the Stuart Trophy, this time with *Deuce III*, but in both races he represented the newly formed Detroit Ice Yacht Club.

Fig. 7. The Hearst International Challenge Cup, donated in 1903 by newspaper publisher and U.S. Congressman William Randolph Hearst.

By the 1940s the Stuart Trophy was arguably the most highly coveted trophy in iceboat racing.[5,6] At this point in time, competitors were mainly from ice yacht clubs in Michigan and Wisconsin. Challenges were issued by the clubs rather than by individuals, and in any given race there were usually two boats racing from each club.

In 1939, the Oshkosh Ice Yacht Club in Oshkosh, Wisconsin, had claimed the Stuart Trophy for Wisconsin, so in 1940, the DIYC put up two boats to challenge the OIYC. The race was held on Green Bay, near Menominee, Michigan.

Figure 8. In 1939, member Joe Lodge lost the Stuart Cup race by only a few agonizing minutes in the fifth race to John Buckstaff from Wisconsin. This photo, taken on the ice of Lake St. Clair, shows Joe (standing) shaking Mr. Buckstaff's hand and presenting him with a pennant that reads, "World Champion Stuart Cup 1939."

Grosse Pointers came to the 1940 Stuart Trophy Regatta on Green Bay in Wisconsin to recapture the trophy for Michigan.

Figure 9. Left to right, Joe Snay, likely *Deuce III's* sail trimmer Charles Van Dyke (a relative of George Hendrie), and former Stuart Trophy champion Joe Lodge, wearing a top hat.

Figure 10. Member John B. "JB" Ford Jr., owner of *Deuce III*.

Figure 11. Left to right, Rex Jacobs, Clare Jacobs, and George Hendrie.

Figure 12 *Deuce III*, left, and *Ferdinand the Bull*, center, ready to race. The iceboat on the right is unidentified.

Figure 13. Early 1914 GPYC iceboat racers Wally Hock, left, and George Hendrie, right. George's wife Rosemary is in the middle. Wally was given the nickname "the teacher," due to his willingness and enthusiasm in teaching his racing skills to younger sailors and iceboaters.

The first DIYC boat was *Deuce III*, the 1938 winner that was now owned by GPYC member John "JB" Ford Jr., and skippered by Wally Hock, a 1914 founding member of the GPYC. Their second boat was *Ferdinand the Bull*, co-owned by Rex Jacobs and George

Hendrie and skippered by George, with Clare Jacobs trimming the sails. The OIYC was represented by *Blue Bill II* and *Debutante III*, the latter having won the Stuart Trophy in 1920 and 1939.

The Stuart Trophy returned to Michigan when George Hendrie finished the 1940 race in first place piloting *Ferdinand the Bull*, with Wally Hock placing second in *Deuce III*. Wisconsin boats *Debutante III* and *Blue Bill II* came in third and fourth, respectively.[7]

Deuce IV and "The Bull"

Deuce IV was commissioned by Clare Jacobs to be a serious racing competitor to brother Rex's *Ferdinand the Bull*. Both boats were built in Harrison Township, Michigan, by the Vanderbush brothers. Their woodworking shop was just a few hundred yards from where iceboaters had been launching on Lake St. Clair in the 1930s, near the intersection of East Jefferson Avenue and Crocker Boulevard.

Following their 1940 win, Jacobs and Hendrie successfully defended the Stuart Trophy with "The Bull" from 1941 through 1947.[8] George Hendrie's son, George Jr., raced with his father as sail trimmer in the 1943 race, again held on Green Bay near Menominee, and remembered the excitement of winning the first three of five potential races to take the trophy. He raced again with his father in 1944 on Lake St. Clair, winning this time in the fifth race. In both races the challenging boats were from the OIYC in Oshkosh: *Debutante III* and *The Flying Dutchman*.

George Jr. also recalled attending the 1947 race on Lake Winnebago near Oshkosh, and remembered that there were light winds on the day of the final race. *Deuce IV*, skippered by Joe Snay, was entered in the series and was favored to win in light wind conditions, but it broke down before the final race.[9] George subsequently watched his father steer "The Bull" to victory himself that day, competing as both skipper and sail trimmer in order to save the weight and be more competitive.

In 1949, again on Lake Winnebago, George Hendrie once again captured the Stuart Trophy, but this time as skipper of *Deuce IV*, with Clare

Jacobs as sail trimmer.[10] It is unclear if Stuart Trophy regattas were held in either 1948 or 1950.

According to Bill Bentsen, a winner of both the Stuart Trophy and the Hearst Cup, the challenging rules for the two awards changed around 1950. Mr. Bentsen, interviewed in 2013 at age eighty-three, said that the qualifications for Stuart Trophy and Hearst Cup challenges were modified to allow the same boat to compete for both awards, even though the races themselves remained separate. During the next two decades, it appeared that ice yacht clubs were either unable or unwilling to challenge, so the challenging process changed to allow individual challenges between iceboat owners. No matter which type of challenge occurred, club or individual, only two boats at a time would now be allowed to face off for either trophy.[11]

On February 24, 1951, the DIYC finally relinquished the Stuart Trophy when George Hendrie, piloting "The Bull" on Lake St. Clair, lost the fifth race by a minute and a half to *Mary B*, which completed the race in forty-four minutes. *Mary B* representing the Four Lakes Ice Yacht Club in Madison, Wisconson was a relatively new boat built in 1948 with nylon sails compared to the "The Bull" with the older style canvas sails. The Bull was leading on the last leg when it hit a wood beer crate stuck in the ice. Part of the crate caught on the steering runner and Hendrie had to stop the boat and kick it off before they could continue which caused him to loose the pivitol fifth race.[4] The skipper, Carl Bernard, had already won the Hearst Cup and Stuart Trophy in other iceboats, and took the Hearst Cup the previous year with *Mary B*. A news article covering the race states that *Ferdinand the Bull* had held the Stuart Trophy for eleven years.[12] This was factually incorrect. George Hendrie held the trophy for eleven years, but in one of those years, 1949, he had captured it in *Deuce IV*.

Around 1957, "The Bull" and "The Deuce" were both sold to iceboaters in Wisconsin. *Ferdinand the Bull* was sold to Harry "Buddy" Melges Jr., of Zenda, Wisconsin, close to Lake Geneva in the southern part of the state. Buddy is considered one of the most successful competition

Fig. 14. *Debutante III* circa the 1940s, winner of the Stuart Trophy in 1920 and 1939. Her home port was the Oshkosh Ice Yacht Club (OIYC) on Lake Winnebago in Oshkosh, Wisconsin.

Fig. 15. *Deuce IV* was trailered to Wisconsin's Lake Winnebago and reassembled there prior to the 1949 Stuart Trophy Regatta.

Fig. 16. George Hendrie, left, and Clare Jacobs, right, preparing *Deuce IV* for the start of the 1949 regatta.

Fig. 17. Contestants for the 1949 Stuart Trophy, left to right: *Debutante III*, *Deuce IV*, and *The Flying Dutchman*. "The Debutante" and "The Dutchman" represented the OIYC.

sailors in history, winning dozens of national and international championships. He was the helmsman in America's successful defense of the America's Cup in 1992 and took both gold and bronze medals in Olympic sailing competitions.[13]

Buddy made some changes to *Ferdinand the Bull*'s rigging and sails, and at some later point added carbon-fiber sails.[14] Racing "The Bull," Buddy won the Hearst Cup in 1961–65, 1971, 1980, and 2001. He won the Stuart Trophy with "The Bull" in 1965, 1968, 1975, 1980, and 2001.

Deuce IV currently holds both the Hearst Cup and the Stuart Trophy. "The Deuce" is 54 feet long with a 52-foot mast and a sail area of 840 feet, making her the largest iceboat still being raced competitively. She is now owned by Rick Henning of Racine, Wisconsin, and was recently clocked by GPS at 119 mph.[15] Both "The Deuce" and "The Bull" race out of the Skeeter Ice Boat Club in Lake Geneva, Wisconsin.

Clearly the Grosse Pointe Yacht Club has moved far from its iceboating history one hundred years ago. Still, it is nice to know that some of our past continues to race on the frozen lakes of Wisconsin, in pursuit of the Hearst Cup or the Stuart Trophy. Perhaps one day we might even see *Ferdinand the Bull* or *Deuce IV* back on home ice, on Lake St. Clair.

ACKNOWLEDGEMENTS

The following people and organizations were very helpful in obtaining this important historical information:

William Bentsen, SIBC (Skeeter Ice Boat Club, Lake Geneva, Wisconsin)

Reid Bielenberg, HRIYC (Hudson River Ice Yacht Club, Poughkeepsie, New York)

Izzy Donnelly, Grosse Pointe Historical Society

Andy Gratton, OIYC (Oshkosh Ice Yacht Club, Oshkosh, Wisconsin)

George Hendrie Jr. and Mike Hendrie, (Detroit Ice Yacht Club, Detroit, Michigan)

Harry "Buddy" Melges Jr., SIBC (Skeeter Ice Boat Club, Lake Geneva, Wisconsin)

Greg Strand, NSIBYC (North Shrewsbury Ice Boat Yacht Club, New Shrewsbury, New Jersey)

Deb Whitehorse, webmaster, Iceboat.org and secretary

4 LIYC (Four Lakes Ice Yacht Club, Madison, Wisconsin)

REFERENCES

1. The actual title was Winner of the Stuart International Ice Yacht Trophy, but since they were the largest and fastest category of racing iceboats in the 1930s and 1940s, those racing for the Stuart Trophy commonly referred to the winning crew and boat as the World Champion.

2. Clarence Monroe Burton, "George Hendrie", Compendium of History and Biography of the City of Detroit and Wayne County, Michigan, (Chicago: Henry & Taylor, 1909) 408-410.

3. Randy Rogoski, "The Inaugural Hearst and Stuart Trophy Regattas of 1904," www.gulllakeiyc.org/history/p3hearst1904 Gull Lake Ice Yacht Club, 1.

4. Conversations between George Hendrie's sons, George Hendrie Jr. and Mike Hendrie, and Larry Stephenson, 2013 and 2014.

5. "Hearst – Stuart News Flash!!! Big Boats are Still Big!!!" www.iceboat.org The Four Lakes Ice Yacht Club, January 13, 2001.

6. The Ice Yacht Challenge Pennant of America was inaugurated in 1881 by the Orange Lake Ice Yacht Club near Newburgh, New York, and was pursued by the largest and fastest iceboats on the East Coast. Holder of the Pennant was considered the world and/or North American iceboat champion. The last regatta held for the Pennant occurred in February 1922. The Lake Orange Ice Yacht Club closed a few years later, and the Stuart Trophy soon took its place as arguably the most coveted trophy in iceboat racing. In 1951, the Eastern Ice Yacht Association took custody and stewardship of the Ice Yacht Challenge Pennant, but the organization later became defunct. Since then, other groups have sponsored races for the Pennant, but the level of prestige it once held one hundred years ago is no longer present.

7. *Oshkosh Daily Northwestern*, February 28, 1940; "Oshkosh Iceboat Beaten," *Milwaukee Sentinel*, Feb. 28, 1940, 14. www.newspapers.com/newspage/43457457/ 13.

8. *The Grosse Pointer*, vol. 8, no. 1, Spring Issue 1947, 39.

9. Newspaper clipping entitled "Detroit Ice Yacht Wins Stuart Cup", circa January 28, 1947, from Carol Bernard Scrapbook Project, P. S1, P. 33, www.iceboat.org.

10. "Detroit Skipper Wins Iceboat Trophy," *The Milwaukee Journal*, March 7, 1949, 30 (P. 6 Sports Section)

11. Phone conversations between William Bentsen and Larry Stephenson, October 2013. Bentsen won the Hearst Cup with ice yacht *Taku* in 1968, 1969 and 1970, and the Stuart Trophy in 1970 and 1971. He was also the recipient of an Olympic Gold Medal as a crewmember on Buddy Melges' sailboat.

12. *Janesville Daily Gazette*, February 26, 1951, www.newspapers.com/newspage/ 12166859 11.

13. "Buddy Melges," Wikipedia, September 17, 2013.

14. Phone conversations between Buddy Melges and Larry Stephenson, October 2013.

15. Daniel Fisher, "Shiver Me Timbers," www.forbes.com March 10, 2007.

Image Achnowledgements

1. George Hendrie Family

2. John Jacobs jr.

3. GPYC

4. George Hendrie Family

5. Andy Gratton

6. Wayne State University

7. Andy Gratton

8–11. Grosse Pointe Historical Society

12. George Hendrie Family

13. *Detroit Free Press*

14.–18. George Hendrie Family

Figure 18. This painting of *Ferdinand the Bull* by Rick Ford depicts a scene from the 1943 Stuart Trophy Regatta held on Green Bay in Wisconsin. "The Bull," crewed by George Hendrie Sr. and George Jr., is pictured in "hiking" mode, lifting its right forward runner blade off the ice. The father and son team won the race, and went on to win the 1944 regatta as well, but later that year George Jr. was inducted into the U.S. Navy, temporarily ending his racing days.

Figure 1. *Typhoon*, Past Commodore Edsel Ford's triple-cockpit express commuter in Ford Cove, Grosse Pointe Shores, Michigan, 1929.

Boats of Note

By Ross B. Stone, with Past Commondores George E. Kriese,
Sloane R. Barbour Jr., and James L. Ramsey

As we reflect on a hundred years of yachting on Lake St. Clair, it is worthwhile to focus at some of the yachts that graced our harbor and to reflect on the transition in technology and design that occurred over that period:

- Hull materials have changed from steel and wood to fiberglass, aluminum and complex composites.

- Propulsion has moved from coal-fired steam burners to sophisticated gasoline and diesel engines.

- Sail materials have changed from cotton and canvas to exotic carbon-fiber compounds.

- Hull design has also evolved from the rounded displacement look to the rakish hydrodynamic shapes of today.

Our harbor has been home to hundreds of truly outstanding yachts, motorboats, cruisers, and sailboats, most of which we would have been happy to include in this offering. As that was not possible, we have attempted instead to identify a sampling of twenty-three of these classic beauties from the past – ten sailing yachts and thirteen powerboats. They were chosen by a panel consisting of the four authors of this article.

PART I: SAILING YACHTS

Apache   **Thomas K. Fisher**

45 ft.   1936; New York 32 Auxiliary Sloop; Olin Stephens design;
Henry B. Nevins, builder.

"The Indian," as she was fondly nicknamed, came to the GPYC in 1939, having been number two in a twenty-boat class designed exclusively for the New York Yacht Club under Cruising Club of America rules. Following two winning seasons at GPYC with Thomas Fisher, she was purchased by Wilfred "Toot" Gmeiner of the DYC and continued to be a major contender on the Great Lakes for some thirty years. *Apache* was later given to "Toot's" two sons, Skip and Doug, the latter a member of GPYC. Seventy-five years later, she is still proudly docked at the DYC, a striking beauty and one of the grand old ladies of Lake St. Clair.

Brilliant   **Henry E. Bodman**

61 ft.   1932; Auxiliary Schooner; Sparkman & Stevens design;
Henry B. Nevins, builder.

One of the most prominent and successful recreational racing schooners on the Great Lakes in pre-World War II years.

Conwego   **Charles Beck**

50 ft.   1930, Eight-meter Class Sloop, designed as a smaller version of the classic 12-meter yachts. Olin Stephens design; Robert Jacobs, builder. One of fourteen 8-meter boats built in the U.S. at various East Coast yards.

Conwego was a consistent local winner. In the mid-1950s she was awarded the season's 8-meter Class Championship and went on to participate in the 1954 Canada's Cup series. There are a number of these boats still actively racing under the pennants of the Buffalo Yacht Club and Royal Canadian Yacht Club in Toronto.

Gypsy   **Thomas K. Fisher Sr., Thomas K. Fisher Jr.**

53 ft.   1936; Double-ended Wood Sloop; Frank Payne design; George Lawley, builder. This unique double-ended beauty was brought to the GPYC by co-owners and captains Thomas Fisher Sr. and Thomas Fisher Jr., following her many years of sailing on the East Coast and Lake Michigan.

Gypsy's record as a cruising boat is the best for any single season on record in Lake St. Clair. It was often asked, "What did *Gypsy* have that the other girls didn't have?" She had her father-son team as captains, backed by the legendary tactical savvy of Carter Sales Jr., often referred to as their "tactical secret weapon." *Gypsy* had also been refitted with the most advanced sailing gear, hardware and state-of-the-art sails.

The 1969 sailing season in the eastern Great Lakes was proclaimed the "Year of the *Gypsy*." She ended that season as "Boat of the Year," besting all competitors in a fleet of two hundred-four boats in the greatest Blue Nose Regatta on record. In October of that year, *Gypsy* left the GPYC for New York, entering and winning several races on Long Island Sound. She then continued south for the Miami-Nassau race and the SOR circuit.

Josephine II
54 ft.

William A. Petzold

1927; John G. Alden design; Reed & Cook Marine Construction, builder.

This fine old classic Alden Schooner was still competitively sailing in the 1940s and 1950s under the ownership of another Club member, Lloyd Ecclestone. She could always be counted upon as a very competitive cruising class boat whenever there was "schooner weather" brewing.

Old Rarity
34 ft.

Susan B. Fisher

1946; Pilot Class Auxiliary Sloop; Sparkman & Stevens design; Fisher Boatworks, builder.

One of the most successful of the Pilot class on both the Great Lakes and East Coast. Aboard *Old Rarity* in 1949, Susan Fisher became the first female skipper to compete in the Port Huron-to-Mackinac race.

Orient
64 ft.

Paul W. Smiley

1938; Auxiliary Sloop; Sparkman & Stevens design; Wing on Shing, builder. Paul Smiley was the owner of Smiley Brothers, a very successful piano company in downtown Detroit. His sloop *Orient* was noted for besting many of the Maxie boats both here in the Great Lakes and on the West Coast during the 1940s and 1950s. Always known as a fierce contender, *Orient* made GPYC history in 1952 when she was first-in and overall winner of the Port Huron-to-Mackinac Race. This was the first time that the winner was flying the Club burgee representing the GPYC. (Other members owned boats that had previously won the race, but had chosen to fly the burgee of other local yacht clubs for the race.)

Roulette II
39 ft.

Past Commodore Roy E. Barbier

1972; World 2-ton Class; C&C designed and built.

Having the same designer and builder was characteristic of the World 2-ton Class of sailboats. It was often said, "*Roulette* never entered a race she couldn't win."

Sassy
78 ft.

E. Russell "Dutch" Schmidt

1984; Ron Holland design; Palmer Johnson builders

As "Dutch" Schmidt's brand new *Sassy* crossed the finish line on Sunday night at 11:30 pm, she shattered the Old Cove Island course record by nearly four hours in the 1984 Port Huron–to–Mackinac race. Corrected time gave her the overall win in the IOR-A Class. The following week, in the Chicago-to-Mackinac race, she was again first over the finish line, but corrected time put her back to fifth place. Three years later, she repeated her overall win in the 1987 Port Huron-to-Mackinac race.

Valkyrie   **Past Commodore Robert E. Thoreson**

41 ft.   1973; Sparkman & Stevens design; Tartan Yachts builder.

There were actually three *Valkyries*: the first, a 30-foot Senior Knarr; second, a 37-ft. Tartan Blackwatch; and finally the 41-foot Tartan. Together, they were some of the most accomplished racing yachts on the DRYA circuit and in the Port Huron-to-Mackinac races. In twenty-five Mackinac races, *Valkyrie* placed nine times, and in 1980 was first in class and first in division. In 1988, her final racing season, *Valkyrie* finished the DRYA racing series in first place. (Researched by Bill Harrington)

PART II: MOTORYACHTS/BOATS

Blue Jacket   **Past Commodore Frank P. McBride**

47 ft.   1987; North Sea Trawler-style, single-screw 250 HP, 6 cyl. Volvo diesel engine, Low Lands Yacht, builder, The Netherlands.

Typical of the growing Great Lakes interest at the time in the seaworthiness and fuel economy of this class of boat. *Blue Jacket* was especially known for the wood-finished beauty of her interior.

Choo Choo V   **Dr. C. J. Williams**

42 ft.   1955; Express Cruiser; Chris Craft designed and custom built for C.J. Williams.

The fifth *Choo Choo* to be docked at the GPYC, from 1945 to 1961, and typical of the Chris Craft cruisers of that era.

Helene   **Charles E. Sorensen**

106 ft.   1927; Defoe designed and built motor yacht.; steel flush-deck; raised pilothouse; single-screw; original power Bessemer diesel; repowered in 1951 with twin 6 cyl. GM diesels; repowered in 1960s with V12 cyl. GM diesel.

Helene actively cruised the Great Lakes until World War II conversion to an Auxiliary Patrol Boat for the Coast Guard. Following a post-war refit and several new owners, she was passed on in the late 1960s to GPYC member Christopher "Marce" Verbiest, and again became a familiar sight on Lake St. Clair. She took part in many GPYC Fleet Reviews as the events flagship, and eventually became a popular charter boat. While under her annual winter layup at Nicholson Terminal in 2012, she suffered severe fire damage and sank. She has currently been refloated and is owned by Nicholson, but remains unrestored; an elderly lady graciously awaiting a white knight to restore her to her former beauty.

Imperial V   **Past Commodore O. James Gagne**

65 ft.   1967; Burger Aluminum flush-deck, twin-screw diesel motor yacht.

Served as flagship of the GPYC fleet in 1969. Although her home port was the GPYC, she cruised extensively on the East Coast and in Florida, the Bahamas, and the Caribbean.

Maradon	**Arthur G. Sherman, Jr.**
89 ft.	

1922; Designed and built by Luders Marine Construction Company; flush-deck, houseboat-style, wood motor yacht; single-screw diesel engine.

Due to a very narrow 14 ft. 10 in. beam, she was always known as a very touchy lady to dock in her long-occupied East Wall berth. *Maradon* served as an Auxiliary Patrol Boat during WWII.

Arthur Sherman owned and operated a pharmaceutical laboratory, but was better known for being the designer and manufacturer of the first mass-produced travel trailer.

Much Too Much	**Arthur H. Schaupeter Sr.**
70 ft.	

1984; Aluminum Sport Fisherman with a 24-ft. beam and twin Mercedes-Benz diesel engines; Striker designed; built in The Netherlands.

Truly a family yacht with four staterooms, three heads and a Jacuzzi tub. All components except the hull and engines were manufactured in the U.S. While based at the GPYC, she cruised extensively on the Great Lakes, as well as on the East Coast, in Florida waters, including the Gulf of Mexico, and in the Bahamas.

Once Again	**Ross B. Stone**
40 ft.	

1948; Matthews designed and built.

A wooden Matthews deluxe enclosed sedan, fully restored and repowered with 350 CID Crusader engines. Cruising speed is eighteen knots. She is a five-time Antique and Classic Boat Society (ACBS) award-winner and the oldest boat currently residing in the GPYC harbor.

Ragtime	**Frederick G. Ruffner**
64 ft.	

1928; Commuter Yacht; Consolidated Shipbuilding Corp. designed and built.

Ragtime has had several extensive refits, including an enclosed bridge, after starting out as a high-speed commuter yacht. She was repowered with 8V-871 GM Diesel engines, with reported speeds of up to twenty-two knots. *Ragtime* is currently reported to be in Bristol condition and cruises extensively on the East Coast.

Rhumb Runner	**Dr. Anthony F. Deluca**
33 ft.	

1982; Fortier-Eldridge & McInnis Down East-style Sport Fisherman.

Traveled from Rhode Island via the Welland Canal to Lake St. Clair and her GPYC dock. She represents the classic style of down-east lobster boat that is presently enjoying growing popularity in the Great Lakes region.

Salador
65 ft.

Frederick A. Coleman

1948; Grebe, flush-deck, enclosed-bridge, twin 200-HP diesel-powered motor yacht.

Grebe yachts were well known around the Great Lakes and the East Coast for their rugged construction and extra fine fit and finish. *Salador* cruised at speeds up to eighteen knots. She had three double staterooms with private baths and crew quarters for two, making her a true home away from home.

Taylor Made
72 ft.

Past Commodores James L. Taylor and James L. Taylor Jr.

1978; Burger aluminum flush-deck, twin-diesel motor yacht.

Because the sitting GPYC commodore's boat is unofficially the flagship of the fleet during his or her year of service, *Taylor Made* is the only boat in Club history to have the distinction of serving in that capacity twice; first for Commodore James Taylor Sr. in 1978, and then for Commodore James Taylor Jr. in 2009. Known especially for the beautiful woodwork of her interior, she has often been referred to as one of the most distinctive yachts on Lake St. Clair.

Teaser
40 ft.

Carl E. Larson

1924; George Crouch-designed; Nevins-built; triple-cockpit express commuter; powered with 650-HP V-12 Liberty engine.

Teaser was originally built for Richard F. Hoyt and was later owned by Edsel Ford I. Member Carl Larson was founder of TRICO Company, which produced the first windshield wiper blades for Henry Ford's Model T. Teaser reportedly was clocked at speeds of up to 60 mph.

Typhoon
40 ft.

Past Commodore Edsel B. Ford

1929; George Crouch-designed; Nevins-built; high-speed triple cockpit commuter. Over the years she sported a series of special V12 engines — Packards, Wright Typhoons, Hall Scotts and Allisons.

One of a two-boat class, she was originally built for Edsel Ford, who wanted a sister ship to *Teaser*, but with a few modifications. Mr. Ford kept her on both Lake St. Clair and in Florida waters. A model of *Typhoon* is presently displayed in the Binnacle Dining Room.

Figure 2. *Apache*, 1936, owned by member Thomas K. Fisher.

Figure 3. *Billiant*, 1932, owned by member Henry Bodman (photo by Morris Rosenfeld).

Figure 4. *Conwego*, 1930, owned by member Charles Beck.

Figure 5. *Gypsy,* 1936, owned by members Thomas K. Fisher Sr. and Thomas K. Fisher Jr.

Figure 6. *Josephine II,* 1927, owned by member William A. Petzold.

Figure 7. *Old Rarity*, 1946, owned by member Susan B. Fisher.

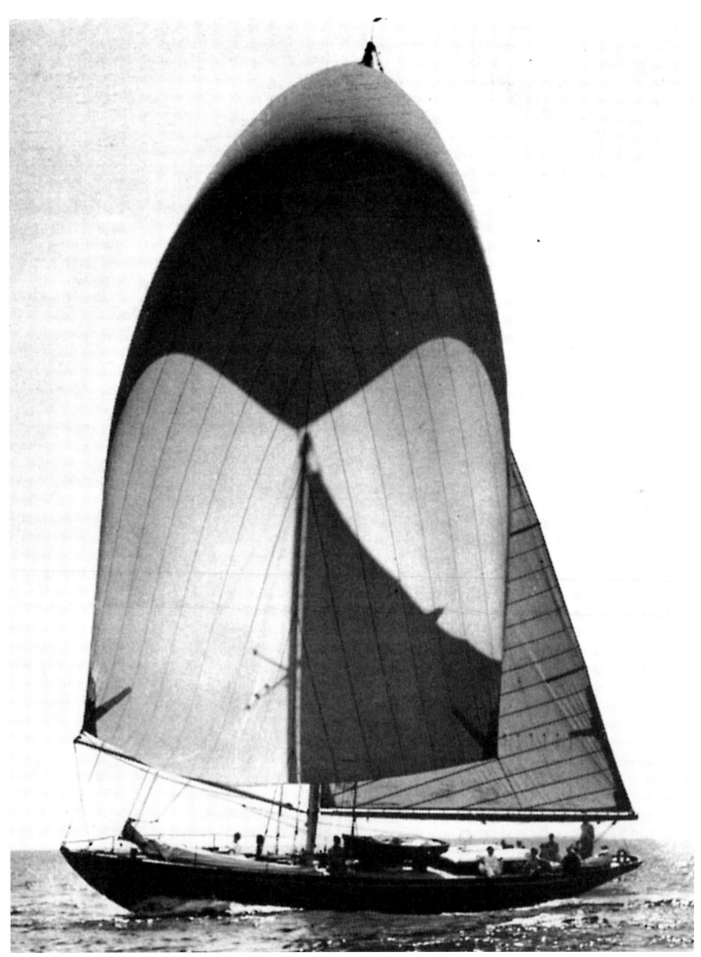

Figure 8. *Orient*, 1938, owned by member Paul W. Smiley.

Figure 9. *Roulette*, 1972, owned by Past Commodore Roy E. Barbier.

Figure 11. *Sassy*, circa 1984, owned by member E. Russell "Dutch" Schmidt.

Figure 10. *Valkyrie,* 1975, owned by Past Commodore Robert Thoreson.

Figure 12. *Blue Jacket*, 1987, owned by Past Commodore Frank P. McBride.

Figure 13. *Choo Choo V*, 1955, owned by member Dr. C.J. Williams.

Figure 14. *Helene*, 1927, owned by member Charles E. Sorensen.

Figure 15. *Imperial V*, 1967, owned by Past Commodore O. James Gagne.

Figure 16. *Maradon*, 1922, owned by member Arthur Sherman Jr.

Figure 17. *Much Too Much*, 1984, owned by member Arthur H. Schaupeter Sr.

Figure 18. *Once Again, 1948*, owned by member Ross B. Stone.

Figure 19. *Ragtime, 1928*, owned by member Frederick Ruffner.

Figure 20. *Rhumb Runner, 1982*, owned by member Dr. Anthony Deluca.

Figure 21. *Salador*, 1948, owned by member Frederick Coleman.

Figure 22. *Taylor Made*, 1978, owned by Past Commodores James L. Taylor and James L. Taylor Jr.

Figure 23. *Teaser*, 1924, owned by member Carl Larson. Note Grosse Pointe Yacht Club in the background.

Figure 24. *Typhoon*, 1929, owned by Past Commodore Edsel B. Ford.

Image Acknowledgements

1. From the Collections of the Henry Ford
2. Skip Gmiener
3. Grosse Pointe Club
4. GPYC
5. Thomas K. Fisher Jr.
6. GPYC
7. Ross B. Stone
8. GPYC
9. Casey Wise
10. Jackie Thoresen
11. Karl Schmidt
12. Jere McBride
13. Dr. John H. Williams
14. Bowling Green Great Lakes Historical Collection
15. GPYC
16. Mystic Seaport Museum
17. Ronald H. Schaupeter
18.–19. Ross B. Stone
20. Dr. Anthony DeLuca
21. GPYC
22. Jim Dorian
23. GPYC
24. From the Collections of the Henry Ford

Figure 1. Seth Arca Whipple
A.A. PARKER TOWING R.W. PARKER – 1892, 25" x 50"
The steamer *A.A. Parker* is towing the barge *R.W. Parker*. Both ships have green wooden hulls and three masts. Shown off the starboard bow of *A.A. Parker* is a lighthouse, and there are two ships in the distance behind *R.W. Parker*. Works such as this were reproduced and hung in virtually every steamship waiting room and ticket office on the Great Lakes. Whipple became one of the best known marine artists whose work was mass-produced during the last quarter of the nineteenth century. Location – Spinnaker Dining Room.

Gallery of the Club's maritime paintings

By Larry W. Stephenson, M.D., GPYC Director Joseph P. Schaden, and John F. Martin

The Grosse Pointe Yacht Club is the proud owner of several extraordinary maritime paintings, most of which were donated by members and are displayed throughout the clubhouse. Additionally, the Club has been the fortunate recipient of a number of other paintings offered on long-term loan. Nineteen images of these works of art have been selected for feature in this gallery, while two others have been deemed important enough to merit their own prominent places elsewhere in this book.

Of those two, by far the largest and most significant painting owned by the Club is that which dominates and defines our Ballroom. *Sea Witch* was commissioned and donated to the Club by our fourth commodore, John H. French. The unveiling of the painting during the celebration of the grand opening of the clubhouse on July 4, 1929, would clearly have been a highlight of the day. To view *Sea Witch* and read more about her history, see chapter two.

Arguably one of the most dramatic of the Club's maritime paintings is *Roaring Forties*. This painting was donated in 1965 by Past Commodore Mervyn G. Gaskin, who was commodore in 1956. Presently it hangs in the Club's foyer. An article featuring *Roaring Forties* was written by Past Commodore Ralph J. Kliber, and is reprinted in chapter six.

The other nineteen paintings were all photographed by member John F. Martin and provided pro bono for this article. *Sea Witch* was also photographed by Mr. Martin for use in its separate article.

Figure 2. Charles Robert Patterson
USS MICHIGAN — ca. 1920, 28.5"x 48"
This oil painting by world-renowned marine artist Robert Patterson depicts the steam gunboat *USS Michigan* of 1844, the first iron-hulled ship built for the United States Navy. It is a starboard view of the ship at an angle of about forty-five degrees on the bow. The ship has a grey-black hull with white rails and buff super-structure, a single stack, sidewheels, and three masts with sails. Location — behind the Spinnaker Bar.

Figure 3. Howard Freeman Sprague
SENECA — 1890, 29" x 45"
This painting of the steamer *Seneca* shows a port side view of the black package freighter with white cabins and four masts. Several other ships are visible in the distance, and birds are in the foreground. The bow of the ship bears the words, "Wards Detroit & Lake Superior Line, Lehigh Valley, R.R." Location — Spinnaker Dining Room.

Figure 4. Howard Freeman Sprague
JOHN V. MORAN – 1889, 30" x 33"
This steam package freighter is a black-hulled wooden ship, seen from the port side, with one stack, one mast, white cabins, and a red house flag with a white "W." On the bow of the vessel are the words, "Wards Detroit & Lake Superior Line, Lehigh Valley, R.R." Location – Spinnaker Dining Room.

Figure 5. R. Gura
UNTITLED – 22" x 32"
This oil painting depicts three single-mast sailboats sailing away from the viewer, apparently seeking a breeze on a hazy day in very calm waters. The brass plaque on the frame reads, "Presented by Past Commodores to GPYC July 1965." Location – Main Dining Room.

Figure 6. Robert Hopkin
OLD DREDGE ON THE ROUGE RIVER — 1908, 13.5" x 21.5"
A depiction of the Rouge River curving from right foreground to right background. The old wooden dredge is tied to the bank in the foreground, along with three or four small sailing craft. Robert Hopkin passed away in 1909, making this one of his last completed works. Location — Main Dining Room.

Figure 7. Caldwell
HAUT MER — 20" x 24"
The water seems to blend into the horizon in this oil painting of a ship, in shades of orange, depicted from the stern, with gulls and what appear to be rocks in the foreground. A plaque at the bottom of the frame reads, "Presented by Commodore J. Earl Fraser April, 1976." Past Commodore Fraser was commodore in 1963. Location — Main Dining Room.

Figure 8. Antonio Jacobson
EDWIN F. HOLMES – 1904, 28" x 42"
A port side view of the black freighter with white forecastle and cabins, a black stack, and two masts. Antonio Jacobson was a Danish-born American maritime artist known for painting more than six thousand vessels between 1873 and 1919. Location – Main Dining Room.

Figure 9.
Jan Pawlowski
SUNRISE OVER THE CLUB – 30" x 40"
This impressionist-style oil painting shows the clubhouse and harbor of the Grosse Pointe Yacht Club at dawn, viewed from the shoreline south of the Club. The brass plaque on the frame reads, "Donated by Commodore John and Marlene Boll 1989." Location – Main Dining Room

Figure 10. Artist unknown
UNTITLED — 22" x 36"
Oil painting of a nineteenth century British clipper ship in choppy waters, flying the colors of the Merchant Navy.
A smaller sailing vessel is in the background, to starboard. Location — Ballroom.

Figure 11. Cooper
UNTITLED — 22" x 36"
A British nineteenth century, two-masted merchant ship sails in dark waters and uncertain skies in this untitled
oil painting. Location — Ballroom.

Figure 12. Sanders
UNTITLED — 22" x 36"
This oil painting of a nineteenth century, three-masted British merchant ship appears to be sailing past, or away from, the port in the background, as the ship in the distance on the right might be sailing in. Location — Ballroom.

Figure 13. Cooper
UNTITLED — 22" x 36"
Oil painting depicting an eighteenth century, two-masted sailing vessel flying the American flag. A small sailboat is in the foreground and a much larger sailing ship is in the background. Location — Ballroom.

Figure 14. Seth Arca Whipple

NORTHWEST – 1883, 20.5" x 26.5"

Northwest sails with her passengers in dark blue water. Blowing high in the wind are several flags. One is the American flag, while the others read: Detroit, Cleveland, Northwest, and M.C.R.R. Seth Arca Whipple was born in New Baltimore, Michigan. Apparently with no formal art training, he managed to paint his way into a lasting place in America's marine art history. Location — Venetian Room.

Figure 15. Robert Hopkin

THE STEAMER ARROW PASSING THE GROSSE ISLE BEACON – 1853, 29" x 36"

Arrow and a sailing vessel are shown going down the Detroit River with a canoe in the foreground. Robert Hopkin was a celebrated artist during the mid to late nineteenth century. In 1907, a group of his peers formed the Hopkin Club in Detroit in his honor. In 1913 it was renamed the Scarab Club, and still exists today by that name. Location — outside the Lakeshore Room.

Figure 16.
Thomas Chilvers
WAYWARD ca. 1885,
32" x 37"
American artist
Thomas Chilvers painted
Wayward and two other
yachts in racing position,
all port side views. There
is an unidentified single stack
steamboat in the background.
Location – outside
Lakeshore Room.

Figure 17. E. Walker
SCHOONER MICHIGAN – 1875, 41.5" x 65"
This oil painting of Great Lakes schooner *Michigan* shows gulls in the foreground and a lighthouse in the distance off
the starboard bow. The schooner was built in 1874 by Detroit Drydock Co. She carried three masts, measured 225 feet
in length and weighed 1056 tons, and was a typical example of large grain schooners built in the mid 1870s. Location –
Lakeshore Room.

Figure 18. R. Lane
UNTITLED — 39" x 40"
This oil painting depicts a two-masted schooner from the starboard side. The small figures on deck seem to be adjusting the rigging. Location — hall on east side of Lakeshore Room.

Figure 19. Wilfred Knox
UNTITLED — 26" x 40"
Born in Birmingham, England, in 1884, Wilfred Knox became one of the most popular English marine artists of the twentieth century. His work was especially known for its fine study of detail and almost poetic movement of the sea, both clearly in evidence in this depiction of two clipper ships. The brass plaque on the frame reads, "Presented by Past Commodores to GPYC July 1965." Location — Ballroom, north wall.

Figure 1. "The Thrill of Victory." GPYC fans and swimmers cheer just as GPYC swimmers win the girls' 200-meter medley relay in a swim meet at Lochmoor Club, June 23, 2014.

GPYC Swim Team

By Ross Stone

The early years

As far back as the early 1900s, the lakefront area at the foot of Vernier Road was a popular destination for a variety of water-oriented activities. There was swimming, sailing, iceboating, picnicking, beach lounging, fishing, and horseshoes to name just a few. By July 4, 1929, the grand opening of our current clubhouse gave Grosse Pointe Yacht Club members a spectacular venue in which to pursue their favorite activities.

When the Club was reorganized and had its "second grand opening" on July 4, 1938, it is interesting to note that all swim activities were centered in the harbor and the open lake along the south wall directly in front of the current harbormaster's tower. The designated lake "swim court" was roped off with multicolored floats, and

had a moored swim platform with rudimentary diving board, water chute and assigned lifeguard. Members called it "Neptune's Garden."

The July 4, 1938, aquatic celebration began with swimming races in the harbor, including three events that were nationally sanctioned by the Amateur Athletic Union (AAU). In the first event, the 200-yard breaststroke competition, Detroit Yacht Club swimmers took all three places, with Ardis Gibson breaking the standing record to become the new National AAU Junior Breast Stroke champion. In the second event, the State 400-Yard Freestyle championship was won by Clayton Main from the Kronk Athletic Club in Dearborn. Three world champion swimmers, Walter Laufer, Rose Boczek, and Arne Borg, competed in the third event. Borg was a member of the Swedish Olympic Team and was attempting to set a new world record in half-mile freestyle, but failed due to the rough conditions on the lake that day.

Rose Boczek was the United States National Indoor Spring Board Diving champion, and by all accounts, was the star of the show as a group of divers put on an exciting exhibition for the crowd. The United States Women's National Junior Water Polo champions also added to the fun with an exhibition of their own.

These events were but a modest precursor to the major role that the swimming program would play in the long history of the Club's growth and development. Competitive swimming is now so much a part of the Club's youth-oriented activities that it is easy to lose sight of its historic relevance. In fact, this centennial year marks the seventy-fifth anniversary of the GPYC swim program.

The tradition officially began in 1939 as Club finances were once again in good order and old and new members were returning. It was time to build a proper in-ground pool that met competitive swimming standards. Pool chairman Leo Fitzpatrick, assisted by Alvan Macauley and the board of directors, raised $25,000 through member subscriptions to begin construction. The

new pool was located in roughly the same footprint as today's pool, but smaller and a little further to the south. It opened on July 4, 1939, and was an immediate hit; competitive swimming among the Club's young people soared in popularity.

MICSA is established

One year later, in 1940, six private clubs in southeastern Michigan banded together to form the "Michigan Inter-Club Swimming Association," commonly referred to as MICSA. The six founding clubs were: Detroit Golf Club, Detroit Yacht Club, Detroit Boat Club, Flint Country Club, Oakland Hills Country Club, and Grosse Pointe Yacht Club. Pine Lake Country Club participated in most competitions but did not join the association.

Today MICSA has fourteen member clubs with two divisions of swim competition and includes three additional local clubs: Country Club of Detroit, Lochmoor Club, and Grosse Pointe Hunt Club.

As a way of showing strong support for the fledgling swim program, the GPYC dedicated four trophies in 1940 to recognize and encourage participants:

Figure 2. Swimming Chairman John Youngblood presents Coach Tom Teetaert with a platter commemorating his team's 1984 50th win in a row, as Vice Commodore James Daoust stands by as announcer.

Figure 3. A banner on the fence tells the story of the swim team's decisive victory against Country Club of Detroit.

The Commodore James Marks Trophy recognized the senior boy and girl with highest competitive point total of the season (age fifteen and over).

The Commodore Herbert Woodall Trophy went to the leading intermediate swimmers (age eleven to fourteen).

The Commodore Frank Couzens Trophy was dedicated to the leading junior swimmers (age ten and under).

The Commodore Lynn Pierson Trophy was given for most outstanding performance in Club and inter-club events.

Later, in 1947, the *Commodore Johnny Allmand Trophy* was dedicated to the outstanding boy swimmer of the season.

Figure 4. Annual award for best overall swimmer in category Boys 10 and 11, won by 2015 Commodore Kevin Granger in 1966.

The MICSA championship was won that first year, 1940, by the Detroit Yacht Club under the leadership of swim coaches Clarence and Betty Pinkston. Clarence was an Olympic champion who had won gold and silver medals in 1920 and two bronze in 1924. His wife Betty (Becker) was also an Olympic champion, capturing gold and silver in 1924 and gold again in 1928. Inspired by the Pinkstons, DYC swimmers dominated MICSA competition during the WWII years and immediately following.

By the early 1950s, swimming had gained significantly in popularity at the GPYC. With a much broader cross-section of both parent members and youngsters, our swim culture gained momentum along with performance expectations.

The Pinkstons were hired with the intention of putting the GPYC swim program on the fast track. The Pinkstons obliged, and over the next eight years Club swimmers began to emerge as contenders with a formidable presence, highlighted in 1956 and 1957 by back-to-back MICSA championships. To this day, the Pinkstons are revered by all those who labored, learned and succeeded under their leadership. The league championship trophy is still named the Pinkston Trophy in their honor.

The Grosse Pointe Yacht Club swim program continued to improve under a series of fine coaches. Coach William Reaume took over the team-building process in the 1960s, followed nearly a decade later by Doctor Tom Mertz.

It was on July 4, 1969, to the roar of a fifty-gun salute, that Coach Mertz and his team celebrated the formal opening of the Club's second new state-of-the-art aluminum pool, with improved race lanes and starting stands, and updated diving facilities. A truly outstanding swimming and diving performance was presented by the team to an appreciative crowd.

The race to 100

In 1973, the program came under the leadership of Tom Teetaert, and something of a swimming dynasty began to take shape. Three seasons later, in 1976, the GPYC team defeated the Detroit Boat Club, scoring the first of what would become a milestone run of fifty dual-meet victories in sanctioned MICSA meets that carried all the way through the 1984 season. During that time, GPYC swimmers held seventeen of the possible forty-six MICSA records.

By the mid-1980s, swimming had become firmly established as one of the Club's leading youth-oriented activities, often attracting as many as one hundred twenty youngsters, ranging in age from five to seventeen. Participants usually stayed with the swim program five years or more. Swimmers and their families represented one of the Club's most active and supportive groups, and it became a given that the swim program was one of the Club's major attractions. The many award-winning seasons were a subject of great pride in the community, and the winning streak would ultimately extend to over one hundred competitive events. The swim team was on a roll and the best was yet to come.

In 1985, a young gentleman by the name of Fred Michalik came to the GPYC as head swim coach, and the dynasty continued its rise to ever-greater achievements. Over the next seven years, Club swimmers reeled in another fifty consecutive victories, winning their one hundredth straight dual meet victory on July 1, 1992, followed by an eighth consecutive MICSA championship later that month. On August 21, the team was honored by a record turnout of members and guests at the Harbor Lights Night Bar-B-Que.

The Club's all-time record-smashing run finally ended at one hundred three straight victories—a feat that may never again be equaled. High praise and special recognition for this remarkable winning record must go to all the participating team members throughout the years, and to the two coaches who were there to make it happen: Tom Teetaert and Fred Michalik.

MICSA comes to the Club

The GPYC hosted the MICSA finals in 1994 and distinguished itself considerably by conducting what was considered to be one of the best-run, most colorfully decorated and fiscally successful events ever held. Over four hundred swimmers competed, cheered on by over a thousand spectators per day during the three-day event. The excitement of the competition ended on the third day with an entry march of all participants by club, with each team captain hoisting their club standard. The march was followed by a massive balloon release, coordinated with a fireboat water cannon display.

Past Commodore Ted Smith served as general chairman, with future commodore Bill Storen and his wife Julie handling the chairs of grounds and facilities and support activities, respectively. Promotional materials were handled by Shelley Schoenherr, who designed special tee shirts for swimmers with the logo "Swimmers Tower Above the Rest." future commodore Jim Anderson constructed a special electronic scoreboard, which he donated to the cause.

As a youngster, Past Commodore Smith had learned to swim at the Club. He was an active member of the swim team in the 1940s and 1950s and carried on with competitive swimming into his collegiate years. In recognition of his many years of support for Club swimming, he was honored as the 1988 Member of the Year. Of the MICSA event, he was quoted as saying, "The MICSA tournaments teach us how to win, how to lose and how to work hard. How could anything else be better?"

The 1997 GPYC swim team captured the MICSA-Blue dual meet division title by upsetting the favored team from Great Oaks Country Club. As League Champions that year, they closed their season with more winning titles than any other club in the fifty-eight year history of the events. The awards banquet was attended by one hundred twenty-eight Club swimmers, each introduced by Coach Fred Michalik and presented with a special achievement plaque. Coach Michalik also received personal recognition for his long-term commitment to team excellence and got a standing ovation from the attendees.

A new pool

It had long been recognized that the Club pool was falling far short of current club standards, particularly for competitive swimming, and that a new facility was needed. After extensive planning and research, preliminary plans were developed and the Club embarked upon the largest capital project in its history.

The old pool was closed on Labor Day weekend 2002, with a gala farewell party and groundbreaking ceremony on September 3. Preliminary viewing of concept drawings for the spectacular new pool had received rave reviews, and excitement ran high all winter and into spring in anticipation of the new pool opening.

As demolition of the old aluminum pool progressed, it was discovered that it had been placed inside the original 1939 cement pool structure. Further excavations uncovered the 1939 pool with its light fixtures nicely preserved and appearing functional.

The grand opening ceremony for the new state-of-the-art, advanced design, number three swimming pool took place on July 4, 2003. The pool ranged from four to twelve feet deep and included eight 25-meter race lanes, a regulation one-meter diving board, a safety-oriented kiddie wading pool with a fountain, and a generously scaled pool deck space for sunbathers as well as event spectators. In light of the Club's history as having one of the top competitively recognized MICSA swim teams, it was a fitting tribute to our young swimmers.

Team building, good fun, and summertime camaraderie

Enthusiasm for the new pool was just one factor that added to the continuing popularity of the swim team during the first decade of the twenty-first century. The dedicated swimmers of the GPYC teams have always been fortunate in having professional-grade coaches and strong parental support as cornerstones to their teams' successes. Competitive swimming isn't just about winning trophies; it's about personal discipline, team spirit and handling adversity. For Fred Michalik, it has also been the importance of a coach's impact on the personal life values of his young charges.

Coach Michalik recalled one day how his encouragement of one swimmer during his long career at the GPYC resulted in an unexpected phone call. He was asked by a proud cadet to attend his upcoming graduation from the U.S. Military Academy at West Point. The soon-to-be commissioned officer explained that he had learned the discipline, determination, and team spirit that were essential to the completion of his cadet training from the guidance he experienced under Coach Michalik's direction. "That call made it all worthwhile," said the coach.

In 2006, the GPYC once again played host to the MICSA finals, and as it had done in 1994, the Club rose to the occasion. Past Commodore Mary Treder-Lang and Mark Basile co-chaired the event, which was attended by all fourteen MICSA clubs. The warm hospitality and efficient organization, as well as the new swim facilities, received rave reviews. Everyone enjoyed the fireworks display, the live music, and the helicopter fly-over. When the final wave was just a ripple, the GPYC team had placed third overall.

The 2008 season was launched with a swim team silent auction that raised $21,000 for the purchase of new computer equipment and an underwater camera imaging system to assist coaches and swimmers in evaluating their stroke and kick techniques.

At the 2009 MICSA finals held at the Birmingham Athletic Club, the proud GPYC team made a splash with their new red shirts with the Club burgee. The team placed fourth overall.

In 2010 the team sported a new name and logo: Sailfish. Early in the season, team members attended special swim clinics conducted by Olympic Gold Medalists and former MICSA swimmers Peter and Alex Vanderkaay. It was readily agreed by participants that this special and expert coaching had a strong impact on the team's performance that year and would continue to do so for several years in the future.

Expectations from 2010 were validated when 2011 became one of the team's successful seasons. The Sailfish, led by Coach Michalik, moved up to a fourth place finish in the MICSA finals, with many new personal achievements throughout the season. The team continued its winning ways with another fourth place MICSA finish in 2012.

The 2013 season saw a record number of swimmers across all classes, and for the third straight year, the Sailfish took fourth place in the MICSA finals. Swim team co-chairs Thad and Ann MacKrell described the 2013 activities this way — "What a season!"

In the centennial year of 2014, the swim team saw many changes. After many successful years of coaching the team, Coach Fred Michalik made the decision to step down, and was replaced by the coaching team of John Fodell, Bill Thompson, Bridget Hubbell and Jacob Montague. "Coach Fo's" Sailfish swimmers finished a 4/2 season and placed fourth at the MICSA finals at the Dearborn Country Club. Two MICSA records were set by

Figure 5.

THE YACHT IS HOT — And the birth of a button

By Shelley Schoenherr

Before the swimming pool was even filled with water for the summer season of 1985, the swim committee met in the original, undecorated "Tower Room" to plan the activities for the season. We were an incredibly dedicated, tight-knit crew, and supportive of Grosse Pointe Yacht Club swimming in every way. A goal that year was to create a "booster button," sell the button in support of Club swimmers, and use the proceeds to cover the cost of a permanent record board at poolside. We wanted to display our pride in the team's achievements, and the sale of the buttons could help us get there.

I remember well designing the button and planning the color of blue in the background to match the blue of a windbreaker worn by committee member and friend, Walt Cytacki. The product of our endeavor was displayed on the clothing racks of Mike's Marine. Buttons were sold at meets and by committee members until enough funds were raised to help offset the cost of the record board.

A year before, I had used "THE YACHT IS HOT" slogan in newsletters and materials that I had written for parents and swimmers, but not until it appeared on the button in the summer of 1985 did the slogan really take off.

And take off it did. "THE YACHT IS HOT" message was seen flying behind an airplane as it circled the Club during several meets, as well as at the finals at Western Golf and Country Club.

The slogan and button were reprinted on the sides of swim caps worn by Grosse Pointe Yacht Club team members for several seasons. For three years, from 1986 through 1988, Past Commodore Schoenherr and I served with Chris and Mike Kirchner as co-chairs of the swim committee, and during those summers we wrote a weekly newsletter for swim team parents and swimmers. You can bet "THE YACHT IS HOT" appeared in each issue, and many team tee shirts were adorned with the slogan in the mid-and late-1980s.

Long after that original record board, which had been proudly purchased through efforts of the committee and was hung at every meet by our swim coach, the team went on to win an unprecedented one hundred three consecutive dual meets. The winning ways of our GPYC swimmers proved that in fact THE YACHT was, and still is, HOT.

Figure 6.

Catie DeLoof, who currently holds seven MICSA records. The finals slogan, "GO with the FO," reflected the team spirit fostered by the energetic and talented coaching staff. With that team spirit, and the friendship and enthusiasm that has always been so much a part of the GPYC swim teams, it is certain that Sailfish swimmers will build on their momentum and continue to grow in the years to come.

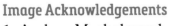

Image Acknowledgements

1. Andrea Mychalowych

2.–3. GPYC

4. Jim Dorian

5. GPYC

6. Shelley Schoenherr

Other photos by GPYC
and Andrea Mychalowych

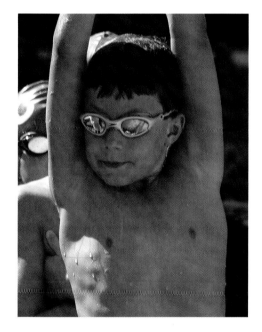

Figure 1. A vivdly attired Opti sailor is seen hiking-out at the 2013 USODA Nationals at GPYC.

The Junior Sailing Program, Yachtsmen's Committee, and GPNEF

By Kelley Vreeken

In the early 1960s, following the formation of a junior sailing committee by the Detroit River Yachting Association (DRYA), a group of GPYC sailors, including Fred Somes Jr. and R. Frederick Kolowich, saw that an organized junior sailing program at the Club was central to its mission and essential to its list of member attractions. A program that taught sailing at all levels to young people would attract the parents of student sailors and also help retain those young sailors as members later in life. Their vision was spot-on.

The first Twenty-five years

The Junior Sailing Program at the Club got off to a strong start in 1963, quickly attracting fifty youngsters, ages seven to eighteen. One of the early participants was 2014 Vice Commodore Kevin Granger, who vividly recalled his formative years there:

"I started in the program in about 1965. We didn't have a sailing director as we do today. It was run by a teacher or college student as a summer job. Member Dr. Bill Jennings once taught sailing at the Club, as did former member

Jimmy Fraser. I, too, was an instructor. There was usually just one or two of us for the entire program, and the classes would run from 9:00 am to noon and then from 1:00 to 4:00 pm. Our classroom was the 'dungeon' under the accounting office, where the door is, just off the main driveway. Our sailing fleet was pretty humble; we only had some Interlakes and a couple of Flying Scots, although Chrysler Corporation, which was into boating in those days, would occasionally donate a boat or two for the summer. We also had one very old steel boat we called the 'Iron Maroo' that served as our coach boat.

"The way the program worked, there were different levels of accomplishment and tests that you could take to achieve them. The beginning level was Seaman, then Crew, then Skipper, Racing Skipper, and Master. I remember studying like crazy back then because I wanted to become the first and youngest person to achieve the master level, which I ultimately did.

"Regattas in those days took place on Saturdays as part of the regular DRYA schedule. There were three distinct courses: A, B and C. The junior sailors would sail the C course and were always the last to start. I remember the Interlake boats were very different from each other in terms of speed potential, and we would have competitions throughout the week to see

Figure 2. Junior Sailing instructor Dr. Bill Jennings steps aboard one of the Club-owned Interlake sloops.

Figure 3. Advanced sailing juniors get to use the Columbia 21 sloops during the 1968 season. Left: Sandy Smith has the jib sheet and Mike Drysdale has the tiller. Right: Out on the foredeck, Dave Helm Jr. and Matt Pierce prepare to set the boat's fluorescent spinnaker.

who would get to sail the fastest one in the regatta. After each Saturday race we were anxious to turn on WJR Radio and hear the wrap-up of the regatta given by GPYC Past Commodore Frank McBride. Frank would announce the winners in the various classes and would sometimes mention us even if we didn't win. He was very good to us. It was always a huge thrill to hear your name on the radio.

"I was lucky enough back then to team up with John Harper and John Walton, and the three of us had an extremely successful junior sailing experience. At one time, we came in second in the Sears Cup, which was the ultimate junior sailing championship. We ended up losing in the last race to a team from Texas. All three of us went on to sail in college; John Walton became an All-American at Michigan State.

"There was no such thing as a 'professional' sailor in those early days, but many of us were offered the opportunity to sail on a wide array of boats in different events and championships. When I was fifteen years old, John Harper and I bought an International Tempest, which at the time was an Olympic-class boat. It was in rough shape, but he and I spent an entire winter restoring the boat so that it would be competitive. We ultimately made two runs at the Olympics, but were not successful, although we did win a silver medal in a pre-Olympic regatta.

"The big thing the program did was to give us the opportunity to sail against teams from all over the world. I remember sailing in Beverly, Massachusetts, against Valery Mankin, who was from Russia and won the gold medal in the 1972 Olympics. I raced many different classes of boats throughout the years and

Figure 4. The Sears Cup is awarded annually to the national junior sailing champion during the U.S. Junior Sailing races. In 1970, young Kevin Granger from the GPYC placed second in the country. Kevin became GPYC commodore in 2015.

Figure 5. In 1970 Kevin Granger won the DRYA award for best overall junior sailboat racer.

also participated in the 1975 Canada's Cup on a boat named *Nike*, which was owned by Bill Timken. *Nike* was a radically designed boat with a crew that included several America's Cup sailors. We were eventually eliminated, however. The ultimate winner was *Golden Dazy*, owned locally by BYC member Dr. Gerry Murphy and skippered by Don Criner. *Dazy's* crew had a young Australian tactician by the name of John Bertrand. John went on to win the silver medal in the 1976 Olympics in the Finn Class and then in 1983 skippered *Australia II* to beat Dennis Connor in the America's Cup. It was the first time in one hundred thirty-two years that the United States had lost the America's Cup.

There have been many more successful sailors that have come out of our junior sailing program since those early years, many of whom were far better than we were."

Figure 6. The 420s are packed and ready to head south for the Orange Bowl in Florida.

Figure 7. Former GPYC junior sailor and Olympian Carrie Howe (right) is all smiles when she is sailing.

By the late 1960s, the three-man Interlake boats were considered out of date, and clubs began adopting the newer and faster Flying Junior class. In the 1970s, Past Commodore Roy Barbier, himself a successful sailboat racer, persuaded yachting committee members and the families of junior sailors to each pledge fifty dollars toward the purchase of Flying Juniors for the program. It was a huge upgrade. By the mid-1990s, under the solid direction of Sailing Director Pat Barry, the Club's junior sailing fleet had grown larger and more diverse, containing Club 420s, Laser Full Rigs, and Laser Radial Rigs. The Flying Junior boats were now used as introductory two-man trainers. Later that decade, the tiny but globally popular Optis were added to the fleet for the benefit of younger sailors.

Over the years, thousands of young people from the Grosse Pointe Yacht Club have learned valuable nautical skills through the junior sailing program. Many have moved on to competitive collegiate sailing and from there to pleasure sailing later in life, all based on sailing lessons learned as youngsters. Two ladies from the junior sailing program have, in particular, achieved notable success with their sailing skills.

Dawn Riley, a young sailor and later an instructor at GPYC, went on to become the first woman to manage an America's Cup campaign and was the first American, male or female, to sail in three America's Cup championships and two Whitbread Round-the-World races.

Carrie Howe, who was also a talented junior sailor at GPYC, went on to excel as a sailor at Boston College and then at the 2008 Olympics in China.

The GPYC Yachtsmen's Committee

As the GPYC Junior Sailing Program grew in size and popularity, so did the cost of maintaining it. In 1988, an organization was formed at the Club that would raise funds to preserve the program and hopefully raise it to new heights. The Yachtsmen's Committee, as it was called, originally consisted of twelve members and was headed then, as today, by Past Commodore James Morrow.

Figure 8. The Great Lakes Boating Festival at the GPYC features boats of many sizes.

The YC's first fund-raising efforts were centered around a get-together known as Yachtsmen's Night, which was a dinner with a notable speaker and a couple of boat manufacturers, namely Sea Ray and Tiara. The speakers at these events included Dennis Connor, Gary Jobson, Peter Isler, Rick Mears and other sports celebrities.

A special fund-raising event was held in 1989 to underwrite the renovation of the Sailing Center. Upgrades included sloping sail storage racks and other improvements. The effort was commemorated with a plaque that hangs in the GPYC main entrance.

From this modest beginning, the event grew steadily in attendance and scope. Yachtsmen's Night expanded to Yachtsmen's Day, then Yachtsmen's Weekend. In 2004, Yachtsmen's Weekend changed its name to the Great Lakes Boating Festival, which opened the gates of the Club to the public for one weekend a year. The new name reflected the fact that the event now offered attractions beyond boats and marine hardware, including wine tastings, vintage cars and motorcycles, and art exhibits.

Today the Great Lakes Boating Festival is one of the largest in-the-water boat shows in the region, attracting hundreds of visitors to the Club over a three-day period. It begins with a spirited "Summer Breeze Party" auction and dinner on Friday night and now, with the raffle of a new Sea Ray, a Rolex, and a Cadillac all provided by sponsors on Sunday afternoon.

Proceeds from the event go to support junior sailing, just as they did when the Yachtsmen's Committee was founded more than twenty-five years ago. Since 1988, the organization has raised nearly three million dollars to support the Junior Sailing Program. By 2014, through contributions and fund-raising, over one-third of all the Club's sailing assets — such as boats, sailing equipment, floating docks, and launch ramps — were purchased with funds raised by the Yachtsmen's Committee.

The GPYNEF is founded

In 2009, the Yachtsmen's Committee donated funds to help form the Grosse Pointe Youth Nautical Education Foundation (GPYNEF), a 501c3 tax-free organization with its own separate board of directors. What set the GPYNEF apart from 501c3 organizations at other area clubs was that the GPYC would maintain control of its junior sailing effort as a program for Club members only. With tax-free status, the GPYNEF encouraged members to contribute to its mission of support for youth sailing, and contribute they did.

The GPYNEF grew steadily in impact. In 2012, the Junior Olympic Sailing Competition and Mallory High School Regional were among a number of events hosted by the foundation. A year later, the GPYNEF became a host and major sponsor of the USODA National Championships, which were held at the Club. Most recently, in August 2014, the foundation hosted the U.S. Youth Sailing Championship, an invitation-only event that drew two hundred of the top junior sailors from around the world to GPYC. As before, the Club and the foundation were praised nationally and internationally as world-class sailing sponsors.

Today, GPYNEF support for sailing extends well beyond the boundaries of the GPYC. Grants from the foundation help fund the following worthy programs and activities:

Challenge the Wind Sailing Program — Brings a learn-to-sail opportunity to Detroit High School students who would not otherwise have the chance.

Figure 9. Challenge the Wind Sailing Program participants.

High School Junior Sailing Programs — Grants from the foundation have expanded the sailing programs at Grosse Pointe North and South High Schools into a spring and fall activity. Previously their sailing was only a spring sport, when the majority of the high school competition was in the fall.

Travel Support — When the Grosse Pointe South sailing team qualified for the High School National Semifinals, GPYNEF helped fund their travel expenses to Minnesota, where they won the Midwest Interscholastic Championships.

Baker Regional High School Qualifier — In 2014, the foundation provided a grant in the amount of $1,000 to help Grosse Pointe South sponsor this event, which brought teams from Michigan, Illinois, Wisconsin, and Minnesota to qualify for the High School National Championships.

Varsity Sailing Equipment Support — When Grosse Pointe South asked for $8,500 to purchase sails for their program, the foundation agreed to contribute one half of the amount if the school would raise the other half. Grosse Pointe South came through and so did GPYNEF.

Figure 10. A GPYNEF matching grant helped fund equipment for Grosse Pointe South High School's Varsity Junior Sailing program.

Figure 11. GPYC harbor during the 2014 Great Lakes Boating Festival.

Figure 12. A live auction at the 2014 Summer Breeze Party helped to replenish the coffers of the GPYNEF.

Figure 13. Two sailors from the Twenty-niner class reach for the mark at GPYC-sponsored 2014 U.S. Youth Sailing Championship.

College Scholarships — The foundation awards up to ten college scholarships every year to young sailors with special academic and sailing skills who participate in a DRYA club or MISSA high school junior sailing program. Eight scholarships were awarded in 2014.

DART — Which stands for Detroit Advanced Racing Team, is comprised of the top twelve Optimist dinghy sailors in the DRYA who received advanced racing training and travelled to regional events to test their skills. After an impressive showing in 2014, DART will continue to receive GPYNEF support.

Regional Regattas — GPYNEF continues to give financial support to specific regattas that are open to the public, providing broad opportunities for competitive sailing at the high school and collegiate level.

Special Grants — The foundation considers grant applications from local sailors who aspire to improve their skills and compete at top-level events. Such events include the Detroit Cup Regatta and Hawks Peacocks Racing.

Figure 14. Detroit Advanced Racing Team, or DART, with coach Connor Corgard, center.

Figure 15. Laser and 420 sailors intersect on a course.

Figure 16. Opti sailors head upwind at the 2013 USODA National Championships.

The results speak for themselves

Over two and a half decades, the efforts of the Yachtsmen's Committee, which now numbers twenty members, have paid off abundantly at the Club. The result is a junior sailing program with an enrollment of over one hundred ten participants each year, all of whom are the children or grandchildren of GPYC members. The fleet of boats in the program currently consists of twelve 420s, seven Lasers, four BICs, forty Optis, two J-22s, nine Boston Whaler powerboats, and two hard- bottom inflatable coaches' boats, with numerous other support equipment.

Not only is the GPYC Junior Sailing Program the largest in the DRYA, it is acknowledged to be the finest program in the Midwest. With the Yachtsmen's Committee and the foundation there to support it, the program will continue to provide value to members and the community. Its success is directly attributable to Past Commodores Jim Morrow and Sloane Barbour, who have led the charge from the beginning twenty-six years ago.

Figure 17. Opti sailors at 2013 USODA National Championships.

IMAGE ACKNOWLEDGEMENTS

1. GPYNEF, photographer David Hein

2.–3. GPYC

4.–5. Jim Dorian

6. GPYC

7. Carrie Howe, Magic Marine

8. Jim Dorian

9. Grayhaven Yacht Club

10. GPYNEF

11. Jim Dorian

12.–13. GPYC, photographer Michele Penoyer

14. Connor Corgard.

15. GPYC, photographer Michele Penoyer

16.–17. GPYNEF, photographer David Hein

18. Jim Dorian

Figure 18. *Thor* owned by Don Fires was the race committee's lead boat at the 2006 U.S. Youth Sailing Championship hosted by the Grosse Pointe Yacht Club.

Figure 1. Bluenose Regatta, September 25, 2010.

GPYC Sailing Trophies

By Ross B. Stone and
Past Commodore Sloane R. Barbour

This history of our Club is chronicled in a variety of ways. Given the strong nautical orientation of a yacht club, one might logically expect that our yachting trophies would be an essential part of our history — and they are. The purpose here is to focus on the trophies awarded for sailboat racing, which has been an integral part of the Club since its inception in 1914 and subsequent joining of the Detroit River Yachting Association (DRYA) the same year.

The DRYA, now known as the Detroit Regional Yacht-Racing Association, was established in 1912, and the GPYC was the fourth club to join, preceded by the Detroit Yacht Club, the Detroit Boat Club, and the Country Club of Detroit. The DRYA organizes sailboat races between member yacht clubs, which now includes twenty-seven clubs in the U.S. and Canada,

extending from Port Huron and Sarnia on Lake Huron down to Toledo on the shores of Lake Erie. George Marsh, our first commodore, served as commodore of the DRYA in 1915, 1916 and 1921.

The authors(RBS and SRB) are the custodians of the Club's many sailing trophies and were asked to choose some to feature in this article. The following trophies were selected.

Commodore John R. Sutton Jr. Perpetual Trophy

Over its forty-six year lifetime, the Com. Sutton Trophy has recognized the outstanding performance of some of the most skillful skippers and competitive yacht designs to sail the Great Lakes. The trophy was awarded continuously, beginning with the 11th Annual Bluenose Regatta Trophy Race in 1949 for Class A, B, and C Best Corrected Time. The first winner was Wendal Anderson in *Escapade* and the final winner in 1995 was N. Munch in *Moonraker*.

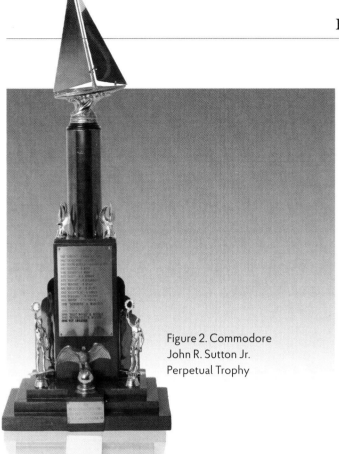

Figure 2. Commodore
John R. Sutton Jr.
Perpetual Trophy

Some of the most memorable winners among the fleet were:
- Wendal Anderson's nationally known *Escapade*
- Henry Burkard   *Meteor*
- Susan Fisher   *Old Rarity*
- H.C. Ford   *Fantasy*
- Karl Ness and
  Maurice de Clercq   *Flying Buffalo*
- E.A. Schmidt   *Sassy*
- George Lyons   *Tigress*
- Norm Sarn   *Revelry*
- Karl Ness   *Happi-Ness*
- Randy Woods   *Espiritu*
- Roy Barbier   *Roulette*
- Rededicated in 1974
  for Cruising Class A
- Rededicated in 1989 for
  IMS Class A-B-C
- Rededicated in 2011
  for Class PHRF 1

Figure 2. Flavell-Putnam
Grosse Pointe Yacht Club
Eight Meter Trophy

John Rummel Trophy

Dedicated in 2004, Bayview Port Huron-to-Mackinac Race, North American 40 Class. The trophy has not been awarded since 2009. It is presently located at the GPYC on the west wall of the east lobby.

- John Rummel   2004 *Majic Star*, Shore Course
                 First to finish NA 40 1st Division
                 First Overall, Shore Course
                 First NA 40 NOOD
                 DRYA NA 40 Season Champion
- John Barbour   2005 *Velero VII*
- Mike Feldman   2006 *Velero VI*
- John Barbour   2007 *Velero VIII*
- John Replogle 2008 *Montombi*
- John Seago   2009 *Seagoing*

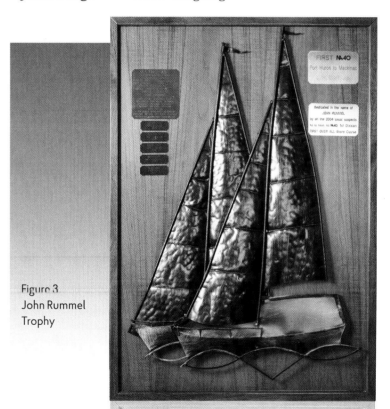

Figure 3.
John Rummel
Trophy

Flavell-Putnam Grosse Pointe Yacht Club Eight Meter Trophy

This classic Tiffany-designed sterling silver cup was donated in 1945 by J.H. Flavell and Ernest C. Putnam to encourage class sail racing at GPYC. The trophy was actively awarded from 1945-1949 and again in 1959. It was rededicated for the PRFC Class in the 1980 and 1982 racing seasons. Its last dedication was in 2011 for the GPYC Bluenose Regattas in the PHRF 2 Class.

Charles J. Glasgow Perpetual Trophy

The trophy was donated by C.J. Glasgow in early 1961. Original dedication was for the GPYC Bluenose Regatta, Best Corrected Time, Small Boat Division.

- Rededicated 1964, Best Corrected Time in Cruising Class D
- Rededicated 1983 for Overall Winner, Bluenose Regatta; last awarded in 1991 to A. Morrison's *Sunshine*
- Reactivated 2011, GPYC Bluenose Regatta for PHRF — A Class

Figure 4. Charles J. Glasgow Perpetual Trophy

Figure 5. Timken Roller Bearing Trophy

Timken Roller Bearing Trophy

Donated in 1941 by Timken Roller Bearing Company. Originally dedicated for the GPYC Bluenose Regatta, Lawley 110 Class, which was an Olympic Class in the 1930s.

- Rededicated 1952 for 22 Square Meter Class
- Rededicated 1958 for the Folkboat Class
- Rededicated 1980 for the J.O.R. "B" Class
- Last awarded in 1982 to Henry Burkard's *Ricochet* from Bayview Yacht Club
- Rededicated 2011 for GPYC Bluenose Regatta, BEN 36.7 Class

WJR Cruising Class B Trophy

Donated in 1939 by Leo J. Fitzpatrick. This trophy was awarded annually from 1939 to 1977 for the Best Corrected Time, GPYC Bluenose Regatta. It was rededicated in 1980 as the PRF B Trophy and last awarded in 1982 to Thomas Kleinhardt in *Forte*, representing LSSC. This trophy is currently available for rededication.

Figure 6. WJR Cruising Class B Trophy

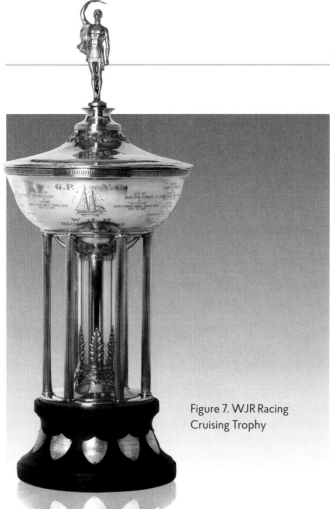

Figure 7. WJR Racing Cruising Trophy

Lake St. Clair Light Trophy

Donated by Stewart T. Hanson in 1952. Originally dedicated for the GPYC Bluenose Regatta for Cruising Class C. Last awarded in 1992 to John Barbour's *Velero*. This trophy is currently assigned to the NA 40 Class.

From 1952 to 1992, some of the more memorable boats and sailors to win this trophy included:

• Karl Ness	*Happi-Ness*
• Tom Hanson	*Dauntless*
• Susan Fisher	*Old Rarity*
• Don Smith	*Yare*
• Skip Boston	*Ranger*
• Henry Burkard	*Meteor*
• Karl Ness and Maurice de Clercq	*Flying Buffalo*
• Herb Mainwaring	*Easterly*

WJR Racing Cruising Trophy

Donated by Leo Fitzpatrick in early 1939 and originally dedicated to the GPYC Bluenose Regatta for Cruising Class E. Last awarded in 1992 to T. Kleinhardt's *Forte*. From 1939 to 1964 and in 1982, the winners of this trophy represented some of the finest sailing yachts and most dedicated, skillful sailors in U.S. yachting history. Many of these yachts are still viable contenders in classic yachting events. Some of the more memorable yachts include:

• J.B. Ford Jr.	*Royono III*
• Tommy Fisher	*Apache*
• George Naumann	*Estrellita*
• Wendell Anderson	*Escapade*
• L. Mitschell	*Soubrette*
• Norm Sarns	*Revelry*
• Carter Sales	*Winsom*
• Clete Welling	*Vitesse*
• Wilfred "Toot" Gmeiner	*Apache*
• Ernie Gates	*Blitzen*
• Paul Smiley	*Orient*
• Gilbert Pingree	*Red Head*
• Clare Jacobs	*Falcon*
• Com. Roy Barbier	*Roulette*

• Rededicated in 2011 to the Bluenose J 120 Class and is currently being actively awarded.

Figure 8. Lake St. Clair Light Trophy

William P. Fisher
Perpetual Member Trophy

Donated 1967 in honor of William P. Fisher by William V., Everell E., Thomas K. Fisher and John Drummy. Originally dedicated to GPYC Bluenose Regatta for Best Corrected Time, Cruising Class A. First winner was Apache, then owned by Wilfred "Toot" Gmeiner, but originally owned by donator Tommy Fisher. Rededicated in 1974 to Overall Winner of the Bluenose. In 1990, the trophy was rededicated as an award to the GPYC Yachtsman of the Year. Qualifications are based on:

- Overall season standing, DRYA regular and long distance races
- Participation in Port Huron and Chicago to Mackinac races
- Participation and standing, Bluenose Regatta
- Strength of competition in respective class
- Overall improvement of performance

Members who have performed in exemplary fashion in yachting-related events are also eligible to receive this award. See appendix six of Yachtsman of the Year.

Figure 9. William P. Fisher Perpetual Member Trophy

IMAGE ACKNOWLEDGEMENTS

1. Tom Kliber
2.–10. Jim Dorian

Figure 10. *Majic Star*, the boat responsible for the John Rummel Trophy, at start of the 2004 Port Huron-to-Mackinac Race.

PART III

Figure 1. GPYC bowling professional Gordy Woods, center, stands in front of the lanes where members Dr. John Seago, left, and Howard Smith, right, each rolled the perfect bowling score — a 300 game.

Committees

Part III of this centennial book is devoted to the Club's various committees and activities, and to the fleet officers. For inclusion purposes, the 2014 heads of all committees and activities, along with all fleet officers, were contacted and given the opportunity to submit a write-up for the book, and a great many did so.

There were no strict parameters, and the responses received vary widely from just a paragraph to several pages. Supplying a photograph to accompany the write-up was optional.

Once the letters went out in January 2014, we received several early responses, but to those who did not respond, we followed up with emails and phone calls in an effort to get as large a participation rate as possible. Thank you to all who contributed.

ARCHIVES
By Robert Hackathorn and Ross B. Stone

Over the course of the Club's one-hundred year history, our archives have been made up of all of the publications, architectural renderings, membership directories, mementos from social functions, and other non-financial and engineering documents.

Until 1997, there was no formal committee to preside over our archives. The Club relied mostly on the diligence of history-minded interested members to keep a reasonably accurate and somewhat complete compendium of the Club's history.

It was in that year of 1997, thanks to the efforts of Past Commodore John Schoenherr's wife Shelley, that a separate committee was formally created to oversee our archives. Mary Huebner was selected as the first chairperson and since that time we have always had a chairperson and committee.

Figure 2. Bocce ball winners, Fourth of July weekend in 2011, wearing the hats given to members to celebrate the opening of the new, enhanced 360-degree seating at the Gazebo Bar.

BOCCE
By Bud and Rene Cornillie

The idea of hosting a Bocce Tournament came from a friendly bocce match between the Cornillies and former members Andy and Pam Bawden back in 2006. The Club now hosts three bocce tournaments every summer. They take place each holiday weekend on the beautiful East Lawn. The Club grooms the grass and sets up pop tents, benches, and a bar. Adult participants of all ages take part on four special roped-off courts. Members sign up with a partner and via a blind draw become a team of four.

Proud chairpersons are Bud and Rene Cornillie and Larry and Mariann Channell. The tournaments have come to be enjoyed as much for their social aspect as for the competition. The Club provides gift certificates for The Grog Shop to the winning participants. The event practically runs itself and every tournament has been great fun for all participants and spectators.

Figure 3. The East Lawn makes the perfect setting for bocce.

BOWLING

By Wayne Wegner and Howard A. Smith

Bowling has been an integral part of the GPYC social scene since 1940, when the first four bowling alleys were completed. With bowling being such an immediate hit, the final two alleys and the pin-setting machines were installed in 1942. The Bowling Center has hosted numerous adult leagues as well as opportunities for the whole family, with bowling parties, junior programs, and other social events. In 1946, a bowling association was formed with other private clubs to provide inter-club competition.

Keeping up with technology, automatic pinsetters were installed in 1956. The Bowling Center continued to see heavy use, and in 1989 the alleys were rebuilt and the automatic pinsetters were updated. In 1998, automatic scoring machines were installed, eliminating the need for manual scorekeeping, allowing bowlers to concentrate on their bowling skills and social interaction. Most recently, in 2012, new ball returns were installed.

EUCHRE

By Tom and Marilyn Stephenson

At some point during the early 1990s, past members David and Emily Linington began the tradition of euchre tournaments among GPYC members. The tournaments occurred until approximately 2002, when there was a lapse for about a year, and then revived in 2003 by euchre lovers and members, John and Stephanie Hirschfeld and Mark Wehrwein and Nora Swoveland. When the Hirschfelds moved away, the tournaments continued to flourish under Mark and Nora until 2010, when Tom and Marilyn Stephenson took the reins and continued the tradition.

The tournaments typically occur on a monthly basis, excluding "boating months," and have been held in various rooms of the Club, including the Fo'c'sle, Tower Pub, Lakeshore Room, Venetian Room, and even the Main Dining Room. The number of participants can vary from as few as twelve to as many as sixty. Partners change each game and are randomly chosen by partner cards and assigned table numbers. Prizes are awarded for the top three individual scores of the evening. The skill level of players varies; many have learned to play the game as children or college students, and some are just learning to play as adults. But all are welcome, and all appear to end the evening having had many laughs with old and new friends. Euchre tournaments continue to be a fun and exciting tradition at the GPYC.

FLEET CAPTAINS (SAIL AND POWER)

By Larry P. Channell

Fleet captains are appointed positions serving at the request of the commodore. While flag officers and board members are charged with the overall serious operation of the Club, the fleet captains play a role closer to cheerleaders.

Although the position of fleet captain at the GPYC may have existed in the early years, no documenting records have been found. At the second organizational meeting of the Club on December 10, 1913, Ignatius B. Hurley was appointed "yellmaster," also known as cheerleader and fleet captain. His job was to keep Club morale high, cheer on the teams, and be responsible for campfire programs. The first record of an official GPYC fleet captain was in 1941, when George Lilygren was fleet captain that year. He had served in the United States Marine Corps during WWI, was the clubhouse air raid warden during WWII, and became commodore in 1946.

In 1990, the fleet captain position split into sail and power. The fleet captains for sail and power promote the operation of their respective fleets and provide a conduit to the flag officers on specific issues, concerns, and desires of their fleet. The fleet captains are typically selected from members who are very active boaters. Being available is an important part of the job. During our centennial year, the fleet captain power was Brian L. Fish and fleet captain sail was Larry P. Channell.

The primary ceremonial function of the fleet captain for sail is to lead the Fleet Review. His or her sailboat leads the fleet to ensure the pack moves slow enough for the slowest boat to participate. Fleet captains are also expected to encourage members to keep their boats in the harbor and to participate in Club activities.

Figure 4. Member Gary Gonzalez and his crew sailing *Dos Mas* to a first-in-class finish in the 2012 Bluenose Regatta.

The Club also sponsors rendezvous and regattas. At some clubs these events are coordinated through the fleet captains. In the case of the Grosse Pointe Yacht Club, the fleet captains participate as necessary in these events. In GPYC regattas such as the Bluenose, the fleet captain for sail should be available to "press the flesh" and promote the event as well as the Club.

FLEET CHAPLAIN
By Rev. Walter A. Schmidt

Being a clergyman, I am probably not the most objective; however, I view the fact that the Grosse Pointe Yacht Club continues the tradition of having a fleet chaplain as one of the fleet officers as very positive. One of the strengths of the GPYC is that we do keep many traditions alive. It seems to me that many in our society are setting aside so many traditions that link us to our heritage, and we are the poorer for it.

I am aware that not all members of our Club are people of faith; however, we do live in a nation that says we are "One nation under God," and we stamp "In God We Trust" on our coins. Thus it seems appropriate to me that we continue the tradition of seeking God's ongoing guidance and direction for our Club. Let me add that no matter what one's faith might be, or the lack thereof, all of the members of the GPYC have been appreciative and supportive of my efforts and words while serving as fleet chaplain. Thank you.

It has been my privilege to serve in this capacity for the past fifteen years. First let me say a sincere word of thanks to the commodores who have had the confidence in me to represent our Club as her chaplain. And in this I am sure that I speak for all of the fleet chaplains who have served throughout the one hundred years of history of our fine Club.

My major responsibilities as fleet chaplain are to invoke God's blessings at the Blessing of the Fleet, the Fleet Review, the Commodore's Ball and the Annual Meeting, plus other events and activities when requested. In addition it has been my privilege to preside at weddings and funerals for GPYC members, and have provided a listening ear for members who just need to talk. I am thankful for having the opportunity to serve our great Club as your fleet chaplain.

FLEET MEASURER
By David Treder

Historically, the duties of a fleet measurer included the measurement of sails, boats, and other equipment, as well as handicapping, interpreting the rules of racing, and the annual review of the racing bylaws.

In modern times at the GPYC, the position is mostly pomp, the one requirement being to assist the commodore in various activities and coordinate certain events for the annual Fleet Review.

In December 1913, at the very first organizational meeting of the GPYC, William Granger was elected to the position of fleet measurer. At the fourth meeting in 1914, Harold "Chappie" Chapoton and Wally Hock were both elected fleet measurers, probably serving through the year 1915. They were both considered excellent iceboat racers and had each won many races.

FLEET SURGEON
By James McCarty, D.P.M.

Having served as fleet surgeon, it's interesting to go back and review the history of past fleet surgeons at the GPYC. Dr. Larry Stephenson did an excellent job outlining the historical duties of fleet surgeons in terms of the military. The U.S. Navy formally established the position of fleet surgeon in 1828. It applies to any physician, not just to those who specialize in surgery. In naval terms, a fleet is defined as a large group of warships commanded by an admiral. The fleet surgeon is stationed on the flagship, while the other ships of the fleet typically have one physician of their own on board. The fleet surgeon is responsible for all medical matters within the fleet and provides medical advice to the admiral as needed.[1]

In regard to yacht clubs, the position of fleet surgeon may be held not only by traditional physicians, but members of other healthcare specialties, such as dentistry, optometry, nursing, nurse practitioner, and physician assistant. In general, the commodore appoints the fleet surgeon and defines his or her duties for the year. Although the position is largely ceremonial, fleet surgeons have given health-related lectures, organized first aid demonstrations, and even taken responsibility for sanitary conditions in and around a clubhouse and harbor. Fleet surgeons at the GPYC have been helpful in upgrading medical equipment within the Club, and establishing and maintaining relationships with local emergency medical services.[1]

As fleet surgeon several years ago, I established a mates' boating course in an effort to educate all boaters to properly operate a vessel. The course was geared to handling emergencies that do happen at sea, as I well knew from personal experience. When I had to leave my vessel to assist a child on another vessel who was overcome by carbon monoxide while underway, my wife was unable to bring our boat to shore. Following this incident, we have now been training spouses for many years in boat handling.

On a lighter note, the fleet surgeon and other fleet officers take responsibility for ensuring a smoothly running year for the commodore. This includes organizing and helping to orchestrate various social events throughout the appointed year.

Reference
1. Larry W. Stephenson, M.D., "The Role of the Fleet Surgeon, Then and Now," *The MAST*, vol. 19, no. 1, January 2009, p.4.

GARDENS AND GROUNDS
By James T. Mestdagh

Before I began as chairperson of gardens and grounds at the GPYC in the early 2000s, my father-in-law, Past Commodore John Boll oversaw the grounds. Our goal has always been to maintain the integrity of the GPYC while enhancing all of the outside areas.

The front island has been transformed and continues to be a visual highlight when driving up to the front door. The flagpole was donated to the GPYC years ago in memory of Anna Thompson Dodge. Because of its size, it was delivered by barge from Rose Terrace, the former Dodge estate. The anchor was commissioned and donated to the Club in 1986. That same year, the cannon was purchased in Buzzard Bay,

Figure 13. Present chairs of the Wine/Gourmet Committee Tom and Marilyn Stephenson, left, former chairs Larry and Carol Stephenson, center, and former co-chairs Kevin Killebrew and Cathy Champion-Killebrew, right, toast another successful wine-tasting. The group has been sponsoring wine events for eighteen years.

referred to it as the wine group or the wine society. In 2003, at the fall meeting, an attempt was made to give it an official name, but nothing could be agreed upon by the members who were present. Then at some later date — no one is quite sure when — it was incorporated into the regular committee list and is now officially known as the wine/gourmet committee. The Stephensons continued to chair the group until 2007, when Kevin Killebrew and Cathy Champion-Killebrew became co-chairs. In 2011, Tom and Marilyn Stephenson took Larry and Carol's place as co-chairs, then took over chairing duties in 2012.

To this day, the group remains very informal and eclectic, with members ranging from wine novices to serious collectors. At present, there is an emphasis on wine education. As the old saying goes, the best wines are those that taste the best and are offered at the best prices. The trick is finding them, and the wine group remains dedicated to that mission.

From its inception to the present, the wine/gourmet committee has been grounded in the modest principles of promoting and enjoying wine. There has been an effort to include all types of wine in all price ranges. Appropriate food pairings, especially at wine dinners, have been offered. Organized events have always been based on these premises. In the early days, an important part of the mission was to maintain a great wine cellar at the Club. Who could have known then that in such a relatively short period of time, a well-stocked wine cellar would become *de rigueur* at any high-standard club. Dr. Stephenson need not have worried after all — good wine is here to stay at the GPYC.

IMAGE ACKNOWLEDGEMENTS

1. John F. Martin

2.–3. GPYC

4. GPYC photographer Michele Penoyer

5. GPYC

6. Marney Ramsey

7. John F. Martin

8. Liz Rader

9.–11. GPYC

12. Nora Williams

13. GPYC photographer Michele Penoyer

Staff

A Salute to a Great Team.

Fig. 1. Thomas G. Trainor, General Manager.

Fig. 3. David Daniot, Executive Chef.

Fig. 2. Timothy Lotito, Chief Financial Officer.

Fig. 4. (Left to right) Susan M. Hughes, Membership Marketing Manager; Aaron K. Wagner, Special Events and Membership Manager; Maureen Nance, Membership Administrator and Marketing.

The pumpkins featured in this section brightened (and menaced?) the Club during Halloween 2014. They were all carved by staff members for display around the clubhouse.

Fig. 5. General Manager Thomas Trainor, Food and Beverage Director Christopher Cassetta, servers, and bartenders, Commodore's Ball 2014. Left to right, first row: Denise Catanzarite, Angela Gates, Carly Spaust, Tyler Love, John Earley, Eric Jamieson, Stanley (Joe) Swierczynski. Second row: Thomas Trainor, Belinda Gilbert, Melanie Lewis, Fina Saroli, Shannon Cicalo, Margaret Santero-Jacobs, Jessica Walkowski, Kayla Bossenbery. Third row: Joe Hooge, David Hilt, Samantha Lasater, Calvin Lewis, Karie Bednarski, Christopher Scicluna, Noah Marion, Wilfred (Tom) Culver. Fourth row: Christopher Cassetta, Denise Koehler, Kishor Oza, Anna Koki, Michael Hadsall, Brendan Bednarski, Lisa Davis.

Fig. 6. Left, Barbara Walkowski, Catering and Events Coordinator; right, Mariann Den Baas, Catering and Events Manager.

Fig. 7. Left, Denise Koehler, Purchaser/Banquet Server; right, Clement Catling, Kitchen Storeroom.

Fig. 8. Left to right, Michele Penoyer, photographer and server; Fina Saroli, server; Denise Catanzarite, server; Robin Hauff, Food and Beverage Manager Emeritus.

Fig. 9. Left to right, David Daniot, Executive Chef; Samantha Lasater, server; Dennis (DJ) Kopp, server, Debra Litzan, Dining Room Supervisor; Tina Hooge, server.

Fig. 10. Front Desk Receptionists, left to right, Patricia Kamensack and Alison Trombley.

Fig. 11. Bussers, left to right, David Hilt, Sarah Cuda, Antonio Grant.

Fig. 12. Kirk A. Risk, Security Supervisor.

Fig. 13. George Spieles, Housekeeping.

Fig. 14. Maintenance staff, left to right, Ronald Adragna, Douglas Stocker, Patrick Gorman, David Browski.

Fig. 15. Executive Chef David Daniot and kitchen staff. Left to right, first row: Frank Ciaramitaro, David Daniot, John Iacono, Bertha Elmore, Tracey Caruthers. Second row: John Paul (JP) Franckowiak, Hamood Alkholani, Linda Dona, Lauren Friedrich, Robin Koehler, Angela Carwile, Jason Boyd. Third row: Duane Walkowski, Michael Nguyen, John Moore.

Fig. 16. Harbormaster Alex Turner and staff, top to bottom: Alex Turner, John Graffius, Christopher Colson, David Smith, Matthew Horeftis, Alec Hughes.

Fig. 17. Pool Manager and Swim Team Coach Frederick Michalik, center, with lifeguards George Daudlin, left, and Stephanie Shea, right.

Fig. 18. Harborside Grill staff. Left to right, front row: Alexandria Bowens, Leah Francis. Back row: Wilfred (Tom) Culver, Kayla Bossenbery, Duane Walkowski, Mary Moesta, Noah Marion, Tyler Love.

Fig. 19. House Set-up, left to right, Ali Algaheim, Mansour Algahaim, Ali Ali Algaheim, Austin Wagner.

Staff members not pictured:

Amanda Blay – Kids' Klub
Catherine Buffa – Accounting
Evan Butler – House/Set-up
Chauncey Chisolm – Kitchen
Wallace Cross – Sailing Pro 2015
Robert Curtis – Security
Sami Daher – House/Set-up
Najat Daher – Kitchen/House
Roniesha Dalton – House
Jorilda Dedelli – Kids' Klub
Gerald Dunn – Security
Walid Elkhourly – Kitchen
Jody Feola – Accounting
Gene Gellert – Security
Catherine Howard – Accounting
Steve Jankowski – Maintenance
Douglas Johnston – Security
Jenee Jones – Server
Colleen Kelley – Dining Room Supervisor
Keiko Kennedy – House
Christopher Lane – Kitchen
Megan Mackiewicz – Server
Michael Milioto – Server
Leen Mosa – Busser
Erica Nixon – Kids' Klub
Patrick O'Shea – Busser
Owen Pfaff – Busser
Donald Riggs – Bar
Misty Schmuckel – Server
Carl Shuster – Security
Rachel Sexton – Server
Jessica Turchick – Kids' Klub
Lawrence Wade – House
Paul Wendling – Kitchen
Milisa Wesley – House
Charles Wilkins – Kitchen

The GPYC employs several people on a seasonal basis only, and although many of those employees are not named here, we would like to thank them as a group for their service to the Club.

IMAGE ACKNOWLEDGEMENTS
Staff

Figs. 1, 3-7, 10, 12-19: John F. Martin
Fig. 2: Jim Dorian
Fig. 8: Tom Trainor
Figs. 9, 11 and pumpkins: Michele Penoyer

Appendices

APPENDIX ONE

COMMODORES
Researched by Larry W. Stephenson and Past Com. James L. Ramsey

1. R. George Marsh	1914–1918; 1925–1926
2. Harry H. Jewett	1919–1925
3. Edsel B. Ford	1926
4. John H.G. French	1926–1931
5. C. Hayward Murphy	1931–1934
6. B.F. Stephenson	1934–1935
7. George M. Slocum	1935–1940
8. Frank Couzens	1940
9. H.J. Woodall	1941
10. H. Lynn Pierson	1942
11. Ward H. Peck	1943
12. James H. Marks	1944
13. C.B. Thomas	1945
14. George N. Lilygren	1946
15. Robert P. Scherer	1947
16. A.P. Teetzel	1948
17. John R. Sutton Jr.	1949
18. C.E. Bleicher	1950
19. J. Edgar Duncan	1951
20. Paul Marco	1952
21. A.R. Motschall	1953
22. Warren H. Farr	1954
23. William O. Kronner	1955
24. Mervyn G. Gaskin	1956
25. Stark Hickey	1957
26. C.L. Jacobson	1958
27. Robert F. Weber	1959
28. William A. Ternes	1960
29. John R. Wilt	1961
30. Paul I. Moreland	1962
31. J. Earl Fraser	1963
32. Edward J. Schoenherr	1964
33. Harold E. Cross, M.D.	1965
34. John W. Paynter	1966
35. Harry J. Chapman	1967
36. John F. DeHayes	1968
37. O. James Gagne	1969
38. Roger K. Smith	1970
39. Ralph J. Kliber	1971
40. Curtis C. Carmichael	1972
41. George M. Cooper	1973
42. Frank P. McBride Jr.	1974
43. George L. Beard	1975
44. Harold S. DeOrlow	1976
45. William D. Plante	1977
46. James L. Taylor Sr.	1978
47. Sheldon F. Hall	1979
48. Paul A. Eagan	1980
49. James D. Mitchell	1981
50. George E. Kriese	1982
51. Roy E. Barbier	1983
52. John C. Woodle	1984
53. James R. Daoust	1985
54. John A. Boll	1986
55. Robert E. Yuhn	1987
56. Theodore H. Smith	1988
57. Fred G. Schriever	1989
58. Tymon C. Totte, D.D.S.	1990
59. Thomas D. Ogden	1991
60. Charles E. Stumb Jr.	1992
61. Herold "Mac" Deason	1993
62. J. James Morrow Jr.	1994
63. Robert E. Thoreson	1995
64. Sloane R. Barbour Jr.	1996
65. John H. Schoenherr	1997
66. Mark R. Weber	1998
67. William J. Storen	1999
68. James A. Anderson	2000

69. John E. De Wald	2001		77. James L. Taylor Jr.	2009
70. Carl Rashid Jr.	2002		78. Mary Treder Lang	2010
71. James L. Ramsey	2003		79. Robert L. Rader Jr.	2011
72. W. Theodore Huebner Sr.	2004		80. Ronald A. Schaupeter	2012
73. Bruce E. Fralick	2005		81. William C. Vogel Jr.	2013
74. Robert J. Kay	2006		82. James N. Martin	2014
75. J. Dennis Andrus	2007		83. Kevin B. Granger	2015
76. David E. Martin, M.D.	2008		(commodore effective November 13, 2014)	

APPENDIX TWO

FLEET OFFICERS

Fleet Captains (Sail and Power)
Researched by Larry P. Channell

The first records we have of GPYC fleet captains begin in 1941.

The single position of fleet captain was split into two positions in 1990: fleet captain sail and fleet captain power.

1941 — George N. Lilygren

1942 — A.G. Herreshoff

1943 — Don Wallace

1944 & 1945 — Vincent Young

1946 – Charles McGregor

1947 — T.W. Fredericks Jr.

1948 — T.A. Davenport Jr.

1949 — Clare S. Jacobs

1950 — E.E. Lundberg

1951 — Aaron L. Evans

1952 — Gilbert B. Pingree

1953 — Valentine Tallberg

1954 & 1955 — Bryan A. Chaplow

1956 & 1957 — Harley F. Riley

1958 — Gordon E. McCabe

1959 & 1960 — Stanley L. Willis

1961 — Charles B. De Vlieg

1962 — Harry J. Chapman

1963 — O. James Gagne

1964 — George A. Gardella

1965 — O. James Gagne

1966 — Allan D. Foster

1967 — Lawrence A. Reif

1968 — John L. Drummy

1969 — William M. Schmidt

1970 & 1971 — Thomas K. Fisher

1972 — George Vandermark

1973 — James L. Taylor Sr.

1974 — Harvey C. Fruehauf Jr.

1975 — Fred G. Schriever

1976 — Arthur Sherman Jr.

1977 — Fred G. Schriever

1978 — Victor J. Barron

1979 — Neil C. Georgi

1980 — Edward W. Wilberding

1981 — John Huetteman

1982 — Peter O'Rourke

1983 — Joseph A. Schrage Jr.

*1984 — Past Com. James L. Taylor Sr.

1985 — Charles W. Davis

1986 — John Mertz

1987 — Laurence S. Baluch

1988 — Vincent LoCicero

1989 — Donald Endres

1990 — Rowland L. Austin and Roger P. Eger

1991 — Deanne Buono (power) and Edwin B. Shaw (sail)

1992 — Thomas M. Campeau (power) and William J. Storen (sail)

1993 — John De Wald (power) and Dennis Foley (sail)

1994 — John Mertz (power) and Edwin B. Shaw (sail)

1995 — Edward B. Connelly

1996 — Michael A. Meda

1997 — Edwin B. Shaw

1998 — Bruce E. Fralick (power) and Robert F. Rehmann (sail)

1999 — John B. Mager (power) and Kevin W. Killebrew (sail)

2000 — Dr. James McCarty (power) and Bruce E. Bradley (sail)

2001 — Patrick S. Connelly (power) and Kenneth A. Flaska (sail)

2002 — Gregory T. Schaden (power) and Dr. Albert Defever (sail)

2003 — Robert L Rader Jr. (power) and Kevin W. Killebrew (sail)

2004 — James T. Mestdagh (power) and Dennis A. Goschka (sail)

2005 — Wayne G. Wegner (power) and Dr. Gary Bill (sail)

2006 – William A. Fleury (power) and Robert F. Rehmann (sail)

2007 — James N. Martin (power) and Steven C. Nadeau (sail)

2008 — Peter G. Beauregard (power) and Dr. Gary Bill (sail)

2009 — Wayne G. Wegner (power) and William J. Champion III (sail)

2010 — Peter T. Gleason (power) and Joseph P. Acheson (sail)

2011 — Philip Trupiano (power) and Ilja Vreeken (sail)

2012 — Joseph J. Haney (power) and Ilja Vreeken (sail)

2013 — Robert F. Wiczorek (power) and Kenneth A. Flaska (sail)

2014 — Brian L. Fish (power) and Larry P. Channell (sail)

2015 — Gary F. Marowske (power) and Larry P. Channell (sail) (effective November 13, 2014)

*James L. Taylor Sr. served as fleet captain in 1973 before becoming commodore in 1978. As fleet captain in 1984, he has the distinction of being one of only two flag officers to later serve as a fleet officer, the other being commodore, then fleet surgeon, Dr. Harold E. Cross. (See list of fleet surgeons)

Fleet Chaplains
Researched by Robert Hackathorn and Larry W. Stephenson

Past Commodore Jim Daoust joined the Club in 1967 and recalled that during his first few years as a member, there was a Catholic priest by the name of Father Richard J. Dorr who would often be giving the invocation at the Blessing of the Fleet and at other Club events. Father Dorr was a Club member from 1968 to 2005.

Past Commodore Daoust also remembered Brother Augustine, fondly known around the Club as Brother Gus. Brother Gus was a member of the Catholic religious Order of St. Augustine and worked in some capacity at Austin Catholic High School. He was never a GPYC member, but had several friends who were members, and through their generosity he enjoyed many happy hours at the Club, especially fishing along the south wall of the harbor. Past Commodore Daoust recalled Brother Gus being actively involved in Club chaplain duties throughout the 1970s.

Brother Gus had served in the U.S. Navy, and perhaps it was at some point during those years that he had acquired one of his most treasured possessions – an old ship's binnacle. When his health began to fail, and his friends learned that he was planning to donate his beloved binnacle to the GPYC, they purchased it from him and donated it to the Club on his behalf. That binnacle now resides on the porch of the Tower Pub, with a bronze plaque honoring the memory of Brother "Gus" Augustine.

The first Club record that has been found regarding the position of a GPYC chaplain is that of Father Albert P. Hillebrand. Father Hillebrand was a Catholic priest who, when he joined the Club in 1964, was principal of Austin Catholic High School. Through the years, his name appeared as GPYC chaplain until his death in 1999. Although he apparently was considered to be a fleet officer, he was never officially listed as such.

Following his death, then-Commodore Bill Storen appointed a committee, chaired by then-Vice Commodore Jim Anderson, to select a new Club chaplain, who would now become an official fleet officer. After interviewing several candidates, the committee chose Reverend Walter A. Schmidt, pastor of First English Lutheran Church in Grosse Pointe Woods. Reverend Schmidt has continued to serve the Club from 1999 to the present, having been most recently reappointed on November 13, 2014, to serve through 2015.

Fleet Measurers
Researched by David W. Treder

1913 (December)—William Granger (for 1914)
1914 — Wally Hock and Harold Chapoton
      (for 1915)
*Although there were most likely fleet
 measurers in the years from 1916 through
 1938, no records of any names have
 been found.
1939 – 1941 — Donald B. Wallace
1942 & 1943 — Gilbert B. Pingree
1944 & 1945 — N.K. Vanosdol
1946 & 1947 — A.G. Herreshoff
1948 — J.H. Flavell
1949 — Aaron L. Evans
1950 — Tore Franzen
1951 — Aaron L. Evans
1952 — George C. Cossaboom
1953 — Alfred John Dalton
1954 — Gordon E. McCabe
1955 — Paul W. Smiley
1956 — Arvid Lundell
1957 — Gilbert B. Pingree
1958 — Gordon E. McCabe
1959 — Dr. Joseph A. Barkley

1960 — Paul W. Smiley
1961 — Aaron L. Evans
1962 — Edmund E. Anderson
1963 — S. Duncan Bradley
1964 — Fred J. Somes Jr.
1965 — James T. Barnes
1966 — Robert B. Sellers
1967 — Milton O. Cross Jr.
1968 — Earl D. Thompson
1969 — Thomas K. Fisher
1970 — Fred J. Somes Jr.
1971 — Jerry K. Girschner
1972 — Dr. John W. Parnell
1973 — Charles E. Exley
1974 — Frederick S. Ford Jr.
1975 — Norbert H. Hollerbach
1976 — William Rodger
1977 — Theodore H. Smith
1978 — Clarence Anderson
1979 — Edward J. Wieferman
1980 — Edward R. Davies
1981 — Peter E. O'Rourke
1982 — Donald N. Savage
1983 — Thomas D. Ogden
1984 — Alfred J. Jehle
1985 — James Touscany
1986 — Jarvis Schmidt
1987 — John G. Martin
1988 — Sloane R. Barbour Jr.
1989 — Dwight D. Labadie
1990 — John D. Mertz
1991 — Douglas E. Busby
1992 — Mark Weber, Ph.D.
1993 — Joseph M. Lucchese
1994 — Hellmuth W.A. Bickenbach
1995 — Dr. Richard A, Herbert
1996 — Robert W. Denner
1997 — Joseph J. Wilt
1998 — Robert J. Kay
1999 — John B. Maliszewski
2000 — Gene Tucker
2001 — Paul C. Lang
2002 — Kenneth W. Kirchner
2003 — William C. Buhler
2004 — Michael J. Wilt
2005 — Michael D. McLauchlan
2006 — William G. Frost
2007 — Dexter J. Kennedy Jr.

2008 — Douglas P. Dossin
2009 — Bradford Tisdale
2010 — David W. Treder
2011 — Michael D. McLauchlan
2012 — Todd D. Andrus
2013 — William J. Dillon
2014 — R. Antoney Bromwell
2015 — Douglas P. Dossin (effective November 13, 2014)

Fleet Surgeons
Researched by Dr. James McCarty

1913 (December) & 1914 — Dr. George Renaud, M.D.

*Although there were most likely fleet surgeons in the years from 1915 to 1938, no records of any names have been found.

1939 to 1943 — Dr. John Prendergast, M.D.

1944 to 1946 — Dr. Clifford Loranger, M.D.

1947 — Dr. Elden C. Baumgarten, M.D.

1948 — Dr. Fred O. Lepley, M.D.

1949 — Dr. Clarence J. Williams, M.D.

1950 — Dr. Harold E. Cross, M.D.

1951 — Dr. Elden C. Baumgarten, M.D.

1952 — Dr. Harold E. Cross, M.D.

1953 — Dr. John E. Clifford, M.D.

1954 — Dr. Clifford Loranger, M.D.

1955 & 1956 — Dr. Karl W. Weber, M.D.

1957 — Dr. Harold E. Cross, M.D.

1958 — Dr. Karl W. Weber, M.D.

1959 — Dr. Clarence J. Williams, M.D.

1960 — Dr. Benjamin W. Stockwell, M.D.

1961 — Dr. Clarence E. Maguire, M.D.

1962 — Dr. William A. Lange, M.D.

1963 — Dr. Cyril R. Defever, M.D.

1964 — Dr. Thomas W. Baumgarten, M.D.

1965 — Dr. Louis J. Gregory, M.D.

1966 — Dr. Frederick B. Watts, M.D.

1967 — Dr. C. Stanley Waggoner, M.D.

1968 — Dr. Karl W. Weber, M.D.

1969 — Dr. Thomas W. Baumgarten, M.D.

1970 — Dr. Louis J. Gregory, M.D.

1971 — Dr. Cyril R. Defever, M.D.

1972 — Dr. Villrad J. VonBerg, M.D.

1973 — Dr. John H. Williams, M.D.

1974 — Dr. John P. Bremer, M.D.

1975 — Dr. John R. Brown, M.D.

1976 — Dr. James M. Pierce, M.D.

1977 — Dr. Tymon C. Totte, D.D.S.

1978 — Dr. George R. Granger, M.D.

1979 — Dr. William C. Jennings, D.D.S.

1980 — Dr. Stuart B. Smith, D.D.S.

1981 — Dr. Donald Pokorny, D.D.S.

1982 — Dr. Richard H. Bryce, D.D.S.

1983 — Dr. Timothy W. Foley, D.D.S.

1984 — Dr. W. Howard Nurse, D.V.M.

1985 — Dr. Ralph B. Soderberg, M.D.

1986 — Dr. Francis P. Blake, M.D.

1987 — Dr. Richard C. Mertz, M.D.

1988 — Dr. Thomas R. Gebeck, D.D.S.

*1989 — Com. Harold E. Cross, M.D.

1990 — Dr. Paul Dzul, M.D.; Dr. Zenon Kossak, D.D.S.

1991 — Dr. Richard Herbert, D.O.

1992 — Dr. Jan Lehman, D.D.S.

1993 — Dr. Peter Fragatos, M.D.

1994 — Dr. Raymond J. Winfield Jr., M.D.

1995 — Dr. William H. Athens, D.O.

1996 — Dr. Peter McCabe, M.D.

1997 — Dr. Larry Stephenson, M.D.

1998 — Dr. James McCarty, D.P.M.

1999 — Dr. Albert R. Defever, O.D.

2000 — Dr. Larry Lloyd, M.D.

2001 — Dr. Kevin J. Grady, M.D.

2002 — Dr. Richard A. Herbert, D.O.

2003 — Dr. Larry W. Stephenson, M.D.

2004 — Dr. Brian J. Hunt, D.D.S.

2005 — Dr. Patrick G. Latham, D.D.S.

2006 & 2007 — Dr. Gary Bill, M.D.

2008 — Dr. Brian M. Litch, D.O.

2009 — Dr. Larry W. Stephenson, M.D.

2010 — Dr. Lisa Manz-Dulac, M.D.

2011 & 2012 — Dr. Thomas R. Gebeck Jr., D.D.S.

2013 — Dr. Gary Bill, M.D.

2014 — Dr. James McCarty, D.P.M.

2015 — Dr. Larry Stephenson, M.D. (effective November 13, 2014)

*Dr. Harold E. Cross served as fleet surgeon three times before becoming commodore in 1965. He has the distinction of being only one of two flag officers to serve as commodore and to later serve again as a fleet officer, in 1989, the other being James L. Taylor Sr. (See list of fleet captains)

APPENDIX THREE

CLUB GENERAL MANAGERS
Researched by Larry W. Stephenson

1. Harry A. Dodge*   May 1929 – May 1932
2. Vernon V. Goetz   May 1932 – 1934
3. Emil Campenhout**   July 1938 – 1946
4. Fred J. Gebstadt   1946 – 1964 or 1965
5. John J. Devers***   1964 or 1965 – 1974
6. David Butterfield   January 1975 – 1976
7. Peter Behr   1976 – 1979
8. Linden Mills   1980 – 1987
9. Jack Sullivan   1987 – 2003
10. Michael Mooney****   2003 – 2008
11. Thomas Trainor   2008 – present

* In the early years, the Club hired executive secretaries to share the responsibilities of the Club managers. John A. King was hired in that capacity in January 1929; he was replaced by Harve Lamont Smith, hired in May 1932.

** During the years the clubhouse was in receivership, William Lancastor and his wife were hired by lien holders to occupy the building as caretakers and lived there from about 1935 to July 1938. One historical document refers to Mr. Lancastor as an assistant manager; another identifies him as club manager.

*** In 1974, then-Commodore Frank McBride hired Dean Parker as acting general manager while a search was being conducted to replace John Devers.

****In 2008, while a search was being conducted for a new general manager, then-Commodore David Martin became the acting general manager for a period of about six months.

APPENDIX FOUR

MEMBERS OF THE GPYC FOR FIFTY YEARS OR MORE
As of 2014
Compiled by Dr. Larry W. Stephenson

Member	Year Joined	Classification
1. Brown, Mrs. Mary	1952	Senior 50
2. Freuhauf Jr., Mr. Harvey C.	1962	Senior 50
3. Gagne Donley, Mrs. Dorothy	1959	Surviving Spouse
4. Lundell, Mrs. Mary	1940	Life
5. McBride, Mrs. Jere	1962	Surviving Spouse
6. Milner, Mr. Earle Ronald	1952	Senior 50
7. Moroun, Mr. Manuel J.	1964	Senior 50
8. Plante, Past Com. William D.	1963	Senior 50
9. Rinke, Mr. Roland J.	1963	Senior 50
10. Rinke Jr., Mr. Edgar T.	1963	Senior 50
11. Touscany, Mrs. Peggy	1962	Non Resident
12. Williams, M.D., Dr. John H.	1948	Senior Social

APPENDIX FIVE

MEMBERS OF GPYC FORTY TO FORTY-NINE YEARS
As of 2014
Compiled by Larry W. Stephenson

Member	Year Joined	Classification
1. Agren, Mr. Wallace J.	1967	Senior
2. Alandt, Mrs. Patricia P.	1974	Surviving Spouse
3. Austin, Mr. Rowland L.	1974	Senior
4. Bania, Mr. Richard J.	1972	Senior
5. Barbour Jr., Past Com. Sloane R.	1966	Senior
6. Butler, Mrs. Regina	1973	Senior
7. Campau, Mr. Thomas M.	1974	Senior
8. Carlino, D.D.S., Dr. George J.	1974	Senior
9. Clark, Mr. George F.	1973	Non-Resident
10. Cole, Mrs. Doris T.	1968	Surviving Spouse
11. Colombo, M.D., Dr. John	1967	Senior
12. Cornillie, Mr. Bernard H.	1968	Senior
13. Cracchiolo, Mr. Thomas A.	1965	Senior Social
14. Cytacki, Mr. Walter S.	1973	Social
15. Daoust, Past Com. James R.	1967	Senior
16. Dossin, Mr. Richard R.	1969	Senior
17. Drummy, Ms. Christine	1968	Senior
18. Eger, Mrs. Elizabeth A.	1967	Surviving Spouse
19. Filipelli, Mr. Richard F.	1973	Senior

20. Fisher, Mr. Thomas K.	1968	Non-Resident
21. Fragatos, M.D., Dr. Peter	1973	Non Resident
22. Gebeck, D.D.S., Dr. Thomas R.	1969	Senior
23. Hammel III, Mr. Godfrey J.	1973	Senior Social
24. Hastings, Mrs. Rosemary	1970	Surviving Spouse
25. Jennings, D.D.S., Dr. William G.	1973	Senior
26. Johnston, Mr. William T.	1971	Senior Social
27. Kriese, Past Com. George E.	1967	Senior
28. Linzell, Mr. Arthur S.	1969	Senior Social
29. Lytle, Mrs. Carol	1968	Surviving Spouse
30. Manoogian, Mr. Richard A.	1968	Senior
31. Mathews, Mr. Charles C.	1974	Senior Social
32. Mc Glone, Mrs. Betty Joan	1967	Surviving Spouse
33. Meacham, Mr. Robert A.	1974	Non-Resident
34. Mertz, Mr. John D.	1969	Senior
35. Miller, Mrs. Elizabeth	1969	Surviving Spouse
36. Moran, Mr. Justin L.	1973	Senior
37. Mossner, Mrs. Joan	1973	Surviving Spouse
38. Orhan, Mr. Xhafer	1973	Senior
39. Packer III, Mr. William M.	1973	Social
40. Reif, Mr. Frederick J.	1972	Senior
41. Retford, D.D.S., Dr. Kenneth H.	1971	Senior Social
42. Riehl, Mrs. Norma L.	1973	Senior
43. Savage, Mr. Donald N.	1969	Non-Resident
44. Schaupeter, Past Com. Ronald A.	1970	Senior
45. Small, Mrs. Faith F.	1972	Surviving Spouse
46. Smith, Past Com. Theodore H.	1971	Senior
47. Sohn, Mr. Raymond F.	1970	Non-Resident
48. Spitzley, Mrs. Sallie	1973	Surviving Spouse
49. Stevens, Mr. Clark V.	1970	Senior
50. Stieler, Mrs. Jacquelyn R.	1967	Surviving Spouse
51. Susalla, Mrs. Hanna	1973	Surviving Spouse
52. Taylor, Mrs. Suanne	1969	Surviving Spouse
53. Taylor Jr., Past Com. James L.	1971	Senior
54. Thams, Mr. Richard W.	1973	Non-Resident
55. Thompson, Mrs. Betty J.	1970	Surviving Spouse
56. Thoreson, Mrs. H. Jacqueline	1967	Surviving Spouse
57. Tisdale, Mr. Bradford	1973	Senior
58. Totte, D.D.S., Past Com. Tymon C.	1966	Senior
59. Treder, Mrs. Mary Louise	1969	Surviving Spouse
60. Tusa Jr., Mr. Michael A.	1972	Social
61. Willis, Mrs. Vonnie	1969	Surviving Spouse
62. Winkler Jr., Mr. Irving T.	1969	Senior

APPENDIX SIX

YACHTSMAN OF THE YEAR
Compiled by Ross B. Stone

In 1990, the William P. Fisher Perpetual Member trophy was rededicated as an award to the GPYC Yachtsman of the Year. The trophy was originally donated in 1967 by William V., Everell E., and Thomas K. Fisher and John Drummy, and dedicated to the GPYC Bluenose Regatta for Best Corrected Time, Cruising Class A. Qualifications for Yachtsman of the year are based on:

• Overall season standing, DRYA regular and long-distance races
• Participation in Port Huron and Chicago-to-Mackinac races
• Participation and standing, Bluenose Regatta
• Strength of competition in respective class
• Overall improvement of performance

Members who have performed in exemplary fashion in yachting-related events are also eligible to receive this award.

GPYC Yachtsman of the Year Recipients

1990 – David Connolly
1991 – Not awarded
1992 – Dr. Roland R. Tindle
1993 – Robert Orr Jr.
1994 – Kenneth Kazerski
1995 – Richard Listwan
1996 – Patrick Beard
1997 – Edward Grant
1998 – Curtis Kime
1999 – Wallace Tsuha Jr.
2000 – Marvin Ihnen
2001 – Wallace Tsuha Jr.
2002 – Steve Nadeau
2003 – Curtis Kime
2004 – Mark F. Symonds
2005 – Past Com. Sloane Barbour Jr.
2006 – Daniel Bracciano
2007 – Not awarded
2008 – Carolyn Howe
2009 – Dr. John Seago
2010 – Past Com. Jim Morrow
2011 – Past Com. Dennis Andrus, Marita Grobbel/Dean and Diane Petitpren
2012 – Kenneth Flaska
2013 – David Schaden / Matthew Schaden
2014 – John Bania / Sean Schotthoefer / Blaise Klenow

APPENDIX SEVEN

DISTINGUISED MEMBER OF THE YEAR AWARD
Compiled by Ross B. Stone

The Distinguished Member of the Year award was established in 1990 by the GPYC officers and board of directors in order to recognize members' outstanding and meritorious service to the Club.

1990 – Douglas McCrackin
1991 – Michael D. Murray
1992 – Edward B. Palm
1993 – Past Commodore Theodore E. Smith
1994 – Joseph J. Wilt
1995 – Leo J. Romzick
1996 – Past Commodore Frederick C. Schriever

1997 – Past Commodore J. James Morrow Jr.
1998 – Clark V. Stevens
1999 – Edwin B. Shaw
2000 – Henry A. Wilson
2001 – Dexter J. Kennedy Jr.
2002 – Past Commodore John A. Boll
2003 – Todd D. Andrus and John P. Bania
2004 – Past Commodore Sloane R. Barbour Jr.
2005 – John J. Ahee
2006 – Michael D. Riehl
2007 – Past Commodore Ralph J. Kliber
2009 – Richard J. Bania
2010 – Past Commodore Frank P. McBride Jr.
2011 – Past Commodore James L. Ramsey
2012 – Alice Kliber
2013 – Peter G. Beauregard
2014 – Dr. Larry W. Stephenson

APPENDIX EIGHT

GPYC COMPILED ROSTER 1914-1935
Researched by Larry W. Stephenson

There is only one GPYC roster known to exist from the 1914-1934 period, and that is for the years 1923 to 1924. This roster was constructed using the 1923-24 roster and by searching GPYC board minutes and other sources. This roster may not be all-inclusive. Names of members who are known to have joined in 1914 are in **bold** typeface. Members' names that appear on the 1923-1924 roster are identified with an (*) asterisk. A few names on this list are classified as "Invited," which means they were given a special invitation by the board of directors to join, but in most cases, it is not known whether or not they joined. Club officers are identified by the following:

C = Commodore
VC = Vice Commodore (highest rank attained)
RC = Rear Commodore (highest rank attained)

A

Acheson, Ira, 1927, Active
Ainsworth, Charles H., 1928, Active
Albrecht, Albert A., 1927, Director
*Aldrich, Dr. C. B., 1927, Director
Alexander, Donald, 1934
Alger, Russell A. Jr., 1925 or early 1926, died 1930
Alger, Russell A. III, 1932, **RC**
Allen, Mark W., 1926, Active
Allen, Robert M., 1926, Class B
Allen, W.H., 1932, Class B
Altland, Daniel F., 1926, Active
Archer, T.P., 1928, Active
*Atkinson, Casey
*Atkinson, Garnet
***Aukland**, John, 1914, Associate, 1927
Avery, Clarence W., 1931, Class B
Ayres, Clarence L., 1926, Director, **RC**

B

Backman, Abe, 1926
Backman, Alonzo, 1927
***Backman**, Ignatius A., 1914, Associate, 1927
***Backman**, Wilfred, 1914, died 1925
Baits, Stuart G., 1930, Class B
Ballantyne, Ford, 1927, **VC**
Barden, Frederick L., 1929
Barie, Robert F., 1930, Class B
Barit, A. Edward, 1932, Class B
Barrett, J. Lee, 1929, Class B
*Barthel, Otto F.
Beaupre, Albert, 1927, Associate
Beaupre, Edwin C., 1926, Associate, 1927
Beaupre, Francis, 1927, Associate
Beaupre, James A., 1927, Associate
Beaupre, Michael C., 1927, Associate
Beaupre, Ormond, 1926, Associate, 1927
*Beaupre, Ralph E., 1927, Associate
Beaupre, Russell, 1927, Associate
Beaupre, Waldo, 1927, Associate
Beaupre, William, 1926
Becker, Charles F., 1927, Director
Beers, Edward J., 1932, Class B
*Belanger, Dr. J.A.
Berger, George, 1932, Class B
Bessimer, Frederick, 1932, Junior
Beyster, Henry E., 1929, Active
Bird, Charles R., 1927, Active
Bitting, Clarence R., 1929, Active
Bodman, Henry E., 1932
Bohan, Frank J., 1931, Class B
Bohn, Charles, 1930
Bonbright, Carl W., 1929
Bonbright, Howard, 1929, Active, Director
Bosquett, T.J., 1928, Active
*Brady, J.H.
Breer, Carl, 1927, Active
Breisshacher, Carl F., 1926
Brennan, 1926
Briggs, Walter O., 1928, Active
Brown, Prescott G., 1927, Active
Brownell, H.R., 1926
Brownell, Peter, 1927, Associate

Brucker, Lewis S., 1932, Class B
Bryant, John A., 1927, Active
Buhl, Arthur H., 1929, Active, Director
Buhl, C. Henry, 1929, Active
Buhl, Theodore D., 1930, Class B
Bundy, Richard J., 1929, Associate
Burns, John McNeil, 1926, Active
Bush, Charles T., 1927, Active, Director, **RC**
Butzel, Fred, 1930, Invited
Butzel, Henry, 1930, Invited
Butzel, Leo, 1930, Invited

C

Callahan, J.J., 1927, Active
Campbell, C.A., 1927, Active, 1932, Class B
Cary, Walter B., 1932, Class B
Carter, George W., 1930, Director
Center, Frank, 1914, 1926
Chalfont, E.P., 1934
Chamberlin, G. Edwin, 1928, Active
Chandler, Clarence J., 1926, Active
*Chapotan, Allan
***Chapotan**, Harold, 1914
Chesterfield, Percy C., 1927, Active
Clancy, Floyd, 1929
Clancy, P., 1926, Class C
Coffin, Howard E., 1926, Active
Collin, Frederic C., 1932, Class B
Colombo, Louis A. Jr., 1932, Junior
Conley, John F., 1927, Active
Connolly, William F., 1928, Active
Coolidge, Frank W., 1926, Active
Coolidge, Frank W. Jr., 1932
Cooper, Gage W., 1926, Active
*Corbett, E.J.
Corrick, J.A., 1926, Active
Cosgrove, Milton J., 1927 active
Cronin, Arthur D., 1932, Class B
Crowley, Daniel J., 1927, Active
*Crowley, J.J.
Cummiskey, James P., 1928, Active
Currie, Thomas E., 1927, Active, Director
Currier, O.L., 1929, Active

D

Dalby, Fred W., 1926, Active, Director
Danaher, R.E., 1927, Active
Day, Al. A., 1927, Active
Deming, Paul H., 1927, Active, Director
Detwiler, Ward A., 1927, Active
Dewey, Frank H., 1926, Active
Diedrich, Albert B., 1928, Active
Diehl, Fred H., 1930, Invited
*Dodge, Horace E., died December 10, 1920
Dodge, Joseph M., 1927, Active
*Dondero, Herman
Douglas, D. Dwight, 1929, Active
Draper, James C., 1929, Junior
Draper, Jesse B., 1928, Active
Draper, Jesse S., 1930
Dreyer, Martin F., 1932, Class B
Drum, A.L., 1927, Active
DuPont, Charles W., 1927, Associate
Dwyer, John Vincent, 1929
Dwyer, Joseph L., 1914

E

Edgar, C.G., 1926
Edgar, James, 1926, Junior
Edwards, Cyrus J., 1926, Active, Director
Ekserfgeon, C.L., 1932, Class B
Emery, Lewis V., 1929, Class B
Endicott, George M., 1930, Class B
Esch, Edward E., 1927, Active

F

Farmer, Robert J., 1927, Active
*Ferguson, Samuel
Fink, George R., 1927, Active, Director
Finn, Joseph V., 1928, Active
Fisher, Alfred J., 1928, Active
Fisher, Charles T., 1927, Active
Fisher, Charles T. Jr., 1929, Active
Fisher, Edward. F., 1928, Active
Fisher, Everell E., 1929, Junior
Fisher, Fred J., 1928, Active
Fisher, Lawrence P., 1927, Active, Director
Fisher, W.A., 1928, Active
Fisher, William P., 1929, Active
Fitzpatrick, William G., 1927, Director
Fleming, Capt. E.C., 1932, Class B

Flood, Aubrey C., 1932, Class B
Ford, Edsel B., 1926, Director, **C**
Ford, John B. 'J.B.' Jr., 1926 or before
Fordon, Ralph, 1927, Active
French, George Russell, 1929
Francis, J. Richard, 1928, Active
French, John H., 1926, **C**
French, John H. Jr., 1932
Freund, Dr. Hugo, 1930, Invited
Freud, Marcus L., 1926, Active
*Frey, Frank

G

Gagnier, George E., 1929, Active
Gaukler, Francis O., 1928, Active
Gauthier, Clayton E., 1926, Associate, 1927
Gauthier, Leighton J., 1927, Associate
*Glendon, J.P.
Grace, Edward R., 1926
Graham, Robert, 1927, Active
Granger, William, 1914
Grant, Howard M., 1927, Active
Grawn, Carl B., 1927, Active
Green, Leslie H., 1930
Greening, Wendell G., 1927, Associate
Grier, John C. Jr., 1929, Active
Grose, Mrs. Percy W., 1929, Active

H

Haas, George J., 1927, Active
***Hager**, Julius, 1914, Associate 1927
Hahn, Gerald, 1928, Active
Halman, George A., 1929 Active
Hamilton, Dr. Birch J., 1927, Active
Hanley, Stewart, 1926, Active
Hanna, Mark R., 1927, Active, Director
***Harrigan**, Edward C., 1914
*Harrigan, J.C.
Harrison, O. Lee, 1927, Active
Harvey, John G., 1927, Active
Hartz, Albert B.
Hayes, Mercy J., 1927, Active
Heftler, Victor R., 1934, Class B
***Hendrie**, George S., 1914, Associate 1927
***Hendrie**, William V.D., 1914, Associate 1927
Henry, O.D., 1914
***Hickey**, Edward J., 1914, Director, **VC**

Hickey, Joseph L., 1927, Director
Hilsendegen, George, 1926
Hirt, Alfred E., 1930, Class B
Hock, Francis J., 1926, Associate 1927
***Hock,** Walter J., 1914, Associate 1927
Hofmann, Arnold E., 1929, Active
Hofmann, Egbert M., 1929, Active
Holland, James G., 1926, Active
Holley, George M., 1929, Active
Hopwood, Warren J., 1927, Active
*Houghton, E.H.
Hoyt, Allen N., 1929, Associate
Hoyt, Bernie P., 1932
Hoyt, Birney, 1929, Associate
Hoyt, Hobart B., 1926
Hoyt, William, 1926
Huck, Lewis C., 1932, Class B
Hughes, Fred A., 1929
Hughitt, Dorothy W., 1932, Class B
Hupp, Robert C., 1914
Hurley, Frances D., 1927, Active
***Hurley**, Ignatius B., 1914
*Hurley, John T., Director
*Hurley, John
*Hurley, Joe
Hutchinson, B. Edwin, 1929, Active

I, J

Jacobs, Rex C., 1929, Active
*Jahn, Julius
Jenney, Frank E., 1931, Junior
Jenney, Fred O., 1931, Junior
Jewett, Edward H., 1932, Class B
*Jewett, Harry M., **C**
Johnson, Courtney, 1927, Active
Johnson, Venable, 1932, Class B
Jolstad, T., 1927, Active
Joy, Richard P., 1929, Active, Director
Judson, Ross W., 1927, Active, Director

K

Kahn, Albert, 1930, Invited
Kanouse, H.W., 1926, Active
Keane, Dr. William E., 1929, Active
*Keenan, James
Keller, K.T., 1928, Active, Director, **VC**
*Kendall, Harry

Kengel, John A., 1926, Active
*Kennedy, H.N.
*Kerby, Earl
*Kerby, Eddie
*Kerby, Fred
Kettering, Charles F., 1930, Director
Kinnucan, Henry, 1932
Kinsel, E.C., 1928, Active
Knudson, William S., 1929, Active
Korneffel, Ferdinand, 1929, Active
Kramer, James Herbert, 1932, Junior
*Kramer, Stanley
Kresge, Anna E., 1930
Kresge, Howard C., 1929 Active
Krimmel, Julius L., 1927, Active
Kunsky, John H., 1928, Active
Kurth, Charles W., 1932, Class B

L

Lambert, John E., 1927, Active
*Larned, Abner E., 1926, Active, Director
*Larned, Bradford, 1914
*Larned, Courtland, 1914
Lauhoff, Henry J., 1932, Class B
Lawrie, Howard H., 1926, Active
Lay, Frank B., 1929, Active
*Leahy, Gibbons
Leithauser, D.J., 1927, Active
Liebold, E.G., 1930, Invited, 1930, Class B
Lindeman, Frank W. Jr., 1932, Junior
Lingeman, Oscar J., 1928, Active
Little, F. Jean, 1932, Class B
Lodge, Joseph, B., 1926, Active
Long, C.E., 1935
Long, Carlisle R., 1914, Associate, 1927
Long, Cornelius J. 'Bud,' 1914, Associate, 1927
*Long, John R., 1914, Associate, 1927, **VC**
Long , William P., 1914
Looker, Oscar F., 1926, Active

M

Macauley, Alvan, 1929, Active, Director
MacDonald, Clay C., 1926, Active
MacDonald, Reginald H., 1927, Active
MacKenzie, Dr. John W., 1926, Active
MacKenzie, Dr. Robert D., 1926, Active
Maise, Herman C., 1927, Active

Maiullo, Anthony, 1932, Class B
Malcomson, George W., 1927, Active
Marks, James H., 1926, Active
*Marsh, R. George, 1914, **C**
Martin, P.E., 1932, Class B
Martin, R.L., 1932, Class B
*Mason, Barney
Mason, M.W., 1930
Maxon, Louis B., 1930, Class B
Mayer, Alfred J., 1932
Mayo, William B., 1929, Active
McAnneney, W.C., 1932
McDonald, Elton F., 1935
*McHie, George
McKee, Max B., 1932
McKenzie, Stanley, 1932, Class B
McLucas, Walter S., 1932, Class B
McManus, Theodore F., 1929, Active
McMillan, James T., 1929
McNaughton, Lynn, 1929, Active
Meginnity, Norman, 1927, Active
Mendelssohn, Louis, 1930, Class A
Mendelssohn, Paxton, 1930, Class A
Mercer, 1926 (iceboat racer)
Mercier, Edwin J., 1932
*Mertz, William M., 1927, Director
Merz, Fred, 1929
Meyering, Henry, 1926, Active
Meyering, Henry Jr., 1926
Miller, W. L., 1929, Class B
Mills, Joseph B., 1932, Class B
Misch, Otto, 1927, Active
*Moliter, E.G.
*Moran, Gilbert M.
Moran, Henry D., 1926, Associate 1927
Moran, Louis A., 1927, Active, Director
Morgana, Charles, 1927, Active
Mott, Charles Stewart, 1929, Active
Mulford, Ora J., 1928, Active
Munger, Frank, 1927, Active
Murphy, Charles Hayward, 1927, Active, **C**
Murphy, Clem W., 1926, Active
Murray, J.R., 1927, Active
Myers, Henry T., 1927, Active

*Shelden, Henry D.
Sherman, Alvin G., 1927, Active
Shreve, C. Upton III, 1932, Class B
Shumaker, Edward J., 1932, Junior
Skelton, Owen R., 1929, Active
Slocum, George M., 1914, Active, **C**
Slocum, Grant, 1914
Smith, Conrad H., 1927, Active, Director
*Smith, Ray
*Smith, Thomas
Snavely, P.D., 1927, Active
Snay, Joe, 1926, Associate, 1927
Snay, Raymond, 1926 , Associate 1927
Sorensen, Charles E., 1927, Active, Director, **VC**
Squire, Alva, 1932, Junior
Stair, E.D., 1927, Active
Stalker, John N., 1927, Active, Director
Staples, G.A., 1929, Active
Stephenson, B.F., 1927, Active, **C**
Stevenson, Elizabeth H., 1928, Active
Stock, Harold, 1932
*Stotter, Max
Stratman, Hugo, 1926, Active
Stroh, John W., 1926, Associate, 1927
Strong, E.T., 1929, Active
Sutton, Gordon O., 1932, Class B
Sweeney, Judge Henry S., 1932, Class B

T

Talman, William W., 1928, Active
Tant, Walter F., 1926, Active, **VC**
Thomas, Luther D., 1927, Active, Director
Thompson, Fred E., 1927, Active
Thompson, Fred H., 1929, Junior
Thompson, Walter, 1929, Active
Tigchon, John H., 1926, Active, Director
Tobin, B. F., 1927, Active
Tomb, Robert C., 1927, Active
Toole, Dr. J.C., 1932, Class B
Topley, Harry A., 1926, Active
Torrey, Dr. Harry Norton, 1927, **VC**

U, V, W

Ullrich, Paul J., 1929, Active
*Van Assche, J.C.
Van Der Zee, A., 1932, Class B
Ver Linden, Edward, 1927, Active
Vernier, Edmund C., 1926, Active
*Vernier, W.B.
Vincent, Col. J.G., 1929, Active
*Volkner, Dr. George
Wade, Thomas G., 1934, **VC**
Walker, Harrington E., 1927, Active, Director
Wallace, Al, 1927, Active
Wallace, A.W., 1929
*Ware, Dr. F.B.
*Warren, B.S.
Webber, Oscar, 1926, Active, Director
Webster, Samuel LeRoy, 1929, Active
Weir, Frank F., 1927, Active
Wessele, R.S., 1932, Class B
Westen, Hugh E., 1929, Active
Wickes, Robert B., 1929, Active
*Willette, Frank
Williams, Ross, 1932, Class B
Wilson, Charles E., 1929, Active
Wilson, Ralph C., 1928, Active
Wilson, Ralph E., 1930
Winningham, C.C., 1929, Active, Director
Woodall, Herbert J., 1926, Active, **C**
Woolfolk, William G., 1932, Class B
Worcester, Willard S., 1930
Wyatt, Harry H., 1930, Class B

X, Y, Z

Young, William J., 1932, Class B
Zeder, Fred M., 1932, Class B
Zimmerman, A.H., 1926, Active

APPENDIX NINE

BOATS OF SIZE
From harbor registries 1966 to present
Researched By Larry W. Stephenson and Ross B. Stone

This appendix includes boats of 60 feet or longer that at some point have been listed in the GPYC harbor registry. Most listed boats have been kept in the GPYC harbor. Members' boats not kept in the harbor may or may not, by owner's preference, be listed in the GPYC harbor registries. There are seven members' boats listed here that were not listed in any known registry, but information about them was supplied verbally, or by other means, to the authors; they are identified with an asterisk (*).

Harbor registries exist for most years from 1938 to 1965, but in most cases do not include boat length. This list spans the period from 1966 to present; registries from 1975-1982 could not be located, nor could those prior to 1938. Although a boat may appear in GPYC registries for many years, boat information supplied annually by the owner sometimes varies, so only one year was chosen for this yacht list.

Owner	Boat Name	Length	GPYC Registry	Builder
Agley, Randolph	*Entrepreneur*	120 ft.	1987	Camper and Nicholson
	Talon	127 ft.	1991	Cantieri Picchanti
Anderson, Carl	*Lady Jane*	64 ft.	2010	Hatteras
Anderson, James	*Motivation IV*	65 ft.	2002	Viking
	Motivation V	74 ft.	2013	Viking
Barron, Victor	*Flying Scot*	63 ft.	1985	Sail
	Baroness	70 ft.	1989	Hatteras
Bailey, Donald	*Rosebud*	60 ft.	2001	Chris-Craft Roamer
Baer, William	*Perfect Lady*	65 ft.	1997	Hatteras
	**Perfect Lady*	84 ft.		Hatteras
Beauregard, Peter	*Fast Lane*	60 ft.	2001	Sea Ray
Bliss, Charles H.	*Caravel*	65 ft.	1969	Grebe
Bliss, Hascall C.	*Maid Marion II*	109 ft.	1966	Matthews
Boll, John	*Rockette*	63 ft.	1996	Sea Ray
	Marzy	85 ft.	2002	Azimut
	My Marzy	115 ft.	2003	Benetti
Bortz, Donald	*Lady Val*	64 ft.	1989	Hatteras
	Lady Val	69 ft.	1994	Hatteras
	Lady Val	94 ft.	1997	North Coast
Britton, William	*Ticonderoga*	72 ft.	1973	Herreshoff
Carter, Thomas	*Serenity*	61 ft.	1986	Hatteras

Owner	Boat Name	Length	GPYC Registry	Builder
Compau, Thomas	*T-Sea*	64 ft.	2003	Grand Alaskan
Coleman, Dr. Henry	*Bodacious*	63 ft.	1993	Hatteras
Connelly, Edward	*Golden Shamrock*	63 ft.	1985	Hatteras
	Golden Shamrock	74 ft.	1990	Hatteras
Coyer, Frank	*Mallard*	70 ft.	1984	Hatteras
Cunningham, Douglas	*Mister C*	63 ft.	1998	Sea Ray
Daskas, Chris T.	*Christina*	68 ft.	2004	Hatteras
Deary, Robert	*Fleetwing*	60 ft.	1971	Unknown
DeFever, Cyril	*Ursa Major*	65 ft.	2010	Malhide Trawler
Devlidge, Charles	*Jig Mill IV*	81 ft.	1966	Burger
Di Sante, Eugenia	*Lady Gene*	60 ft.	1992	Pacemaker
Doren, Mark	*Loro Tego*	61 ft.	1993	Garden
Ferrera, Rocco	*Sherri Lynn*	63 ft.	1969	Unknown
	Connie R	71 ft.	1971	Unknown
	Connie R	82 ft.	1972	Burger
Ferris, Louis Jr.	*Tour De Force*	61 ft.	2013	Viking
Fisher, Thomas	*Psyche*	62 ft.	2002	Viking
Ford, Donald	*Wicked Witch III*	66 ft.	1984	Derecktor
Ford, Elena	*Unity*	130 ft.	2002	Palmer Johnson
Fox, Timothy	*Patricia III*	60 ft.	2014	Ocean Yachts
Friedt, Glenn	*Pelican III*	63 ft.	1971	Unknown
Gagne, James	*Imperial V*	63 ft.	1967	Burger
Gagne, Steve	*Triumph*	61 ft.	1984	Cuthbertson and Cassian Yachts
Gardner, Marc	*Charge It*	70 ft.	2009	Unknown
Geissbuhler, John	*Compromise*	60 ft.	1994	Hatteras
	Magician	62 ft.	2002	Viking
Gibson, Alex Jr.	*Gibson Girl*	69 ft.	1971	Allied
	Gibson Girl	78 ft.	1978	Trumpy
Grecken, Steve	*Equation*	70 ft.	2013	Lazzara
Giffin, David	*Summer Suite*	90 ft.	2000	Broward
	Summer Suite	100 ft.	2002	Broward
Grobbel, Jason	*Irish Eyes*	60 ft.	2013	Viking

Owner	Boat Name	Length	GPYC Registry	Builder
Grouschow, Kathleen	*Donald Duck*	65 ft.	2013	Viking
Hansemann, Rene	*Resolute*	63 ft.	2013	Hatteras
Holzer, Thomas	*Connies Absolut*	63 ft.	1995	Sea Ray
Hunwick, Ronald	*Here Tiz*	60 ft.	1974	Chris-Craft
Hyatt, Gerald	*Hyatt House II*	60 ft.	1977	Chris-Craft
Jones, Wayne	*Perfect Lady*	65 ft.	1997	Hatteras
Joslyn, Robert	*Interlude*	60 ft.	1998	Hatteras
Kennedy, Dexter	*Nightingale*	66 ft.	1994	Burger
Kreuger, Gregory	*Sauerkraut*	61 ft.	2005	Viking
	Sauerkraut	61 ft.	2009	Sunseeker
Lauzon, Thomas	*Just Because*	68 ft.	2003	Sea Ray
Lawrie, David	*C Mar*	65 ft.	1970	Matthews
	Matt	65 ft.	1984	Matthews
	C Mar	63 ft.	1996	Burger
	C Mar	80 ft.	2003	Bagliette
Lees, George	*Georgie*	72 ft.	1987	Chris-Craft
Leuliette, Timothy	*Nausikaa*	68 ft.	1980	Nordhaven
Liggett, Robert	*AM-FM*	72 ft.	1977	Hatteras
Love, John	*Queen Bee*	60 ft.	1989	Chris-Craft Roamer
Lowery, Michael	*Predator*	60 ft.	1993	Viking
Maguire, Bruce	*Malia*	61 ft.	1966	Stephens
Mager, John	*More Toys 4 Us*	73 ft.	1996	Hatteras
	Toys 4 Us	91 ft.	2004	Broward
Manoogian, Alex	*Mallard*	73 ft.	1995	Hatteras
Manoogian, Richard	*Lady Jane*	64 ft.	1985	Hatteras
Markey, Dennis	*Hut Maker*	60 ft.	1993	Carver
McDonald, Bruce	*Sea Spot*	60 ft.	1992	Hatteras
	Sea Spot III	67 ft.	2002	Hatteras
	Trilogy	91 ft.	2008	Stephens
McKinley, William	*Denale*	70 ft.	2005	Nelson/Marek
Mead, Kenneth	*Vexation*	61 ft.	1987	Hatteras
	Rendezvous	95 ft.	1997	Broward
	Renegade	70 ft.	2001	Santa Cruz
	Renegade	68 ft.	2002	Sunseeker
	Renegade	75 ft.	2005	Sunseeker

Owner	Boat Name	Length	GPYC Registry	Builder
Meager, Michael	*Nancy's Dream*	80 ft.	2000	Hatteras
Meathe, Cullen	*⋆Summer Wind*	91 ft.		Stricker
	Off Duty	126 ft.	2008	Motor Yacht
	The Real Deal	80 ft.	2011	Donzie
Mertz, Richard	*Alyssa*	60 ft.	2003	Neptunus
	Alyssa	65 ft.	2011	Neptunus
Mestdagh, James	*Jester*	62 ft.	2011	Bertram
Millidrag, George	*Princess Tina*	131 ft.	2009	Broward
Milligard, Dennis	*Capricious*	68 ft.	1995	Hatteras
Mitchell, William	*Mitch Mate I*	75 ft.	1977	Burger
	Mitch Mate II	105 ft.	1978	Fedship
	Mitch Mate III	112 ft.	2001	Fedship
Moore, Charles	*Diamond Star*	67 ft.	1971	Burger
Moore, Ronald	*Soft Touch*	67 ft.	1978	Burger
	Soft Touch	85 ft.	1993	Broward
Morrison, Thomas	*Prima Donna*	64 ft.	2014	Viking
Mascone, Mark	*Nuo Posto*	70 ft.	2006	Hatteras
Newkirk, Howard	*Espirit*	60 ft.	1991	Viking
Olson, John III	*Halo*	65 ft.	1995	Hatteras
	⋆Passion	105 ft.		Broward
Olson, Oscar	*Miss Olsonite*	62 ft.	1974	Pacemaker
	Miss Olsonite	66 ft.	1984	Pacemaker
Palm, Edward	*⋆Equation*	65 ft.		Farr Trans-Pack
Packer, William	*White Heron*	65 ft.	1967	Abeking Rasmusen
Packer, William III	*Remedy*	61 ft.	1995	Hatteras
	Remedy	63 ft.	1998	Hatteras
Piceu, Roger	*My Beth*	72 ft.	2014	Marlow
Quint, David	*Seaquence*	60 ft.	2014	Sea Ray
Riehl, James Jr.	*Eagle One*	61 ft.	2007	Viking
Riehl, Michael	*Reel E Hooked*	64 ft.	2010	Viking
Roberts, Glendon	*Glori Bee*	62 ft.	1966	Burger
	Glori Bee	70 ft.	1967	Burger
Ruffner, Frederick	*Mary Ann*	76 ft.	1984	Trumpy
	Rag Time	64 ft.	1986	Consolidated
	Electra	96 ft.	1989	Lake Union Drydock

Owner	Boat Name	Length	GPYC Registry	Builder
Sappington, Michael	*O-U-One*	63 ft.	2003	Hatteras
Scaglione, Albert	*Fourth of July*	80 ft.	1999	Sandrenzo
Schebil, James	*Shy Fox*	61 ft.	2004	Viking
Schaden, Greg	*Indulgence*	63 ft.	1997	Hatteras
	Indulgence	61 ft.	2011	Viking
Schaupeter, Arthur	*★Ottelia*	135 ft.		Lawley & Sons
	Much To Much	70 ft.	1984	Striker
Schmidt, Russell "Dutch"	*Sassy*	61 ft.	1973	Cuthbertson and Cassian
	Sassy	78 ft.	1984	Palmer Johnson
Schrieber, Walter	*Opel M*	81 ft.	1969	Burger
Schriever, Fred	*Hi Pat*	60 ft.	2001	Tolly Craft
Shelden, Alger	*Strathbelle*	87 ft.	1966	Burger
Sherman, Arthur Jr.	*Maradon*	90 ft.	1968	Luders Yacht
Simon, Brian	*She Devil*	74 ft.	2012	Sunseeker
Soave, Anthony	*Mallard*	70 ft.	2011	Hatteras
Sohn, Roy	*Rama*	68 ft.	1988	Burger
Stefani, Michael	*Bellagio*	60 ft.	2004	Ocean Yacht
Strange, Edward Jr.	*Stranger*	71 ft.	1967	Unknown
Summer, William	*Thunder Ball*	93 ft.	2005	Alauga
Szott, Thomas	*Zot Yot*	61 ft.	2007	Viking
Taylor, James Sr.	*Taylor Made*	66 ft.	1978	Pacemaker
	Taylor Made	74 ft.	1979	Burger
Taylor, James Jr.	*Taylor Made*	74 ft.	2010	Burger
Taylor, Maurice	*Mallard*	70 ft.	2006	Hatteras
	★Sea Bear	126 ft.		Christensen
Taylor, Thomas	*Lady TV*	60 ft.	1970	Hatteras
Thomsen, Howard Sr.	*Irish Princess*	63 ft.	1982	Hatteras
Thomsen, Howard Jr.	Name Unknown	65 ft.	1992	Tolly Craft
Thomsen, Jay	*Lady of the Lake*	61 ft.	1982	Tolly Craft

Owner	Boat Name	Length	GPYC Registry	Builder
Thomason, Michael	*Andale*	80 ft.	1997	Palmer Johnson
	Twilight	91 ft.	1998	Palmer Johnson
Trerice, Howard	*Lady K*	60 ft.	2011	Viking
Uznis, John	*Evelyn U*	66 ft.	1977	Burger
	Evelyn U	86 ft.	1983	Burger
Van Elslander, Archie	*Pepper XIII*	82 ft.	2000	Mangusta
	⋆Pepper XIII	112 ft.		Westport
Verbiest, Christopher	*Helene*	106 ft.	1967	Defoe Ship Building
Werthmann, Norman	*Verlaing*	63 ft.	1966	Viking
Wheeler, Thomas	*Destiny*	124 ft.	2003	Broward
Wickman, Axel	*Tempo*	60 ft.	1966	Unknown
	Tempo	65 ft.	1969	Unknown
Wilt, Michael	*Lady Susan*	60 ft.	2001	Hatteras
Yates, William	*Livy Lou*	77 ft.	2011	Hatteras
Yuhn, Robert	*Red Apple*	60 ft.	1988	Bruce King Cutter

Ottellia owned by member Arthur Schaupeter. Photo courtesy of Past Commodore Ron Schaupeter.

References and Endnotes

References Chapter 1

1. Vera Brown, "A Bit of Spain", reproduced from 1929 Detroit newspaper article, *Grosse Pointe Yacht Club Yearbook 1943*.

2. "35-Year Chronological History," *The Grosse Pointer*, August 1949. At the Commodore's Ball on May 21, 1949, Mrs. R. George Marsh, widow of the GPYC's first commodore, presented the Club with Commodore Marsh's scrapbooks of the Club's early history. She also included the first burgee, which she had sewn by hand. The presentation was featured in the June / July 1949 issue of *The Grosse Pointer*. The August 1949 *Grosse Pointer* issue contained an in-depth article on the Club's early history, with new information that presumably was acquired from the scrapbooks. Unfortunately, the scrapbooks and the burgee have all gone missing. In gathering information for the centennial book, a considerable effort was made to locate these items, including an open letter to the membership, but to no avail.

3. GPYC Public Relations Committee, "A Flood in 1952...And 38 Years of GPYC History," *The Grosse Pointer Membership Album*, 1952.

4. Commodore Roger K. Smith and Commodore Ralph Kliber, "The Making of a Yacht Club Heritage," *The Grosse Pointer*, 1979 Album.

5. Robert R. Morris, *Grosse Pointe Yacht Club, A Beacon of Tradition for 75 Years, 1929–2004*, Walsworth Publishing Company, Marengo, IL, 2004, 24.

6. Commodore Ralph Kliber, "Revisiting Past Events," *The Grosse Pointer*, November 1989, 38–41. This article by Past Commodore Ralph Kliber contains the photograph that is labeled both "The Founders" and "Founding Fathers of the Grosse Pointe Yacht." Chapter One shows the photograph as fig. 3, along with fig. 4, a copy of the minutes from the first meeting of the GPYC. The photograph and minutes were given to the Club in 1989 by William C. Roney Jr., who had discovered them in the home of his father, William C. Roney Sr., following his death in 1984. The senior Mr. Roney served as the Club's secretary for the first four meetings, and possibly until as late as 1917 when he left to serve in the U.S. Navy during WWI.

When the minutes were found, they were contained in a hardbound notebook. Pages one to six were the minutes from the first four meetings of the Club. Pages seven to thirty-one are missing. Pages thirty-two to thirty-three contain the minutes from a meeting on August 22, 1917. There are no more pages present until page one hundred fifty-six, which is numbered but blank. In 2014, Dr. Larry Stephenson interviewed William C. Roney Jr. and asked about the missing pages. Mr. Roney was unaware of any missing pages and speculated that they could have been removed either before he donated the book to the Club or after the fact.

7. Robert R. Morris, *Grosse Pointe Yacht Club, A Beacon of Tradition for 75 Years, 1929–2004*, Walsworth Publishing Company, Marengo, IL, 2004, 19.

8. S. Calhoun Smith, *Ice Boating*, (Princeton: D. Van Nostrand Company, Inc., 1962), 9–34.

9. Madeleine Socia and Suzy Berschback, *Grosse Pointe 1880–1930*, (Chicago: Arcadia Publishing, 2001), 22.

10. James Gallagher, "Lakeshore Drive and Vernier Road, A Special Place," *A Beacon of Tradition*, (Kelvin Publishing, St. Clair Shores, MI, 1986), 4.

11. "Old Hotels, Road Houses and Picnic Grounds," *WPA Sponsored History of Grosse Pointe*, (U.S. Government, 1936), 28–29.

12. "Parks," *WPA Sponsored History of Grosse Pointe*, (U.S. Government, 1936), 5–6.

13. Susan Brown, "Palace by the Sea," *Heritage, A Journal of Grosse Pointe Life*, vol. 2, no. 4, August–September 1985, 15.

14. *Turn-of-the-Century DYC Becomes Cornerstone of Detroit Area Yacht Clubs,* "Main Sheet," June 1985, 66.

15. Robert R. Morris, *Grosse Pointe Yacht Club, A Beacon of Tradition for 75 Years, 1929–2004,* Walsworth Publishing Company, Marengo, IL, 2004, 20.

16. Many personal telephone and in-person conversations between Larry W. Stephenson and George Hendrie Jr. July-December, 2013.

17. Miner A. Gregg, "Grosse Pointe Ice Yacht Clubs," *The Rudder,* January 1906, 63–64.

18. A Further Unscrambling of the Confusing Origins of the GPYC

    In January 1901, "twenty-three prominent yachtsmen" gathered at Matt Kramer's Roadhouse on the corner of Jefferson Avenue and Kensington Road, in what is now Grosse Pointe Park, to form a club. The new club was to be centered on winter ice and summer water sports with a focus on competition between members as well as other clubs. They gave their new club a name: the Grosse Pointe Yacht Club. (A)

    At the next meeting, officers were elected and rules were drawn up to govern iceboating competitions for the remainder of the season. An article from the Detroit *Free Press* lists twenty-two charter members by name, none of which have been found on any known membership lists from the GPYC that would be formed in 1914.

    No other references to a Grosse Pointe Yacht Club in those years have surfaced, but five years later, in December 1906, the *Free Press* reported on a huge rift that was developing between members of a Grosse Pointe Ice Yacht Club. It seems that this club had been meeting in various roadhouses, but now a house near Vernier Road had been leased for meetings against the wishes of many members. (B,C,D,E) These disgruntled members threatened to leave the club, and in February 1907 they did, forming the Grosse Pointe Ice Boat Association. The new club met at Ed Vernier's roadhouse at Vernier and Lake Shore, while the GPIYC continued to meet at their leased house. (F)

    In January 1908, the *Free Press* reported that a meeting of the GPIYC was held at the Bingham Lakeside Inn in Mt. Clemens, where a large number of local iceboaters were admitted and plans were discussed to reincorporate under the name Detroit and Mt. Clemens Ice Yacht Club, or something similar. The article mentioned a Lake St. Clair Ice Yacht Club, which also held meetings at the same inn. (G)

    Extensive research has not revealed any other references to the name Grosse Pointe Yacht Club until the initial meeting of our founders in 1913 that went on to become today's GPYC. The logical assumption is that the main focus of that 1901 Grosse Pointe Yacht Club quickly became iceboating and the club renamed itself the Grosse Pointe Ice Yacht Club to firmly associate itself with the sport.

    All of the following referenced articles appeared in the Detroit *Free Press.*

    A. "New Yacht Club Formed," Jan. 21, 1901.

    B. "Other Grosse Pointe Clubs Still on the Ice," Dec. 7, 1906.

    C. "Ice Yachtsmen in Broil," Dec. 25, 1906.

    D. "Hot Meeting is Looked For," Dec. 28, 1906.

    E. "Breach Between Two Parties is Widening," Dec. 29, 1906.

    F. "Ice Yachters are Divorced," Feb. 3, 1907.

    G. "New Members Admitted," Jan. 13, 1908.

19. Clarence M. Burton, "George Osius," *History of Wayne County and the City of Detroit,* Vol. 3 (S. J. Clarke Publishing Co., Chicago-Detroit, 1930), 722–724.

20. Bronze tablet, front hall, Grosse Pointe Shores Municipal Building. Dedicated November 20, 1915.

21. "Testimonial to Honorable George Osius, 1928", Burton Historical Collection, Detroit Public Library, 3 (reading room file).

22. Ibid., 5.

23. Taped interview between George Hendrie and Jean Dodenhoff, Grosse Pointe Historical Society, 1988.

24. Clarence M. Burton, "Robert George Marsh," *History of Wayne County and the City of Detroit*, Vol. 5 (S. J. Clarke Publishing Co., Chicago–Detroit, 1930) 359.

25. "Commodore R. George Marsh Funeral Rites Were Held Wed." Obituary, *Grosse Pointe Review*, April 22, 1937.

26. Gary Freeman, "A Sporting Life," *Heritage, A Journal of Grosse Pointe Life"*, vol. 4, no. 1, February–March 1987, 55–59.

27. John A. Bluth, "Harry Mulford Jewett, DAC's Renaissance Man," *DAC News*, vol. 86, issue 8, October 2001, 94–95.

28. Mary Rodrique, "'Four Horsemen' Led Outstanding DAC Track Squads", *DAC News*, vol. 91, issue 9, October 2007, 56–57.

29. Obituary, Harry Mulford Jewett, *Detroit Free Press*, June 17, 1933.

References Chapter Two

1. "The Roaring 1920s," Wikipedia, www.wikipedia.com, Apr. 12, 2014.

2. "The Dawes Plan 1924 — Inter War Period Causes of WWII," www.interwars.weebly.com/dawes-1924, April 12, 2014.

3. James Gallagher, "Lakeshore Drive and Vernier Road, A Special Place," *A Beacon of Tradition*, (Kelvin Publishing, St. Clair Shores, MI, 1986), 7.

4. Ralph Henry and Henry Richmond, "A Building on the Board: A Selected Group of Drawings Showing the Progress From the Sketch to the Finished Working Drawings of the Grosse Pointe Yacht Club, on Lake St. Clair," *Pencil Points*, December 1929, 829–839.

5. George Kriese, "A Meneely in our Belfry," *The Grosse Pointer*, Fall 2008, 8, 20.

6. George M. Slocum, "The Commodore's Annual Message," *The Grosse Pointer*, Vol. 1, No. 7, 1939, 7.

7. Vera Brown, "A Bit of Spain," *The Grosse Pointer Yearbook 1943*, 92–96.

8. *Detroit Yacht Club 125th Anniversary History Book*, 1993, 23.

9. GPYC Board of Directors Minutes, April 26, 1934.

10. As with Active, Life and Non-Resident classifications, candidates were required to be nominated by three sponsoring members, but the Associate category had a notable exception: two of the sponsoring members had to be members of the board of directors. This added qualification would seem to indicate that the board wished to maintain tight control over who could — or could not — become an Associate member.

11. "Edsel Ford," www.wikipedia.com, April 8, 2014.

12. *Detroit Free Press*, April 28, 1926; November 18, 1952.

13. *Detroit News*, September 20, 1934, November 17, 1952.

14. Clarence M. Burton, "Charles Hayward Murphy," *History of Wayne County and the City of Detroit*, (S.J. Clarke Publishing, Chicago-Detroit, 1930) vol. III, 108–109.

15. Lucile Benson "Geo. M. Slocum in Person," *Detroit Saturday Night*, Mar. 12, 1938, filed under Slocum, George M., Reading Room file, Burton Historical Collection, Detroit Public Library.

16. "Slocum Takes Chair for Music Festival," *Detroit News*, Apr. 24, 1935.

17. Anthony Weitzel, "Notes on People and Characters," *Town Crier*, filed under Slocum, George M., Reading Room File, Burton Historical Collection, Detroit Public Library.

18. "The Short Road to Profit," 15-page pamphlet circa 1920s, filed under "B.F. Stephenson," Reading Room file, Burton Historical Collection, Detroit Public Library.

19. Scott Taylor Hartzell, "Developer Built Fortune in Detroit, Lost One in Florida," *St. Petersburg Times Online*, July 23, 2003.

20. "Real Estate Magnate, B.F. Stephenson, Dies," *Detroit Free Press*, May 15, 1954.

21. Detroit Phone Directories, 1938, 1939.

22. Clarence R. Burton, "Clarence L. Ayres," *City of Detroit, 1701–1922*, (S.J. Clarke Publishing, Chicago-Detroit, 1930) vol. III, 1922, 180.

23. "Biography of Clarence L. Ayres; Wayne County," *Biographies, Detroiters, A Biographical Dictionary of Leading Men in the City of Detroit*, Second Edition, (A.N. Marquis & Co., Chicago, IL, 1914).

24. Ralph J. Kliber, "50th Anniversary Publication, Grosse Pointe Yacht Club," *The Grosse Pointer*, vol. I, no. 7, 1979, 11.

25. William Monahan, "WPA Sponsored History of Grosse Pointe," 14-page manuscript at U.S. Coast Guard Station, Lake St. Clair, Grosse Pointe, Wayne County, Michigan, Dec. 4, 1938, (U.S. Government, 1938) 2, document located at the Grosse Pointe Historical Society.

26. Ibid, p. 8.

27. Ibid, pp. 2,3.

28. Ibid, p. 9.

29. Ibid, p. 7.

30. Ibid, p. 11.

31. Ibid, p. 12.

32. Ibid, p. 13.

33. Ibid, p. 14.

References Chapter Three

1. Commodore Paul I. Moreland, "Trials and Triumphs," *A Beacon of Tradition: The Complete History of Grosse Pointe Yacht Club* (Kelvin Publishing, St. Clair Shores, MI, 1986), 17.

2. Robert R. Morris, *Grosse Pointe Yacht Club: A Beacon of Tradition for 75 Years, 1929–2004* (Walsworth Publishing, Marengo, IL, 2004), 35.

3. Commodore Ralph J. Kliber, "New Beginning for Yachting," *A Beacon of Tradition: The Complete History of Grosse Pointe Yacht Club* (Kelvin Publishing, St. Clair Shores, MI, 1986), 42.

4. "Fourth of July Marks Ninth Anniversary and Eighth Annual Regatta of G.P.Y.C.," *The Grosse Pointer* 3, no. 1 (July 1938): 1–4.

5. "A Message from the Commodore," *The Grosse Pointer* (November 1938): 5.

6. "A Tenth Anniversary and an Ambition Realized," *The Grosse Pointer* 1, no. 7 (July 1939): 7.

7. "The Grille Room of the Grosse Pointe Yacht Club," *The Grosse Pointer* 1, no. 4 (1939): 29.

8. "The Commodore's Annual Message," *The Grosse Pointer* 1, no. 4, 1939: 11.

9. Adrian Martin and Larry Stephenson, *Operation PLUM: The Ill-fated 27th Bombardment Group and the Fight for the Western Pacific* (College Station: Texas A&M University Press, 2008), 1.

10. Kathi Ann Brown, *No Ceiling on Effort: The Harvey C. Fruehauf Story* (Spectrum Creative, Fairfax, VA, 2011).

11. "The Commodore's Message," *The Grosse Pointer* 2 (1940): 11.

12. "Frank Couzens," www.en.wikipedia.org/wiki/frank_couzens, May 22, 2013.

References Chapter Four

1. *The Grosse Pointer* 3, no. 71941): 79.

2. Ibid., 13.

3. H. Lynn Pierson served as president of the Detroit Harvester Co., president of the Detroit Board of Commerce, chairman of the Detroit Committee for Economic Development, and president of the Detroit Athletic Club.

4. *The Grosse Pointer* 4, no. 101942): 11.

5. *The Grosse Pointer* 5, no. 51943): 19.

6. "The Coast Guard at War, Auxiliary XIX," May 1, 1948, Historical Section, Public Information Division, USCG Headquarters, Washington, DC, 23–24.

7. Edwin Theisen, Past Commodore and Club Historian, Detroit Yacht Club, Past Commodore and Historian, Detroit Regional Yacht Racing Association (formerly Detroit River Yachting Association), telephone conversation with Larry Stephenson, October and November 2013.

8. *The Grosse Pointer* 6, no. 21945): 19.

9. *The Grosse Pointer* 9, no. 141948): 7.

References Chapter Five

1. "Decorating Program at GPYC," *The Grosse Pointer*, vol. 12, no. 1, 1951, 10.

2. Ibid., 11.

3. Photo caption, *The Grosse Pointer*, vol. 16, no. 4, 1955, 13.

4. Minutes, Board of Directors Meeting, June 14, 1956.

5. "Transformation," *The Grosse Pointer*, vol. 18, no. 1, 1957, 36.

6. Ibid.

7. "Tentative Entertainment Schedule for 1959," *The Grosse Pointer*, vol. 20, no. 1, 1959, 27.

8. "Commodore Gaskin's Annual Report," *The Grosse Pointer*, vol. 18, no. 1, 1957, 12.

9. "New GPYC Terrace Lounge Opened," *The Grosse Pointer*, vol. 21, no. 2, 1960, 5.

10. "A Flood in 1952...and 38 Years of GPYC History," *The Grosse Pointer*, vol. 13, no. 3, 1952, 103.

11. Robert R. Morris, *Grosse Pointe Yacht Club, A Beacon of Tradition for 75 Years, 1929–2004*, (Walsworth Publishing, mareng, IL), 18, 19.

12. Frontispiece, *The Grosse Pointer*, vol. 13, no. 3, 1952.

13. "Sports Dinner Climaxes Swimming Season," *The Grosse Pointer*, vol. 14, no. 4, 1953, 12.

14. "Automatic Pinsetters Ordered for GPYC Alleys," *The Grosse Pointer*, vol. 17, no. 1, 1956, 53.

15. "GPYC's First Mackinac Victory," *The Grosse Pointer*, vol. 13, no. 4, 1952, 11.

16. "International L-16 Races at GPYC," *The Grosse Pointer*, vol. 13, no. 4, 1952, 13.

17. "Record Fleet of 170—But Few Finishers," *The Grosse Pointer*, vol. 15, no. 3, 1954, 34–35.

18. "World Series of Yachting at GPYC," *The Grosse Pointer*, vol. 16, no. 2, 1955, 4.

19. "Some Orchids for GPYC," *The Grosse Pointer*, vol. 17, no. 1, 1956, 40.

20. "GPYC Boats Score Double-Victory in Mackinac Races," *The Grosse Pointer*, vol. 21, no. 4, 1960, front cover.

21. Minutes, Board of Directors Meeting, February 24, 1955.

22. Minutes, Board of Directors Meeting, December 3, 1957.

23. "The Commodore's Report," *The Grosse Pointer*, vol. 19, no. 1, 1958, 31.

24. Commodore Robert Weber, "What Is the Grosse Pointe Yacht Club?" *The Grosse Pointer*, vol. 20, no. 1, 1959, 7.

References Chapter Six

1. John F. DeHayes, "A Yacht Club and More, A Beacon of Tradition, *The Complete History of Grosse Pointe Yacht Club*, (Kelvin Publishing, St. Clair Shores, MI, 1986) 46.

2. "New GPYC Terrace Lounge Opened," *The Grosse Pointer*, vol. 21, no.2, 1960, 5.

3. Paul I. Moreland, "Trials and Triumphs," *A Beacon of Tradition, The Complete History of Grosse Pointe Yacht Club*, (Kelvin Publishing, St. Clair Shores, MI, 1986) 20.

4. Ibid

5. Minutes, Board of Directors Meeting, November 6, 1963.

6. Minutes, Board of Directors Meeting, February, 1964.

7. Minutes, Board of Directors Meeting, June, 1964.

8. Minutes, Board of Directors Meeting, August, 1964.

9. Minutes, Board of Directors Meeting, March 4, 1965.

10. "GPYC Harbor Control Tower is Unique," *The Grosse Pointer*, vol. 24, no.2, 1963, 84.

11. Minutes, Board of Directors Meeting, June 3, 1965.

12. Ibid.

13. Minutes, Board of Directors Meeting, May 6, 1965.

14. Ibid, 61.

15. "44 New Wells for Us," *The Grosse Pointe*r, vol. 28, no.2, 1967, 126.

16. "Get the Idea, Ladies?" *The Grosse Pointer*, vol. 28, no.1, 1967, 51.

17. "Membership: We Gained 49 Additional Members," *The Grosse Pointer*, vol. 28, no.4, 1967, 59.

18. Paul I. Moreland, "Trials and Triumphs, *A Beacon of Tradition, The Complete History of Grosse Pointe Yacht Club*, (Kelvin Publishing, St. Clair Shores, MI, 1986) 21-22.

19. "The 795," *The Grosse Pointer*, vol. 29, no.1, March 1968, 123.

20. "Pool's Open!" / "More Construction," *The Grosse Pointer*, vol. 30, no.3, 33-34, 1969, 36-37.

21. Paul I. Moreland, "Trials and Triumphs," *A Beacon of Tradition, The Complete History of Grosse Pointe Yacht Club*, (Kelvin Publishing, St. Clair Shores, MI, 1986) 22.

22. "It Was a Record Regatta," *The Grosse Pointer*, vol. 22, no.2, 1961, 36.

23. "A Lady with a History – Coming to GPYC," *The Grosse Pointer*, vol. 23, no.1, 1962, 45.

24. Ibid, 25-33, 40.

25. "Commodore Hickey and Commodore Moreland Dedicate New Trophies," *The Grosse Pointer*, vol. 24, no.3, 1963, 2.

26. "Mrs. Slocum's Annual Breakfast at GPYC," *The Grosse Pointer*, vol. 24, no.1, 1963, 40.

27. "Carnival at GPYC," *The Grosse Pointer*, vol. 24, no.3, 1963, 35.

28. Ibid, 10.

29. "Clambakes and Opener," *The Grosse Pointer*, vol. 28, no.2, 1967, 115-116.

30. Margie Reins Smith, "Proper Luncheons and Dances, Bright, Brash Feasts and Bashes," A *Beacon of Tradition, The Complete History of Grosse Pointe Yacht Club*, (Kelvin Publishing, St. Clair Shores, MI, 1986) 33.

31. "First Snow Ball Hits Home," *The Grosse Pointer*, vol. 29, no.1, 1968, 59; "The Ball," 39.

32. "A Mod Party Lets In a Little Psychedelic Light on Hippies," *The Grosse Pointer*, vol. 28, 1967, no.4.

33. "GPYC Boats Score – Victory in Mackinac Races," *The Grosse Pointer*, vol. 22, no.4, 1961, cover.

34. "It Was a Record Regatta," *The Grosse Pointer*, vol. 23, no.2, 1962, 36.

35. "GPYC Hosts Mallory Races for 1964," *The Grosse Pointer*, vol. 25, no.2, 1964, 114.

36. Paul I. Moreland, "Trials and Triumphs, *A Beacon of Tradition, The Complete History of Grosse Pointe Yacht Club*, (Kelvin Publishing, St. Clair Shores, MI, 1986) 21.

37. "Yachting: A View From the Dock," *The Grosse Pointer*, vol. 27, no.3, 1963, 65.

References Chapter Seven

1. Robert R. Morris, "The 1970s," *Grosse Pointe Yacht Club: A Beacon of Tradition for 75 Years, 1929–2004* (Marengo, IL: Walsworth Publishing, 2004), 61–62.

2. Paul I. Moreland, "Trials and Triumphs," in *A Beacon of Tradition: The Complete History of Grosse Pointe Yacht Club* (St. Clair Shores, MI: Kelvin Publishing, 1986), 23.

3. Robert R. Morris, "The 1970s," *Grosse Pointe Yacht Club: A Beacon of Tradition for 75 Years, 1929–2004* (Marengo, IL: Walsworth Publishing, 2004), 62.

4. George E. Van, "The Spring Flight of our Birds," *A Beacon of Tradition: The Complete History of Grosse Pointe Yacht Club* (St. Clair Shores, MI: Kelvin Publishing, 1986), 36.

5. Ibid.

6. Robert R. Morris, "The 1970s," *Grosse Pointe Yacht Club: A Beacon of Tradition for 75 Years, 1929–2004* (Marengo, IL: Walsworth Publishing, 2004), 63.

7. George E. Van, "The Spring Flight of our Birds," *A Beacon of Tradition: The Complete History of Grosse Pointe Yacht Club* (St. Clair Shores, MI: Kelvin Publishing, 1986), 36.

8. "Gypsy Sails to Victory in Stormy Bluenose Race," *The Grosse Pointer* 31, no. 4 (1970): 105, 107.

9. George Van, "Turn Off the Power and Set Sail," *The Grosse Pointer* 32, no. 2 (1970): 31.

10. "Boston's Lone Ranger Wins Mackinac Class D," *The Grosse Pointer* 32, no. 3 (1971): 35.

11. George E. Van, "Turn Off the Power and Set Sail," *The Grosse Pointer* 33, no. 3 (1972): 31.

12. George E. Van, "In Both Mackinac Races: First-to-Finish Honors Come Home to GPYC," *The Grosse Pointer* 33, no. 3 (1972): 37.

13. George E. Van, "They're Coming Home—Winners!" and "...And May the Best Boat Win," *The Grosse Pointer* 33, no. 4 (1972): 22–23; 29–31.

14. George E. Van, "Sailors Put It All Together," *The Grosse Pointer* 34, no. 4 (1973): 21.

15. Ibid., 22.

16. Ibid.

17. George E. Van, "Victory in Italy," *The Grosse Pointer* 35, no. 4 (1974): 88.

18. George E. Van, "This Racing Summer," *The Grosse Pointer* 36, no. 2 (1975): 11.

19. George E. Van, "The Mackinacs: A Culmination of Summer Yachting on the Great Lakes," *The Grosse Pointer* 36, no. 3 (1975): 37–38.

20. "The Club Revs Up for Powerful Racing," *The Grosse Pointer* 34, no. 4 (1973): 19.

21. Ralph J. Kliber, Commodore Interview Series, GPYC Archives, Transcript 21.

22. Margie Reins Smith, "Proper Luncheons and Dances—Bright, Brash, Feasts and Bashes," in *A Beacon of Tradition: The Complete History of Grosse Pointe Yacht Club* (St. Clair Shores, MI: Kelvin Publishing, 1986), 33–34.

23. "The Tinseltown Thing," *The Grosse Pointer* 31, no. 4 (1970): 99.

24. Ibid.

25. "150 Revel at the Elizabethan Feast," *The Grosse Pointer* 32, no. 1 (1971): 31.

26. "Clambake Is a Lot of Fishy Fun," *The Grosse Pointer* 32, no. 2 (1971): 22.

27. Ibid., 28.

28. Ralph J. Kliber, Commodore Interview Series, GPYC Archives, Transcript 25–26.

29. Frank P. McBride Jr., Commodore Interview Series, GPYC Archives, Transcript 130; George L. Beard, Commodore Interview Series, GPYC Archives, Transcript 4.

30. Peggy McBride, "Even a Pregnant Cheerleader Shows Up at This American Bandstand Party," *The Grosse Pointe*r 35, no. 2 (1974): 26.

31. *The Grosse Pointer* 39, no. 4 (1978): 71, 86, 91.

32. *The Grosse Pointe*r 38, no. 1 (1977): 69, 77.

33. Robert R. Morris, "The 1970s," *Grosse Pointe Yacht Club: A Beacon of Tradition for 75 Years, 1929–2004* (Marengo, IL: Walsworth Publishing, 2004), "The 1970s," 63.

34. *The Grosse Pointer* 32, no. 1 (1971): 41.

35. Maureen Geutle, "Les Plasirs de Grosse Pointe,"*The Grosse Pointer* 36, no. 3 (1975): 20; and The Grosse Pointer 345, no. 1 (1973): 29.

36. *The Grosse Pointer* 34, no. 3 (1973): 38.

37. "Ann Sutton and John Anderson are Top Bowlers," and "Heartland Regatta Honors Skippers," *The Grosse Pointer* 32, no. 2 (1971): 18, 26.

38. "Chatham Powerboat Gathering Features Large Turnout," *The Grosse Pointer* 33, no. 2 (1972): 11.

39. *The Grosse Pointer* 35, no. 2 (1974): 15.

40. Frank P. McBride Jr., Commodore Interview Series, GPYC Archives, Transcript 129; George L. Beard, Commodore Interview Series, GPYC Archives, Transcript 6.

41. "Tower Dedication Shows Progress on Anniversary," *The Grosse Pointer* 35, no. 3 (1974):

References Chapter Eight

1. George Kriese, Commodore Interview Series, GPYC Archives.

2. Paul I. Moreland, "Trials and Triumphs," in *A Beacon of Tradition: The Complete History of Grosse Pointe Yacht Club* (St. Clair Shores, MI: Kelvin Publishing, 1986), 23.

3. "The Verdict Is In: Club's Bubbling Program Is a Success—And We Don't Mean Champagne," *The Grosse Pointer* 41, no. 6 (June 1981): 19.

4. "Historical Flagpole, Grounds Improvements Make GPYC Shipshape," *The Grosse Pointer* 43, no. 11 (November 1982): 17.

5. Peter E. O'Rourke, "Full Voting Rights Given Female Members by GPYC Directors," *The Grosse Pointer* 45, no. 4 (April 1984): 31–32.

6. John Kelvin, "New Gate House Revives Ancient Look of Club's Design," *The Grosse Pointer* 45, no. 9 (September 1984): 33.

7. George Van, "Breaking an Imaginary Finish Line Tape—And the Real Port Huron-to-Mackinac Record—Dutch Schmidt Had a Broom Tied atop His Mast, Slightly below the Stars and Stripes, and Near the Racing Team's Banner. By That Time All Knew *Sassy* Had Made a Clean Sweep of the Race," *The Grosse Pointer* 45, no. 9 (September 1984): 18–19.

8. John Boll, Fred Schriever, Commodore Interview Series, GPYC Archives.

9. James Daoust, Commodore Interview Series, GPYC Archives.

10. "Member Takes It All in Offshore Racing World Championship," *The Grosse Pointer* 47, no. 12 (December 1986): 25–26.

11. "Former GPYCer Makes His Mark as World-Class Racer," *The Grosse Pointer* 48, no. 4 (April 1987): 30.

12. Theodore Smith, Commodore Interview Series, GPYC Archives.

13. "GPYC Pool Gets a New Look," *The Grosse Pointer* 49, no. 7 (July 1988): 44.

14. Fred Schriever, "Clubhouse Activities Reflect Members," *The Grosse Pointer* 50, no. 2 (February 1989): 5.

15. Fred Schriever, "The Year in Review," *The Grosse Pointer* 50, no. 11 (November 1989): 33–35.

References Chapter Nine

1. Tymon C. Totte, "Address at Commodore's Ball," *The Grosse Pointer* 50, no. 1 (January 1990): 7.

2. Tymon C. Totte, Commodores' Interview Series, GPYC Archives.

3. Minutes, Board of Directors Meeting, September 20, 1990, Addendum—Deed of Gift, "Distinguished Member of the Year," Article III.

4. "Eighth Annual Red Wings Night Scores a Victory," *The Grosse Pointer* (May/June 1996): 10–11.

5. "Trumpets Sound for 62nd Annual Commodore's Ball," *The Grosse Pointer* (1991), Album, 17.

6. Thomas D. Ogden, Commodores' Interview Series, GPYC Archives.

7. "Fleet Captain Dee Buono Reflects on Events of the Past Year," *The Grosse Pointer* (November/December 1991): 19.

8. Charles E. Stumb Jr., Commodores' Interview Series, GPYC Archives.

9. Charles E. Stumb Jr., "Commodore's Message," *The Grosse Pointer* (July 1992): 3.

10. "GPYC Swims to 100th Victory," *The Grosse Pointer* (August 1992): 11.

11. "World Class Regatta Held at GPYC," *The Grosse Pointer* (September 1992): 7.

12. Minutes, Board of Directors Meeting, September 30, 1993.

13. James J. Morrow, "Commodore's Message," *The Grosse Pointer* (November/December 1993): 5.

14. James J. Morrow, Commodores' Interview Series, GPYC Archives.

15. "MICSA Swimmers Tower above the Rest," *The Grosse Pointer* (Spring 1994): 7.

16. Pat Barry, "Sailors Savor Success: GPYC Sailing Program Completes Its Most Successful Season in Years," *The Grosse Pointer* (Fall 1994): 6–8.

17. Robert E. Thoreson, "The Harbor—Now Is the Time," *The Grosse Pointer* (January/February 1995): 3.

18. "I Can Do That! Boat Handling for Mates Course," *The Grosse Pointer* (September/October 1995): 8.

19. Sloane R. Barbour Jr., Commodores' Interview Series, GPYC Archives.

20. "Tower Pub Opens to Rave Reviews: A Great Room with a Spectacular View," *The Grosse Pointer* (January/February 1996): 10.

21. "Harbor Renovation Is Here at Last," Commodore's Message, *The Grosse Pointer* (January/February 1996): 3.

22. "Harbor Renovation Bulletin: Second Membership Meeting Produces Positive Reaction," *The Grosse Pointer* (May/June 1996): 17.

23. John H. Schoenherr, Commodores' Interview Series, GPYC Archives.

24. Platinum Clubs of America, www.platinumclubsoftheworld.com/platinum-clubs-america, February 26, 2014.

25. James L. Ramsey, "Renovated Southwest Harbor Is Open for Business," *The Grosse Pointer* (July 1997): 7–9.

26. Minutes, Board of Directors Meeting, October 29, 1998.

27. "Swim Team Celebrates Success," *The Grosse Pointer* (December 1997): 15.

28. "Harbor Renovation: Rebuilding the Wall," *The Grosse Pointer*, Summer Wrap-up 1998: 4–6.

29. William J. Storen, "Our Crown Jewel of the Great Lakes," *The Grosse Pointer* (Summer 1999): 2.

30. "Archival Dedication—Thank You," *The Grosse Pointer* (Summer 1999): 18.

31. William J. Storen, Commodores' Interview Series, GPYC Archives.

32. Minutes, Board of Directors Meeting, January 28, 1999.

Refrences and Endnotes

Chapter 10

1. The "Number-one Yacht Club in America." What's behind the title?

When the GPYC was first named the top yacht club in the country in 1997, the internal reaction was not immediately euphoric. Typically the response ranged from skepticism to puzzlement to "It's too good to be true."

The announcement seemed to raise more questions than answers. As members, we tend to think highly of our Club (and pay monthly dues to show our affection). But we can also be our own toughest critics when things don't go as they should. And what about the people who bestowed the award— what was their motivation? We all have had experience with mailings telling us we have won a huge prize, only to learn that it is a veiled attempt to sell us something.

What did the award mean? What was it based on? Was it legitimate or not? Were we really that good? All were valid questions.

As the board and management studied the selection criteria, skepticism gave way to realization: The award was for real. It wasn't based on someone's arbitrary judgment, but instead by a survey of the Club Managers Association of America (CMAA), consisting of the managers and presidents of the country's most respected private clubs. The survey was conducted among six thousand private clubs in the U.S. by the Club Leaders Forum, an organization that recognizes excellence in the private club industry.

Of the four thousand clubs currently in the survey, the top two hundred thirty-five vote-getters are designated as Platinum Clubs of America. The Grosse Pointe Yacht Club has been voted a Platinum Club every year since the survey began.

Platinum Clubs are divided into these categories—Golf Clubs, Country Clubs, Athletic Clubs, City Clubs, and Yacht Clubs—and then ranked within their state or geographical region. If they score well enough, they are ranked nationally.

Regardless of category or region, all clubs are graded on the following criteria: quality of membership, tradition and culture, amenities, governance, and quality of management and staff. The process seeks to identify best in class and best overall.

Based on the input from thousands of these surveys, the nation's top clubs are selected every three years. The GPYC was named the most highly regarded yacht club in America in 1997 and held the title for fifteen consecutive years. In the opinion of hundreds of club professionals and club presidents nationwide, our yacht club was the best of the best, ahead of the New York Yacht Club, St. Francis Yacht Club, San Diego Yacht Club and San Francisco Yacht Club.

Winning that honor once might be considered a fluke. But winning it consecutively every three years, especially in light of the competition, is an achievement.

It should also be mentioned that the top golf, country, city, athletic, and yacht clubs in each region are also compared head-to-head to determine who is best overall, regardless of category. In 2000, the survey named GPYC the top club in Michigan, period, ahead of such respected institutions as Oakland Hills CC, Birmingham CC, Detroit Athletic Club and Country Club of Detroit. Since then, the GPYC has never finished lower than second in these state rankings.

The cynics among us may persist in finding such recognition doubtful. But others reason that praise from one's professional peers is the highest form of acclaim. As one sage observer put it, "Awards are never important until you don't win any."

XYZ.